BLOOD AND FIRE

BLOOD AND FIRE

THE UNBELIEVABLE
REAL-LIFE STORY OF WRESTLING'S
ORIGINAL SHEIK

BRIAN R. SOLOMON

Copyright © Brian R. Solomon, 2022

Published by ECW Press
665 Gerrard Street East
Toronto, Ontario, Canada M4M 1Y2
416-694-3348 / info@ecwpress.com

Editor for the Press: Michael Holmes
Copy-editor: Rachel Ironstone
Cover design: David Drummond

LIBRARY AND ARCHIVES CANADA CATALOGUING IN PUBLICATION

Title: Blood and fire : the unbelievable real-life story of wrestling's Original Sheik / Brian R. Solomon.

Names: Solomon, Brian, 1974- author.

Identifiers: Canadiana (print) 20210354011 | Canadiana (ebook) 2021035402X

ISBN 978-1-77041-580-5 (softcover)
ISBN 978-1-77305-882-5 (ePub)
ISBN 978-1-77305-902-0 (PDF)
ISBN 978-1-77305-903-7 (Kindle)

Subjects: LCSH: Sheik, 1926-2003. | LCSH: Wrestlers—United States—Biography.

Classification: LCC GV1196.S53 S65 2022 | DDC 796.812092—dc23

PRINTED AND BOUND IN CANADA

PRINTING: MARQUIS   5 4 3 2 1

So many associated with Detroit wrestling have been lost since I began this journey, and this book is dedicated to their memories.

First and foremost, to the sons of The Sheik, Eddie Jr. and Tommy Farhat, who I had hoped would one day see that all I ever wanted was to pay tribute to their incredible father.

To the accomplished and beloved Detroit wrestling historian Mark Bujan, who was one of the first people to reach out to me when I started this project, and one of the most helpful. He wanted nothing more than to see the finished product, and I can only hope that this book would've lived up to his expectations.

To Pampero Firpo, Killer Tim Brooks, Bobby Davis, Tony Marino, and Dominic Denucci.

And finally, to Terry Dart, who never did find out why Sheik broke his camera.

CONTENTS

AUTHOR'S NOTE

More than anything, The Sheik was known for his strict adherence to kayfabe, professional wrestling's time-honored code of secrecy. No one protected his persona, or "lived his gimmick," more than he did. And no one worked harder to keep his personal life away from the ring secret from the fans. Because of this, it goes without saying that writing a biography of the man would be a formidable undertaking—and perhaps this is part of the reason why none has ever been published, or even attempted with any success.

In order to do what had never been done before, I made every effort to delve as deeply as I could into research—not just into his professional career, but his actual life, to find out who the real Edward Farhat was. As with any biography, research and interviews made up the most important part of the process. And I think I was able to put together as complete a picture as I could with the tools at my disposal and thanks to the scores of people who knew and worked closely with him who were willing to speak to me. The one element that eluded me throughout the process was direct participation from the living members of the immediate Farhat family, who declined to take part despite my best efforts to include them. While this did not surprise me, given I had already been familiarized with their reclusive nature and dedication to protecting The Sheik's legacy, it did disappoint me, as it would've undoubtedly provided an even more complete picture than what you now hold in your hands.

Nevertheless, I fully respect their decision and the reasons behind it. I must also acknowledge that this project came along at a time of great suffering and loss in the family, as both of The Sheik's sons passed away before it was complete. I had been in touch with Eddie Farhat Jr. in the early stages of the writing process, and while there was definitely reticence, I did sense he was on the verge of relenting a bit, when suddenly he was faced with the unthinkable loss of his brother. We lost contact after that, and any hopes for his changing his mind ended with his own tragic passing less than six months later.

That said, I have chosen to take a very transparent approach to the narrative of this story. There are areas that remain mysteries, and I will indicate when that is the case. There are areas where the truth is still a bit unclear, and I will also indicate when that is the case. In some instances, The Sheik was so successful in kayfabing people that there are some indisputable facts I've uncovered that contradict the accepted timeline of his life as it currently stands. This necessitates a direct, first-person style, rather than the omniscient narration that is typical of most biographies. In other words, I intend to be completely up-front with you, the reader, about what I know and what I don't know, and also how I know what I know. I believe this to be the best way to honor The Sheik's legacy, while also telling the most complete and truthful story I can. I stand by the work I've done as the best possible summation of the man's life, given the resources and living witnesses available to me.

"People say that wrestling isn't real.
Well, somebody forgot to tell that son of a bitch!"
—TERRY FUNK

FOREWORD

Being part of the Sheik's clan earned us a lot of respect from the boys, while we were coming up. My first two or three years in the business, introductions were met with a special look in people's eyes. There was a tight group of five of us that had the honor of beating the crap out of each other in The Sheik's ring: Thom, George, Dango, myself, and Sabu. A few other wrestlers would pass through, often never returning, or showing up once every three months, comparing us to safer schools. That's how we realized we wrestled much, much stiffer than ... well, everybody.

One of our first shows was in Fort Wayne, Indiana. Dango and I had a tag team match against a couple of young guys that were acrobatic like us and had some really cool moves. Before our match, everybody thought it'd be a good idea to rib our opponents and tell them that we thought everything was real and they better be careful. I'm guessing that after feeling a few of our slams and kicks, they believed it was true because very early in the match, our opponents surprised us by not kicking out of a random pin, to end the chances of anyone getting hurt.

There was no getting hurt in the ring for Sheik's boys. While training, when one of us complained that we needed to stop and take a few minutes to shake something off, Sheik would tell us that he was stabbed in the leg in Puerto Rico by a crazy fan and continued the match. We were always amazed at his stories, and we loved hearing them while we sat around the dinner table after training. It felt like we were part of a significant group of very few, select people. We were a family. Still, Sheik kept all of us constantly intimidated, even Sabu.

I remember trying to peek over Sheik's shoulder in the locker room before a show in Vermont in 1991. We wanted to see what was in Sheik's mysterious briefcase, and he had it partway open on his lap while he sat in a folding chair. As we crept our way closer to peek inside unnoticed, he slammed the case shut while snapping around toward us yelling, "WHAT ARE YOU LOOKING AT?"

We ran like little kids.

Later that night, Sheik wrestled Abdullah the Butcher, and the match called for the entire locker room to run out and aid in a big pull-apart on the floor. Sabu and I decided to stay away from everyone out there because we knew what to expect. Afterward, all the boys came back surprised because they didn't realize they had been cut and thought the blood belonged to someone else. They all got sliced by Sheik or the Butcher, or both. Same two blades for the entire locker room. When Abby came back from the chaos, he was pissed and yelled at me and Sabu because when we came out, to avoid the melee on the floor, we hit the ring and started doing high spots. It's funny to think of how inconsiderate that was of us, and how pissed Abby was. I don't think Sheik saw us in the ring.

His words and his teachings will always stick with me. Still, I didn't realize how little I knew about my mentor until reading *Blood and Fire*. In fact, the only time I remember him showing a soft side was when his granddaughter Susi was visiting. He loved her so much and was so warm and inviting to her. It was almost embarrassing for us, like we shouldn't have access to this side of him. He would almost be in baby-talk mode, he was so happy, but I don't remember ever feeling comfortable enough to joke with him about it or anything.

Blood and Fire gives us such an extensive look at the most original wrestler to grace the industry and the most important man of my career. I learned so much about his business journeys and his personal life too. I find it incredibly interesting to learn what was happening in Sheik's life when our paths crossed.

It's incredible that no one has ever written a book about Sheik, but I'm so glad because no one could've done what Brian Solomon accomplished. It's so well written, it's an enjoyable read while at the same time delivering astounding numbers and facts, such as dates, addresses, tickets sold, and wrestlers' fees. If there's more than one version of a story, Brian will give them all to you. The immense amount of research that was put into this book is apparent on every page, all the way through.

Knowing Sheik more now, as I do, I have a greater understanding of what parts of me he built. He gave me the mindset to raise the bar, in the industry and in life. I also see much more of him in Sabu then I did before, in different areas of life.

I'm thankful for this book, and I hope many people enjoy it as much as I do.

—ROB VAN DAM

INTRODUCTION

O n the banks of the Detroit River in Cobo Arena, a crowd of nearly
ten thousand Motor City residents waits with bated breath. The
typical clang and furor of a packed house has briefly quieted in
the anticipation of the moment. In the center of the arena stands a wrestling ring, currently occupied by a short, chubby gentleman wearing the
black-and-white striped shirt of the referee; a tall, skinny young man
in a horrendous tuxedo and glasses, holding a microphone; and, standing tentatively in the corner, a short, stocky middle-aged wrestler with
flowing brown locks, in nondescript blue trunks and boots. Every now
and then, he looks up from the canvas to the locker room entrance about
fifty feet up the aisle. A couple of years ago, they were making him wrestle in a Batman costume in Pittsburgh. In about five minutes, he'll be
longing for those halcyon days.

"And now for our next match here at Big Time Wrestling!" announces
the man with the mic. He lifts his hand in the air and then lowers it in the
direction of the blue-booted grappler before continuing. "The following
contest is a special attraction, scheduled for one fall! Introducing first, in
the corner to my left, from Italy, weighing 235 pounds . . . Tony Marino!"

With a nod, Marino half-heartedly raises his arm to the crowd,
fingers semi-clenched in a weak fist. A smattering of hopeful cheers
breaks through the silence but quickly dies down. Suddenly, the sound
of a door slamming open can be heard, as the long black curtains that

1

obscure the locker room entrance are quickly parted. To the rising chorus of preemptive boos and hisses that begins to fill the auditorium, stepping out onto the hardwood floor are two figures who are definitely not among Earl "Big Cat" Lloyd's Pistons.

The first to be illuminated by the spotlight is a sweaty hobgoblin waving the red, white, and black colors of Syria. He sports a yellow and brown checkered polyester suit of a variety that would be unlikely to set the buyer back by very much. The fat cigar clenched between his teeth doesn't seem to be impeding his angry growls to the unappreciative masses as he leads the way for his charge. With his greasy mass of curly hair, a silver-dollar-sized Star of David medallion hanging from his neck, and thick-framed brown sunglasses, he is the anti-Semite's worst mental image of the crass, obnoxious, loudmouth Jew come to life.

But whatever minimal restraint the crowd had previously been showing in its vociferous antipathy is completely abandoned once emerges into the light the individual for whom this flag-carrying cretin was merely preparing the way. Draped in the traditional white cotton kaffiyeh headdress and billowing red and gold Bedouin robe, he doesn't so much walk through the curtain as explode, screaming in unintelligible syllables as if in mid-conversation with some mad deity. He gesticulates wildly, a hint of drool seeping out into his neatly trimmed beard, black with just a touch of gray. As he lunges forward, wild-eyed, children scatter, the police escort and security staff seemingly there mainly to protect *them* from this raving lunatic.

"And now, making his way down the aisle, his opponent," the ring announcer resumes his intonations as the duo continues its erratic progress to the ring. "Accompanied by his manager, Eddy 'The Brain' Creatchman . . . from Syria, weighing 242 pounds, The Noble Sheik!"

Creatchman scampers up the corner ring steps and through the ropes first, continuing his grumbling and muttering, a cloud of cigar smoke wreathing his head. While The Sheik makes a similar ascent, the manager heads to a neutral corner, rests his flagpole against the ropes, and gently places an intricately embroidered prayer mat on the canvas. The Sheik meanders around the inside of the ring in a rough approximation of a circle as Marino, referee, and ring announcer give him a wide berth, the ring announcer soon making the wise choice of exiting the scene, his work, conveniently, done.

Having spotted the mat in the corner, The Sheik immediately quits his wandering and makes his way over, casting a steady glance to the crowd before falling to his knees. The frenzied boos, epithets, and general howls of disapproval that had already been pouring from the rafters now rain down in torrents, along with cups, crumpled papers, and whatever else fans can get their hands on. As he bows three times in ceremonious fashion, The Sheik groans, "ALLAAAHHHH!!!" followed by a stream of what may be other words, which cannot be made out over the cacophonous din.

Suddenly, catching everyone in the building completely off guard, particularly those currently in the ring with him, The Sheik leaps up from the prayer mat, grabs the flag still leaning against the ropes next to him, lunges behind Marino, and proceeds to break the wooden pole over his back, sending his screaming would-be opponent to the canvas. Sheik then grabs one of the broken pieces of the flagpole and presses it across Marino's throat as the referee desperately tries to pull him off and Creatchman leaps up and down with joy. The referee finally manages to pry the wooden shard from Sheik's hands and quickly kicks it under the ropes and out of the ring. He backs Sheik into the corner as the stunned Marino, on all fours with his head down, takes a moment to try and catch his breath. The crowd is already whipped into a raging froth, and the match has not yet even officially begun.

After shooing Creatchman back down the ring steps to the floor, the referee looks both ways, taking in this brief moment of peace as The Sheik removes his kaffiyeh and robe and tosses them over the top rope to his manager. His headdress gone, The Sheik reveals a shock of salt-and-pepper hair, as well as a thick mass of scar tissue covering his entire forehead, marked by deep vertical grooves running from his hairline down to his bushy black eyebrows. He wears short black wrestling trunks emblazoned with a white camel, and matching boots, their tips turned up in little points. Marino makes his way to his feet just as the ref finally calls for the opening bell. For a fleeting moment, as the two men circle each other, what is happening in the ring resembles a wrestling match. They lock up in what is ironically termed "the referee's hold," each man placing his right hand behind his opponent's neck and his left inside the fold of his opponent's elbow. Betraying an actual knowledge of wrestling fundamentals, The Sheik transitions from the hold into a side headlock.

Dragging Marino by the head, The Sheik makes his way over to the ropes and strategically turns his back on the referee. Freeing one of his hands, he balls it into a fist and starts bouncing it off the top of Marino's head, simultaneously raking his face back and forth across the top strand. The referee begins an angry count of five, threatening to disqualify Sheik if he continues, which merely causes Sheik to clamp down on the headlock and drag Marino over to another corner of the ring. As if on cue, Creatchman jumps up onto the ring apron with some unknown grievance that grabs the referee's attention, just long enough for Sheik to reach into his trunks and produce a finely sharpened pencil. Gasps of real concern can be heard as Sheik puts the business end of the pencil against his opponent's forehead. As Marino flails his arms helplessly, Sheik's eyes roll back in his head and he takes his opponent down to the canvas, hunching over him and jabbing the pencil up and down into his head in a stabbing motion.

Creatchman's ploy exposed, the referee abandons the manager on the apron and runs over to pull the pencil-wielding Sheik off Marino's prone body. As he does so, Marino lifts his face from the mat to reveal a roadmap of crimson rivulets, his eyes tightly closed and his mouth open in a grimace as blood drips from his head, staining the canvas red. The ref manages to get between the two men, but as he attempts to grab the pencil from Sheik's hand, all he succeeds in doing is giving the bloody and indignant Marino an opportunity to steal the pencil himself. As Marino holds the pencil up in triumph, the whites of his eyes keenly visible in the mask of plasma and sweat that is now his face, the gasps of the crowd quickly turn into an explosion of exultation. Marino shoves the referee aside and leaps toward The Sheik, driving him back into the opposite corner as he brings the pencil down in a wide arc. Towering over Sheik as he sits helpless in the corner while the referee works to keep Creatchman out of the ring, Marino brings the pencil down repeatedly.

Sheik crumples to the mat, holding his head in both hands. Marino backs away, and Sheik puts hands to his side, revealing that his face, too, is now coated in blood. The referee stumbles over, looks both men up and down, shakes his head back and forth, and motions for the bell to be rung. He then leans over the top rope and calls out instructions to the frightened ring announcer, who has been cowering at a ringside table watching all this unfold.

"The time, four minutes and forty-one seconds," declares the ring announcer on the house mic, as the referee returns to his desperate attempt to keep Sheik and Marino apart, Creatchman now joining the fray. "The referee has disqualified both men. This match is ruled . . . a draw!"

The rain of trash resumes. The Sheik steadies himself against the ropes and gets to his feet. A repeated clang of the bell resounds through Cobo Arena as both referee and Creatchman pull the struggling Marino away from Sheik and back into the center of the ring, blood now streaming down his chest. While this is going on, attention is briefly drawn away from The Sheik, but that changes when he takes a step toward the restrained Marino, hands clasped together. In a flash, Sheik opens his hands and hurls what appears to be a small orb of flame directly into Marino's face.

Screams of terror erupt from the already apoplectic crowd. Women hide their faces in their husbands' and boyfriends' arms. Children cry as their parents shield them from what is happening. Creatchman and the referee flee to opposite corners of the ring, releasing Marino as he drops to the mat in agony. The flame disappears as quickly as it appeared, but Marino is still writhing on the mat, screeching as he holds his face tightly with both hands. The Sheik now stands over him, blood and drool dripping from his face, his tongue hanging out one side of his mouth, the pupils of his eyes pointed at the ceiling. Through it all, the bell continues to sound, loud and futile.

As the scene unfolds, watching from behind the curtain that leads to the locker room is a thin, attractive middle-aged woman with blond hair, snazzily dressed in white jacket and matching pants. A look of concern crosses her face, but not for long; she's seen him in similar circumstances so many times, and deep down she knows he'll be fine, but it doesn't make it any easier to watch. She's gotten used to it, and in years past was in fact much closer to the action herself, acting as The Sheik's beautiful, mysterious ringside valet. Back then, she went by several names, including Princess Fatima and Princess Salima. Now, she is known only as Joyce Farhat. Although no longer The Sheik's valet, she continues to fulfill another role, the same one she has for the past twenty-three years: that of The Sheik's wife. And while she, like everyone else, usually calls him Sheik, at home, behind closed doors, he will always be just Ed to her.

His name is one of many details to which Joyce Farhat is privy, and of which those ten thousand rowdy Detroit fans, and millions of others worldwide, remain intentionally uninformed. Although he is indeed of Middle Eastern descent, Ed Farhat was born and bred in the good old United States—just about ninety miles west of where they are standing now, in fact. The son of Lebanese immigrants, he was raised not as a Muslim, but as a Catholic, and the only language he speaks fluently is English. Like many sons of immigrants, he was a patriotic American who served his country in World War II, even going so far as attempting to fake his birth certificate so he could join the service at age seventeen. In addition to being a loving husband, he is also a proud family man with two sons at home: nine-year-old Tommy; and twenty-two-year-old Eddie Jr., who recently received a degree in business administration from Michigan State University. But even more than his status as husband and father, fans might be most surprised to learn of Ed's acumen as a businessman—for Ed is also the owner and operator of Big Time Wrestling, and one of the most powerful wrestling promoters in the country. In this anonymous role, he has been producing professional wrestling events for the paying public, both live and on television, throughout the Midwest for the past eight years. Each of the wrestlers who appear under the auspices of Big Time Wrestling, including Tony Marino, whom he has just reduced to a burned and bloody heap in the middle of the ring, works for Ed. The very fans screaming for his head may not realize it, but they have The Sheik to thank for their weekly entertainment in more than one way.

In a world built on illusion, no one lived and breathed the illusion like Ed "The Sheik" Farhat. During an era when pro wrestling's secrets were truly sacrosanct, there was no secret as heavily guarded as the true nature of the man whose barbarous and animalistic reputation made him the most feared and famous wrestling villain on the planet. The line between fantasy and reality was blurred to a degree that was extreme even by wrestling standards, and to a certain degree remains blurred to this day. His story is unique in the annals of the business, which is truly saying a lot. He was a character that could only have been produced by that paradoxical world, a setting where his nightly behavior and the acts he committed, which would have landed him in jail in any other context, instead elevated him among the most revered legends to ever step through the ropes.

CHAPTER 1

HEADED FOR THE MONEY

"There ain't no nice guys in this business.
There ain't no people. There's dollars."
—THE SHEIK

In the heart of Michigan, on six and a half square miles of land, sits the town of Charlotte, population ten thousand. The population was roughly half that on the cool, cloudy evening of October 26, 1938, when three young boys from Lansing were picked up by police while hitchhiking along Route 27. They had collectively run away from home four hours prior, making it thirty-five miles southwestward across the state—falling a bit short of the grand, cross-country adventure they had planned.

The boys were identified as thirteen-year-old Roosevelt Haspeny, eleven-year-old Freddie Rahar, and the ringleader, a skinny twelve-year-old Syrian kid named Edward Farhat. The three neighbors and friends were brought to the Eaton County Courthouse, where they cooled their jets until their worried parents were notified of their whereabouts and came to pick them up, effectively bringing their ambitions to a grinding halt, at least for the moment.

When questioned by Sheriff Milton Kreig about exactly what they had in mind, Eddie declared, "We're going out to California, where it's summer all the time and where there's a lot of money."

Eddie's journey was cut short on that fateful day, but in another decade it would start anew, and fulfill all the dreams he had as a kid, and much, much more. Even at that tender age, he knew what he wanted, and he knew he wasn't going to find it in Lansing. That restless spirit that led him, as a seventh grader, not only to put out his thumb and see how far it would take him, but to recruit others to join him for the ride, would stay with him. It would eventually get him to the sunny climes of California . . . as well as New York, Chicago, Houston, St. Louis, Toronto, Phoenix, Boston, Montreal, Philadelphia, Indianapolis, DC, Nashville, Baltimore, Louisville, Milwaukee, Atlanta, Miami, New Orleans, Honolulu, San Juan, and Tokyo, among many other places. He would find the money he was looking for—more than his young brain could've ever imagined in those days—and live like the prince he portrayed himself to be.

The dream wouldn't last forever, and he would lose it all in as dramatic a fashion as he achieved it. But along the way, he would change his chosen business forever, become one of the greatest attractions ever seen, and create a legend still talked about in hushed tones nearly two decades after his death. In order to do it, he would have to destroy that little boy, wipe him from existence, and in his place create a fearsome monster that would travel the globe, leaving chaos in its wake, but also leaving cashboxes filled to overflowing with the hard-earned cash of people who would pay to see it.

And it all started, as most stories of great men do, with a little boy trying to prove something to himself.

CHAPTER 2

DOWN FROM THE MOUNTAINTOP

A collection of rock-hewn structures nestled amidst the hills of the mountainous Jabal Amel region of Lebanon, some 2,500 feet above sea level, the village of Tebnine dates back to ancient times, when it was populated by Phoenicians and Canaanites. Ravaged during the Crusades of the early Middle Ages, it later came under the rule of the Ottoman Empire, which controlled the surrounding territories for more than four centuries. In those days, Lebanon was not a sovereign state, but rather viewed as a subsection of Syria, which is why

many of those who emigrated from there to the United States during the great period of epic migration in the late nineteenth and early twentieth century, were referred to as Syrian rather than Lebanese.

By no means one of the more impressive villages of Lebanon, with a population not enough to fill the old Cobo Arena in Detroit even halfway, the humble Tebnine nevertheless produced a family whose most famous child would fill that arena to capacity on a biweekly basis for years on end. Like millions did, that family would leave their native home looking for a better way of life in a land of opportunity—and all would find it, each in his or her own way. For the youngest son, Edward, that opportunity would arise in a uniquely American industry and entertainment: professional wrestling. By exploiting and subverting his foreign heritage, he would attain the American dream in the most unorthodox of ways, finding wealth, power, and influence in the nation where his parents had chosen to make their new home.

By the early twentieth century, the grip of the once-mighty Ottoman Turks was slipping as the Middle East and Europe experienced a period of uncertainty and instability that would eventually slide into the First World War. Though under majority Muslim rule, the Ottoman Empire nevertheless was known for its tolerance of other faiths over the centuries; however, this had begun to change as local rule became more erratic. Life became especially challenging for minority groups such as the Maronites, a Catholic-Christian sect founded in the fifth century that owed its allegiance not to Mecca but to Rome, made up of ethnic Arabs who had resisted conversion to Islam. Tebnine had long been home to a significant Maronite population, which had flocked to the somewhat secluded village for protection generations earlier. Nevertheless, brutal massacres had been known to occur, as the Maronites would be randomly targeted by both the Muslim majority as well as the Druze, another monotheistic minority sect.

Davoud Khalil Farhat, son of Khalil and Mary Farhat, was one of those Tebnine Maronites who saw the writing on the wall. After growing up and working on his father's hilltop farm, he left the village for the first time in May 1904 at age twenty-two, making his way to Beirut, where he hopped on a small transport ship to the French coastal port of Le Havre. From there he boarded the fabled French steamship *La Gascogne* on June 4 and made the nine-day voyage across the Atlantic to Ellis Island. It was a gutsy move for a provincial farmer's son who could neither read nor write and didn't even know the exact date of his birth. In fact, he didn't even have the fifty dollars required to avoid being detained, and he was held on the island for three days before being released into the custody of his uncle, a Michigan resident who took Davoud to stay with him at 212 Lahoma Street in downtown Lansing.

The move was not a permanent one yet. Presumably, Davoud, like many others in the Old World, had heard tales of the bounty America had to offer, the stories of new starts and hopes for escape from whatever struggles had defined people's lives for generations. The Lansing and greater Detroit areas were developing prominent Arabic immigrant populations thanks to the promise of a comfortable middle-class life away from strife and upheaval. Decades before the days of its own economic collapse and infrastructural failure, Detroit was ground zero for the automobile industry, then in its earliest infancy. The new industry was poised to change the world and usher in an era of progress and prosperity, especially for the laborers who got in on the ground floor.

Over the next few years, Davoud would return to Tebnine while still putting out feelers in the country he intended to make his new permanent home. During his time back in Tebnine, he met a local girl, Latife Tobia, daughter of Michael and Malake Tobia. Davoud and Latife were wed on August 27, 1907. At the time, Latife was only fifteen years of age, and Davoud was almost ten years her senior—not unusual for the time period or their culture, and it is entirely possible that the marriage may have been arranged, although this is not known for certain.

Davoud continued to divide his time between Tebnine and Lansing, earning money while establishing a new life back home with Latife, who remained in the village for the time being. Although they didn't spend a great deal of time together in those years, they did spend some— evidenced by the birth on July 5, 1908, of their first child, a baby girl they called Zieckie.[1] Over the next five years, Davoud got a firmer footing in Michigan as matters got more dire in Lebanon, with the Ottoman Empire in decline and the entire region on the brink of war. The transition was helped by the presence of a large number of cousins and other extended relatives who had already made the move, as well as the arrival of Davoud's younger brother, Assad Khalil.

And so, the time finally came for Davoud to bring his new family to America and leave the old country behind for good. At twenty-one years of age, with her younger sister and four-year-old daughter by her side, Latife traveled from Lebanon to Liverpool, England, where she boarded the SS *Merion*, an ocean liner bound for Philadelphia. After a twelve-day trans-Atlantic journey (which any parent will tell you could not have been fun to endure with a preschooler), Latife arrived in the United States on June 30, 1913, and was reunited with her husband.[2]

And this time, it was for good. Davoud and Latife became David and Eva. The biblical world of Mount Lebanon and its Iron Age trappings lay behind them; which was ironic, since the iron and steel of Detroit and its booming auto works would become their new home. The Ottoman Empire would fall after World War I, putting Lebanon under the control of the French for a time before it finally managed to establish its own freedom and independence. For David and Eva Farhat, however, the struggle was over—they were already free.

CHAPTER 3

GROWING UP FARHAT

"Mrs. David Farhat's heart is bigger than her home."
—*LANSING STATE JOURNAL, MAY 10, 1953*

The early twentieth century was a time of massive immigration and assimilation in America as Jews, Italians, Poles, Greeks, Swedes, Chinese, and countless other ethnic groups carved out their piece of the pie, usually settling in urban centers like New York, Boston, Milwaukee, Chicago, and San Francisco. For the Farhats, it was the Lebanese enclave in suburban Detroit, more specifically the Greater Lansing area, where they would spend more than twenty years absorbing the culture and adapting to life as new Americans before their youngest son, Edward, the boy who would go on to become The Noble, Exalted Sheik, was even born.

Far from the farmland of Jabal Amel, David found his niche as a metal worker, pouring iron molds first for the Motor Wheel Corporation and then, starting in 1914, for the Capital Casting Company, where he would spend the next thirty-five years, until his retirement. With David socking away as much as he could in the years since he had been coming to America to make his living, the Farhats were able to purchase a home in downtown Lansing—a rarity in those days when many newly arrived families were compelled to live in cramped tenements and ramshackle shanties. Mortgaged for $5,000, their home at 828 Williams Street,[1] a stone's throw from the Grand River, would remain the heart and soul of the extended Farhat family for almost half a century—right into the years when The Sheik had become a national TV celebrity. With Dave's cousin George and his wife, Martha, living next door and other assorted

Farhats mere blocks away, it quickly became a warm and welcoming environment—more than a "home away from home," it was simply home.

Over the years, the house would expand, going from three bedrooms to seven, as well as having two complete kitchens. And given how the family would grow now that David and Latife were living together full-time, it's not hard to understand why: Their second daughter, Olga, would be born a year after Latife's arrival in America, and their first son, Lewie, a year after that. Their third daughter, Julia, came along in 1917, followed by Joseph (later nicknamed "Topper") in 1918 and Elizabeth in 1919. By the start of the 1920s, the Farhat home contained David and Eva; their six children; Eva's mother, Malake; one of David's cousins; plus a boarder whose rent helped them pay down their mortgage. Although most didn't have as much space as the Farhats did, this living setup was not uncommon among immigrant clans in those days, with sprawling extended families providing support and security in a foreign land that became less foreign with each passing year.

To help support the family, Eva took a part-time job as a cook at the Downey, a luxury Lansing hotel at the corner of Washington Avenue and Washtenaw Street. David became a member of the Syrian-American Workmen's Association, a Detroit-based labor organization catering to the growing population of ethnic Lebanese working industrial jobs in the region. And there would be even more mouths to feed in the new decade, with a third son, Moses, coming into the world on New Year's Day, 1921, and a fourth, Amal, two years later. In 1924, the Farhats produced a fifth

David and Eva Farhat,
The Sheik's father and mother.

son, whom they named Edmund, which would in later years be the cause of some confusion thanks to its similarity to the name they bestowed on their sixth and youngest son. The similarities would end there.

On June 9, 1926, Edward George Farhat was born to thirty-four-year-old Eva and forty-four-year-old David Farhat, the tenth child of their still-growing brood of first-generation Americans.[2] The precise location of his birth is unclear. There were two hospitals in close proximity at the time: McLaren Greater Lansing and Sparrow, with the latter being the more likely place of birth due to the presence of the only pediatric ward in the region. However, in the 1920s, home deliveries with the aid of a midwife were common, especially among immigrant families who were still comfortable with such methods from the old country.

The youngest son, little Eddie, was not the last of the bunch: his baby sister, Genevieve (or "Eva" like her mother), was born at the end of 1928, bringing the grand total to eleven Farhat children, born over a span of twenty years. As an example of how dramatic the age differences were between the oldest and youngest siblings, a mere nine months after Genevieve's birth, first-born Zieckie was married at age twenty-one. She and her husband, Solomon Rashid, would continue to live in the family home, along with their son Jimmy (the first of more than thirty grandchildren for David and Eva).[3]

Eddie grew up in what was by all indications a warm and hardworking household; the family attended St. Mary's Roman Catholic Church regularly and, by the time he was a boy, had already become a respected fixture of the local community and a shining example of an immigrant success story (even if they were a far cry from the wealthy Syrian oil barons he would later claim kinship to as part of his wrestling persona). So large was the family that David built a special table himself to place in the main dining room so that everyone could enjoy meals together happily and comfortably. Eva, ever the joyful matriarch,[4] became known throughout the neighborhood for her cooking, serving up traditional Lebanese dishes like kibbe and fattoush salad to her many children and their many friends. On Sundays and holidays, the house would be even fuller than usual, with extended family and friends all partaking in the feast. So well-known was her cooking that she would regularly volunteer to cater local events. While the kids were asleep, she would make upwards of forty pounds of flour into flat Syrian bread, baking late into the night. For the rest of his years, Edward would take with him a lifelong love of Lebanese cuisine, as well its close cousin, Greek cuisine.

Retaining pride in their heritage while also embracing the ways of their new home, the Farhats symbolized the epitome of the American dream. Members of the Al-Ashab Syrian Progressive Club, a local organization dedicated to the peaceful merging of Syrian and American cultures, they were known throughout Greater Lansing society, especially for their charming and talented children.[5] Though not much is known of his childhood, by all accounts Edward was an active child who enjoyed building model boats, which he would race in the nearby river. He also spent time with his friends, playing and indulging his model boat interest at the historic Scott Park in downtown Lansing, later representing Scott Park in a 1939 county-wide youth model boat racing competition sponsored by the Lansing Board of Education and FDR's Works Progress Administration.

Born just three years before the catastrophic stock market crash of 1929, Edward was a child of the Great Depression, although the Farhats navigated those treacherous waters better than most immigrant families. David never appears to have been out of work, and at least four of the six Farhat sons, Lewie, Joseph, Amal, and Edmund, appear to have received college educations. However, along with older brother Moses, Edward did not. He also seems to have received the least amount of education of all the Farhat children, and it's possible that the Depression may have had something to do with this. There is some confusion as to exactly how much education he received: A 1940 census report, taken when Edward was thirteen, lists his last completed grade as the fifth. At the time, the boy was three years past the age for fifth grade, which may mean that he had been left back or that he had already been pulled from school. His military records, however, indicate that he got as far as eighth grade, while his death certificate indicates eleventh. I'm inclined to believe the military record is the most accurate.

The scenario was not totally uncommon for the era, when exceptions to the laws requiring students to remain in school till age sixteen could be made. However, usually these early withdrawal exceptions were made due to serious disciplinary or performance issues. In Eddie's case, the reasons remain unknown. But the result was that Eddie's extended education took place, as the old cliché goes, in the school of hard knocks, growing up just a little bit more streetwise than his more privileged older siblings, a kid whose early toughening up would certainly serve him well in later years. Like many Depression-era children, he took refuge in the escape provided by Hollywood, and it's known that he was particularly struck by the 1937 jungle adventure movie *Elephant Boy*, starring thirteen-year-old Indian Muslim swashbuckling sensation Sabu.[6] It's not hard to imagine the preteen Eddie Farhat sitting in the old Orpheum Theater in Lansing's Washington Square, enthralled by the exotic Far East environs and by a dark-skinned boy like himself, not far from his own age, taking center stage in an era when most Hollywood headliners were lily-white and as American as apple pie. This may have been the boy's first exposure to the allure and draw of Eastern exoticism on American audiences. If so, it was a lesson not lost on him in later years.

One year after seeing *Elephant Boy*, Eddie would stage his own Hollywood-style adventure with his infamous cross-country hitchhiking attempt. And even though it didn't succeed, the seed had been planted. The boy had a thirst for new experiences, for traveling, for glory and adventure. In the years soon to come, he would quench those thirsts as few can ever hope to.

CHAPTER 4

FORGED IN THE FLAMES OF WAR

"'Buy bonds, and keep 'em flying,' is the motto of Mr. and Mrs. David K. Farhat, 828 Williams Street, and their six sons and five daughters."
—LANSING STATE JOURNAL, AUGUST 15, 1943

By the start of the 1940s, with the threat of America entering another World War looming, Edward Farhat was a boy in his early teens, his formal education over but his life education only beginning. There has been quite a bit of confusion regarding the subject of his schooling—along with several other topics related to a man whose lifelong goal was secrecy. Stories have commonly circulated of his attending Michigan State or some such other local university, of being a standout football star, even of teaching university classes himself. Records do not bear any of that out, but it likely has to do with reporters and other researchers mixing him up with his older brother Edmund. It was Edmund, just two years Edward's senior, who achieved possibly the highest level of education of any of the Farhat boys, graduating from Ferris State University and attaining a master's in education from Michigan State. It was Edmund who was a standout high school and college football and basketball player, who played Triple-A softball, and who eventually became athletic director and superintendent of Muskegon Catholic Central High School.[1]

Such confusion was common even during the heyday of Edward's Sheikdom, and the erroneous story even made it into print, making it reasonable to assume that The Sheik chose to be silent on the issue, and perhaps even encouraged such confusion, adding to his fascinating mythos as it did. But the reality is that, for whatever reason, Edward seems to have gotten somewhat short shrift, as the later children of enormous families often do.[2] Is it possible, as is sometimes the case with youngest sons, that Edward, a young boy in a family of high local stature, passing the time home with his parents while his older brothers got busy achieving great things, was saddled with feelings of inferiority? If so, that would certainly explain the blazing fire that seemed to be lit underneath him as he approached full manhood. It was a fire whose heat would be felt by many adversaries he later saw as obstacles in his way. First among them would be Hitler and Hirohito.

The Farhats prided themselves on being loyal Americans—and that loyalty would be put to the test on December 7, 1941, when forces of the Empire of Japan launched an attack on the Pearl Harbor naval base in Hawaii, hurling the United States into World War II. Edward was only fifteen at the time, but he watched his older brothers go off to serve and longed to do the same. Topper, already a married father of twins, was the first, leaving his job at the Olds Motor Works to enlist just prior to Pearl Harbor, ascending to the rank of sergeant and helping to train new recruits. Moses, also an Olds employee and new father, enlisted as a private and saw extensive action in Italy.[3] Amal and Edmund, who were working at the time as government clerks after school, received officer's training and

Brothers in Service

Edmond   Amal   Moses   Joseph

"Buy bonds and keep 'em flying," is the motto of Mr. and Mrs. David K. Farhat, 828 William street, and their six sons and five daughters. Four sons are now serving in the armed forces. They are Corp. Edmond Farhat, 18, and Corp. Amal Farhat, 20, who are stationed at Shenango, Pa. Prior to entering the service they were employed at the secretary of state's office. Edmond was graduated from St. Mary's high school where he participated in sports, and he also played ball in the city league.

Pvt. Moses Farhat, 22, is stationed at Camp Gruber, Okla. Prior to entering the service, he was employed at the Olds Motor Works. He attended St. Mary's school, and took an active part in sports, also playing with the city league. He is married and the father of one child.

Sgt. Joseph 'Top' Farhat, 25, is stationed at Boston, Mass., where he is training recruits. He was graduated from Central high school. He played basketball and softball in the city league for five years, and was also manager of the softball team of the Syrian-American Workmens' association. Prior to entering the service two years ago, he was employed at the Olds Motor Works. He

is married and the father of twins. Lewie Farhat, 27, is a defense worker at the Nash-Kelvinator plant Edward Farhat, 17, is employed at Estill's cafeteria. He tried to enlist in the marine corps, but failed to pass the physical examination.

A son-in-law, Pvt. Raymond Dennis, is also in the service and is stationed in Texas.

Julia Farhat is employed in the navy department at Reo Motors Inc., and Betty Farhat is employed at the Olds Motor Works.

The father, David Farhat, is a moulder at the Capital Castings company, and they are all reported to be war bond buyers.

GROUP FROM CITY AT MAXWELL FIELD

MAXWELL FIELD, Ala., Aug. 14 —Sixteen youths from Lansing, Mich., and East Lansing, have reported to the army air forces preflight school for pilots at Maxwell Field, Ala., to begin the third phase

Lansing State Journal, *August 15, 1943: Four of Edward's five older brothers are pictured in an article touting the wartime efforts of the inspirational Farhat immigrant family.*

attained the rank of corporal. Lewie and Julia did defense work, building helicopters and trucks for the military. All the adults of the family were war bond buyers, putting their hard-earned money into the war effort as so many did. The immigrant family was once again held up as an example of first-generation Americans proudly supporting their adopted country.

By the age of seventeen, with the war in Europe at its height, Edward was working at Estill's Cafeteria, a popular Lansing restaurant located in the basement of an Elks Lodge. A well-known legend dictates that he capitalized on the similarity of his older brother's name by using Edmund's birth certificate to enlist in the Marines while underage. However, records indicate that his attempt to enlist failed, as he did not pass the physical exam. It's unknown whether this was due to actual medical reasons, or simply that his subterfuge was discovered and he was rejected for his age.

Nevertheless, his time would come on August 17, 1944, when he was drafted into the United States Army two months after his eighteenth birthday. Owing no doubt to skills learned from his father and older brothers, who were working in metal foundries and auto factories, Edward was identified as a candidate for tank operations, and assigned to the 93rd Cavalry Reconnaissance Squadron, as part of the 13th Armored Division. He was sent to Camp Bowie in west central Texas, where he trained for eight months. It was also during that time that he took an interest in an amateur sport that none of his athletically accomplished brothers had ever tried: wrestling.[4] While Edward received basic training as a soldier and

Eddie Farhat's selective service draft card.

training as a wrestler as part of the 93rd, Allied forces had completed the beach invasion at Normandy, France, and were making their way gradually toward Germany and the heart of the Third Reich.

In January 1945, the 93rd Cavalry was sent overseas to join General George S. Patton's 3rd Army in its advance across France. One of the newer recruits, Edward didn't join them for three more months. At the beginning of April 1945, after having attained the position of Technician Fifth Grade, he was sent to the New York Port of Embarkation at Camp Kilmer, New Jersey, then departed from New York on the USS *Marine Devil*, a cramped troop transport that spent twelve days on the Atlantic before pulling into the bombed-out French port of Le Havre—ironically, the exact location from which his father had first embarked for America some forty years prior.[5]

By this point, the 93rd and the rest of Patton's 3rd Army were deep in German territory, with the Nazis on the run. Eddie and the rest of the newly arrived troops made their way across countless wrecked and burned vehicles, uncleared minefields, barbed wire entanglements, and towns with hardly a building still standing, finally meeting up with the rest of their compatriots across the Danube River near the town of Langenerling. Driving a tank across the scorched earth of Bavaria, Eddie made his way through the heart of a nation on the verge of surrender. On the day Hitler killed himself in his Berlin bunker, April 30, Eddie Farhat and the 93rd crossed the river Isar at Plattling, later capturing bridges over the Rott and Vils rivers before stopping the next day at the village of Simbach near the Inn river, where the Nazis blew up the bridge while Eddie and his fellow cavalrymen were only fifteen feet away from crossing. From there, the plan was to capture the Austrian city of Salzburg—but German defeat at the Battle of Berlin on May 2 halted all plans. Three days later, the Germans surrendered in Bavaria, and, finally, the unconditional surrender of Germany was signed in Reims, France, on May 7, bringing an end to the war in Europe.

With hostilities halted, the troops went into cleanup mode, and for the next couple of months there was more time for leisure, which often took the form of athletics. It was common for different squadrons and divisions to play each other in organized sports, and as part of the

93rd squad's wrestling team, Eddie took on opponents from throughout the surrounding area, with the 185-pounder emerging undefeated in twenty-two encounters on his way to becoming heavyweight wrestling champion of the European Theater of Operations (ETO). It would be the first title of many, many more to come—and definitive proof that The Sheik really did know how to wrestle, despite what some of his detractors would later say.

It was also during his time in Europe that Eddie first became keenly aware of an issue that would remain important to him throughout his life—the disparity of treatment between white and Black people in America. He was struck by the racial segregation of the troops and the difference in their wartime experience. Perhaps some of it had to do with his own Arab heritage, which allowed him to be considered "white" by most of the general populace in 1940s America, despite not having a European ethnicity. "He watched the Black guys get treated differently in the war," explained Rudy Hill (aka The Rude Boy), a Michigan-based indie wrestler who grew close to The Sheik in his later years. "He developed a lot of compassion for people because of the injustices he got to see. He said that the Black and brown guys would get pushed to the front of the line in battle. He told me that's where he learned that people are people—Black, white, whatever."

But the end of the line for the ETO didn't mean the end of the war. In July, the 93rd—and in fact, the entire 13th Armored Division—was ordered to be deployed to the Pacific Theater of Operations (PTO) for an all-out offensive against the Empire of Japan, America's original antagonist and the last of the Axis powers. Operation Downfall had all the earmarks of a suicide mission, and that had to weigh heavily on the men's minds as they made their way to Camp Atlanta in France, and later back to the port of Le Havre (with a merciful Paris leave in between). The USS *Explorer* ferried Eddie back across the Atlantic to Boston, where he arrived on July 27, 1945. The squadron received a thirty-day leave, during which Eddie got to visit his family in Lansing for the first time in almost a year, not knowing if he would ever see them again.

However, things didn't turn out as dire as they originally seemed— at least for Eddie Farhat and the men of the 13th. On the mornings of August 6 and August 9, 1945, while Eddie was back home with his family, the United States dropped atomic bombs on Hiroshima and Nagasaki, leading to the official surrender of Japan the following week. Before Eddie reported for duty at Camp Cooke in California at the end of August, the Second World War had drawn to a close. The invasion of Japan that would've spelled certain death for so many American soldiers never happened. Eddie continued to serve stateside for five more months before receiving an honorable discharge. On January 27, 1946, after 528 days of service, PFC Edward G. Farhat officially returned to civilian life after leaving the Separation Center in Fort Sheridan, Illinois. He came home with several accolades from his time in the service, including a Bronze Battle Star. He'd also been awarded a medal for good conduct. Considering the career that awaited him after the war, it's reasonable to assume it would be the last time he would ever be recognized for that.

CHAPTER 5

STEPPING INTO THE RING

*"Eddie Farhat, the Lansing G.I. for whom observers are predicting
a bright future in the grunt and groan industry..."*
—LANSING STATE JOURNAL, JANUARY 18, 1947

A s one of America's most populous urban centers, and the heart of the booming automobile industry, Detroit had been a hotbed for professional wrestling dating back to the early years of the twentieth century. Promoters and other businessmen who helped shape the distinctly American enterprise in its earliest years knew they could draw huge crowds of paying customers with the right kinds of attractions. As early as 1912, Buffalo promoters Maurice Collins and Dick Fleming brought Dr. Benjamin F. Roller and Polish powerhouse Stanislaus Zbyszko, two of the most famous wrestlers on the planet, to the Detroit Light Guard Armory before a record-setting crowd of over four thousand (during a time when larger sports venues were nearly unheard-of). Then there was the legendary halfback for the University of Detroit Mercy and the NFL's Detroit Panthers' own "Dynamite" Gus Sonnenberg of Ewen, Michigan, who revolutionized wrestling with his flying tackle in the late 1920s and made several triumphant returns to the Great Lakes State as world heavyweight champion.

The history of pro wrestling is a history of heated promotional rivalries, and the first of these to grip the Detroit area occurred in the 1930s, when two major promoters vied for control. The more prominent of these was Nick Londes, a boxing and wrestling impresario who was part of what was known as The Wrestling Trust, a powerful national syndicate of promoters and bookers that also included Paul Bowser out of Boston,

Jack Curley out of New York, Tom Packs out of St. Louis, and Ed White out of Chicago. Another key to Londes's dominance was his control of a cavernous new fifteen-thousand-seat Detroit sports venue at 5920 Grand River Avenue: the Olympia Stadium. Home to the Detroit Red Wings of the NHL, the Olympia became one of the leading sports facilities in the country, and Londes eventually became its executive director. His Motor City promotional rival was Adam Weissmuller, a standout welterweight wrestler of the 1920s who had wrestled for Londes before transitioning to the business end of things when trachoma[1] took much of his vision. Weissmuller, the brother of famed movie Tarzan Johnny Weissmuller, was himself affiliated with a slightly less powerful wrestling circuit that included Al Haft of Columbus, Ohio; Chicago's Fred Kohler; barnstormer Billy Sandow;[2] and the notorious itinerant trickster Jack Pfefer. Along with his business partner Louis Markowitz, Weissmuller's home base was the Arena Gardens, a roller rink on Woodward Avenue near 8 Mile Road.

Drawing talent from the likes of Curley and Bowser, Londes was able to bring world heavyweight champs like Ed Don George, "Golden Greek" Jim Londos, and "The Irish Whip" Danno O'Mahoney to the Olympia. Weissmuller, a former lighter-weight wrestler himself, specialized in presenting junior heavyweights—but that all changed in 1936 when German grappler Dick Shikat went into business for himself at Madison Square Garden against O'Mahoney, refusing to "do business" with the Wrestling Trust and taking the heavyweight crown from the stunned Irishman in an unplanned finish. In doing so, he wrested the title out of the control of the Trust and offered his services instead to the Haft-Kohler-Sandow-Weissmuller alliance, giving Weissmuller exclusive Michigan booking rights to the champ.

Londes did what he could to block the maneuver, attempting to have the state athletic commission suspend Shikat under flimsy pretenses, but nothing could stop Shikat from drawing record crowds for Weissmuller, leading to a highly anticipated title defense against Arteen Ekizian, known in the ring as Ali Baba. A colorful character of Armenian extraction, Baba had massive appeal to Detroit's sizeable Middle Eastern population. With his shaved-bald head and giant handlebar mustache, not to mention his ring name of choice, he played into American stereotypes of Eastern and Arabic culture to his great advantage—the first competitor to rise to fame in the Detroit area by doing so. (Although it is not known whether Eddie Farhat was a wrestling fan as a little kid, if he was, he would have most certainly been exposed to Ali Baba in a big way.) The Shikat-Baba bout was such a big deal that it gave Weissmuller the leverage to muscle Londes out of the Olympia and hold the match there, where, on April 24, 1936, Ali Baba captured the world heavyweight title in what was the biggest match in Detroit wrestling history up to that point.

Although Baba would only hold the title for two months, it helped tip the scales of power in Detroit wrestling to Weissmuller. He also garnered huge fan support, despite the protestations of so-called wrestling purists, by encouraging more outrageous characters, roughhouse tactics, and other sensational gimmickry that didn't always quite fall under the traditional definition of "wrestling." This was epitomized by popular brawlers like Danny McShain, and especially a wild-haired, wild-eyed chair-swinging dynamo from Hartford, Connecticut, named Bull Curry.[3] With his unforgettable bushy eyebrows and hirsute physique, Curry became a sensation in Detroit in the 1930s, throwing the rulebook out the window and truly pioneering an anything-goes, ultra-violent form of wrestling that wouldn't be termed hardcore until many decades later. In some ways, it was Curry who paved the way for the next Motor City madman, The Sheik, with whom Curry would eventually develop a close bond over their common approach to working and their shared Lebanese heritage. The wild-and-woolly style popularized by Curry and others would remain a hallmark of Detroit wrestling for nearly half a century.

But just as things were gaining momentum for Weissmuller, a mysterious stomach ailment put him in the hospital, then caused his premature death at the beginning of 1937.[4] Louis Markowitz assumed control of Weissmuller Wrestling Enterprises (the first "WWE") and continued to promote into the 1940s. Meanwhile, he would receive some competition of his own in the form of Harold Lecht, a former prizefighter who had been working as an assistant and something of a protégé of Weissmuller, under the professional name Harry Light.

Two years after Weissmuller's death, Light broke away and formed the Harry Light Wrestling Office, promoting cards at Detroit's Fairview Gardens. The name he used for his particular product would be one that would stand the test of time in the Detroit area: Big Time Wrestling. Light was assisted by two trusted right-hand men whom he had recruited from among Weissmuller Wrestling Enterprises' troupe of wrestlers: One was Jack Britton, an Italian-Canadian former boxer and grappler who was Light's road agent, managing the day-to-day operations at live events.[5] The other was Bert Ruby (born Bertalan Rubinstein), a Hungarian immigrant who had come to America during the Depression and whose wrestling career began in the early thirties when he was discovered while pumping gas in Toronto. Known for wrestling barefoot, Ruby performed double duty for Light, both competing as an active wrestler and working in the front office as talent booker as well as trainer, the role that would eventually bring Eddie Farhat into his orbit.

By the 1940s, there was a jumble of promotions vying for power in the greater Detroit area. Markowitz held onto the Arena Gardens as a holdover from the Weissmuller days until finally being pushed out by Light after World War II. Chicago kingpin Fred Kohler, once a friend and partner of Weissmuller, was now trying to horn in on western Michigan, including towns like Benton Harbor, which were under the control of 1930s main event superstar turned promoter Jumping Joe Savoldi. Even the legendary Ed "Strangler" Lewis, a former five-time world heavyweight champion and perhaps the biggest star in wrestling up to that point, tried his hand at running the Arena Gardens for a time in 1943.

This was the byzantine professional wrestling landscape that young Eddie Farhat would step into following his service. But long before completely taking over that entire landscape, he was just another returned GI trying to settle back into normal domestic life after going toe-to-toe with Nazi Germany. While some older brothers like Topper and Edmund got to pursue advanced degrees, nineteen-year-old Eddie had to go to work, taking a job on the assembly line at Lansing Car Assembly, putting together Oldsmobiles along with his brother Moses and his uncle George. He was a member of the United Auto Workers (UAW) Local 652 and remained so for years. A war veteran before his twentieth birthday, back to living at home with his parents, he could've easily become just another Motor City auto plant lifer—but that was not to be his destiny, thanks to his continued interest in the thing that had first brought him attention in the army.

Eddie started training as part of the men's program at the Lansing YMCA, building himself up from 185 to 210 pounds of muscle packed on to his stout five-foot-eight frame (although he was billed in later years as five-eleven, his military records indicate otherwise).[6] He started taking part in demonstrations of wrestling put on at the Y from time to time. It's also possible that he was sitting in on workouts with the Michigan State University wrestling team in nearby Lansing.[7] Although it is unknown exactly where this occurred, shortly after Eddie's return from the war in early 1946, he was discovered by Bert Ruby, who was scouting local talent for Harry Light.

Young and good-looking, with an impressive Army wrestling pedigree, it's easy to understand why Ruby would've considered Farhat a prime recruit. For a kid who seemed adrift, and who wanted something more from life than the assembly line, it must've appeared as a great opportunity for a little excitement, not to mention the chance to bring home some extra money. Ruby took the nineteen-year-old under his wing, showing him the finer points of professional wrestling, which, despite utilizing some of the important skills derived from the amateur game, was a very, very different animal. To this end, Ruby also introduced Farhat to Lou Klein, a former amateur standout who had smoothly transitioned to the pro ranks before the war and, in addition to being a regular performer for the Light organization, also broke in young prospects and helped them make the same transition he had.[8] As did most rookie performers, Farhat spent months in training with Ruby and Klein three times a week, learning the physical aspect of the business as well as its inner workings, during a time when the true nature of the business was protected by the thick curtain of kayfabe, wrestling's time-honored code of secrecy that Farhat would one day wear like a cloak.

In an early 1990s interview with Japanese wrestling historian Fumi Saito, The Sheik indicated that he had his first professional matches under a mask as "Black Mephisto," desiring to protect his identity due to pro wrestling's sordid reputation in the amateur ranks. This story could not be corroborated anywhere else, and there is no record of a Black Mephisto wrestling anywhere at this time. While this does not completely discredit Sheik's claim, as there are many small-time shows from that far back that have been lost to the mists of time, it's also possible that Sheik was in working mode during parts of the interview, as many old-timers trained in kayfabe were still very protective of behind-the-scenes aspects of their career—and no one more so than Sheik.

Eddie Farhat's earliest known professional wrestling match took place on a Tuesday evening, January 14, 1947, in the Prudden Auditorium, a 2,200-seat building adjacent to the Lansing Chamber of Commerce that was a center of civic life for the Greater Lansing community. On a card presented by Gus Cummings, who ran the building utilizing talent provided by Harry Light, Farhat took on fellow ex-serviceman Joe Knight, a former judo champion and a wrestler on the Michigan State squad, in what was billed as a "special exhibition." Fans on hand that evening could've had no idea of what the future held for that clean-shaven, dark-haired local boy, appearing under his own name—a name he would later discard and bury. The two men battled to a draw that night and were brought back to the Prudden Auditorium one week later in separate matches, with Farhat taking on fourteen-year Canadian veteran Eddie Lee Balbo in the opening match of a card that also featured his trainer

Local Grappler

LANSING STATE JOURNAL

Eddie Farhat (above) has joined the ranks of professional wrestlers and appears again Tuesday night on the Prudden auditorium program as the Veterans of Foreign Wars present a tag-team match with four wrestlers and Farhat against Al LeClerc, a Canadian, in a best-two-in-three fall bout. The show starts at 8:30 o'clock.

Lansing State Journal, *February 4, 1947:* *The earliest known photo of Farhat as a wrestler (here at twenty years of age), plugging his upcoming third professional match.*

Lou Klein, who presumably watched the progress of his student that night with great interest. By his third bout for Cummings, a prelim victory over Al LeClerc before a scant three hundred spectators, it was announced that Farhat had officially "turned pro."

Farhat continued to make appearances at the Prudden Auditorium through much of 1947, often competing in opening matches on shows that included Klein or Ruby, or both, who continued to monitor his progress for Light. There is no question that Light was hungry for new talent, with dwindling attendance in Detroit compelling him to expand his interests into surrounding towns such as Flint, Kalamazoo, and Grand Rapids. Also making things interesting for Light was the introduction of television, a new medium about whose benefits or detriments to the wrestling business promoters were still divided. KTLA in Los Angeles had kicked off the TV wrestling boom in 1946 with a weekly program showcasing the stars of Johnny Doyle's Southern California promotion, and Light was soon to follow with a live show debuting in the fall of 1947 on WWJ-TV from the Arena Gardens.

Before long, TV presence had placed Light at the unquestioned top of the food chain in the often-tangled Detroit promotional scene. This prominence in the business allowed him to get in on the ground floor of something truly special on July 18, 1948, when he joined Al Haft, Iowa's Pinkie George, Minnesota's Tony Stecher, Kansas City's Orville Brown, and St. Louis's Sam Muchnick as one of the founding members of the National Wrestling Alliance, a conglomerate of promoters whose goal was to eliminate the chaotic competition that had characterized the 1930s and '40s by organizing the business into a cooperative network of territories recognizing one world heavyweight champion.

With Light's promotion on the rise, Farhat continued to build his name as a local boy made good, even if the money wasn't really much to write home about. "He would work for a ham sandwich and a pop because he loved the business," explained his son Eddie Jr. in a 2009 radio interview.[9] While maintaining his day job at the Olds plant, he continued participating in YMCA athletic demonstrations. Much like his brothers, he remained athletically active simply for pleasure, participating in whatever local neighborhood sports he could find, both formal and informal.[10] With Bert Ruby's approval, he was about to rise up the ranks for Harry Light, who was looking for viable attractions to populate his newly minted NWA territory. However, he would not do so as plain old Eddie Farhat from Lansing, Michigan. The transition required something dramatically different, something special, something that was sure to draw attention, while also creating a distinct boundary between Eddie's personal and professional lives. A transformation was about to occur, from which there would be no turning back.

CHAPTER 6

ENTER THE ARABIAN MADMAN

"The great ones are who they are. Lou Thesz was Lou Thesz.
The Sheik was The Sheik."
—TERRY FUNK

One of the key aspects of Eddie Farhat's life that eluded all my research was exactly when, where, and how he met Joyce Jean Fleser, the beautiful young Williamston woman who would become his wife, wrestling valet, business partner, and closest confidant. What we do know is that they were introduced by mutual friends, and, early in the relationship, she was the one to pursue him (which is ironic, considering the subservient role she would later play by his side on television). Despite its obscure origins, it would become the relationship that would most define his life, for better and for worse. She was the daughter of Ellen Lynch Fleser and Francis Louis Fleser, a truck driver for the Industrial Transport Company and the owner of Fleser's Hangar, a nightclub and restaurant in downtown Lansing.[1] At the time of their wedding, Joyce was less than six months past her eighteenth birthday, four years her groom's junior. This may have been part of the reason her father did not, at first, approve of the relationship, in addition to their vastly different cultural and family backgrounds. The two were married on June 25, 1949, at Holy Cross Catholic Church on Lansing's west side, with Eddie's older brother Edmund serving as best man, his brothers Amal, Topper, and Moses, as well as his nephew James Rashid, standing as ushers. The reception was held at the Fleser home, with Eddie's sizeable Lebanese family no doubt a cultural contrast to Joyce's more Americanized Irish clan.

At age twenty-three, Eddie was moving out of his parents' home for the first time, heading two miles east and setting up house with Joyce at 2320½ East Main Street in Lansing. The wrestling gig he was using to make extra money while maintaining his day job at the factory had become a bit stagnant, but with a new bride and plans to start a family, Eddie put a plan in place to help kick it out of neutral. Although it is unknown who came up with the original idea, it is reasonable to assume that in addition to Eddie himself, his mentors Bert Ruby and Lou Klein and possibly his employer Harry Light had a hand in it as well. This idea helped take Eddie from an obscure kid wrestling in local gyms to a wrestling immortal renowned on the world stage.

Pro wrestling had thrived on colorful characters for decades, but by 1949, with the TV wrestling craze in full bloom across the country, said colorful characters were more in demand than ever before—the more colorful, the better. The Argentine high-flyer Antonino Rocca was wowing fans on the East Coast with his barefoot acrobatics; "Nature Boy" Buddy Rogers out of Camden, New Jersey, created a preening, platinum-blond template that set the mold for generations to come; "Mr. America" Gene Stanlee was a sculpted Adonis from Chicago whose ring entrances lasted almost as long as his matches; Chief Don Eagle parlayed his true Mohawk heritage into widespread fame and the world heavyweight title. And standing steam-curled head and feathered shoulders above them all was George Raymond Wagner, a middleweight carnival wrestler from Houston who saved his career from obscurity by becoming Gorgeous George, the Toast of the Coast and a bona fide mainstream celebrity of the highest order.

Although he would in later years bill himself as "The Original Sheik," Eddie Farhat was not, in fact, the first individual to take on the mantle of a wrestling sheik. Back in 1932, a Lebanese and Latino wrestler named Julian Arturo Herrera Haddad began calling himself Sheik Mar Allah and making a name for himself in Mexico, Texas, and California, among other places. He was known to sometimes wear a turban, a fez, or a kaffiyeh, the traditional Arabic kerchief headdress, to the ring, but often appeared out of costume like any other wrestler. More relevant to Farhat's development was Arabic wrestler Emir Badui, who had been part of Jack Pfefer's traveling troupe. Badui debuted in 1935, but by 1947, with Pfefer's encouragement, he began adopting a sheik persona, going by many names over the years, including Sheik Badui, Sheik Ben Ali, Prince Emir, and Sheik Clarence.[2] Badui fully committed to the persona, appearing in traditional Bedouin regalia and growing a thick Vandyke beard. He made several appearances in 1947 and 1948 in the Lansing area, and it would be reasonable to assume he and Farhat crossed paths and that Badui made a strong impression on the aspiring rookie.

In those days, the connotation of "sheik" would be very different to fans than it would later become in a post–Iran hostage crisis America, when fear of Muslim terrorists fueled an Islamophobia that was exploited by wrestling promoters for money, like so many other American insecurities and fears. The original connotation was one of romance and exoticism—following World War I, the US had begun doing more oil business with the Arab world, bringing an unprecedented awareness of Arab culture and traditions to white Christian Americans who were fascinated by its mysterious *other*ness. This fascination reached nuclear levels with the 1921 release of *The Sheik*, a film starring iconic Hollywood sex symbol Rudolph Valentino (based on the best-selling 1919 novel of the same title). The film was a smash success, making Valentino into the object of desire for millions of women and kicking off the "desert romance" genre, which emphasized the mystery and allure of Arab lands and the wealthy oil barons who presumably populated them.

All this is to say that Eddie Farhat had a lot of inspiration and motivation with which to craft his own Sheik persona, capitalizing on his Semitic looks and real-life Middle Eastern background. The persona would evolve over the years in many ways. In the very beginning, it involved trading in his clean-cut look for a thick but neatly manicured black beard and mustache and donning a dark turban, Bedouin robes, and trunks emblazoned with the silhouette of a camel. To give the impression of a foreign dignitary, he would not speak English—or, more accurately, he would not speak at all. As with many wrestlers presented as foreigners in those days, he was positioned as a villainous figure, or heel in the parlance of the business. In short, he was no longer local kid and babyfaced former G.I. Eddie Farhat. Of course, Farhat was not Muslim but Catholic—however, in the fictionalized world of professional wrestling, that mattered little. It was the stereotype, the cultural archetype, that mattered.

What was Eddie Farhat's first appearance as his Sheik character is a matter of some conjecture. He told his one-time manager and close confidant Dave Burzynski that it happened in 1949 against his trainer Lou Klein; however, no official record of this match has been found.

The first known, confirmed appearance took place just two days before his wedding, on a Thursday night, June 23, 1949, at the Marion Armory in Marion, Ohio, almost two hundred miles south of his usual haunts in the Lansing area. (Could it be that he wanted to first try it out far from where he thought he might be recognized?) On that night, he was billed as "The Arabian Sheik," a "newcomer from Europe," and finished off his opponent, Dale Wayne, in just six minutes of the third fall of a match in which "fans were asking for his blood," according to the *Marion Star* the next day. Farhat continued making appearances over the summer of 1949 in several smaller Ohio and Michigan towns, still called, simply, The Arabian Sheik. It was also around this time that the newlywed Farhats discovered they were expecting a baby, giving Eddie even more motivation to push ahead with The Sheik experiment and see where it went.

After a few months of trying out his new persona on the local scene, December 13, 1949, became the first known date on which Farhat stepped into the ring using a slightly altered name, and one that would stick: The Sheik of Araby. His Prudden Auditorium days behind him, he now found himself working the undercard for Harry Light and Bert Ruby at their main venue, the Arena Gardens, defeating local enhancement talent Al Warshawski[3] on a show main evented by his trainer, Lou Klein. The new name, an attempt to tap more directly into the pop culture fixation on the Arabian world, came from the title of a 1921 song by Harry B. Smith, Francis Wheeler, and Ted Snyder, originally written to capitalize on the success of the Valentino movie and popularized by singer-comedian Eddie Cantor in the Broadway revue *Make It Snappy*. One look at the lyrics gives a thorough idea of the romanticism tied to The Sheik mystique in those days:

> Over the desert wild and free,
> Rides the bold Sheik of Araby.
> His Arab band, at his command,
> Follow his love's caravan.
> Under the shadow of the palms;
> He sings to call her to his arms:

"I'm The Sheik of Araby,
Your love belongs to me.
At night when you're asleep,
Into your tent I'll creep.
The stars that shine above,
Will light our way to love.
You'll rule this land with me;
The Sheik of Araby."

While stars are fading in the dawn,
Over the desert they'll be gone;
His captured bride close by his side;
Swift as the wind they will ride.
Proudly he scorns her smile or tear;
Soon he will conquer love by fear.[4]

As The Sheik of Araby, Farhat's bookings began to quickly increase. By the start of 1950, he was appearing for Light and Ruby throughout the general area in towns like Port Huron and Saginaw, as well as school gymnasiums and other small venues within the Detroit city limits. Usually in the opening bout, he often found himself pitted against Warshawski, as well as Jack Britton, Ruby, and Klein, building his skills against familiar opponents. The new character began generating a buzz in local newspapers, then the best marketing tool for wrestling promotions. In 1951, he even enjoyed a brief stint with the Cristiani Brothers Circus, second-largest circus in America behind Ringling Bros. and Barnum & Bailey. In a throwback to pro wrestling's earliest days in the carnivals, The Sheik of Araby would accept open "challenges" from the audience, invariably coming from incognito circus performers planted in the crowd.

On March 26, nine months and one day after their wedding, nineteen-year-old Joyce gave birth to a baby boy, Edward George Farhat Jr. At age twenty-three, the man now known as The Sheik of Araby was a husband and a new father, balancing work on the auto assembly line with a burgeoning career on the local wrestling scene. As a whole, the Farhat clan was thriving in those days: Lewie and Amal were opening up their own Syrian restaurant on West Saginaw Street (with their mom helping supply the cuisine), and Edmund had embarked on a teaching career. But there was tragedy also, as Eddie's oldest sibling, Zieckie, died on November 11 at only forty-three years of age.[5] She would be the only one of Eddie's immediate family who would not live to see him become a superstar. It's amusing to speculate on what the rest of the family's views might have been toward Eddie's rather unorthodox career path in those early days. If it was true that he felt a bit overshadowed by his overachieving older brothers, it certainly was one way to attract attention and make a name for himself, even if that name was not the one on his birth certificate.

It was also during his first year as The Sheik of Araby that Eddie crossed paths with another up-and-coming Detroit-area wrestler who would quickly become his very best friend in the business. Arthur Lawrence Beauchene was another Ruby trainee who was already beginning to dazzle fans with his flying headscissors and other aerial tactics that earned him the name "Leaping" Larry Chene. In the ring, they were enemies, working against each other in both tag team and singles encounters—Farhat the nefarious bad guy, while the clean-cut Chene, with his unassuming and instantly likeable face, was the good guy, or babyface in grappling vernacular. Meanwhile, away from the ring they quickly bonded, having a great deal of shared experience as far as breaking into the business, and both with high hopes for where it might take them. That real-life-versus-wrestling dichotomy would become a running theme throughout Eddie's career, as his closest friends would often be those with whom he warred most fiercely in the ring.

Harry Light brought The Sheik of Araby to the Olympia Stadium, then Detroit's primary wrestling venue, for what may have been the very first time on November 29, 1951, for a card benefiting injured veterans of the then-raging Korean War. Before fifteen hundred fans, he appeared in the tag team opener, joining with Jan Gotch to take on familiar adversaries Chene and Ruby, on a show headlined by national megastar Gene Stanlee against Joe Christie. This led to his taking his first step outside of the Michigan wrestling scene, and it was a big one. On New Year's Day of 1952, he headed to Indianapolis for a show promoted by Billy Thom, a tough retired welterweight pro who had also been wrestling coach at Indiana University. There he got his first taste of the main event, taking on no less than Buddy Rogers, one of the industry's elite performers and attractions. Farhat lost, but it didn't matter—the point was, he was getting noticed. Three days later, he traveled to St. Louis, the very heart of the National Wrestling Alliance, where he competed in the tag team opener on a Kiel Auditorium card headlined by Canadian dynamo Whipper Billy Watson against Tarzan Kowalski, a lanky newcomer who was soon to be rechristened "Killer." That would be his first time working for promoter Sam Muchnick, the NWA president he would one day call a peer.

Aside from the exposure, the most important development that would come out of Farhat's venture out of state would be catching the eye of James E. Barnett. An industry wunderkind who had begun working in wrestling publicity right out of high school, Barnett was the young office assistant to Chicago wrestling kingpin Fred Kohler, who by this point had become the most powerful and influential promoter in the country thanks to his weekly program *Wrestling from Marigold*, a ratings power-house seen on television screens across the entire United States. The Indiana wrestling circuit drew much of its in-ring talent from Kohler in those days and had a close working relationship with the Chicago office—it's entirely possible that this is where Barnett first noticed Farhat and brought him to the attention of Kohler, who was always on the hunt for flamboyant and charismatic characters to populate the cast of his blockbuster show. Needless to say, The Sheik of Araby was just the kind of act Kohler was looking for. Farhat and Barnett would have much to do with each other professionally in the decades to come—as colleagues, as partners, and as rivals. But it all started with an enviable opportunity—a chance for The Sheik of Araby to reach a much larger audience and become a national sensation in the process.

CHAPTER 7

THE SHEIK GOES NATIONAL

*"The Sheik really knew how to play the game. There's a lot of jealousy in
the wrestling business, but nobody could touch this guy in his prime,
and that's a fact. There was nobody like him."*
—"FLYING" FRED CURRY

Professional wrestling has had a lot of so-called golden ages. But for
fans of a certain age, the "Golden Age of Wrestling" means only
one era: the early to mid-1950s, when a frenzy for the grunt and
groan game gripped the nation as never before, thanks to the fledgling
medium of television. Suddenly finding themselves with hours of airtime
to fill, TV network execs snatched up whatever they could find—old
movies and cartoons—in addition to producing their own programming using the relatively primitive technology available. Sporting events
were deemed valuable because they were ready-made, with no need for
production, just waiting to be filmed and broadcast. And of all sports,
boxing and wrestling were the simplest; the action took place in a small,
confined area, with a small number of competitors, only requiring one
or two cameras placed in the right positions to capture it. And because
wrestling was not burdened with having to be a legitimate competitive
sport, as boxing was, its proponents could fill their programming with
whatever colorful antics and personalities were necessary to hold the
audience's attention. And hold it they did.

During those early years of television, pro wrestling was the hottest
show on the tube, and pro wrestlers were among the first bona fide TV
celebrities. For the first time, people didn't have to buy a ticket and go
to the arena but could enjoy the ruckus in the comfort of their own
living rooms. The audience for wrestling expanded beyond hardcore

fans and added legions of folks who wouldn't have ordinarily gone to live events but tuned in and became hooked; the casual wrestling fan was born. The camera allowed wrestlers to be more histrionic than before, and microphones allowed them to speak, adding the art of the promo to the skills any successful wrestler needed to have. Heels became more heelish; gimmicks became personas; matches became wilder and more performative than ever.

There were lots of regionalized wrestling TV shows that popped up in those years, but the most popular and most influential of them all was *Wrestling from Marigold*, which aired nationwide on the DuMont Network, one of the original three major TV networks along with CBS and NBC. A relatively small Chicago venue at the southwest corner of Grace and Halsted Streets on the former site of a nightclub, the Marigold Arena was wired for television by Windy City wrestling impresario Fred Kohler. The TV program, airing every Saturday evening and watched by millions of Americans with as much fervency as they watched Milton Berle, Lucille Ball, and Howdy Doody, made Kohler the most powerful promoter in the country. Each week, viewers tuned in and thrilled to the exploits of such performers as Verne Gagne, the squeaky-clean former Olympian who became the NWA's first United States Champion; Reggie Lisowski, the tough-as-nails brawler who would later make Milwaukee famous as "The Crusher"; Hans Schmidt, the rangy grappler who was actually Canadian Guy Larose but ascended to prominence playing a goose-stepping Nazi; Pat O'Connor, the stocky New Zealander who would parlay his natural gifts into a run as NWA World Heavyweight Champion; and Lord James Blears, a purported British aristocrat and former merchant marine who had escaped Japanese captivity during the war.

Into this televised world of cowboys and Indians, barroom hooligans and prancing sissies, sneaky Japanese and flying Frenchmen, stepped Ed Farhat as the newly minted Sheik of Araby—a product of the Midwest, draped in mystery and ready to make his mark on the wrestling world. After donning his turban and robes in 1949, Farhat had been generating buzz and gradually getting himself on the radar of important people in the business. The NWA and its board of directors, led by Sam Muchnick, had taken notice of him, even booking him in an NWA World Heavyweight title match against champion Lou Thesz in Saginaw, Michigan, in the summer of 1952. Even though the match was rained out, The Sheik of Araby was becoming a known commodity.

Thanks to the involvement and advocacy of Jim Barnett, Farhat was brought to the Chicago scene to go to work for Kohler, along with a few other Detroit-area grapplers, including Farhat's mentor Bert Ruby, his trainer Lou Klein, and his best friend Larry Chene. He made his first Chicago appearance on May 7, 1952, at the Rainbo Arena, Kohler's second most important wrestling venue, run for Kohler by promoter Leonard Schwartz. In an encounter that went to the thirty-minute time limit, The Sheik of Araby tangled with Klein[1] in the middle of a card headlined by Antonino Rocca taking on aging West Coast legend Man Mountain Dean, that also featured Angelo Poffo, a local boy and son of Italian immigrants whose vaunted wrestling family would have much to do with The Sheik in years to come. The reaction to Farhat was so strong that the following month he was slotted into the main event at the Rainbo, losing to Rocca in two straight falls.

Along with Kohler, Farhat began landing bookings for Midwestern stalwart Al Haft, who ran much of Ohio, West Virginia, and western Pennsylvania at the time and was another cornerstone promoter for the NWA. And then finally, on October 17, 1953, he made his first televised appearance on *Wrestling from Marigold*, defeating Kohler enhancement talent Johnny Gilbert. Millions of Americans simultaneously got their first exposure to The Sheik of Araby that night, and it would be the first of many appearances through the mid-1950s, on both the Marigold show and a second program from Chicago's International Amphitheatre, hosted by the droll producer-announcer Russ Davis.

Six years into his professional wrestling career, Ed Farhat had gotten his first taste of the big time. He quickly became part of a cast of characters known to loyal viewers all over the country—one of the unforgettable participants in the Golden Age of Wrestling, which would hold a lot of water in later years, as these would be performers that fans would never forget, even long after *Wrestling from Marigold* was off the air. It's hard to overestimate the impact this would have had on Farhat's career and

The Sheik of Araby, as the national TV audience would come to know him in the early 1950s.

on his personal life. Up until this point, he had been hanging on to his membership in the UAW and his day job at the factory—but by the end of 1953, professional wrestling was his full-time and only job. The Sheik of Araby was becoming more than a pro wrestler; he was becoming a celebrity.

With the TV cameras fixed upon him, capturing his every move and mannerism, he began doing what any great performer would—playing to them. At the suggestion of one of the cameramen, he began acting a bit crazed, rolling his eyes and making wild facial expressions. He would even inform the crew when and where he was going to do it, to make sure it got caught on film.[2] Although relatively tame compared to what would come later, this was the beginning of the unhinged madness that would come to characterize him. Even his wrestling style was changing: although he was still executing traditional holds and maneuvers (this would also change), little flourishes were added, such as the so-called camel walk—a series of wiggles, twitches, and shimmies that he would break into as he paced the ring before locking up with his opponent.

He'd do whatever it took to get attention, and promoters responded in kind. He was starting to get better and better bookings, including a match against future world champ Pat O'Connor in Amboy, Illinois, in November 1953. That same month, he and Gypsy Joe[3] were named by

Kohler as NWA Midwest Tag Team Champions—it was the first of many titles that Farhat would hold throughout his career. Kohler made the choice mainly because he needed a strong heel tag team to carry the title after previous holders Ben and Mike Sharpe left the area. The title was recognized throughout the towns Kohler ran in Illinois, Wisconsin, Indiana, and Ohio. They would hold it for ten months before being dethroned by Billy Goelz and Cowboy Carlson in Rockford, Illinois, on September 28, 1954.

By the summer of 1954, the regular opponents for The Sheik of Araby included the likes of Gagne, Rocca, and other top-flight attractions. He had broadened his radius of operations to include Tony Stecher's Minnesota territory, forerunner to Gagne's American Wrestling Association. And if there was ever a sign that he was a star on the rise, it was the proposed boxer-wrestler matchup between The Sheik and former heavyweight champ Joe Louis that almost took place in Fon Du Lac, Wisconsin, on July 28, 1954. Louis, then down on his luck and looking to pro wrestling for a payday, had been touring the country taking on several wrestlers in exhibitions, but when the Wisconsin State Athletic Commission got wind of the proceedings, they put the kibosh on the match, stating Kohler had not gone through the proper channels.

National television exposure had made The Sheik of Araby a coveted act for promoters even beyond the Midwest region where he had made his living up to this point. If it took a leap of faith to commit to wrestling as a full-time profession, that leap was further vindicated in October 1954, when Farhat was brought to the Lone Star State by Morris Sigel, a Russian-Jewish New Yorker and former junk dealer who had somehow positioned himself as the kingpin of Texas wrestling after relocating down south in his twenties. Houston was the epicenter of Sigel's wrestling empire, and The Sheik of Araby was soon making appearances at the Sam Houston Coliseum, as well as in cities such as San Antonio, Galveston, Corpus Christi, Dallas, and Waco, where Sigel supplied the talent for local promoters like Ed McLemore, owner of the legendary Dallas Sportatorium. Thanks to the flourishing partnership of the NWA, such a talent exchange between Sigel and Kohler was easier than ever and helped a top-shelf talent like Farhat, who had proven himself in one region, take his show on the road and make a bigger name for himself across other NWA territories.

The Sheik of Araby was such a hit in Texas that, for a time, Farhat relocated there, bringing Joyce and Eddie Jr. down as well. At just twenty-eight and twenty-four, with a four-year-old in tow, the Farhats were a young couple in a place totally alien to them. But they weren't completely alone—Sheik's great friend Larry Chene had preceded him there by a few months and was already doing fairly well for himself. He and his wife, Mary, who had just welcomed their brand-new daughter, Carole, into the world, also welcomed the Farhats into their apartment, and the two young families lived together in Texas for nearly eight months, which brought Sheik and Chene closer together than ever. However, much as before, the two men could not make their friendship public, as their in-ring rivalry was still blazing hot.

Success came quickly in Texas, as Sigel put the Texas Heavyweight Championship on The Sheik of Araby on October 22, 1954, with a win in the Sam Houston Coliseum over strapping bleached-blond Washingtonian Johnny Valentine—a ruggedly handsome and double-tough babyface who would come to work often for The Sheik later in his career. He held it only a month, which was not uncommon for that title, being as it was a star-making stepping-stone to greater things, as it had been for the likes of Mike Mazurki, Bobby Managoff, Lou Thesz, Buddy Rogers, Antonino Rocca, Danny McShain, and Verne Gagne. It was the first major singles title of Farhat's career. It would most certainly not be the last.

Texan fans had gotten their first look at The Sheik, and they liked what they saw—or rather, they hated him so intensely they couldn't wait to have him back again. From then on, Texas became one of his regular and most lucrative touring stops. Meanwhile, when Sheik returned home with his family in the summer of 1955, he found that his cachet had increased somewhat as a result of his travels—Kohler began using him regularly in semi-main events on television and around the horn. Jim Barnett by this time had become much more than Kohler's assistant and now was a full-on business partner, running towns in Indiana and elsewhere, and would often bring Farhat in.

One such booking would take place at Buck Lake Ranch, two miles west of Angola, Indiana, on August 12, 1955, and is the first recorded meeting between Farhat and a man who would become a heated adversary both in the ring and in business. William Afflis was a local talent, a cinderblock wall of a man who had played four seasons for the Green Bay Packers in the early 1950s before turning to pro wrestling and quickly becoming a hot young prospect for Kohler and Barnett as Dick the Bruiser. Much like The Sheik, he became a major star off the steam of Kohler TV, and he parlayed that into a career as a major touring attraction, as well as a promoter in his own right, whose ambitions would later place Farhat and his own promotional interests directly in his crosshairs. But on this night, they were just two up-and-coming wrestlers—Farhat a veteran of eight years finally hitting his stride, and Afflis a green-as-grass rookie with just a few months under his belt, but whose barroom brawling style and unforgettably rough and raspy voice (the result of a larynx injury suffered on the gridiron) would help him catch up in very short order.

Meanwhile, Farhat continued to work the local Detroit scene for Harry Light, who still held sway in that neck of the woods, as well as Bert Ruby, who by that point had amicably broken away from Light and was running his own shows in the smaller towns of the greater Detroit area under the brand name of Motor City Wrestling. In October and November 1955, Farhat made triumphant returns to Lansing for Ruby—the first time he had wrestled in his hometown area again since achieving national fame on the DuMont Network. The *Lansing State Journal* reported on the homecoming, even going so far as breaking kayfabe in its enthusiasm to declare that The Sheik of Araby was actually Lansing's own Ed Farhat. Interestingly, local reports also list the "cobra hold" as his trademark maneuver, which may have been a reference to what would later be known as the cobra clutch, a sleeper-type submission hold Sheik was using at the time as a finisher (and which he may have invented.)

Although he had already been getting national TV exposure for a couple of years by this time, many point to a match that occurred in the fall of 1955 as the one that really put him to the next level and began his ascent from the middle of the card to the top. The date was November 18, and the site was Chicago's International Amphitheatre, where fans waited in anticipation as a blizzard raged outside. At last, after a canceled booking three years earlier, The Sheik of Araby was getting a shot at the NWA World Heavyweight Championship, in those days at its very zenith as pro wrestling's unquestioned, undisputed supreme prize. As it had been since the late 1940s, it was still in the possession of the great Lou Thesz, the son of a Hungarian shoemaker from St. Louis, who was the ultimate standard bearer of the NWA, representing everything it purported to stand for, with his no-nonsense, pure grappling approach and the clean-cut, classic appearance of a mainstream sports figure. By the 1950s, Thesz was already something of an anomaly in the kooky, theatrical world of wrestling—an actual wrestler who rejected the antics and histrionics adopted by so many others he referred to merely as "performers."

Like NWA president Sam Muchnick, Thesz believed in putting over the legitimacy of the world championship, and he wasn't thrilled about having to defend it against someone like The Sheik, whom he viewed as a "gimmick wrestler" rather than a serious athlete. Word spread backstage that perhaps the champ didn't respect The Sheik and planned to get a little rough with him (Thesz was not above slapping around or applying a legitimately painful hold or two to an opponent he deemed unworthy to be in the ring with him). Before the match, there was a brief locker room confrontation, in which Thesz warned Farhat that if he "tried any of his shit," he'd break his legs. Farhat indicated there was no way he'd let that happen.[4] Once they got in the ring, Farhat brazenly went through his usual pre-match "Sheik of Araby" ritual as Thesz seethed. Then the bell rang, and it quickly became apparent that Farhat was quite out of his league—Thesz pounced to take the first fall in very short order, stunning The Sheik with the ease with which he could basically do whatever he wanted to him.

Realizing he was in serious trouble, not just of losing (which was the planned finish anyway), but of being seriously injured and humiliated, Farhat did the unthinkable (but in keeping with his wild and unpredictable Sheik character): he fled the ringside area and ran right out of the building into the raging snowstorm. Part of the crowd followed him, intent to see what he would do. Finding a parked bus half-buried in a large drift, he burrowed through the snow and under the bus, where he reportedly remained hidden for hours.[5] Police and EMTs were called to the scene, as well as news reporters keen to cover the unheard-of spectacle. "With Thesz, if any actual wrestling took place, Sheik had no chance," explains historian Fumi Saito, who heard the story directly from Sheik. "That was the smartest way to handle it."

Smart indeed—despite obviously being counted out and losing the match, The Sheik of Araby attracted enormous attention to himself that night. Newspapers covered the unlikely story on a national level, reporting on a wild and crazy wrestler who hid from his opponent under a bus during a snowstorm. Even Thesz had to marvel at Sheik's showmanship and the savvy way he brought publicity to him. Although they wouldn't cross paths often again until much later in their careers, Thesz grew to admire Farhat for his business sense. "Lou in the end respected my father a ton," Eddie Jr. recalled. "They became very good friends, even though they had very different views about pro wrestling. I think my dad's career really took off the night he wrestled Lou. It was like someone turned the light switch on, and every promoter in the country had to have him."

Just a little earlier that year, *Wrestling from Marigold* had been canceled by the DuMont Network, bringing an end to nationally televised wrestling. Kohler and Barnett continued promoting throughout the Illinois-Wisconsin-Indiana circuit, but their TV would now be only regional, as would most everyone else's for the next couple of decades. The dynamic wrestling boom of the early to mid-fifties may have been dying down just a bit from a mainstream perspective, but The Sheik's career was hotter than ever. And between the Kohler-Barnett and Light-Ruby territories, he had developed a strong home base of operations.

Playing into the increased publicity and attention he had been enjoying, Farhat made more changes to the act—an ongoing process in his early career. These were changes largely made to capitalize on TV cameras and make The Sheik of Araby that much more colorful and exotic—as well as to increase his heel heat. To further enhance and highlight his character's foreign-ness in the eyes of white Christian Americans, by around 1956 he began bringing a prayer rug with him into the ring and taking a few moments before each match to kneel, bow, and pray to Mecca in the traditional Muslim fashion. As with heel performers who portrayed Nazis, Japanese, Soviets, and other mistrusted groups and played up their supposed nationality/ethnicity, this was the kind of thing that was sure to trigger knee-jerk xenophobic reactions in 1950s audiences (and beyond). Ironically, in the largely Judeo-Christian landscape of mid-twentieth-century America, the lion's share of the populace had probably never come into contact with Muslims in everyday life and had little awareness of their authentic culture. Unlike the other groups mentioned, they had little reason historically to despise Muslims or Arabs, particularly in the era before terrorism or any other events that magnified Islamophobia in the United States. Nevertheless, the strange otherness, and implied flouting of Christian norms, was enough to whip most crowds into a frothing frenzy before the bell even rang, which in those days meant Farhat was doing exactly what he was hired to do. It goes without saying that his own real-life Catholic faith only further underlined the irony of the proceedings.

DAVE BURZYNSKI

"You couldn't take your eyes off the television," remembers long-time fan, promoter, and wrestling talk-show host John Arezzi. "There was not one other personality in the history of the wrestling business that played the gimmick without ever dropping the gimmick. No one knew what he was going to do. There's a handful that you never forget: Blassie, The Sheik, Bruno, Mil Mascaras, they were just so believable."

Arezzi's comments point to another aspect of Farhat's developing persona in the 1950s that would grow stronger over time and become one of the hallmarks of his mystique: his strict adherence to the code of kayfabe. In order to make The Sheik of Araby gimmick work, Farhat had to *become* the character, giving himself to it in a way that even went beyond what was common in the days when wrestlers fiercely protected the nature of the business and their own private lives. Pro wrestling was still being presented largely in sports-like fashion—unlike how it might have been with other forms of entertainment, if fans had known that the grim and wild-eyed Sheik of Araby was actually World War II vet and Lansing resident Ed Farhat, it likely would've meant the death of the gimmick, as well as much of his marketability. And so, he began playing it to the hilt, not even breaking character when he was in public and away from the arena.

"You believed him," says veteran wrestler, promoter, commentator, trainer, and all-around Zelig of the business Les Thatcher, who grew up watching The Sheik on TV as a kid in Cincinnati. "He lived his gimmick, as we used to say. After a match he would come out of the ring, and although there was always security, he didn't need it. Because the people would part like the Red Sea. They thought he was nuts. I heard that when they stopped at a gas station, Joyce said 'fill it up.' At a restaurant, she ordered from the waitress. Everybody thought that's what he was. He was an Arab and didn't speak English."

His persona coming more into focus, The Sheik of Araby passed another milestone of his early career on May 11, 1956, when he stepped in the ring for the first time with a man who would remain intertwined with his career for just about as long as he had one—and whose career would last just as unfathomably long. Their in-ring feud would rage on and off for nearly thirty-five years, in two different countries, over at least sixteen different states and provinces (plus Washington, DC) and in roughly seventeen different major wrestling territories. Cities ranging from New York, Buffalo, Atlanta, and Orlando; to Detroit, Cleveland, Milwaukee, Kansas City, Toronto, Chicago, and Memphis; to Phoenix, Los Angeles, San Diego, Honolulu, and dozens more would witness their epic rivalry—considered by most historians to have been the longest-lasting in the history of the business. Yet, just as it had been with Larry Chene, Sheik would also count this "rival" among the nearest and dearest friends he would make in his lifetime.

Born Houston Harris in Little Rock, Arkansas, in 1924, he grew up in Benton Harbor, Michigan, and briefly played baseball in the Negro leagues. While working in a steel mill, he was discovered by Benton Harbor wrestling promoter Joe Savoldi, who helped get him trained for the ring and gave him the name Bobo Brazil. Standing nearly six and a half feet tall with 250 pounds of muscle on his hulking frame, he had no trouble at all making a name for himself—first in Canada, and then in California, where, by the mid-1950s, he was already a major attraction. The naturally charismatic and humble career babyface so enamored himself to fans of all races that he became one of the first African-American performers to break the color barrier, regularly facing white opponents, competing in main events, and being marketed as a star to fans of all persuasions. For this reason, he later came to be known as the "Jackie Robinson of professional wrestling."

Their first match took place at the Benton Harbor Naval Armory and ended in a count-out victory for Brazil in the third and deciding fall. It would be their only known encounter of the 1950s, but the 1960s and 1970s in particular would be filled with hundreds of matches between the two—usually ending in similarly chaotic finishes.

DAVE BURZYNSKI

The Eternal Struggle: The Sheik vs. Bobo Brazil.

While back in his native stomping grounds, Farhat took advantage of his growing name recognition—and bank account—to open his own restaurant-nightclub in Williamston, right outside of Lansing. Called Sheik's Oasis, it was launched in financial partnership with his father-in-law, Francis Fleser, who already had lots of experience, having owned and operated a nightclub in the area for years. With the family splitting their time in those days in Texas, Chicago, and Lansing, there weren't many opportunities for Sheik to actually visit his Oasis, but he made a point to show his face there a few times a year, much to the delight of patrons. "My God, it was packed," remembered Eddie Jr. in a 2017 Facebook post. "I remember we were all at the restaurant [once], and Dad said to everyone, 'I have guests coming for dinner.' Well, sure as heck, around 5pm, in walk the Everly Brothers." Despite attracting celebrity clientele, Sheik's Oasis went out of business by the end of the 1950s—but by then, Sheik was on the verge of much bigger things anyway.

As for young Eddie Jr., then just starting school, it wasn't always easy being the son of a professional wrestling star: "Dad left going to my school to my mom. Mostly it was my grandma, my mom's mom. Dad was just on the road so much. He tried, but back then he just was not going to get close to outsiders. In those days, he was just Dad to me. I didn't really realize what he had going." As would happen often through Sheik's life, the price of keeping kayfabe could be steep. Joyce, meanwhile, began to get heavily involved in community life. She became an officer in the Sigma Beta Iota chapter of Epsilon Sigma Alpha, a collegiate and service organization for women. Formal teas and other social and charitable functions for the chapter would often be held in the Farhat home—a sight that would have surely caused any follower of The Sheik of Araby's career to do a double, triple, and quadruple take.

But the demands of the road continued. The Farhat family was back in Texas in the fall of 1956, which meant more time spent with the Chenes. This time, Sheik also brought another close friend, Lou Klein. By February of the following year, the services of The Sheik of Araby were sought out by Eddie Quinn, a former boxer and taxi driver who had gotten his start in Massachusetts but was now the chief wrestling promoter in the Canadian province of Quebec. Most importantly, Quinn had been granted exclusive rights by the Montreal Athletic Commission to present wrestling at the Montreal Forum, longtime home to the Montreal Canadiens and perhaps the most venerated hockey venue of all time. Quinn famously favored colorful and sensational wrestlers over scientific grapplers, which made Farhat a perfect fit. Sheik made his Montreal Forum debut on February 6, 1957, with a draw against amiable Hawaiian Sam Steamboat and was back again the following week with a win over Cowboy Len Hughes, once a top star of the Maritimes now on the tail-end of a twenty-five-year career. Farhat was liked by Quinn, who also used him in other towns he ran, like Ottawa, Ontario. This would begin Sheik's long-running success not just in the Montreal territory, but throughout Canada.

On the local front, The Sheik of Araby was still a fixture for Kohler and Barnett, even enjoying a one-week stint as Midwest Junior Heavyweight Champion in August 1957 (he lost it to his best pal, Chene, in Milwaukee). Another reason for him to stay local that month was his parents' surprise fiftieth wedding anniversary—and in typical fashion for David and Eva Farhat, the celebration was held at their sprawling home on Williams Street, with more than two hundred guests present, including their ten surviving children, thirty-three grandchildren, and one great-grandchild, who got together to present them with brand-new wedding bands to commemorate the occasion.[6] Sadly, a mere fourteen weeks later in that same Williams Street home, on December 4, 1957, David K. Farhat died of heart failure at the approximate age of seventy-five. It had to have been special and important to Edward that his father at least got to see his youngest son, the scrappy street kid who never finished school, make good as a success in the wrestling business—but not even he probably foresaw how much further up the ladder he was destined to climb.

The next step on that ladder came at the start of the new year, when The Sheik of Araby was called for the first time to what was traditionally the most lucrative and high-profile region for professional wrestling, the Northeast. By that time, the most powerful promotional faction in the region was an NWA-affiliated company called the Capitol Wrestling Corporation, based out of Washington, DC, and owned and operated by a second-generation Irish-American impresario from Rockaway Beach named Vincent James McMahon, whose father, Jess, had been tied in for years with Tex Rickard, kingpin of boxing promotions in New York. McMahon had gained power in the Northeast due to his Thursday night TV program, *Heavyweight Wrestling*, being picked up in New York and adjacent markets by the DuMont Network, looking for a local summer replacement for Fred Kohler's TV broadcast. As a result, McMahon's talent was now in demand, leading Kohler—who had once been top man on the totem pole—to seek a partnership with the newcomer. But the lynchpin in McMahon's cementing of Northeast control was his partnership with old warhorse Joe "Toots" Mondt, a once-feared and dangerous grappler whose innovations helped change the business in the 1920s and whose byzantine business dealings across the country had kept him an integral part of it ever since. Mondt held sway over the most famous arena in the United States, Madison Square Garden, and because he, too, now needed McMahon's wrestlers to bolster his sagging business, that meant that McMahon had the leverage to muscle in on the Garden as well.

It's possible that Kohler's link with McMahon was what helped Farhat get booked with Capitol, but even without the link, The Sheik of Araby was a natural because he fit in with the sensational, rough-and-tumble product that McMahon was supplying to fans and local promoters throughout the Northeast. His first appearance for McMahon made an instant splash, as he debuted on the *Heavyweight Wrestling* TV program on Thursday night, January 30, 1958, with a victory over Donn Lewin, one of three wrestling brothers whom Sheik would come to know quite well. He spent the early months of 1958 touring the Northeast, working for McMahon loyalists like Ed Contos in Baltimore and Willie Gilzenberg in New Jersey, as well at Sunnyside Gardens, a venerable boxing and wrestling venue in Queens booked directly by McMahon and Mondt.

But that all paled in comparison to the opportunity he got on February 24, 1958, when he got called up to the hub of Capitol's operations at Madison Square Garden itself, on 8th Avenue and 49th Street in the heart of midtown Manhattan. There, under the same lights that had shone down on the likes of Jack Dempsey, Joe Louis, and Rocky Marciano, The Sheik of Araby appeared before 18,156 fans on the third match from the top, losing to ballet dancer turned professional wrestler Ricki Starr. Typical of wrestling at the Garden, it was a stacked card featuring the best in the business: a main event pitting Antonino Rocca and Miguel Perez, perhaps the hottest tag team attraction of all time, against fearsome Greek brothers Chris and John Tolos; "Flying Frenchman" Edouard Carpentier against Dick the Bruiser; Pat O'Connor facing the towering Canadian behemoth Killer Kowalski. The night left a profound impression on Farhat, as it was the kind of talent-packed event that would become the hallmark of shows he would later promote with similar success. Sheik got not one but two Garden bookings in the winter of 1958, coming back the following month to tangle with rugged Hawaiian Bolo Hakawa.

Farhat made a great first impression in the Capitol Wrestling territory, leaving the door open to several returns to the area. Vince McMahon had become just the latest in a series of major power brokers in the wrestling business who liked what they saw in The Sheik of Araby. To anyone watching closely, it might have seemed like a career that was at its peak. How ironic it would have been then if anyone had known that, even at age thirty-one, The Sheik's career was nowhere near its crescendo; and that, in fact, the 1950s would be looked back on as only the early prelude to the thundering maelstrom that was to come.

CHAPTER 8

MOTOR CITY MAYHEM

*"To me, he was the greatest heel of all time. Every one of us that tried
to emulate him were pretty successful, because we were taking
from the greatest of all time."*
—KEVIN SULLIVAN

A s the 1950s drew to a close, the Farhat family continued to
thrive despite the loss of its patriarch. Amal and Lewie were
the owners and operators of Farhat Brothers Grocery store;
Edmund, ever the athlete, was now athletic director of Muskegon
Catholic Central High School; Topper had landed a job with the
Michigan State Highway Department that he held for the remainder
of his working life; Moses remained hard at work as an Oldsmobile
employee, the last of the brothers to stay in the auto industry. Edward's
unlikely success in the pro wrestling business surely must've made for
interesting conversation around the extended family dinner table, and
it was only just beginning.

In the years immediately to come, he would use his high national
profile to gain a stronger foothold in the Detroit wrestling world than he
had ever enjoyed before, thanks in part to the new presence on the scene
of a longtime associate and employer who already knew his value. This
greater presence eventually led to his becoming the lord and master of all
wrestling in the Motor City area and beyond, both in the ring and out.
But that was still a little way off. En route to making that happen, he was
a man hell-bent on proving himself even further, as a drawing attraction,
of course, but also as someone with a good head for business, who was
destined for more than being just one of the boys.

He would begin to prove this not just in his own local region, but in other regions as well, some of which already knew him, and others to which he was still a new commodity. The loss of national television was making the business more regionalized than ever before, each territory with its own thriving fiefdom and strong localized television. And The Sheik of Araby was making a major splash in many of them, becoming a bona fide touring attraction in the process, and further honing his act along the way.

One place where he spent a significant amount of time was the Northeast, in Vince McMahon's Capitol Wrestling corridor of operations. After having tested the waters in the winter of 1958, Farhat returned in the fall and spent the majority of the rest of the year as well as the entirety of 1959 working for Capitol. The area had been a proving ground for Antonino Rocca, Johnny Valentine, The Graham Brothers, Ricki Starr, Dick the Bruiser, and others, and would serve much the same function for The Sheik of Araby. The region was packed with perhaps more major metropolitan areas than any other part of the country, and promoters there looked to McMahon and Toots Mondt to provide them with talent, making the Capitol Wrestling Corporation something like a miniature version of the National Wrestling Alliance (even though Capitol was itself a member of the NWA). In New York, Sheik performed for fans in Kingston and White Plains as well as out on Long Island and in boroughs like Brooklyn, Queens, the Bronx, and of course Manhattan, where he became a monthly fixture at Madison

Square Garden; New Jersey fans witnessed him in Newark, Patterson, and Jersey City; Connecticut fans in New Haven, Bridgeport, and Waterbury. Add towns like Baltimore, Maryland; Reading, Pennsylvania; Alexandria, Virginia; and the home base in Washington, DC, and it was more than enough to keep The Sheik busy five or six days a week.

Madison Square Garden, October 20, 1958: The Sheik of Araby tangles with Antonino Rocca in his third Garden appearance. Sheik's tag team partner Bull Curry can be seen behind him on the ring apron. That's the leg of Miguel Perez in the foreground.

For much of this stretch, the longest Northeast run of his career, he was paired with another of the squared circle's maniacs, Wild Bull Curry. A fellow legend of Detroit wrestling, Curry had nevertheless rarely crossed paths in the ring with The Sheik of Araby before, outside of a pair of raucous encounters in Galveston, Texas, in the winter of 1955. With their keen eye for bombast and drawing power, McMahon and Mondt saw The Sheik and Curry as a natural tag team and put them together with Bobby Davis, a pompous and pompadoured loudmouth from Columbus, Ohio, who was busy inventing the role of the modern wrestling manager. Together, they faced off against the megateam of Antonino Rocca and Miguel Perez at Madison Square Garden in October 1958, battled Eddie and Dr. Jerry Graham in a memorable heel vs. heel encounter on Washington TV, and challenged extensively for the US Tag Team Championship held by two handsome Jewish kids from Buffalo, Don Curtis and his junior partner Mark Lewin.

The bond formed between Sheik and Curry during those months stayed with them for many years to come, also owing in large part to their shared Lebanese heritage. The families grew close as well, and Bull's son, Fred Curry, who would later go on to his own enormous wrestling success as well, still fondly recalls the first time he met The Sheik, while sitting ringside at age fifteen for one of the team's matches against Curtis and Lewin in the Currys' home state of Connecticut: "I was out there watching the matches, I look up and there's The Sheik. He looks down at me and says, 'If you come to Michigan, come visit me someday.' I didn't think anything of it then. I was kind of petrified!" Despite his under-standable adolescent trepidation, the seeds of that encounter would later pay off in spades for the younger Curry.

Beyond teaming with Curry, Farhat's stock continued to rise in Capitol as a singles competitor. He was put in several main event matches around the circuit with Rocca, Capitol's golden goose, including two different TV main events in Capitol Arena, an aging eighteen-hundred-seat building in downtown Washington, DC, where McMahon's televised program was held every week. He made ten appearances at Madison Square Garden during this period, including two back-to-back main events in the spring of '59, teaming with old foe and freshly turned heel Johnny Valentine to take on Rocca and Perez.[1]

As Farhat got more clout, one development that begins to emerge, particularly during the Capitol period, is he begins winning the large majority of his matches. Losing, or jobbing as it is known in the business, is an inevitable part of every wrestler's career, especially in its early years. Part of what began to make The Sheik of Araby so intriguing is that unlike most heels, who would peak for a few weeks and then be soundly thrashed by the babyfaces to the delight of the crowd, he usually walked away from his matches with his hand raised, one way or another. It is not known how much this was due at the time to Farhat's own insistence, but it is likely that it played a part, since so few heels were booked this way. It's also known that in later years when he had even greater power, Sheik almost never lost a match. We definitely see the beginning of that already happening this early, even if he was still losing to top stars like Rocca, as well as McMahon and Mondt's newest discovery, Bruno Sammartino, a humble, muscle-bound weightlifter from Abruzzo, Italy, who would eventually go on to become the greatest drawing card Capitol ever had and a bona fide Italian-American cultural phenomenon. Farhat and Sammartino first met at the Island Garden Arena in West Hempstead, Long Island, on January 16, 1960, with Bruno taking the match via disqualification. Only three months in the business, Sammartino was already being groomed for great things, and would certainly cross paths with Farhat many times in later years.

Farhat's wisdom in limiting the jobs promoters would ask him to do is easy to see. Whereas many heels ran the risk of running very hot and then cooling down really quickly after being inevitably thwarted by babyfaces, he kept his character mysterious and menacing by rarely going down in defeat. Enhancing this mystery and menace was a new practice he started adding to the act at the very end of the 1950s. Taking a page from the playbook of professional magicians, he began using a simple yet effective parlor trick involving flash paper and a small device he would wear on the ends of his fingers. The device contained flint, so when he struck his fingers together while holding the flash paper, the sparks generated would then ignite the paper and create the illusion of a giant ball of flame that would be "thrown" in the direction of his opponents during matches. Naturally, this maneuver would draw a disqualification if the referee spotted it, but when done right, it had a shocking effect on the crowd, making it appear as though the exotic and deadly Sheik of Araby possessed a sinister supernatural power. It may not have been wrestling, but it was theatricality at its finest, and the chance that the fire might be thrown (although it was quite rare back then) made The Sheik of Araby even more of a must-see attraction than before.

Other changes to Farhat's persona and to the act began to take shape in the late 1950s. His turban would be replaced with a kaffiyeh or traditional Arab head-scarf—more accurate to the trappings of an

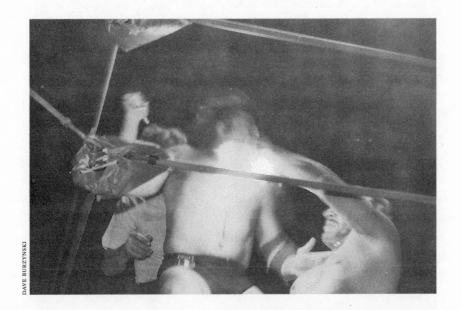

actual sheik. He took to wearing boots with upturned, pointed toes, to suggest the footwear of sheiks and Saracens of old. For the first time, his wife, Joyce, sometimes joined in on the act, taking advantage of her diminutive stature and slim figure to take on the role of Princess Salima,[2] the meek and humble bride of The Sheik of Araby, who accompanied him to the ring and did his every bidding, supplicating herself to him all while he mistreated and berated her in garbled, grunting gibberish that was supposed to be Arabic. Her face veiled and her body draped in multicolored robes, her very presence was meant to rile audiences into outrage and sympathy as they watched a brutish foreigner abuse this young, attractive woman he had apparently enslaved. It was the beginning of Joyce's involvement in her husband's career, and a clear example of how dedicated she was to supporting his endeavors, no matter what she was called upon to do.

Right before leaving the Northeast, Farhat made one more tweak that would turn out to be a game-changer. At the suggestion of Vince McMahon, he shortened his ring name, dropping the Araby portion.[3] When Ed Farhat appeared to take on Angelo Savoldi on the January 13, 1960, edition of *Heavyweight Wrestling from Bridgeport*, Capitol's number two weekly TV program, he was introduced simply as "The Sheik." With

Capitol Arena, December 11, 1958: Princess Salima (aka Joyce Farhat) blesses the ring with incense as her Sheik (and husband) prepares to take on Skull Murphy in a vicious heel vs. heel main event for promoter Vincent J. McMahon.

the exception of a handful of matches later in 1960 and 1961, he would be called that for the remainder of not only his career, but his life.

Home was beckoning The Sheik, and after leaving Capitol he took to refocusing his energies on "homesteading" and putting down deeper roots in the Michigan-Indiana-Ohio-Wisconsin area. In addition to his wife and son being back home in Lansing, family obligation had also taken the form of the passing of his mother, Eva, who died on October 12, 1959, at the age of sixty-seven, during the tail end of his Capitol run. A weeklong break in Farhat's bookings at the time indicates he likely was able to get away to be with the family—and it was only three months later that he made the decision to return home for good. The big house on Williams Street had now lost both its original owners and would remain in the family for just a few more years before being sold in 1963. The Farhat siblings were now in charge of the family, and in his position as big-shot wrestling star, Edward, once the baby, began taking on more of a patriarch role.

The landscape had changed a bit in his absence, as is often the case in the wrestling business. Larry Chene, once Sheik's fellow struggling rookie, had returned from Texas and become one of the biggest stars on the Detroit wrestling scene after getting over huge for Bert Ruby working local shows while on a holiday break visiting family. Fred Kohler's power in the business was waning, having lost his television spots and gotten largely ostracized by the NWA, and relying heavily on his partnership with McMahon and Mondt to keep himself afloat. Meanwhile, his former assistant and business partner Jim Barnett was growing in power and was making life very difficult for the man who had controlled wrestling in Detroit for nearly fifteen years, Harry Light.

In late 1958, Barnett came into contact with Johnny Doyle, an old pro in the promotional game who had gotten his start in the 1930s booking talent for Philadelphia impresario Ray Fabiani, and who had also briefly worked as talent booker for Toots Mondt in New York. Where Doyle had really made his name was in Southern California, where he spent years as the promotional partner of NWA member Cal Eaton until eventually running afoul of Eaton and getting pushed out of the Los Angeles territory. As a result of his experience, Doyle had no love for the NWA and its monopolistic practices and was looking for a young upstart like Barnett to help him launch something that would truly flout the sacred territorial protections of the NWA and ruffle the feathers of members who thought their pieces of the national pie were protected.

The Barnett-Doyle Corporation was formed in April of 1959, with interests in places as far flung as San Francisco, Denver, Omaha, and Minneapolis. They specifically had their sights on areas of Michigan, Indiana, and Ohio that were still largely run by NWA members Light, Kohler, and Al Haft, respectively. With the NWA already having been made vulnerable by an FBI-led anti-trust investigation, Barnett and Doyle set up shop as an outlaw promotion and quickly went to work assuming control of the region. In Detroit, they took over promotions at the venerable Olympia Stadium, pushing out Light after over a decade of his running the "Old Red Barn."[4] Barnett knew well the value of television thanks to his early association with Kohler, and pretty soon his product was airing out of nearby Windsor, Ontario, Thursday nights on Detroit's CKLW Channel 9, with the product presented sometimes as "All-Star Wrestling," but also using the name originated in the area by Light, "Big Time Wrestling."[5] Pretty soon, Barnett and Doyle had control of Michigan, Indiana, and much of Ohio—Light was completely out of the business, while Bert Ruby was still able to run his Motor City Wrestling in the smaller towns, with his own TV on WXYX Channel 7 Saturday afternoons.

In addition to the value of television, another lesson Barnett had learned from his time with Kohler was the power of the printed word. Back in the forties he had gotten his start running the business's first true magazine, *Wrestling as You Like It*, which also doubled as a program sold at Kohler's events. Once he and Doyle took over their new territory, one of the first things they did was to get a high-quality program magazine off the ground. Eventually called *Body Press*, it was initially run by Detroit newspaperman Art Hagen, who also contributed most of the articles under various pseudonyms to protect his reputation in the "legitimate" media world. Although only sold at live events, it was more than just a program, boasting roughly twenty pages of content, with dazzling photographs and stories pushing all the area's top stars. It most definitely added value to Barnett and Kohler's product and helped it become a major hit with fans. For these reasons, it would continue publication well beyond Barnett and Kohler's tenure in the territory.

As Sheik's fortunes increased, he and Joyce moved from Lansing to Williamston, the town where she had grown up, purchasing an impressive home at 3275 East Grand River Avenue. He soon became a regular fixture of Barnett and Doyle's promotion, albeit typically still on the mid-card. His in-ring act continued getting wilder and weirder, as in addition to the praying and bowing, he would now often stare quizzically upward and point at the ceiling, as if gesturing to some unseen force or deity. In addition to the cobra clutch and the Arabian backbreaker, he added a new finishing hold that involved sitting on his opponent's back while draping one of their arms over his knee, clasping their chin with both hands, and pulling back until a submission occurred. It was a variation of a hold often credited to Mexican-American luchadore Gory Guerrero, who began using it in the 1940s along with his frequent tag team partner, the legendary Santo. (The Sheik had wrestled Guerrero once in New York in January 1958, and it's possible that he had learned the hold directly from him.) Guerrero called it el de a caballo, roughly translated as "the one on horseback," but The Sheik named it the "camel clutch"[6] in keeping with his gimmick. It would become his signature finishing maneuver for most of the rest of his career.

Wresting historian and lifelong fan Tom Burke remembers what it was like first seeing The Sheik on TV in those days as an impressionable kid: "We used to get Big Time Wrestling out of Indianapolis, on channel 8 out of New Haven. Sheik had his wife, Joyce, with him as Princess Salima. He beat the hell out of her. My mother was outraged. When The Sheik would come into the ring, they would have an incense burner that Joyce would carry. The commentator Sam Menacker mentioned that maybe what was in the incense urn was marijuana and that's why he would go crazy."

In addition to regular dates for Barnett and Doyle throughout the states they controlled, Sheik broadened his travels in 1960. Taking advantage of the warm weather in the dead of winter, he took a couple of bookings for Clarence "Cowboy" Luttrall, the former wrestler from Jacksboro, Texas, best known for getting annihilated by an aging Jack Dempsey in a 1940 boxing exhibition, who now ran the wrestling rackets down in Florida. He took dates in Kansas, Iowa, and Nebraska for Joe Dusek, one of the famous Dusek Riot Squad, wrestling's original brother faction, who now operated as a promoter out of his home base in Omaha. In the summer of 1961, he took a series of weekly dates for Georgia wrestling bigwig Andrew Lutzi, a former student of catch wrestling pioneer Farmer Burns who had changed his name to the more WASPish "Paul Jones" during his wrestling career and kept it that way throughout his lengthy promotional career in the Peach State.

He even remained loyal to his old boss Fred Kohler, still making monthly appearances in Chicago, including two major extravaganzas at Comiskey Park, home of the Chicago White Sox and a site that hadn't hosted pro wrestling since the epic 1911 "Match of the Century" between Frank Gotch and George Hackenschmidt. In the first of these, Sheik defeated influential Samoan superstar Prince Neff Maiava before 30,275 fans—the largest North American crowd of his entire career—on the undercard of a show headlined by NWA World Heavyweight Champion Pat O'Connor defending the title against Yukon Eric, the man who had famously lost part of his ear eight years earlier in a match with Killer Kowalski. The novelty of the Comiskey return having apparently worn off, a little more than half that many fans returned the following month to witness a rare loss for The Sheik against the 601-pound scuffler from Morgan's Corner, Arkansas, Haystacks Calhoun, himself also a major touring attraction.

Most importantly for his career at that point, Sheik came into the orbit of Ignacio "Pedro" Martinez, the six-foot-four retired Mexican grappler who had once been Toots Mondt's partner in the Manhattan Booking Agency and now ran the Buffalo Athletic Club, which controlled wrestling in western New York State, as well as right down the I-90 corridor in Erie, Pennsylvania, and Cleveland, Ohio. Butting up as closely as it did to Barnett and Doyle's territory, it was a great place for The Sheik to grab some additional bookings without straying too far from home, and he did quite well there from the beginning, drawing great business and getting invited back often. The relationship between the Detroit territory and the Buffalo territory would continue with Sheik as the unifying force for years to come.

Meanwhile, Barnett was hard at work making the man he had first helped get onto national TV in Chicago become an even bigger star than ever. In April 1960, Sheik received two back-to-back shots against O'Connor for the heavyweight crown at the Olympia. Antonino Rocca, who was getting booked less and less by McMahon and Mondt in the Northeast due in part to the rise of Sammartino, came in for a series of matches against The Sheik in the spring of 1961 in Indianapolis, Cincinnati, and elsewhere around the horn.[7] When Barnett and Doyle landed Briggs Stadium, home of the Detroit Tigers, for a big outdoor super-show in the summer of '61, they booked The Sheik to win over twenty-four-year-old Canadian newcomer Emile Dupree on a card that also featured O'Connor defending against the Mormon giant Don Leo Jonathan, and Sheik's soon-to-be archrival Bobo Brazil facing the man who was by that point Barnett and Doyle's top attraction, Dick the

Bruiser, upon whom they had bestowed the United States heavyweight title, the top prize in the territory.

An example of what would sometimes be called a tweener, Bruiser was often booked as a rule-breaking heel but was becoming so popular with fans for his roughhouse tactics and tough guy persona that he would sometimes be booked as a babyface. This would explain why he spent a lot of the early 1960s both tag teaming with Sheik for Barnett and Doyle, as well as facing him in some knock-down, drag-out affairs throughout the area (and in other places). Bruiser was becoming such a big star for Barnett and Doyle, in fact, that he would soon entertain the notion of supplanting them.

By the middle of 1961, the NWA World Heavyweight strap was in the possession of the tan, bleached-blond, and eminently hated Buddy Rogers, who had taken it from O'Connor in June at another Fred Kohler Comiskey show, this one drawing a crowd that set a modern attendance record. Rogers was the first true heel that the NWA board had approved to hold the honor, but being world champ meant having to defend against good guy and bad guy alike, and so even the despicable Sheik got a few cracks at the gold: a two-out-of-three falls encounter at the Olympia on August 18, as well as a shot in Fort Wayne, Indiana, in October and another the same week in Dayton, Ohio, for Al Haft, Rogers's mentor and Buckeye State wrestling kingpin for more than forty years.

And the NWA title wasn't even the only version of the world heavyweight crown that Sheik was vying for at the time. One-time Kohler megastar Verne Gagne, having been stymied in his own political campaign for the title, purchased the Minnesota territory from NWA cofounder Tony Stecher, renamed it the American Wrestling Association, and broke away entirely from the NWA, declaring himself the inaugural AWA World Heavyweight Champion, recognized throughout a northern Midwest swath that then included Minnesota, the Dakotas, Iowa, Nebraska, and parts of Wisconsin. Despite the schism, The Sheik proved adept at breaking political boundaries without suffering any discernible consequences, taking dates against Gagne for the AWA title in Lincoln, Nebraska, in April and Omaha in September, as well as several more shots during the early 1960s.

Viewed by most as a legitimate world title challenger and at least a solid upper mid-card worker everywhere he went, Sheik nevertheless suffered a bit from the stigma often attached to "gimmick wrestlers" in those days, in that he was good enough to draw money with, but not worthy of actually holding the top prize or even of really being the top star. Still, he was used consistently by Barnett and Doyle as their promotion continued to thrive, and he remained loyal to them even as they battled Sheik's former boss Harry Light. When in the summer of 1961, in a last-ditch effort to save his company, Light maneuvered his way back into his old stomping grounds at the Olympia, Barnett and Doyle looked to a brand-new facility on the banks of the Detroit River. Starting with Barnett and Doyle and continuing for years after, it would become the heart and soul of Detroit wrestling for the next two decades.

Built on the exact site where, on July 24, 1701, Antoine de la Mothe Cadillac first set foot on the land that would later be Detroit and claimed it for France's King Louis XIV, the sleek, modern construction of concrete, steel, and glass was begun in 1956 and completed four years later. Named for Detroit's mayor at the time, Albert Cobo, the arena was part of a larger exhibition hall meant to house conventions, concerts, sporting events, and other civic functions, like so many other shiny new venues popping up all over the country at the time. A wonder of modern design, Cobo Hall was built specifically to stand above the also newly constructed Lodge Freeway and boasted a parking area on its roof, high above the teeming streets below. Part of the complex, encompassing approximately forty thousand square feet, with a seating capacity of close to 12,500 for boxing and wrestling, Cobo Arena became the home of the NBA's Detroit Pistons (who played their first four seasons at the Olympia before the move). It housed its first event, the forty-third Auto Industry Dinner, on October 17, 1960, and its first concert, a performance by rock 'n' roll legend Jerry Lee Lewis, on May 17, 1961.

On September 23, 1961, Barnett and Doyle moved into Cobo Arena with the venue's first pro wrestling event, topped by Dick the Bruiser, who took the United States title back from Verne Gagne in the main event before 8,018 fans. From then on, Cobo was Barnett and Doyle's to run, while Light tried to stake his claim to the Olympia on the other side of town. Light pled his case to the NWA, which considered Barnett and Doyle to be an "outlaw" operation and therefore put their support behind Light in his bid to reassert his claim as the officially sanctioned NWA representative in the Motor City. As it often did in cases of promotional wars, the NWA called on its members to send talent from all over the country to help Light turn the tide, and so his Olympia shows featured wrestlers sent from Fred Kohler in Chicago, Vince McMahon in New York, Toots Mondt in Pittsburgh, and others. But it made no difference—even with shows featuring NWA talent from across the nation, Light's Olympia events were drawing roughly half the crowds that Barnett and Doyle were at Cobo. The promotional war was a swift one. Outlaws or not, Jim Barnett and Johnny Doyle were the unrivaled kings of Detroit wrestling by the start of 1962, running both Cobo Arena *and* Olympia Stadium.

It was during this proto–Big Time Wrestling era that The Sheik and Bobo Brazil came to be booked against each other more often, although Barnett and Doyle seemed to see fit to match them in nearly every major stop in their circuit *except* Detroit (that would come later). It's easy to speculate that this was partly due to Detroit's large African-American population, as promoters in those days were still somewhat hesitant to book white and Black wrestlers against each other, for fear of a race riot. Meanwhile Pedro Martinez, himself America's only major non-Caucasian promoter at the time, had no issue booking Sheik and Brazil several times in his territory's main venue, the Buffalo Memorial Auditorium, as well as elsewhere. The public throughout both areas was getting a taste of the growing chemistry between the two performers, setting the stage for epic confrontations in the years soon to come.

In fact, Martinez was the promoter using The Sheik most often in those days, aside from Barnett and Doyle. He appeared in Martinez's two-week Wrestlethon tournament in the Memorial Auditorium in December '61, making it all the way to the finals before losing to German grappler Kurt Stein (the future Kurt Von Brauner). He was also routinely matched with the enormously popular Italian superstar Ilio DiPaolo—who also happened to be Martinez's son-in-law, which meant that the usually unbeaten Sheik had to do the honors during most of their encounters.

But win or lose, Sheik was a top draw for Martinez during those days, and his drawing power in the Buffalo-Cleveland circuit would hold strong from then on.

Meanwhile back on the home front, Farhat was first brought into Cobo Arena—the building that would one day be known as "The House that Sheik Built"[8]—on January 20, 1962, for a tag team match, joining with fellow career heel and former military wrestler during the war, Rochester's "Handsome" Johnny Barend, to defeat future Mid-Atlantic legend Johnny Weaver and his "brother" Sonny.[9] It was the opening match of a card headlined by Dick the Bruiser—again, indicative of the pecking order at the time. Nevertheless, The Sheik was a regular on Barnett and Doyle's TV, and it was still common to see Princess Salima at his side, with relatively local shows allowing Joyce to remain close to home to tend to Eddie Jr. Something of a pause in the on-air relationship of The Sheik and the Princess occurred at the end of the summer of 1962, when Joyce learned that a second little Sheik was on the way.

Eddie Jr., soon to be a big brother, was also discovering that being the son of a hated TV wrestler could have its disadvantages: "To be honest,

WILSON LINDSEY

CKLW-TV Studio, early 1960s: The Sheik and his Princess make an appearance during the Barnett-Doyle days of Big Time Wrestling for a Windsor, Ontario, taping.

sometimes it wasn't very nice," he told Gary Cubeta in 2009. "When you're young, going to school, ages six to sixteen, everybody wants to beat you up because your dad's The Sheik. It wasn't very fun. Everybody thinks because you're a celebrity that life was much better on our side of the track. But he was just a human being. He was a dad when he came off the road. He was a good father, but he was always on the road, so he could only do so much. When I was a kid, with little league games and such, my grandpa would always take me to those things, because Dad was always away."

The pattern of Farhat's necessary absence from family life only intensified as The Sheik became more of a touring attraction in further-flung parts of the country. In April 1962, he was flown out to the West Coast for the first time in his career, brought in by outlaw San Francisco Bay Area promoter Roy Shire, a ruthless wrestler-turned-businessman who had just won a war for control of the Northern California area. Much like Barnett and Doyle, Shire was running in opposition to the NWA and looking for talent to help pop the shows at his San Francisco Bay home base, the Cow Palace. The Sheik served this purpose nicely and came in for one show each month for the remainder of the year, including shots against chiseled top babyface Pepper Gomez for Shire's version of the United States title, as well as team-ups with Shire's number-one heel and lead drawing card, the "Blond Bomber" Ray Stevens. This was the beginning of a phenomenon that only grew as The Sheik's legend did—promoters from territories where Sheik didn't normally wrestle enlisting his occasional services as a special attraction designed to score a few high-revenue houses to give a boost to their bottom line.

Farhat was a man becoming more and more keenly aware of his worth and ability to play the political game, and Barnett and Doyle saw it too. By the end of 1962, he was more than just a worker, he had been appointed as their booker—a crucial backstage role that involved helping to make the matches and formulate the angles or storylines that would help drive paying customers to want to see those matches and, of course, deciding who won and lost. It instantly made him more of a locker room leader, as he now had a reasonable amount of power in terms of helping or hindering people's careers. "Long before he bought into the territory, he was running it," remembers Canadian wrestler-turned-carpet-magnate Bernie "The Cat" Livingston, who worked with and for The Sheik numerous times. "The writing was on the wall for years, even before it was well known that he was running the territory, he was the one you'd talk to, or one of his men would talk to you."

Naturally, with that kind of power came the ability to self-aggrandize as well, and Sheik wasted no time in booking himself against Mark Lewin, a top babyface in the territory against whom he already had worked extensively in tag team matches back in the Capitol days. A so-called white meat babyface of the highest order, the tall, clean-cut, good-looking all-American Lewin was perfect to match with the sinister, raving, bloodthirsty, flame-throwing Sheik. Their first singles match took place on October 10, 1962, at the Tyndall Armory in Indianapolis, a town run for Barnett and Doyle by Native American promoter Balk Estes. They met in a series of encounters from the fall of '62 well into '63 in places like Cincinnati Gardens, another Estes-run venue, as well as back at Cobo Arena. That set the stage for countless other matches in future years, as Lewin became another of The Sheik's classic archrivals.

As he gained a certain level of respect, his level of comfort and familiarity with the boys increased. In those days, some of the older and more experienced workers in the locker room would still occasionally call him Eddie, although that would change as the years went by and he established more seniority and the leverage to insist upon being called Sheik in keeping with the professional persona that was becoming more intertwined with his private one. There was another familiar nickname reserved for trusted friends and associates—"Zib," an Arabic vulgarity that stuck to him because that's also what he loved calling everyone else.[10]

"He was so personable," remembers Les Thatcher, who first encountered The Sheik in those days as a rookie wrestling for Jim Barnett in Indianapolis, after having watched him on TV as a kid. "I never had a problem with Eddie at all. He was one of the first guys I worked with for Barnett my first day at TV. I couldn't begin to tell you how many times I worked with him. He was always friendly. And he had a sense of humor. I never had a cross word with the man. But he seemed to transition from Eddie to The Sheik without any problem. He'd be sitting in the dressing room and talking like you and I are talking now, and someone came and said you guys are on, and when you got to the ring, it was The Sheik. It wasn't Ed Farhat."

Farhat's burning desire to advance his career was no doubt only further stoked by the imminent arrival of his second child. After defeating twenty-eight-year-old future AWA World Champion Nick Bockwinkel in under six minutes at the Cow Palace, he hightailed it from California back home, where the next day, April 21, 1963, Joyce gave birth to their son Thomas. Sheik's match record reveals a rare week-long gap at this point, indicating that Farhat more than likely stayed home for a few days to spend time with his wife and brand-new baby boy before venturing back on the road. Now the father of a thirteen-year-old and a newborn, Farhat was more intent than ever on climbing the ladder of success and reaching not only new heights but new markets where The Sheik could run wild. This included continuing his relationship with Roy Shire on the West Coast, as well as with fading powers Fred Kohler and Al Haft in the Midwest.

It also included branching out to somewhere totally new, where he would spend nearly a full year, do gangbusters business, and open the eyes of more than a few people as to his viability as a consistent main event performer and attraction. The Sheik had been to Texas before, but not the Amarillo-based Western States Sports, a territory located in the west of the expansive Lone Star State, independent of the Houston-Dallas contingent that had used Sheik in the past. The operation was owned and operated by Dory Funk, a grizzled son of Hammond, Indiana—not far from Farhat's neck of the woods—who had embraced a cowboy persona after experiencing great success wrestling in Texas following his service in World War II. Funk was joined by his business partner and booker, Jack Pfefer protégé Karl "Doc" Sarpolis.[11] And then there were his two sons—recent West Texas State grad Dory Jr., who had just joined the family business, as well as Terry, still in his second year at West Texas—both of whom Dory had every intention of building his wrestling promotion around, much as many other promoters had done with their sons, willing or no.

Thanks to a working relationship between the Funks and Jim Barnett, The Sheik was first brought down to Amarillo on September 5, 1963, and slotted directly into the main event at the Sports Arena against handsome Oklahoman Joe Blanchard, like Funk an out-of-stater who had experienced great success in Texas. On that night, however, he fell to The Sheik in under six minutes. Fans were immediately enthralled by the mysterious madman, who might as well have been from another planet, with his glaring hundred-yard stare, pseudo-Arabic gibberish, headscarf, prayer mat, and flame-throwing ways. With the exception of a one-month break when he came home for the holidays, Sheik remained in Funk's territory for the majority of the next twelve months, selling out shows in Amarillo as well as other Funk towns like Abilene, Odessa, and in particular Lubbock, where he drew record-setting crowds at the Fair Park Coliseum, an arena built into the site of the historic South Plains Fairgrounds near the edge of Yellow House Canyon.

"He had a connection with my father," remembers Terry Funk, who was a fresh-faced lad of twenty when he first met The Sheik. "He was a tremendous box office attraction. That's why he would come into Amarillo, and it would be an automatic sellout in all of the towns that he went to, every one of them. I don't know if it was the character, if it was his actions in the ring or what it was, but he had a magnetism that attracted people and paying customers. Everyone loved to go to the arena whenever he was on the card, hoping he'd get the shit knocked out of him. But that seldom happened."

Funk and Sarpolis had great confidence in Sheik's drawing power and ability to generate nuclear heat, which can be seen in the astonishing way he was booked: a win over rookie Dory Jr., the promoter's son, in straight falls on October 3 in six minutes; a victory over Dory Sr. himself a week later to take the North American Championship, which he held for a solid six months, including the month he spent back home; joining forces with other mega-heels like Fritz Von Erich, the rangy Texan footballer born Jack Adkisson who had joined the Nazi wrestling villain brigade, and Sputnik Monroe, the stripe-haired hipster from Dodge City who became an unlikely champion of desegregation in Southern arenas; a DQ win over Verne Gagne, fresh off a recent loss of the AWA World Heavyweight crown; challenging old foe Lou Thesz, in possession of the NWA heavyweight prize one final time, before another sellout

Lubbock crowd. In one particular Lubbock match, Sheik scandalized the audience by throwing one of his infamous fireballs in the face of sentimental favorite Dory Jr. Shocked and appalled though they might have been, the people kept coming back to see if he would do it again.

For this particular Texas run, Sheik didn't bring his family down with him, as by this point Eddie Jr. was going to school back in Michigan (Larry Chene and his family, who had hosted the Farhats in the past, had relocated permanently back to the Detroit area). But family or no, the paydays were too good to pass up. Sheik returned home for brief stints each month throughout 1964, spending time with Joyce and the boys and also taking dates at Cobo Arena and TV tapings in Windsor, Ontario, designed to keep his face in front of Detroit fans despite his extended absence. Other than these occasional breaks, his time was spent building his legend in Texas and proving for the first time that he could be a consistent main-eventer—something that not even Barnett and Doyle had allowed him to do. As far as the Funks were concerned, it had everything to do with The Sheik's ability to rile up fans like no one else, by committing to his persona full-tilt and creating an aura of total unpredictability.

"It wasn't his height. It wasn't his weight. What did he have?" Terry Funk ponders. "Yes, he was The Sheik. But you have to have something more than that. You have to have charisma and talent, and that's exactly what he had a combination of—plus, he had no fear. I truly mean that. He would go to the extent that the fans wanted to kill him, and he would go out right through the crowd! I've seen him make mincemeat of a lot of people; he put a lot of fear in the crowd's eyes. You know what I think his appeal was? When he came out of the dressing room, he scared everybody shitless. Including me! And that's no lie."

Much like his occasional tag team partner Sputnik Monroe, one thing about wrestling in Texas that Sheik took exception to was the way in which African-American fans would be corralled up in the balcony while white fans got to enjoy the floor seats, during those days when Jim Crow laws still held sway in the South. Having grown up in a racially mixed neighborhood where children of all ethnicities interacted freely, this kind of separation, and the inherent disenfranchisement that went along with it, was abhorrent to Farhat. One oft-repeated anecdote recounts how Sheik, during one of his engagements, hopped out of the ring mid-match and proceeded to climb up the balcony and tear down the fence that penned in the Black spectators. He was able to get away with this behavior by passing it off as part of his wild-and-woolly act; something the crazed and uncontrollable Sheik would do to foment chaos. And even though heels in the South would sometimes side with Black fans as a cynical tactic to draw heat, in Farhat's case it was also done to send a message, which was heard loud and clear despite being shrouded in kayfabe.

It was while working for the Amarillo office that Farhat first met Jack Cain, brother-in-law of Dory Funk Sr., then working for the promotion as a referee. Whatever it was, he saw something he liked in Cain, as the seeds were sown then for a working relationship that would blossom soon enough, as Cain would eventually come to work not *with* Farhat, but *for* him. Big things were on the horizon for The Sheik in the autumn of 1964, when an intriguing business proposition called him home from Texas for the time being. After years of making a name for himself on the Detroit scene and beyond, Sheik was on the verge of becoming so much more than a wrestler. He was about to become the boss.

CHAPTER 9

BIG TIME

"This is a business. If you ain't in it, you out of it, baby."
—THE SHEIK

There are lots of BC/AD moments in pro wrestling history; watershed events that changed the course of the business, and after which things would never be the same. Jack Pfefer breaking kayfabe to the *Daily Mirror* in 1933; the death of Georgia booker Ray Gunkel in 1972; Hulk Hogan winning the WWF World title in 1984; Shane Douglas throwing down the NWA World title belt in 1994; among many, many others. Another of these, and the one most relevant to this story, is what happened in Johnny Doyle's luxury condo in downtown Detroit in October 1964. It was there that Ed Farhat, professionally known as The Sheik, for the tidy sum of $50,000, became the owner of Big Time Wrestling and the controlling power of a wrestling empire that covered parts of Michigan, Ohio, Indiana, and West Virginia but was commonly known as the Detroit territory. It was also the moment when he went from being a successful mid-card heel to one of the hottest main event attractions in the country; from a typical wild man of professional wrestling to *the* wild man of professional wrestling. This was the moment he took the leap from wrestling stardom to wrestling immortality.

The 1960s was a time of parity and opportunity for wrestling's territorial system. Without national television, there was no one company with overwhelming power over the others; different regional circuits and organizations were thriving all over North America, and business was cooking on all cylinders. The NWA had more members than ever before,

THE SHEIK

despite the fact that some companies were choosing not to affiliate with it. In the Northeast, Vince McMahon's Capitol Wrestling had broken away from the NWA and rebranded itself as the World Wide Wrestling Federation. Verne Gagne's Midwestern AWA was steadily expanding. In addition to Roy Shire in San Francisco, Southern California had the LA-based World Wrestling Association run by Cal and Aileen Eaton and later Aileen's son, Mike LeBell.

Then there was another World Wrestling Association, inspired by the California one but established in a far less sun-kissed environment. Dick the Bruiser, once the top draw for Jim Barnett and Johnny Doyle, had experienced success with Eaton in Los Angeles, capturing the WWA version of the world heavyweight title. His burgeoning star power and championship acclaim gave him the idea to return home to the Midwest and try to pull the rug out from under Barnett and Doyle right in their own backyard. In those days, Barnett and Doyle's Midwestern terri-tory was broken up into two distinct sections or offices, one based in Michigan and the other in Indiana. Joining forces with fellow Eaton main-eventer, former footballer, and the man credited with inventing the abdominal stretch, Wilbur Snyder, Bruiser first set his sights on the latter section. He and Snyder set up shop in Indianapolis and proceeded to gradually take over the Indiana territory by force, calling their new company the World Wrestling Alliance, with Bruiser still claiming to be the WWA World Heavyweight Champion (this subterfuge was aided by the lack of information technology in those days, which meant that fans in one territory had little knowledge of what was going on in other parts of the country). Working relationships with the Los Angeles office as well as Gagne's AWA helped give them tremendous momentum from the start and put their outlaw promotion on the map right out of the gate. By November 1964, Balk Estes, Barnett and Doyle's Indianapolis promoter, had officially closed up shop, ceding total control of the area to Bruiser and Snyder. "Bruiser was an intimidating guy," remembers Scott Romer, who would one day become his son-in-law. "He carried pistols. He also had a lot of power with the athletic commissions."

Barnett and Doyle still held on to the northern portion of their territory, but their days were numbered there as well, partly due to circumstances beyond the professional wrestling business. It's safe to assume that Barnett in particular was vulnerable to incursions by Dick the Bruiser and others because his attentions were divided as he battled a potential sex scandal bubbling up, with him caught right in the middle. It wasn't easy being an openly gay man in a business dominated by testosterone and hyper-masculinity, let alone one who was so flamboyantly effete. The diminutive, bespectacled, and nattily attired Barnett always loved living the high life (whether he could afford it or not), and at one point had purchased an opulent home on posh Lakewood Drive in Lexington, Kentucky, which he shared with his companion Lonnie Winter. The house was a mere five-minute drive from the University of Kentucky, which became convenient when Barnett became mixed up with the University of Kentucky football team, bribing them with expensive gifts and women; inviting the young players to wild, booze-fueled parties; and cajoling them into having sex with him and some of the closeted gay celebrities who moved in his circle, including Hollywood icon Rock Hudson.

When word of the severe improprieties reached University of Kentucky officials, who had recently had to deal with a point-shaving scandal with their football team and were anxious to avoid getting dragged through the mud again, they demanded Barnett cease immediately and get the hell out of town. But it wasn't as simple as that, as the newest scandal certainly looked like it would have some legs. It soon became apparent that it was in Barnett's best interest to not just get out town but to get as far away as possible. He began looking into divesting himself of all US interests in the wrestling business and starting up a promotion in Australia, on the literal other side of the world. After convincing Johnny Doyle of the profitability of his plan, Australia being virgin territory when it came to wrestling, all that remained was finding a buyer for the Detroit office. They had lost Indiana by force—they would be damned if they couldn't get someone to go the honorable route and buy them out in Detroit so they could at least walk away with something.

That buyer turned out to be none other than their own booker, The Sheik, who had earned their trust and respect. They also had confidence in him because he had proven he had more business acumen than most of the talent; much like Dick the Bruiser and wrestlers like Verne Gagne, Roy Shire, Paul Jones, Dory Funk, and others, he possessed in him a restless ambition that wouldn't allow him to be simply one of the boys in the locker room. Ed Farhat wanted more for himself and for his family than that and sought to seize an opportunity for power and money on the other side of the wrestler-promoter dynamic. He sought to enter that highest echelon of authority in the business and take control of one of the most lucrative and high-profile territories in the country.

After a year spent mostly in western Texas, The Sheik started taking some other bookings in September 1964, the Barnett-Doyle deal looming. While negotiations were underway, he spent time back on the West Coast making some appearances for Shire. He took a couple of rare dates for St. Louis promoter and NWA president Sam Muchnick—a former sportswriter who was not the biggest fan of Sheik's antics, or sensationalism in wrestling in general—including a match on Muchnick's acclaimed TV show *Wrestling at the Chase*, incongruously filmed before patrons in tuxedos and evening gowns at the Chase Park Plaza Hotel in downtown St. Louis.

He also came into contact with another office that would have a tremendous long-term impact on his career, as well as a strong working relationship with the company he was about to buy. The Sheik had worked many shows in Southwestern Ontario, just a stone's throw from Lansing across the Canadian border, mostly for Barnett and Doyle, and Bert Ruby and Harry Light before them. But it wasn't until September 17, 1964, that he first set foot in the Maple Leaf Gardens, the cavernous arena on the northwest corner of Carlton and Church Streets in Toronto's historic downtown core that had been home to the Maple Leafs hockey team for decades. A four-hour drive from downtown Detroit, it was the heart of Maple Leaf Wrestling, a territory owned by Frank Tunney, a convivial if somewhat unambitious promoter who, despite his limited aspirations, had spent a year as NWA president and was considered the friendly peacemaker of the group of often-antagonistic businessmen who made up the alliance.

Times were getting tough in the Queen City, with Tunney drawing some of the smallest houses he ever had since taking over the Queensbury Athletic Club from his ailing mentor Jack Corcoran, the godfather of Toronto wrestling, some fifteen years prior. He'd been known to bring in Detroit-based talent in the past, but he may have been hesitant to bring in The Sheik due to his affiliation with the outlaws Barnett and Doyle, nonconfrontational promoter that he was. But with those two heading out of the country, and Sheik's decision to join the NWA if and when he took over, the doors opened to Tunney bringing him in for an undercard match against Eric Froelich, a German wrestler working as a barefoot babyface—quite a rarity in those days, with the memory of World War II still keen in the hearts of many fans. This kicked off the beginning of a working relationship between Tunney and Farhat that would really yield fruit by the latter part of the decade but still saw Sheik work several matches at Maple Leaf Gardens in late 1964 and early '65—initially on the undercard, but that would change once The Sheik's fortunes did.

Eager to make the deal, Barnett and Doyle accepted the offer made by Farhat and his father-in-law, Francis Fleser, who had done business with his son-in-law in the past and reportedly fronted the money to be put up in the form of a down payment, with regular installments to be made going forward. It appears that Barnett was the first of the two promoters to leave for Australia, hurried as he was by the impending University of Kentucky scandal hot on his heels. That left Johnny Doyle on his own to sit down at his home in Lafayette Towers, a stylish apartment complex in downtown Detroit's upscale Lafayette Park district, with Ed and Joyce Farhat, and make everything official.

Photographer Wilson Lindsey was then still a teenager getting his start taking ringside pictures for Doyle, to be used in the *Body Press* program. Johnny and his wife, Marge, had practically taken in the starstruck youngster, who spent a great deal of time around Detroit wrestling talent like The Sheik, and also around the Doyles' condo, which had become like a second home to him. "They almost adopted me," Lindsey says. "It turned out to be just a wonderful situation. And of course, The Sheik was one of the main acts, so I saw him quite a bit in the course of doing the job. He was always very nice and very open, and he was definitely one of my favorites at that time."

Lindsey was an inadvertent witness to wrestling history when he happened to be hanging out at the Doyles' place the day the Farhats showed up to make the deal to purchase the territory, and he paints a vivid picture of a giddy Sheik on the verge of taking the defining step of his career: "He was in a *joyful* mood. In fact, everyone was. And they signed the deal there at Johnny's condominium. Johnny had a small Hammond organ there in his home, and The Sheik turned it on and started playing the keys with his nose. It was hilarious—he had us rolling! Anyway, that was the tenor of the whole meeting. It was a lot of fun."

What The Sheik actually got that day for his $50,000—a down payment of $10,000 followed by $1,000 monthly installments for forty months, which he paid religiously—was usage of the Big Time Wrestling name, Barnett and Doyle's TV contracts with CKLW Channel 9 and other local TV stations throughout the area, and their exclusive rights to promote at Cobo Arena. Along with that came implicit control of wrestling in places like Flint and Grand Rapids, Michigan; Lima, Canton, Dayton, Toledo, and Cincinnati, Ohio; Charleston and Wheeling, West

Virginia; Angola and Hammond, Indiana; as well as numerous other small towns within the purview of the territory, using the same strong relationships with the local promoters that Barnett and Doyle had already established over the years. Such things would be a bit hard to enforce on a legal basis, but pro wrestling was a backroom business in those days, and much like the world of organized crime, territories were respected and maintained, even if they weren't entirely legitimate. This was why Bruiser was able to take his piece of the pie through force and intimidation without consequence, while Sheik saw fit to go about it in a more honorable way—as much as there could be honor among wrestling promoters.

After the sale, Johnny and Marge Doyle soon followed Jim Barnett out to Australia, where they put their money into World Championship Wrestling, a promotion that would take the island nation by storm and become a television sensation still talked about to this day by fans who enjoyed it during its run in the sixties and seventies. Sadly, Doyle suffered an untimely death a mere five years after settling Down Under, first sustaining a heart attack, after which doctors discovered inoperable cancer. Barnett would go it alone for a while, but his scandalous exile from the States wouldn't last forever—he and Sheik still had some business to transact down the road, and not all of it good. More on that later.

But just at the moment when Sheik was experiencing dizzying heights, he would also have to grapple with unspeakable lows. The very same month that Sheik purchased Big Time Wrestling, during the early morning hours of October 2, 1964, to be exact, his best friend, Larry Chene, who had broken into the business with him under the tutelage of Bert Ruby, and who by that point was the number-one star of Ruby's Motor City Wrestling outfit, tragically died in an automobile accident. After a losing effort against barrel-chested superheavyweight Larry "The Axe" Hennig on an AWA card in Moline, Illinois, Chene had committed to making the staggering 430-mile overnight drive to get back to his wife, Mary, and their six children in Detroit. But a combination of slick roads and excessive speed (he had already received a ticket earlier in the evening) meant he would only make it less than a hundred of those miles. On I-80 outside Ottawa, Illinois, his car flew off the road and into a telephone pole, killing him instantly.

It was a devastating loss to the Midwestern wrestling community, especially in the Detroit area, where he had become a beloved hero. And although the terrible Sheik and "Leaping" Larry Chene had clashed countless times and spilled copious amounts of blood in wrestling rings all over the country, when Mary Chene found herself confronted with a $1,400 funeral bill that she could not pay, it was The Sheik who quietly covered all expenses, being careful not to ruin his dastardly image. He had been in St. Louis the day it happened, wrestling Italian junior heavyweight Lorenzo Parente to a draw before fourteen thousand fans, on a card headlined by Lou Thesz defending the NWA World title against Fritz Von Erich.[1] He rushed home the next day. Jim Myers, then a high school football and wrestling coach in Madison Heights, Michigan, moonlighting for Bert Ruby under a mask as The Student, was on hand for the services at St. David Roman Catholic Church, in the old Italian section of Detroit: "The thing I remember most about going to his funeral was I'd never seen The Sheik before, and he's a pretty strong legend ... He flew in, and was dressed in a silk suit with real small glasses to cover his tears."[2] Myers would later go on to great fame using the name bestowed upon him by The Sheik not long after that: George "The Animal" Steele.

The loss of Larry Chene at that precise moment was something of a watershed moment for where Detroit wrestling was about to go. With The Sheik taking over the territory and preparing to position himself as the top heel, all signs had pointed to his wanting to use Chene as his top babyface and ultimate foil—a hot money-making feud that could've gone on for years and come to define the company much like his legendary upcoming rivalries with the likes of Bobo Brazil, Mark Lewin, Fred Curry, and others eventually did. But fate had other plans, and Sheik would have to embark on his new career adventure without his best friend and in-ring adversary. Things were about to begin changing in the Motor City and beyond, both for the landscape of the wrestling business and for Sheik's own position within it. Under the official corporate umbrella of World Wide Sports, a holding company he created within the auspices of Farhat Enterprises, Ed Farhat now owned Big Time Wrestling, and it would become a brand name etched in the minds of area fans like never before. There was no doubt about it: a new era was dawning.

After having spent many months in other places, Farhat began making his presence more felt in the Detroit area, reintroducing fans to an even more ratcheted-up and crazed version of the already unhinged Sheik they knew and hated. He started making "unplanned" appearances in the CKLW studios, disrupting matches and having to be restrained by police. As part of this ingenious angle, it was declared that TV execs had banned him from wrestling—which in the wrestling world was typically only a way to increase fan interest in seeing him. In fact, and perhaps as a parting gift to Farhat before lighting out for Australia, Johnny Doyle himself (or someone in his employ) penned a fascinating article for the *Body Press* magazine, putting over Sheik's insane antics while also paradoxically providing a decidedly kayfabe-breaking glimpse at the real man behind them:

> This lunatic on the mat is difficult to explain to those few who know him. Away from the arena, you wouldn't recognize him as the same man . . . He idolizes his two boys, helps his ten [sic] brothers and sisters unstintingly and sobs out loud watching any sad scene on old television movies. Last summer, I took twelve of my dearest friends to The Sheik's home in Williamston, Michigan. The Sheik had set up a ping-pong table, a badminton court, had a horseshoe tournament, organized a softball game for the children and supervised a giant barbecue and picnic. He waited on everyone hand and foot and completely charmed all . . . The Sheik built his own swimming pool, surrounded by Oriental tile and artificial palm trees, coconuts and all. In their own home, the roles of The Sheik and Princess Sahl-Ami [sic] are completely reversed. She rules the roost, gives the orders, and no one ever had a more abject, slavish subject than the Princess has in the person of The Sheik."[3]

Doyle's bizarre shoot aside, Farhat was consciously retooling his Sheik persona as he had done in the past. Whereas he had employed traditional wrestling holds during his formative years in the 1950s, by this point he was relying more on wild brawling tactics—biting, clawing, and gouging his opponents, as well as including the use of a foreign object, usually a pencil wrapped liberally in athletic tape and strategically hidden from the referee. As the years went on, his pencil would become so ubiquitous as to be instantly associated with The Sheik in the minds of fans, like a twisted calling card. He drooled, he shouted, he seemed to have little to no regard for the "rules." As his matches became more overtly violent, blood became a much more common sight, both on his adversaries and, even more often, on himself.

The act of blading—in which wrestlers discreetly cut themselves with razor blades hidden somewhere on their person in order to produce the illusion of injury and convince fans of the reality of the simulated brutality they're witnessing—had been around in the business since at least the 1930s. It was probably really popularized in Texas in the 1940s by Sheik's old friend and idol Wild Bull Curry along with his archrival, "Irish" Danny McShain, the lantern-jawed ex-boxer and inveterate streetfighter from Little Rock, Arkansas, who is also credited with introducing the chair shot. By the 1960s, blading had become much more common in wrestling, and The Sheik was without a doubt one of its greatest and most notorious practitioners. Cutting off a small corner of the blade and wrapping it in tape to prevent cutting too deeply, he would typically hide one in the waist band of his trunks, or even tape some to his fingers for greater ease of use.

FROM THE PERSONAL COLLECTION OF DAVE BURZYNSKI.

Many were the times that The Sheik's rampages grew so out of control that local police—often not smartened up to the proceedings—had to step in to restore order. Through it all, to protect the business and his livelihood, Sheik never broke character.

His forehead was the usual target of the bloodletting, as it was with most performers, except that in Sheik's case he made little effort to make the cuts horizontal near his hairline as was usually done to minimize visible scarring—opting instead to slice himself broadly and vertically across the top of his face, turning it into a proverbial crimson mask of blood mixed with sweat (and also resulting in an unmistakable patchwork of keloid scars that was already beginning to disfigure him).[4]

The Sheik was certainly no stranger to blading before then, but it was when he took over Big Time Wrestling and put himself at the top of the card that the use of color greatly increased, becoming an expected part of almost every Sheik match. It was an easy way to generate heat and excitement—also, for those with the stomach to go through with it, a shortcut to use in place of an overabundance of athletic maneuvers. In other words, a splash of scarlet on an appropriately grimacing face could have the same energizing effect on a crowd (and the box office) as a match full of deftly performed slams, suplexes, and tumbles, as was expressed in the popular expression in the business in those days, "Red equals green."

The Sheik of the mid-1960s was in many ways The Sheik in his ultimate form, the way most fans would best remember him in his prime. By this point, he had all the trappings that would be most associated with his act: the fire mysteriously hurled from his fingertips (though still used only sparingly for effect), the full-dress regalia, the prayer mat routine, the dreaded camel clutch, and lots and lots of blood. His working style at this point was a mix of traditional wrestling, classic heel stalling tactics, and brazen rule-breaking, with the actual wrestling starting to take more of a backseat in favor of the crazy stuff. But it was the crazy stuff that drew. While most wrestlers experience the prime of their careers in their early to mid-thirties, Sheik was closing in on forty and still on the rise. Owning his own wrestling company was certainly a part of that, to say the very least.

In the early years of Sheik's Big Time Wrestling, Sheik himself acted essentially as owner and booker, crafting the angles that would generate heat between opponents and keep fans tuning in and paying for tickets. In those days, angles were typically reserved only for the upper-card talent, with most of the lower-card talent relying strictly on the tried-and-true heel-face dynamic to draw heat and hold interest, without many more bells and whistles needed. Although in later years Sheik would hire others to do the booking for him, as most promoters did, he always retained total control of his own storylines, or programs, as they were called. With that kind of power and autonomy, it meant that the days of regular losses in the ring would become a thing of the past—Sheik had protected himself from excessive jobbing before, but now that he held the proverbial pencil (both literally and figuratively), he would make sure that losses were all but nonexistent. In his mind, this was the best way to protect his persona and his drawing power. By hook or by crook, The Sheik would always win, which was rather unusual for a heel, since fans usually paid their money to see the bad guys lose. It was far from uncommon for wrestler-promoters to book themselves on top—Verne Gagne had been doing it in the AWA for years, as did Dory Funk, Dick the Bruiser, and Fritz Von Erich, who had joined Ed McLemore in running the Dallas office not long after Sheik took over Detroit. But virtually no one would do it to the extent that The Sheik was about to in the coming years.

Part and parcel with this extreme protection of his position came the ever-stricter tightening of the kayfabe curtain. To be sure, this was the era of pretty strict kayfabe to begin with, when promoters worked diligently to convince spectators of the reality of their product and wrestlers kept their personal lives and gimmicks strictly separated, not wanting to spoil the illusion for fear that it would hurt business. But even in those days, Ed Farhat would go to nearly unheard-of extremes to cultivate belief in the persona of The Sheik, going further than nearly anyone else to almost literally *become* his character in the eyes of the outside world. Being his own boss would now give him even greater license and ability to do so without contradiction. He was known to never, ever break character in public, to be fully and truly *on* one hundred percent of the time. Even in his everyday life, he began answering only to Sheik, rather than his birth name, even among family—anyone who called him Ed would be met with either zero response or a glaring look from his piercing brown eyes under those heavy black brows, sufficient warning to never slip up again. People calling the house knew to ask for Sheik, because if they asked for Eddie, "Wrong number!" would be the response. "Dad always said, if you're gonna be in the business, and you're gonna be this person, then that's who you have to be," explained Eddie Jr. "You can't be two different people. He lived it. Grandpa Sheik, Uncle Sheik, no one called him by his real name, out of respect. He wouldn't answer you."

Sometimes it might take more than a glare. "There was once this collegiate heavyweight wrestler, who was really good, and thought professional wrestling was fake," recalls preeminent wrestling journalist Dave Meltzer, who remembers seeing Sheik as a young fan in California. "He went backstage and called him Ed Farhat. Sheik put the blade to his throat and goes, 'I'm The Sheik, and if you ever call me Ed Farhat again, I'll slice your throat.' The guy was scared shitless!" Several stories like this one have circulated in hushed tones over the years, of Sheik not being afraid to physically threaten fans in order to preserve his image. He played it to the hilt at all times, and the result was that fans really did believe he was this terrifying, almost inhuman monster, the eccentric scion of a wealthy Middle Eastern oil family intent on burning as much flesh and spilling as much blood as he could, incapable of or unwilling to speak any intelligible language, who would slice you open just as soon as look at you.

Dave Burzynski,[5] who would later go on to become a close associate and friend of The Sheik, as well as a manager under the name "Supermouth" Dave Drason, was just a wide-eyed young Detroit superfan in those days and recalls The Sheik in all his glory in vivid detail: "His entrance was easily a good five minutes, if not more . . . Hearing the crowd, just the noise that he created just by walking out of that dressing room door and down the aisles . . . Sometimes you'd have a fan or somebody standing up to block his path, and all he'd have to do is just make a sudden move and give a stare, and these guys would back off and run, crapping their pants. There were times he would stop and look around, or look up in the air. And more catcalls would come. Then just getting into the ring, he would start pacing back and forth, going along the rope, strutting, stopping, pointing up in the air. People wondered what the hell he was looking at! His manager would ask the crowd to quiet down, and of course they'd get louder and louder. He would bow and pray before the match, and as a fan, the way I saw it was, he's asking Allah for forgiveness for what he's about to do, because he knew there was going to be violence and bloodletting."

Sheik's extreme adherence to kayfabe led many to speculate over the years that he even worked his family and friends and everyone else in his private life, presumably snarling and staring his way through dinner, chewing up contracts and spitting them out, setting fire to the drapes, and whatever else their minds might conjure. If anything, this was perhaps the greatest tribute to his total commitment to the act. Needless to say, and to finally debunk the myth, this was not actually the case, as no one could reasonably take it that far—after all, Sheik had a family to support and a business to run, even if fans in those days didn't know he was running the show behind the scenes. A shrewd promoter and showman, he was all business backstage, with his own private office inside Cobo Arena, where he would hold court, right up until the point he emerged from that curtain before the fans and completely transformed into the creature they expected to see, remaining so until the moment he returned through the curtain again.

In order to preserve the illusion and not reveal the true nature of Farhat's ownership of the promotion, a figurehead was needed. Not only would it damage fans' belief in his deranged character to know the truth, but in those days of kayfabe it looked bad for a currently active wrestler to publicly acknowledge ownership of a wrestling company, as it might indicate a conflict of interest to fans who still wanted to believe (not to mention the state athletic commissions that still tried to regulate pro wrestling as a sport). Selected for the role was his father-in-law and real-life financial backer, Francis Fleser, who would be put forth as the "official" president of World Wide Sports and promoter of Big Time Wrestling—a bit of trickery that held up for the entirety of the company's existence. And even though family members called him Sheik, they knew Ed Farhat was all about family, taking over the role once held by his parents, hosting enormous gatherings at his home on Sundays and holidays whenever possible, enjoying his new position as the godfather of the extended Farhat clan—even if rumor had it he did enjoy sometimes working the more extended members of the family and other acquaintances who may not have been fully clued in as to where illusion ended and reality began.

One last change in the act had everything to do with family and with the new responsibilities attached to being the boss. Once the sale went through and the Farhats were in charge of the business, Joyce made the decision to step away from her role as the inscrutable Princess Salima, hanging up her shawls and veils for good. Part of this had to do with the growing demands of domestic life, as Eddie Jr. was now in high school and there was also the little toddler Tommy to chase after. But even more than this, Joyce was taking on the enormous responsibility of running the day-to-day operations of Big Time Wrestling, including everything from continuing publication of *Body Press*, to counting ticket receipts, to making sure everyone got paid, and, in short, being the power behind the throne. "Joyce was the business behind the business," confirms Brian Bukantis, a writer and photographer who eventually interacted extensively with her while running *Body Press*. "She ran it. She was sweet, very nice, very cordial, but all business. She knew what she wanted. She took care of the money. She was the person that ran the ship." This was especially important with her husband not only being focused on booking and performing, but also constantly on the road to other territories, as the demands for his appearances from other promoters only increased alongside his notoriety.

After working several dates back in Texas for the Funks, as well as Ontario for Tunney, The Sheik returned home to get down to business. His first official date as owner of the Big Time Wrestling circuit, as best as can be estimated, took place November 4, 1964, in Cincinnati. The bald and bespectacled Les Ruffin, who had bounced around Massachusetts rings in the 1940s for Boston wrestling impresario Paul Bowser before turning to the promotions game himself, had worked for Barnett and Doyle, and Fred Kohler before them, running the Cincinnati Gardens, a twenty-five-thousand-square-foot building of brick and limestone that was home to minor league hockey as well as the NBA's Cincinnati Royals.[6] As with many promoters on the circuit, Sheik had inherited Ruffin from the previous owners of Big Time Wrestling, and they continued the working relationship for years to come. On this particular night, he and Ruffin drew a little over four thousand fans for what had to be a hard-hitting main event pitting Johnny Valentine, perhaps wrestling's toughest brawler of all time, against NWA World Champion Lou Thesz, one of its most dangerous shooters. (Such a match was made possible by Sheik applying for membership in the NWA, meaning that the Michigan-Ohio territory was no longer an outlaw promotion.) The Sheik himself also appeared in the third match from the top, besting a still wet-behind-the-ears Les Thatcher.

Three days later, what appears to be the first Cobo Arena card officially under the new Farhat regime took place, with Sheik making short work of Canadian journeyman Al Ward (wrestling as "Alexander the Great") once again in the third match from the top. The main event that evening featured Valentine teaming up with Richard Gland, a former chiropractic student and reported card-carrying member of the Ku Klux Klan from Delaware who achieved fame wrestling as Dick "Bulldog" Brower, taking on the duo of Von Erich and a man known very well to fans in the Detroit and Toronto areas: Lord Athol Layton. A tall, strapping Englishman whose aristocratic bearing matched his ring name, Layton had spent some of his formative years in Australia, opening a pub after he got back from World War II, before the wrestling game brought him to North America. He had since become a major star for Tunney in Toronto and formed a memorable tag team in the 1950s with fellow Brit Lord James Blears. His perfect command of the Queen's English had helped him cross over into the realm of TV commentating not only for Tunney but for Barnett and Doyle in Detroit too. Sheik inherited his services as both a wrestler and a commentator, and it was Layton's dulcet voice that fans would most come to associate with Big Time Wrestling, both in its original Thursday night time slot and the later Saturday afternoon slot it switched to after The Sheik takeover.

In a 2020 Facebook post, Eddie Jr. remembered making the fateful drive down from Williamston to Detroit with his parents that day: "You could tell he was excited and was thinking about that night's card. What a mind he had. He always pushed talent to be at their best or they wouldn't be used. He was very aware the fans paid to see Big Time

Lord Athol Layton tries in vain to get a word with The Sheik after a studio match from the early days of Big Time Wrestling in the 1960s.

Wrestling, and come hell or high water, a great night they would get. When the night ended, he was in a great mood. He said to my mom in the car, 'Detroit is hungry, and it's time to pop this city.' That night was 6,000 fans, from 3,500 when Barnett and Doyle ran." By the following Cobo show some twenty days later, Sheik had put himself into the main event at the Detroit arena, a victory over Brower. He would remain in that top Cobo spot for the next fifteen years.

As Sheik had surmised, Detroit was indeed hungry, and the city continued heating up under the new regime, by the summer of 1965 doing regular crowd numbers that beat what was customary under Doyle and Barnett. Television tapings continued to be held in Windsor, Ontario, with biweekly shows at "beautiful, air-conditioned Cobo Arena" as it was memorably advertised, typically on Saturday nights. In addition to Cobo and the Cincinnati Gardens, other venues on the regular circuit included the beige and boxy Toledo Sports Arena, run by swarthy former wrestler and manager Martino Angelo; the brand-new Hara Arena, a 5,500-seat structure built on the former site of a fruit orchard in Dayton that would eventually be run by Eddie Jr.; the church-like Canton Memorial Civic

Center, run by former boxer and steel plant manager Vince Pelkowski, aka Vince Risko, and later by Jack Cain; and the Michigan State Fairgrounds Coliseum, on the site of the nation's oldest annual state fair, which housed Big Time Wrestling on those occasional dates when Cobo was otherwise booked.

Even from the beginning, Big Time Wrestling boasted a roster of talent that made it easy to understand why the houses were popping right from the get-go. In addition to Valentine, Brower, and Layton, Sheik brought in such workers as Bobo Brazil, Mark Lewin, and Haystacks Calhoun, all of whom he had crossed paths with many times before. There was the nearly seven-foot-tall Frank "Tex" McKenzie, a Jack Pfefer discovery from Edmonds, Washington; the brash and bleached-blond Reginald "Sweet Daddy" Siki of Montgomery, Texas, perhaps second only to Brazil in breaking down color barriers in the business; Sailor Art Thomas, the former pro bodybuilder and merchant marine from Gurdon, Arkansas; the bald and brutal Killer Karl Kox of Baltimore, inventor of the brain buster; and the young and handsome Johnny Powers, a protégé of the late Larry Chene who would later become both a promotional ally and rival of The Sheik. Sheik even made good on his early promise to Fred Curry, now a high-flying rookie whose clean-cut appearance couldn't be any more different from that of his legendary dad, Wild Bull Curry, who came along as well to resume his old in-ring partnership with The Sheik and continue his decades-long reign of terror in the Motor City.

For the all-important development of new talent, Farhat enlisted the aid of one-time trainer and longtime friend Lou Klein, by then a grizzled twenty-five-year veteran known as "The Man of a Thousand Holds." At his gym in the Detroit suburb of Allen Park (where he also owned the local Tastee-Freez), Klein worked with potential hopefuls, schooling them in the rigors of the ring and, if they made it through the grueling initiation outsiders were put through in those days, also schooling them in the inner machinations of the business to prepare them to go to work. Klein was also given the responsibility of running the so-called spot shows—smaller-scale cards and fundraisers held at local high schools, halls, and armories in towns that weren't regular stops on the circuit. As far as an actual "front office" for World Wide Sports, it was set up on Grand River Avenue in downtown Williamston—about a mile down the road from the Farhat home, where a lot of the business would be transacted anyway.

The Sheik's increased influence was evident the night of December 27, 1964, when he returned to Toronto to win the Tunney promotion's version of the United States Heavyweight title from Johnny Valentine before about nine thousand fans in the main event at the Maple Leaf Gardens. In those days, partly in order to placate frustrated promoters who had to wait long periods of time for the world champion to pass between their borders, the NWA allowed member promotions to recognize their own iterations of the US title, which meant that there were a bunch of them throughout North America—even, as paradoxical as it may be, in Canada. This particular version had only been in existence for less than three years, and Valentine had already held it five times during that short span.[7] Although Sheik only held it a week before losing it back to Valentine at the next Maple Leaf Gardens show, it was something of a trial run—after all, Big Time Wrestling had its own United States Heavyweight title, and, unlike in Toronto, Sheik had total control over booking *that* one.

Big Time Wrestling's version could be reasonably traced back to the original, undisputed NWA United States Heavyweight title, officially sanctioned by Fred Kohler in Chicago during the height of his national TV exposure in the 1950s. When Jim Barnett broke away from Kohler to form the independent Big Time Wrestling in the Detroit area, he took then–US Champion Dick the Bruiser with him (Kohler stripped Bruiser and recognized Buddy Rogers as his champion). It was that stolen version of the title that became the centerpiece of wrestling in Detroit and would be for the next two decades.

Sheik may not have had the power to put the NWA World Heavyweight title on himself, and maybe the NWA's bias against "gimmick wrestlers" would continue to prevent this from happening, but in Detroit, The Sheik now held ultimate sway and, in his mind, dominance of the United States title was essential to cementing his spot as a main event talent of national significance. That dominance began on February 6, 1965, at Cobo Arena, when The Sheik captured Detroit's version of the

US Championship—coincidentally, also from Johnny Valentine. "I was sitting in the front row," remembered the late Terry Dart, who would one day capture The Sheik as a photographer but on that night first encountered him as just a fan. "It was a two-out-of-three fall match, and Bulldog Brower was hiding under the ring. During the third fall, he came out, kneedropped Valentine off the top rope, and Sheik won the bout and the title." With the exception of a couple of brief vacancies and switches designed to build interest in upcoming rematches, he would hold the title for the majority of the next six years. And that was only to be the first of what are "officially" recognized as twelve reigns as NWA United States Champion for Big Time Wrestling, although some count as many as fourteen or more. In many ways, the US title would come to define Sheik just as much as the blood, the fire, the prayer mat, and all the rest of it—virtually inseparable from the image of the Syrian madman. In that sense, it certainly did the job it was intended to do.

Farhat took to his new role as the boss quite naturally, and it helped that the talent already knew him as a person of influence from when Barnett and Doyle were still running things. And although much of the locker room didn't see the changeover coming, they certainly were aware once it went into effect. With The Sheik calling the shots, there was absolutely no question as to who was in charge. The tough street kid with a chip on his shoulder and something to prove was still there, and that aspect of his personality could sometimes be on full display. "He was a boss that, if you were in the loop and he thought you were worth it, there was nobody better," remembers Fred Curry, who Sheik definitely felt was worth it. "He made his enemies too. I was in a show with him in Indiana in the early days, and he's arguing with one of the wrestlers, Mr. Kleen.[8] The Sheik was a gutty type of guy; he'd fight you. They got in an argument and started pushing each other around, and Sheik grabbed him by the back of the head, shoved his head in the toilet and flushed the toilet. He was a funny guy."

The regime change was not always a pleasant one. Wilson Lindsey, then still a teenager, continued working for Sheik after the buyout and recalls a transition that was a bit bumpy, partly due to Sheik and Joyce, but also due to Eddie Jr., which Lindsey attributes to both being aspiring rock musicians: "My association with The Sheik was always fantastic until the deal went down between him and Doyle. Then the whole tenor of working for the company changed . . . It was uncomfortable. Sheik was very warm and very friendly generally, but in the course of that changeover, things just became a lot less easygoing. His wife was calling the shots. And she was pretty critical toward me personally . . . It was awkward. I didn't necessarily like the situation anymore. And his son took a dislike toward me for some reason. He just kind of inserted himself in my movements. I had had free rein pretty much in the dressing rooms and access to virtually anything I needed as a photographer and a writer. Then he got in the way and was constraining my movement. At the time, Junior had a rock band, and I don't know if he felt some kind of competition with me as a musician . . . Why, I'm not certain. But whatever the case was, it was an uncomfortable relationship."

The Sheik's leadership methods may have been rough around the edges at times, but the results were clear. Houses were up, business was improving overall, and The Sheik as a top attraction was capturing the imagination of the fan base. The Sheik had been accepted as a member of the National Wrestling Alliance, mending the rift caused by Barnett and Doyle's outlaw promotion and bringing the Michigan-Ohio territory back into the NWA fold. Nevertheless, Farhat's new relationship with the other power brokers of the wrestling business was a bit rocky from the start. Lifelong promoters were hesitant to trust or respect a mere worker who had climbed the ladder and grabbed a seat at their table, particularly promoters who had never themselves been in the ring. This was especially true of a worker who had made his name as a staring, slavering, flame-throwing lunatic, as can be witnessed in this very telling February 15, 1965, letter from NWA president Sam Muchnick of St. Louis to the newly relocated Johnny Doyle:

> We have Valentine here on Feb. 19 and so does The Sheik
> in Detroit—a double booking . . . I never discuss business
> with my wife, but did mention the mix-up. She said: 'You
> and Johnny can work this out.' I said 'Johnny is gone and
> there is another promoter.' She said: 'Who is he?' Frankly,

I was too embarrassed to tell even my wife that The Sheik, who is not supposed to talk English, is the promoter in Detroit. That in a nut-shell tells you what is happening to our business. And it proves to me that if we had all stuck together what a great organization the Alliance would have been. Things are so confused now. Wrestlers behind the scenes have been in promotion for many years—but now it is getting open and I can't imagine what the result will be.

Doyle's response one month later is a combination of candor and admiration for the man who had recently bought him out, and it also reveals an early example of skepticism over his booking practices that would only ring louder in the industry in years to come:

I read with interest your comments about letting The Sheik promote in Detroit. I really didn't think much of the idea but I had nowhere to turn. Most of the old time, reliable promoters will not stray far from their own territories and there doesn't seem to be any young promoters coming along except wrestlers. I must say I am amazed at the way The Sheik is programming the town. The gate receipts are up a little so maybe he is doing the right thing although many of the boys have written me they think he is shotgunning the town and will kill it inside a year. I hope not as we have our payments spread out over a long time.[9]

But of course, The Sheik wasn't the only Barnett-Doyle star-turned-promoter in the region. Dick the Bruiser and his junior partner Wilbur Snyder held the southwestern portion of the territory with their Indianapolis-Chicago circuit, the World Wrestling Association. Backed by Verne Gagne out of Minneapolis, with whom he had carved up the old Kohler territory, Bruiser sought early on to muscle in on the Detroit leg of the circuit, thus completing his hostile takeover. The earliest incursion took place in the spring of 1965, when he struck a deal with Olympia

Although they were often forced to get along as co-members of the National Wrestling Alliance, Farhat and NWA president Sam Muchnick had a decidedly tepid professional relationship.

Stadium president and Red Wings higher-up Lincoln Cavalieri. The Olympia had been dark for wrestling ever since Barnett and Doyle had stopped running there the year before in favor of Cobo Hall, and Cavalieri, fresh off landing two concert appearances from The Beatles the previous fall, was now anxious to bring the grunt 'n' groan game back to his venue. Bruiser was all too eager to oblige and ran three monthly shows at the Olympia with his troupe of talent that included wrestlers from Gagne's AWA and featured Bruiser defending his WWA World Heavyweight title against Pat O'Connor, and four-hundred-pound Eddie "Moose" Cholak, a Korean War vet who had been a breakout star on *Wrestling from Marigold* a decade before.

Bruiser made sure to run each show on a weekend that Sheik wasn't running Cobo, to avoid direct competition. And the competition couldn't have been that contentious, as just one week after his first show at Olympia, Bruiser made an appearance in the main event at Cobo, teaming with The Sheik himself to take on Haystacks Calhoun and Johnny Valentine. By the summer of '65, Bruiser had retreated from the Motor

City to his homestead of Indiana, ending the brief and uneventful cross-town rivalry and ceding total control of Detroit to The Sheik. At least for the moment; the power struggle between the two ambitious alpha wrestler-promoters would eventually be revisited, and this trial run would turn out to have been the mere calm before a mighty storm.

While fending off Bruiser's testing of the waters, Sheik was also busy consolidating control of not just Detroit but the surrounding Michigan towns. Some of these towns were still being run by Sheik's old mentor Bert Ruby, who had fled to the suburbs after breaking away from Harry Light. Barnett and Doyle had allowed him to continue operating while they were running things, even occasionally co-promoting events in the area—but this would not be the case under The Sheik regime. Some accounts claim that Farhat bought Ruby out just as he did Barnett and Doyle, but there are other accounts that would indicate he pushed Ruby out against his will, thus meaning the end of Motor City Wrestling and also, if true, bringing an ignominious conclusion to the relationship between Farhat and the man who had brought him into the wrestling business in the first place. Once Ruby was out, Farhat's Big Time Wrestling truly was the only show in every town.[10]

In his first full year as an NWA promoter and a breakout main-eventer, The Sheik saw his bookings across the country already begin to increase. Unlike some other wrestlers like Verne Gagne and Fritz Von Erich who became bosses and essentially stopped touring, he didn't hunker down in his home territory. In fact, quite the opposite occurred, as his days as a touring attraction were really only just heating up. He returned to western Texas for the Funks in January, February, May, and October, including some titanic heel vs. heel encounters with Sputnik Monroe; in February and March he came to Kansas City to work for another fellow wrestler-promoter, the equally rough-around-the-edges Bob Geigel, a future NWA president whose Heart of America promotion had pushed out previous territorial kingpin and NWA founder P.L. "Pinkie" George; also in March, he came to San Antonio for Ed McLemore, and Sam Muchnick held his nose to book him for a tag team match in St. Louis on *Wrestling at the Chase*;[11] just six days after his St. Louis date, he was in Pittsburgh for ancient German-born impresario Rudy Miller, whose Studio Wrestling outfit was a satellite of Vince McMahon's WWWF.

In July 1965, he returned to the WWWF proper, for the first time since the name change, for a special one-shot appearance at Madison Square Garden, teaming with rookie Smasher Sloan, a McMahon creation, against Miguel Perez and Rocca-wannabe Argentina Apollo before 17,134 fans on the undercard of a show headlined by Bruno Sammartino defending the WWWF World Heavyweight crown against Big Bill Miller, a three-hundred-pound former veterinarian from Ohio who so impressed The Sheik that he later brought him to Detroit as a contender for his United States title. Whereas just a few years earlier Sheik had been just another regular on the McMahon traveling troupe, this time he was something special, brought in to help boost attendance and also lend some juice to Sloan, an up-and-coming heel on the WWWF circuit. It was a sure and telling sign of the progress Farhat had made in the intervening years.

On the home front, in addition to the Windsor tapings, he added a second weekly TV taping for Big Time Wrestling in Detroit itself. On August 21 at the Cincinnati Gardens, Sheik faced the kid who had once watched him from ringside as a teenager, "Flying" Fred Curry, for what appears to have been the first of what would be scores of times. "I knew one thing," remembers Curry of those grueling wars with his boss and real-life mentor. "I had to train like hell. I couldn't blow up, I couldn't be out of condition. I had to keep moving. I had to throw dropkicks, I'd have to take bumps out of the ring, I had to take the fire, I had to take the pencil. I had to overachieve, because I was in the ring with a guy that continually overachieved, which bumped me up about five notches. You had to be out there performing, or you wouldn't be out there anymore. If you were good, you better be terrific, or you weren't gonna have another match with him. If you couldn't get those fans standing up, he had no use for you."

But of all the opponents The Sheik started programming himself against, none was more significant than Bobo Brazil. The two had met before over the years, but it was in 1965, with The Sheik at the helm of Big Time Wrestling, that their legendary rivalry really hit its stride; in fact, there wouldn't be a year after this in which they *didn't* wrestle each other until well into the 1980s. No villain can become truly great without a worthy hero to oppose him, and the enormously beloved Brazil fit that bill perfectly. Like Batman and the Joker, Holmes and Moriarty, Van Helsing and Dracula, King Kong and Godzilla, or Ahab and the white whale, their wars raged—first throughout the Big Time circuit in Detroit, Cincinnati, Benton Harbor, Dayton, Toledo, and Charleston, West Virginia, and then eventually spilling out into territories across the country. The United States title was the perfect prize around which their hundreds of battles usually revolved, but the explosive violence and mayhem unleashed and all the blood spilled (almost always on Sheik's part, as Brazil usually preferred not to blade), transcended any mere wrestling championship. When The Sheik met Bobo Brazil in the ring, fans knew they were in for an epic conflict, particularly in the early years when both could still go, and go prodigiously. "It was one of the biggest drawing angles for years," says Al Snow, then just a small child but eventually an up-and-coming performer in the Ohio-Michigan area himself. "And Bobo Brazil towered over him, which was unusual for the babyface . . . He was a naturally impressive man, he was built. And Sheik drew money as a heel beating him up!"

Detroit wrestling historian and lifelong Big Time Wrestling fan Mark Bujan watched them clash countless times and got to the heart of what made the feud click: "Sheik and Bobo were probably best friends, and they realized they could make money together. Bobo was a Black guy in Detroit, with a big African-American following here. He was always in the main event. The Black folks really turned out, and so I think the both of them realized they could make a lot of money here, and they did. He lived here in Michigan, and they just took advantage of that and it worked . . . They'd build it for weeks in advance. The Sheik's philosophy would be booking three matches in a row against the same guy . . . He would love the buildup. The next one will be a Texas Death match, third one would be a cage." It's worth noting, as others have pointed out, that this booking philosophy was similar to what Vince McMahon was doing in the WWWF with Sammartino, only in reverse, with a heel on top instead of a babyface.

While making appearances throughout his territory, Farhat always made a point to return home that night rather than staying at a hotel if possible, even if it meant hours of driving, so intent was he on spending as much time as possible with his family and being able to wake up with his sons in the morning. One of the difficult downsides of life as a successful wrestler was (and is) missing out on so much of one's family life due to time spent on the road, and Farhat was determined to avoid this as much he could, so ingrained in him were the values of family. These values were put to the test on October 23, 1965, when his older sister Betty suffered an untimely death at age forty-six, leaving her twelve-year-old son, Paul Ritchie, without a parent, as her husband had abandoned the family years before. Ed and Joyce stepped into the breach and became Paul's legal guardians, bringing him into their home and raising him alongside Eddie Jr. and Tommy as their own for the next decade.

Following the death of Betty and the adoption of Paul, Farhat stayed local for the next few months, before finally hitting the road again in March of 1966. This time, he was brought into the largest wrestling terri-tory in the South, a sprawling Kentucky-Tennessee-Alabama circuit called Mid-America. It was run out of Nashville, a city no stranger to the promotions game, by Nick Gulas, a Greek-American born into an entrepreneurial family who had gotten his start promoting both wres-tling and big band concerts in the 1940s, aside his longtime partner Roy Welch, patriarch of the largest wrestling family in the history of the business. Welch hid his involvement in the front office from the public due to his status as an active performer, thus making Gulas the face of the company. Gulas-Welch Enterprises landed The Sheik for two dates, the first being a TV squash match on their live show out of Bowling Green, leading up to a match in Birmingham against Amarillo wrestler and former Texas light-heavyweight and middleweight Golden Gloves Champion Alex Perez, which went to a draw.

This quick-and-easy pattern of a TV appearance to establish The Sheik to local fans, followed by a house show match or two, was the common approach in those days for special attractions like The Sheik. The rest of 1966 saw him being used in similar ways in Kansas City as well as back in the Amarillo area, where he remained as loyal as ever to the Funks, who had been the first to show consistent faith in him as a main-eventer. He made two more Madison Square Garden appearances for McMahon, a five-minute victory over another former Golden Gloves Champion, Ronnie Etchison, in March, and a second five-minute win over career journeyman Ricky Sexton in December. He even made a TV appearance for McMahon, the first in over six years, returning to the Capitol Arena in DC in October for a tag team match pitting himself and the WWWF's number-one heel, a hulking Italian-American Ithaca College wrestler named Bob "Gino" Marella, who had transformed himself into the "All-Asiatic Champion" Gorilla Monsoon of Manchuria, against the fan favorite dream team of WWWF World Champion Bruno Sammartino and Bobo Brazil.

Another WWWF alum, Bill Miller, was brought into Big Time Wrestling in September 1966, challenging The Sheik for the United States Championship at Cobo Arena in a match that ended in a double-disqualification, resulting in the title being held up for two weeks before Sheik regained it with a decisive win over Miller at the next Cobo show. In his spot at the top of the food chain, Sheik was in a position to help newcomers and veterans alike by giving them work and a push. He did both in October, first by tag teaming with a man who would one day arguably succeed him as the most famous wrestler from Detroit, the future George Steele (then still under a mask as "The Student"), whom he joined to face Fred Curry and popular former hockey player from Ontario Billy Red Lyons, at the UAW Union Hall in Lima, Ohio, a regular stop in the heart of the Big Time circuit. Then, he reunited his iconic tandem with the legendary Wild Bull Curry, joining his fellow Lebanese wild man for a couple of team encounters at Cobo that represented the first time the two had stepped in a ring together since the Capitol days some seven years prior.

In those early years of Big Time Wrestling, each year was more successful than the last, and 1967 continued that pattern. In addition to proven Detroit regulars like Brazil, Fred Curry, and Killer Karl Kox, Sheik also groomed another potential star performer who had been around the business for a number of years but experienced a dramatic career renaissance thanks to a little gimmick retooling in the mid-1960s. Dearborn native Dick Garza had been a professional bodybuilder, winning Mr. Michigan in 1954 and later competing for Mr. America and Mr. Universe titles. Bert Ruby discovered him in 1957, and before long he was appearing on Ruby's Motor City Wrestling cards as well as at Olympia Stadium shows for Barnett and Doyle, typically in an opener or mid-card match. It was Verne Gagne who helped turn things around for him when he brought him to the AWA in 1964, giving him the persona of Mighty Igor Vodik, a friendly, somewhat simple Polish immigrant whose innocent nature belied his freakish strength.[12] This simple change was Garza's ticket to the main event, even leading to a one-week stint as AWA World Heavyweight Champion. Not long after, Farhat brought him to Big Time Wrestling, shortening his name to Mighty Igor and even further accentuating his simple-minded sweetness to make him a major draw for young fans, who rooted him on as he battled the nefarious Sheik in a conflict of pure good against the ultimate evil. He would become one of The Sheik's most prolific opponents.

In a show of continued cooperation between Big Time Wrestling and the WWA, Dick the Bruiser brought The Sheik to Indianapolis for an appearance on February 25, 1967—his first since the two men had split the territory between them. Sheik also continued his healthy relationship with his fellow promoter Vince McMahon, flying into New York for five different appearances at Madison Square Garden in 1967, including a January win over the now-solo Miguel Perez, a June win over former tag partner Smasher Sloan, and a twenty-minute time limit draw with Edouard Carpentier in September.

He also came to Montreal for the first time in nearly a decade. Old-school Quebec promoter Eddie Quinn had been succeeded by the latest in the "scourge" of wrestler-promoters, Johnny Rougeau, whose International Wrestling Association had taken over promotions at the Montreal Forum in the mid-1960s. The pecking order was a little different there, as Carpentier was the major attraction, which explains why Sheik did a very rare job for him in his Forum return match on August 28, 1967. The Sheik made several Montreal appearances for the remainder of the year and into early 1968, most notably capturing the IWA International Championship by defeating Gino Brito (son of former Harry Light assistant Jack Britton) in a tournament final on October 23. It was a championship that traced its lineage directly back to the world heavyweight championship recognized by the Montreal Athletic Commission from the 1930s to the 1950s, making the two weeks The Sheik held it the closest he would ever come to holding a world title in his nearly fifty-year career.

Nevertheless, as Farhat was in the midst of proving, and had been proving for some years, titles didn't mean everything. And even if promoters didn't see him as "world champion material," there were ways to get around that, and around them. He now had the power to make himself a legend—to will himself into being a superstar of national, and even international, proportions. He had joined the industry's elite club, whether the other members liked it or not. The thirteen-year-old boy from Lansing who ran away from home to get to "where the money is" had finally found it.

CHAPTER 10

ON TOP OF THE WRESTLING WORLD

"[The Sheik] drew more fans and sold more tickets in more places for a
longer period of time than anyone else in the sport's history."
—JIM CORNETTE

I t's become a cliché of every book focusing on any topic related to
American history or popular culture to refer to the late 1960s as a
time of seismic change, development, and tumult. And like many
clichés, it became one because it's true. Perhaps no other period in the
twentieth century saw so much of a dramatic shift in cultural norms,
mainstream entertainment, and social issues, as well as chaos in daily
life. At the end of 1967, films like *Cool Hand Luke* and *Bonnie and Clyde*
demonstrated a grittier, more violent shift in tone in Hollywood; on the
radio, the sounds of The Supremes, Jackie Wilson, and The Temptations
represented the dominance of the Motown sound, cultivated in the same
city that gave rise to The Sheik himself. Another Detroit power broker,
Jimmy Hoffa, whose rise to prominence as a union activist and president
of the Teamsters coincided with Ed Farhat's rise to prominence in the
wrestling industry, found himself behind bars thanks to his infamous
mob ties. Protests against America's involvement in the Vietnam War,
then in its fourth year, had begun to take form across the country. A
nation still not quite recovered from the assassination of President John
F. Kennedy had just a few more months before enduring the murders of
his brother Bobby and Dr. Martin Luther King.

With civil rights at the forefront like never before, the so-called long,
hot summer of 1967 saw a grand total of 159 race riots erupt in cities
and towns all over America. And none was worse than the one that set

PRO WRESTLING ILLUSTRATED/KAPPA PUBLISHING

Detroit's Near West Side aflame beginning in the early morning hours of Sunday, July 23, 1967, when police raided a blind pig, or unlicensed bar, located within the offices of the United Community League for Civic Action, igniting a catastrophic conflict between police officers and mainly African-American city residents that raged for five days. Michigan governor George Romney called in the National Guard, and President Lyndon Johnson sent the 82nd and 101st Airborne divisions in an attempt to quell the worst riot in American history since the Civil War. When the smoke finally cleared on the 12th Street Riot, forty-three people had lost their lives, 1,189 were injured, 7,231 were arrested, 2,509 business were looted, and 412 buildings burned to the ground. The issues that led to the riot were about more than just a raided drinking establishment; they had everything to do with decades of suppressed anger over housing discrimination, income inequality, widespread poverty, and the many other forms of racial injustice that had been transforming Detroit ever since a massive influx of African-American residents that began during the Second World War.

Having grown up in a racially mixed neighborhood, plus being of non-white descent himself, Farhat had always been sympathetic to the plight of the racially oppressed—also, like many a successful wrestling promoter, he wasn't above leveraging it to make a few bucks, as his never-ending ring wars with the ultimate Black fan–favorite, Bobo Brazil, will attest. In fact, less than six miles south on the Lodge Freeway, mere hours before the hostilities began, The Sheik was defending his United States title against Brazil in Cobo Arena before 10,076 screaming fans of all races, losing by disqualification after laying out the referee nineteen minutes into the third and deciding fall. Just two days later, while the fires blazed and the bullets rained in Detroit, The Sheik and Brazil battled again with similar results just two hours south on I-75 in Lima, Ohio, and then again in the Cincinnati Gardens on the 29th, less than twenty-four hours after the riots were finally stopped.

Most telling of all was the next Cobo show on August 5, when Farhat finally made the call to drop the United States title after holding it for two and a half years, losing a Texas Death match to Bobo Brazil before 7,283 jubilant Detroiters. Losing itself was rare enough for The Sheik, but putting the championship on Bobo Brazil was no accident or coincidence in light of recent events. Dave Burzynski was there as a young fan that night, and in a 2021 article for SlamWrestling.net, remembered speaking to The Sheik about it years later: "[T]hough it wasn't in the original booking plans, he thought, 'What could be better than to give the fans what they hoped and dreamed?' A time to see a man of color be lauded as a champion, giving fans of multiple races and color the thrill of a lifetime. As he saw it, he could help heal the city of Detroit by this small gesture of taking the fall and crowning a new champion." The fact that this was a gift to a hurting city was reinforced even further by Sheik's decision, once things had settled down a bit just six weeks later, to take the gold back from Brazil in a steel cage match. To soften the blow, the title change took place not in Cobo, but rather in Dayton's Hara Arena, to be announced to the live crowd the following night before Sheik's Cobo title defense against Mark Lewin.

While it may seem like insensitive trivializing to discuss racial strife in Detroit in relation to professional wrestling, the fact is that Big Time Wrestling was a uniter at a time when the city was beginning to explode and eventually crumble along racial lines. Fans of all colors packed Cobo

Arena every two weeks to thrill to their favorites and direct their collective disdain at their most hated targets—chief among those being The Sheik, of course. The city would never be the same after that horrible week in the summer of '67, but for many tens of thousands of its residents, wrestling provided an outlet—a release that didn't involve Molotov cocktails or firehoses. Blacks and whites disagreed on many things, but all agreed that The Sheik was the living embodiment of evil and deserved a pounding from Bobo, from Lewin, from Mighty Igor, from Fred Curry—from whoever stood on the other side of the ring from him. The Sheik was the lightning rod that could absorb all that tension and dissipate it for a few hours on a Saturday night in the Motor City.

Retired corrections officer and National Boxing Hall of Famer Ernie "Big E" Brown was a Black kid in Detroit in those days, just trying to keep his grades up so his mom would let him save his money for a $3.50 blue seat at Cobo. He remembers the climate very well: "Let me tell you—I never heard a racial slur at the wrestling matches. Ever. Even when we'd take the bus back, there'd be whites, Blacks, and we were talking about the matches, just enjoying ourselves. No racial fights ever when I went to the matches. We had the good guys and we had the bad guys, and that's how you rooted. Everybody just enjoyed it, and we were discussing matches all the way home. We had a respect for [The Sheik]. He wasn't a big guy, but when he went against Ernie Ladd, Mighty Igor, Haystacks Calhoun, he was able to escape losses. When The Sheik wasn't on the card, it seemed like the card was lacking a little bit. When he was on the card? Man, the place was rockin'. It really was."

All across the flourishing North American territorial system, major stars were being cultivated—stars who ruled the roost in the areas where they spent most of their time and who became such powerful draws that they had the ability to travel beyond their familiar borders and be known commodities throughout the wrestling world. Western Canada's Stampede Wrestling had Archie Gouldie, known in some circles as the Mongolian Stomper, who held the North American Championship a record fourteen times; in Mexico's Empresa Mexicana de Lucha Libre there was El Santo, the silver-masked icon who became a cultural hero in Mexico on the level of John Wayne or Babe Ruth; Championship

Wrestling from Florida had Eddie Graham, formerly a tag team specialist for Vince McMahon, who achieved such notoriety in the Sunshine State he eventually took over the promotional reins from Cowboy Luttrall; out in Southern California they had the masked Destroyer, known to his friends as Dick Beyer, a rangy former Syracuse University stand-out whose legend had even expanded across the Pacific to Japan; in the Mid-South-based Tri-State Wrestling there was the double-tendoned marvel Danny Hodge, the only man to ever win national titles in both boxing and wrestling, who spent over a decade as NWA World Junior Heavyweight Champion.

And in the eastern Midwest by the end of the 1960s, the name of The Sheik belonged right on the list alongside those others—and above most of them. It was in this cultural and pro wrestling landscape that Big Time Wrestling experienced its most booming, successful years and that The Sheik's name meant an instant box office boost for any promoter anywhere able to book a date with him. He didn't need an angle, storyline, or established feud; the only buildup required was to mention his name on television; he had the ability to walk into any arena on the continent, cold, with whomever they put him against, and not only increase the number of people in the building but guarantee their rapt attention and passionate reactions while there. In short, he was The Sheik. And that was all that was needed.

In those days before social media and the internet, the wrestler's greatest tool for spreading his name nationwide and making himself into a star even for those who had never had a chance to see him yet, was the robustly thriving wrestling magazine industry. Each month, upwards of a dozen different periodicals could be found on newsstands on virtually every corner in every town in America, featuring articles on talent from far and wide; their covers brandishing unforgettable, grinning, grimacing, glaring, and often gory faces, daring fans to buy them, rush home with them, and devour every single page with relish. It was there that fans learned about all the hottest stars not just on their own local TV but in places that may as well have been a million miles away. Naturally, they would want the chance to see these exotic names, and when their own home promotion brought them to town, they flocked to buy tickets.

Throughout the late 1960s and well into the 1970s, The Sheik was among magazine publishers' very favorite subjects and adorned more covers than virtually anyone, probably rivaled only by Bruno Sammartino, who benefited greatly by being the top star in New York, where most of the magazines were based. Scarcely a month went by when a wrestling fan approaching the magazine rack wouldn't be confronted by the image of The Sheik—staring menacingly into space or biting into an opponent's forehead, his face often covered in blood. Those covers commanded instant attention, and it can't be overstated how important they were to spreading the legend of the inscrutable and diabolical Sheik, who traveled the countryside burning and stabbing—and who might one day come to an arena near you.

Renowned sports author and magazine mogul Lou Sahadi spearheaded several top wrestling periodicals at the time, most notably *Wrestling World*. He came into The Sheik's orbit thanks to his many visits to New York—not to mention that much like the Currys, he, too, shared Farhat's cultural heritage: "I met Eddie when he used to come into the Garden. He was Lebanese and I'm Lebanese, so that was a natural tie-in right there. Every match that came into Madison Square Garden, I covered, so I got to know a lot of the wrestlers. Him and I hit it off really well. He was a great showman. Every time after the matches, we'd go out to eat, and they were first-class restaurants. One was the London Chophouse, which is a high-end restaurant. He liked Lebanese lamb, so we'd go to a lot of Greek restaurants. I'd meet him at the Garden early . . . Sheik had the Garden electrified; he was that kind of a personality. He was like Buddy Rogers, he could turn a crowd on like that, with the snap of a finger. Eventually he invited me to come into Detroit and said, 'Why don't you cover some of my shows?' And so, I went out there and did some shows with him. He put me up in the Sheraton-Cadillac Hotel. Didn't cost me a nickel. I used to write two or three stories out there with his wrestlers. They all respected him highly and didn't give him any lip. He was a perfectionist."

It's easy to see why magazines with Sheik on the cover sold so well, and in a business where sell-through is key, it was a no-brainer to keep going back to the well. "He was very colorful," Sahadi explains. "He was a guy that would absorb a lot of cuts, so you always had good photos . . . He was cooperative; he'd do anything you wanted. I wouldn't put somebody on the cover that I didn't think would sell!"

One of Sahadi's main competitors in those days was Stanley Weston, a Damon Runyon–esque figure who had gotten his start in the stock room for Nat Fleischer's *The Ring* magazine, later hand-painting a string of memorable covers for the "Bible of Boxing." By the 1960s, Weston was one of the most successful wrestling magazine publishers in the business, boasting such titles as *The Wrestler* and *Inside Wrestling*. At the end of the decade, a Jewish kid from Queens, Bill Apter, who had started as just a fan reading those magazines, came to be a photographer and eventually an editor for them, his name becoming so synonymous with Weston's publications that they came to be known as "Apter mags." Apter started working for Weston in the midst of Sheik-mania: "He was exciting. Mr. Weston's covers before I started were more sensationalism than after I started. Blood and sex sold on the cover. The Sheik was a master of having his opponents bleed—so it went on the cover. And those covers sold well . . . Even if he wasn't on the cover, he was an inside story."

In order to get those cover shots, intrepid photographers were often required to brave the fury of The Sheik to get close enough to snap. Backstage in front of a backdrop was one thing, but when Farhat was working in front of a crowd and between those ropes, all bets were off. Needless to say, he would never break character, and so photogs often considered requesting combat pay for what they'd have to endure. Many are the tales of Sheik unleashing his fury on terrified lensmen. "Shooting his matches was frightening, because I never knew when he might turn and start attacking the photographers, because he was known for that," remembers Apter. "He never did attack me, but he did with some of our guys in Detroit and Toronto. It was never considered fake or weird what he did—it was scary. He was the best at what he did. He kept true to his persona—not a gimmick—24/7."

Wrestling historian, author, and publisher Scott Teal was also a photographer in those days, and he first encountered The Sheik in the locker room at a Nick Gulas show in Tennessee: "Later that night he had his match, he's in the ring at TV . . . He got out of the ring at one point.

I was on the other end of the ring, leaning on the apron taking pictures. I had just been in the dressing room, shook hands with him, he talked to me like a normal, calm, collected human being. Like a businessman. He got out of the ring, he looks at me, and his eyes get wide and he starts to walk toward me. I knew better than to just sit there, because it would just kill his gimmick if I didn't run. So, I took off to the other corner, and he followed me around the ring almost one whole circuit. I finally stopped when he stopped. When he first got out of the ring and looked at me, I don't care how much I had talked to him, how much I knew about wrestling, how long I had been around; when he opened his eyes wide, looked at me and took a step toward me, there was something inside me that said, 'You had better run.' It crossed my mind: Is this guy really crazy? Here I'd been around the business forever. But he had this persona that scared you . . . He was so authentic in what he did. You could've been traveling up and down the road with him in the car, but when you get to the arena and he looks at you like that, there's a little voice inside you wondering if this guy is real or not."

And then there was London, Ontario's Terry Dart, as passionate and earnest a wrestling fan as one could ever hope to find, who was loved and cherished by everyone—except The Sheik. "He was saying his prayers in the ring on the prayer rug he had," Dart recalled of the most infamous moment of his photography career. "I was focusing my twin-lens camera, the kind you have to look down through the top to focus. I was reloading film, he rolled up his prayer rug and smacked me in the face with it, knocking me into the first few rows of seats. Broke my camera all to hell. So, I went to a lawyer and told him. The lawyer asked his name. I said nobody knows, we just call him The Sheik. The lawyer said unless you know his real name, you're out of luck. This happened more than once. Taking pictures of him fighting Bobo Brazil, Sheik came out and broke the camera again. Broke all five of my cameras! I think he was targeting me, but I never got a clear answer. The guy that wrote the book *Drawing Heat*[1] mentioned me because he knows me, but every time I asked him why The Sheik was doing this to me, he would change the subject. I'd go up to the ring, and as soon as The Sheik saw me, he would spit at me. It was ridiculous! I can't forgive The Sheik, and I never will."[2]

Not everyone was a fan of The Sheik and his antics, including some of his fellow promoters. As the Muchnick-Doyle letters demonstrate, there was skepticism about his membership in that elite fraternity from the start, and it only continued as time went on. Like most of their relationships with each other, it was love-hate: his colleagues may have held their collective noses, but they couldn't deny his ability to draw money hand over fist, both for himself and for them. Each year, the NWA would hold a convention, where everyone would mingle and debate important issues, and Farhat took pleasure in drawing attention to himself in his flashy, expensive, tailored three-piece suits and designer shades, dripping with gold and jewelry around his neck, and on his wrists and fingers. He was a man who had made his fortune and wasn't afraid to flaunt it, and for some of the more austere members of the Alliance, this didn't always sit well. When the conventions would be held in Las Vegas, Sheik's high living would be on its greatest display, as he became known for spending lots of time at the tables, a high roller in spite of the admonishments of his colleagues who urged him to be more careful with his money.[3] Some found him uncouth and crass for these reasons, and it's hard not to view some of it through the lens of ethnic or racial prejudice, as Farhat was one of only two major territorial promoters in the United States or Canada at the time who wasn't of Caucasian background, the other being Buffalo's Pedro Martinez.

Farhat was aware of the implicit animosity toward him and wasn't afraid to name it, whether accurately or just via his own perception. "He thought of some of the other promoters as white trash," remembers Japanese wrestling historian Fumi Saito from his early 1990s interview with The Sheik. "He was living in the Midwest, and he was a really Arabic-looking man. So, among all those white people, he probably felt left out. He said Verne Gagne was total white trash. Bill Watts was white trash; Fritz Von Erich was white trash. I think that's part of the reason that his best friend was always Bobo Brazil."

The Sheik could be a complicated man—even more so because he hid his true self from public life so carefully. His goal was to make sure only those close to him really knew him, and he largely succeeded in that goal to a very impressive degree. What remain are secondhand stories from those who managed to come into close contact with him over the years, and they paint an often-contradictory picture. For example, he achieved a reputation that persists to this day of being one of the stingiest payoff men in the business. Many performers have reported feeling burned by the lousy pay they would get working for Big Time Wrestling, to the point that it would discourage them from remaining employed there. However, there are others—admittedly in the minority—who had no such issues working for The Sheik. Taken altogether, it seems safe to characterize the payoff issue thusly: The Sheik was a promoter who valued those who drew a lot of money for him, those in his inner circle, and would usually pay them accordingly. For the rest of the talent, specifically those he may have felt (whether correctly or incorrectly) were not as important to the house that night, it was a very different story.

"Eddie Jr. used to make a speech: 'If you don't like it, you can fuckin' leave,'" remembers Lanny Poffo, who later came to work for Sheik with his dad, Angelo, and younger brother, Randy. "I remember hearing that a lot. It was coming from his dad too. It was said that his payoffs were not good. But I felt that I was overpaid! Louie Klein used to . . . have little spot shows where the new guys would wrestle on the main event and the students would be on the card without getting paid. They always took care of my dad and me, but I understand big stars like Tex McKenzie would always be grumbling. The locker room was always full of dressing room lawyers, always a hundred percent pissed off ninety percent of the time. My time taught me not to sink into that negativity—it can be demoralizing." Les Thatcher had a slightly different experience and remembers being coaxed to work a Hara Arena card in Dayton while home visiting family and later receiving a paltry check in the mail: "The funny thing is, Sheik used to bitch about payoffs. But then I remember working for him, and I thought, 'Damn! You're making up for your bad payoffs by not paying us well!'. . . I wasn't interested in taking bumps for twenty-five dollars."

The company would become infamous for spot show payoffs as low as ten bucks. And because Joyce was the one actually writing all the checks, they became caustically known among the boys as the "Joyce $10 Payoffs." Bernie "The Cat" Livingston, who spent weekends wrestling and weekdays running his family's carpet business in Port Credit, Ontario, accepted working for The Sheik for what it was: "He was the boss. If he promised you something, especially pay-wise, you could expect that as good as in the bank. He wasn't the best on payoffs, but if you worked for him, you knew how much you were gonna get, and that's exactly what you got. If you didn't wanna work for that payoff, you just didn't go and work for him."

And yet, Ed Farhat the human being was known by many to be a kind and generous man. An oft-repeated story in the business comes from the late Harley Race, the son of Missouri sharecroppers and an eight-time NWA World Heavyweight Champion, who recalled how when at age seventeen a devastating car crash took the life of his new bride and crushed his leg, nearly ending his wrestling career in its rookie year, it was The Sheik who began sending him weekly checks to help him get through it, despite not even knowing him personally at the time. "He was very big-hearted, very giving," said Killer Tim Brooks, who would later get to know him quite well as both a boss and a tag team partner. "He treated his employees with respect. He was a good businessman."[4] His photographer and future manager Dave Drason saw both sides: "If he liked you, he was good to be around. If he didn't like you, basically just stay away, because you didn't wanna be on his bad side! I remember Bobby Heenan telling me that when he was just a kid taking ring jackets and stuff like that, selling sodas and popcorn in Indianapolis, when Sheik was on the show, he would always tip Bobby ten or twenty bucks. You know, 'Hey, can you watch my car?' He always took care of Bobby."

Tommy Sullivan was a twenty-year-old kid from the North Hills section of Pittsburgh who one day knocked on the door of fellow Pittsburgher Bruno Sammartino and asked him how to become a pro wrestler. Bruno brought him to Vince McMahon, who in turn sent him to the doorstep of The Sheik:

> I got a room at the YMCA and hitchhiked to his house in Williamston, Michigan. When I first saw him, it was a hot summer of 1967. He lived in a big home with a swimming pool and wrestling ring in the hot sun. Bobby Shane and Al Costello got me on the mat instantly. It was The Sheik's

private ring. I didn't pay anything . . . He came out, a smile on his face. Friendly. You could see his forehead. The rings on his fingers. It was like meeting Yasser Arafat. He looked like him . . . I was all mat-burned. Sheik's wife put salve on me. Very kindhearted. Sheik had me over for dinner and drove me to the arenas . . . Sheik was a main event guy inside and outside the ring. First class. Reached for the stars. Did it with dignity. Presented himself at a high level and therefore was at a high level . . . Sometimes he'd talk like a street guy but he was a matter-of-fact kind of guy. Not a jerk . . . He had a temper, though. And when he got into character, you believed it. You thought he had a camel outside. You felt that if you punched him, sand would come off him . . . He stayed aloof and was very selective of whom he got close to. He was a businessman but he was very good to me. Very kind, very generous.[5]

After his training, Tommy found his way back to McMahon, who presented him as mid-card babyface John L. Sullivan. Just a few years after that, he hooked up in Ontario with Jimmy Fanning, a flamboyant wrestler from Tullahoma, Tennessee, who went by the name "Handsome" Jimmy Valiant. Before long, Sullivan had changed his name to "Luscious" Johnny Valiant, and the two began performing as a brother tag team, first for Dick the Bruiser in Indianapolis, and later for the WWWF, becoming one of the most successful duos of the 1970s. His story is just one of many of those whose journey to superstardom began with The Sheik.

Meanwhile, with his former princess busy writing the checks, The Sheik had been going solo for a couple of years, but eventually felt the need for another representative to escort him to ringside. This time, instead of a meek supplicant he could use to draw sympathy heat from the crowd, he wanted someone who could more actively stoke the flames of fan hatred, who could court disdain by speaking as his mouthpiece, giving the till-now wordless Sheik a vocal representative. He found that mouthpiece in the form of Irwin "Ernie" Roth, a former DJ and weatherman from Canton, Ohio, who had gotten his first introduction to the wrestling business in the late 1950s when he was discovered by crooner Johnnie Ray while taking tickets at the Canton Theater and introduced to his friend Buddy Rogers, who in turn introduced him to Columbus promoter Al Haft. Haft was the first to put Roth's diminutive size (all of five-foot-seven and 130 pounds) to good use as a heat-magnet manager, shaving his head bald, giving him an earring, and naming him "Mr. Kleen." A few years later, Jim Barnett and Johnny Doyle brought him to Detroit for the first time as the pompous J. Wellington Radcliffe, complete with spats, walking stick, and bowler.[6]

At the time Farhat selected him to be his manager, Roth had stepped away from the role for a couple of years and was working for Big Time Wrestling as an announcer for the locally produced studio show in Dayton, Ohio, on WKEF Channel 22, having totally dropped his gimmick and playing the part of plain old Ernie Roth, straight-laced wrestling commentator. Farhat, having remembered Roth's ability to generate heat by using his legendary gift of gab to run down opponents while hiding behind his charges in classic cowardly heel fashion, crafted for him the persona of Abdullah Farouk, the sinister handler who had been sent by The Sheik's family in Syria to manage the affairs of the Arabian madman. Dressed in notoriously garish suits and ties, sporting dark sunglasses and a fez cocked atop his head, he initially bore a passing resemblance to George Zucco as the guardian of the monster Kharis in Universal's 1940s Mummy movie series, which Farhat would've seen as a teenager, and which may have been the inspiration for the character.

Roth took to the role immediately, and by the beginning of 1968 had become an inseparable part of Farhat's presentation, his sneering, cackling face the perfect villainous counterpart to Sheik's inscrutable deadpan expression. Exhorting the virtues of the "Noble, Exalted Sheik," Abdullah Farouk (nicknamed "The Weasel" by the appropriately exasperated TV announcer Lord Layton) would taunt his adversaries and the fans and wasn't above slipping his man a concealed foreign object when the ref wasn't looking. Before long, he was earning a reputation as one of the best talkers in the business, which is exactly what someone like The Sheik, who never spoke, needed to complement his act. The heat drawn by The Sheik, already at nuclear levels, was sent into the stratosphere thanks to the devious and malignant presence of Farouk at his side. They were wrestling's match made in hell. "Farouk was one of the greatest managers of all time," sums up Drason, who later succeeded him beside Sheik. "He didn't have to do much to get heat. He taught me the art of the promo. What to say, how to say it, the subject matter. It should never be about you, it should always be about The Sheik."

As the decade drew to a close, Farhat continued populating his territory with new and even more colorful characters for his fans to enjoy. There was the six-foot-nine defensive tackle for the Kansas City Chiefs, "Big Cat" Ernie Ladd, who wrestled in the off-season before turning to wrestling full-time; Montreal's George "Crybaby" Cannon, aka Man Mountain Cannon, a rotund grappler and variety show host who drew heat by pretending to weep during matches; the sullen and leather-clad Hell's Angels, Ron and Paul Dupree, two-time holders of Big Time Wrestling's version of the NWA World Tag Team titles, who wrestled as brothers but were privately lovers;[7] and arrogant, jive-talking Claude "Thunderbolt" Patterson, an African-American heel who controversially exploited Detroit's simmering racial animus by using a white manservant named Man Hamilton and being introduced as hailing from "the Watts section of Los Angeles" (he was actually from Iowa).

His product now well-established in the Detroit area, Sheik was able to do what all promoters did in those days when each territory was a completely self-contained regional entity, and educate the local fans on the action they could expect to see. Since professional wrestling is based on illusion and simulation, fans could be taught with relative ease exactly what to accept as "pro wrestling." Some territories, like St. Louis, Florida, and the AWA, for example, based their product on sound, scientific mat wrestling; in Jim Crockett's Carolina-based Mid-Atlantic territory, tag team wrestling was the order of the day; fans in Mexico came to expect lots of high-flying acrobats in their lucha libre. Under The Sheik, Big Time Wrestling came to be known for wild-and-woolly action; clearly defined heels and babyfaces with colorful gimmicks and personas; brawling and bloodletting on a grand scale. In certain ways, as many have noted, the style that became popular in the Motor City was very much a precursor of the violent "hardcore" style of wrestling that came into vogue in the 1990s thanks to the rise of companies like ECW, CZW, and Japan's FMW—and The Sheik was the godfather of that style, which trickled down to the rest of the card like the rivers of scarlet running from his forehead.

You generally didn't go to a Cobo card to see lots of nuanced chain-wrestling, fancy takedowns, and leverage holds. You came to see the good guys beat the snot out of the bad guys, you expected mayhem and chaos, and that's what you got. As a businessman, The Sheik knew his audience, namely the working class, blue-collar people living in the heart of America's automotive industry, and he knew how to give them what they wanted. Consequently, Big Time Wrestling got a reputation in the industry of being a "punch and kick" territory, where talent knew they wouldn't be expected to display their technical prowess as much as they might working other parts of the country, but they better be ready to fight. "That was their style," explains journalist James Painter, who spent the early years of his wrestling career working in Detroit as Big Jim Lancaster. "They would start using illegal maneuvers and punching right at the beginning of the match, unlike Funk and Brisco type of matches. Those matches never occurred in the territory, but when they rarely would, the fans responded to them very favorably. There's just a handful of matches that occurred like that. That's the way The Sheik ran the territory. He was a punch and kick guy, he never wrestled anybody, so it's just a lot of heels like that, forty seconds into the match they're punching guys. Forget working holds or trying to work high spots or having a match that lasts longer than ten minutes . . . Sheik taught people that that was the only type of wrestling that there was, and you weren't gonna watch guys go to an hour broadway on top like they did in Florida. The fans just came to figure, that's what we're gonna get."

In this respect, Big Time bore a resemblance to another territory that had a "punch and kick" reputation and generally emphasized colorful characters over wrestling realism, the WWWF. It's clear that Farhat learned a lot from Vince McMahon and was inspired by the time he spent working for him. Not only did his product have certain similarities, but so did his booking approach, building main event programs around one top star who would face the incessant challenges of opponents coming into the territory and trying to knock him off his perch—usually with a main event or two that ended indecisively, followed by a final blow-off match with a dire stipulation that saw the top star finally overcome the odds. Of course, the key difference was that McMahon was doing it with an enormously popular babyface that fans wanted to win, namely Bruno Sammartino, while in Detroit it was a deeply reviled heel, The Sheik, who was fending off challengers left and right and built up to be seemingly unbeatable, while fans desperately prayed for him to lose. For the time being, this booking approach was working like a charm, but it wouldn't always remain so.

In addition to defending his United States title against the usual suspects, like Bobo Brazil, Mark Lewin, Mighty Igor, Lord Layton, and Fred Curry, in 1968 The Sheik also positioned himself on the opposite side of the ring from a man who had been his on-again off-again tag team partner for a decade, Fred's dad, Wild Bull Curry. While not so much fully turning Curry babyface per se, Sheik clashed with Curry around the Big Time Wrestling horn in a true battle of wrestling's most uncontrollable maniacs, yet fans took to cheering for the bushy-haired Bull for the simple reason that he wasn't The Sheik, the object of their ultimate hatred. This practice of taking another top heel and turning him face to work a program with him was something Sheik would do time and again, specifically for the purpose of making sure that he always remained the number-one villain in the territory and that no one ever got more heat than he did over any sustained period. It was another tried-and-true strategy that couldn't be argued with, while it was still working.

Outside the territory, Sheik made a handful of appearances at the Montreal Forum in the first half of 1968 to tangle with his old rival and Quebec favorite Edouard Carpentier, and he also worked a couple of dates for Dick the Bruiser in Indianapolis. But more important would be the sojourns he made to the two opposite sides of the country. On the East Coast, he would plunge into his first main event program for the WWWF and his longest stretch working for that company since taking over his own territory. And on the West Coast, he would debut in Southern California, an area that was virgin territory for him, but where he would come to enjoy more success than just about anywhere else in the United States outside of his own backyard.

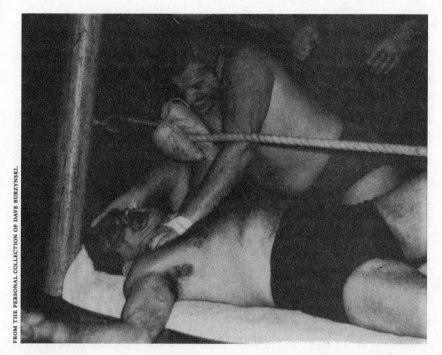

After spending years as tag team partners, The Sheik and Wild Bull Curry engaged in a violent feud that raged throughout Michigan and Ohio in the late '60s and early '70s.

Roughly four hundred miles south of the Cow Palace, the heart of Roy Shire's Northern California territory that had hosted Sheik several times over the years, stood Los Angeles's Grand Olympic Auditorium, a ten-thousand-seat boxing and wrestling venue originally built for the 1932 Olympic Summer Games. With its close proximity to Hollywood, it had been known as a hot spot for movie stars and other celebrities to check out the action, and the boxers and wrestlers who appeared there were often tapped to appear in movies when such types were needed.[8] It was without a doubt one of the most high-profile arenas in the country, and it also housed the offices of Worldwide Wrestling Associates, an independent promotion that controlled wrestling in Southern California and was run by brothers Mike and Gene LeBell (primarily Mike), along with their mother, Aileen, and their trusted booker, Jules Strongbow, original partner of Aileen's husband, Cal, who had passed away in 1966.

The WWA had chosen to leave the National Wrestling Alliance after the NWA's FBI anti-trust investigation in 1956 and had been giving it a go on their own ever since. When The Sheik was first brought in during the summer of '68, the WWA was mere months away from finally rejoining the Alliance, but for the time being they were still independent and still recognized their own world heavyweight champion, which happened to be none other than someone with whom Sheik was deeply acquainted: Bobo Brazil—a top attraction out on the coast for at least a dozen years by that point. In typical fashion, The Sheik made his LA debut with a TV squash match against California enhancement talent Jerry Monti on July 10, followed nine days later by a two-out-of-three falls main event at the Olympic for the WWA World title, which Brazil retained by disqualification.

This also meant that The Sheik and Joyce got to spend a week in Los Angeles, which was a perk of working the territory that cannot be understated. From the beginning, the love affair between Hollywood and The Sheik, a man who enjoyed the finer things in life, was apparent. Jeff Walton, Mike LeBell's publicist and eventual right-hand man, had just come to work for the Los Angeles office at the time of Sheik's first trip out there and can still recall the unlikely experience of taking him around Rodeo Drive on shopping sprees: "The Sheik loved Beverly Hills, as funny as that sounds. He loved shopping [there] with his wife, Joyce. They would come in almost once a month when they could. This is why he started working the area. He figured, well, I'll come in on a Thursday, and we'll go back Friday night after the matches, so he's back in Detroit by Saturday. He would buy boots, jackets, pants, everything custom-made and designed. And he loved spending time with Mike LeBell. They were around the same age, so they would drink and just have a great time.[9] If we would've been able to do what they do today with contracts and signing, he probably would've stayed, and he would've been tremendous for us. Because he was always good for us."

As Walton indicated, the Los Angeles area would become a regular stop for The Sheik going forward, starting with this handful of appearances in 1968. But later that year, Sheik made the shift from Los Angeles to New York, and did so with a level of commitment that hadn't been seen from him in years. Essentially, The Sheik worked out a deal with Vince McMahon to come into the WWWF on a pretty much full-time basis through much of the fall, and even into the early months of 1969, flying in weekly or biweekly while still managing to make local appearances at Cobo and other regular stops on the Big Time Wrestling circuit. The incentive was that this time, for the first time, he would be taking part in a main event program, tangling on the top of the card with the number-one attraction in the most lucrative region in the country: WWWF World Heavyweight Champion Bruno Sammartino.

At the time, Eddie Jr. had recently graduated high school and had just begun pursuing a degree in business administration from Michigan State University. He remembered his dad's Northeast venture like this: "In the late sixties, Vince Sr. was losing the New York territory. It was just not drawing. [He] didn't have anybody that could work against Bruno that could draw a decent house. And he talked to Dad, and Dad said, 'Listen, here's what I'll do. I'm OK here in my territory, I've got workers who can cover for me. I'll come and work for you against Bruno, and we'll pop the [territory].' Lo and behold, he went there for three months and he popped it, from Boston to Baltimore to New York with Bruno. And Dad never took one cent. He said, 'That's my gift to you,' and he took off." While Eddie Jr.'s memory on the matter may not have been entirely accurate, as Sammartino had been drawing houses at Madison Square Garden that year against the likes of Ernie Ladd, George "The Animal" Steele, Bull Ramos, and "Kentucky Butcher" John Quinn that were comparable to what he would draw with The Sheik, it is true that the Sammartino-Sheik program saw a noticeable uptick in business in some of the other cities in the territory.

It began in October with a series of three weekly TV squashes of enhancement talent at Capitol Arena in Washington, DC, to help reintroduce the WWWF audience to the menace of The Sheik, accompanied by Abdullah Farouk in the territory for the first time. This led to his first meeting with Sammartino in the main event at Madison Square Garden. This was not the old Garden that had stood on 8th Avenue and 49th Street for more than forty years, where The Sheik had appeared in the past, but rather a brand-new rotunda of gleaming steel and glass, not unlike Cobo Arena in structure but about fifty percent larger, standing one mile south at 34th Street, on the site of the old Penn Station. That initial encounter before 10,443 fans saw Sheik emerge victorious via count out when both combatants brawled outside the ring and Bruno failed to beat the referee's count to get back inside. The week after the expectedly inconclusive match, Sheik made two DC appearances, first joining Gorilla Monsoon to battle Sammartino and Brazil, then a TV squash match on Halloween. At the start of November, he was first brought for a couple of TV squashes to the Philadelphia Arena, where the ornery, penguin-like Phil Zacko, who had been running Philly since the fifties, coordinated McMahon's secondary television program. This led to a tag team main event at the Baltimore Arena, a venue that had seen McMahon push out the venerable Contos family, which had run Baltimore for thirty years, during his Northeast expansion earlier in the decade. There, Sheik and Monsoon were pitted against Bruno and the mammoth Haystacks Calhoun. This two-out-of-three falls match clearly demonstrated Sheik's keen backstage politicking, as he completely avoided being pinned—not only having his partner Monsoon take the pin in the second fall, but actually scoring a very rare pinfall over Sammartino himself in the third and deciding fall (thanks to outside interference from Gorilla, naturally).

Madison Square Garden, October 21, 1968: In the first of their three MSG main events, WWWF World Champion Bruno Sammartino punishes Sheik with a hammerlock (above) and his dreaded bearhug (facing).

The feud still alive and well, Sheik teamed with the Isle of Malta's favorite son, Baron Mikel Scicluna, at the next set of Washington TV tapings to take on the champ and his ally and fellow ethnic draw, Greek superstar Spiros Arion. This built directly into a hotly anticipated November rematch with Bruno at MSG which, to the undoubted disappointment of the more than twelve thousand fans present, saw The Sheik disqualified for biting in just over six minutes. As was common for the WWWF booking structure in those days, the program built to a third epic confrontation at the Garden in December, which would be contested under no-disqualification Texas Death rules, in which the loser would be the one declared unable to continue.

Another legendary future heel, Kevin Sullivan, was just a twenty-year-old YMCA wrestler from the west side of Boston at the time—a pro wrestling fan from childhood who was fascinated by the differences between what he saw on television and what he experienced on the mats competing for New England AAU championships. Mere months away from his own entrance into the mysterious world of the professional ranks, he was one of the fans on hand during one of Sheik's WWWF appearances, this one at "the other Garden," Beantown's fabled arena built by boxing impresario Tex Rickard in the West End district, run by promoter Abe Ford, whom McMahon had put in place

once he took over the town after the death of former Massachusetts grappling kingpin Paul Bowser. "The Sheik came into the Boston Garden to wrestle Spiros Arion," Sullivan remembers. "Arion looked to me like an athlete, and he was. Spiros was a man's man, and they kept him in a very good position. He was Bruno's partner, he was undefeated, and The Sheik came in there and when he came down the aisle, I thought the building was going to collapse. There was an energy, a force field I had never seen before, and I've been a sports fan my whole life. And when he hit that ring, the building exploded—and he hadn't done anything yet! Then he jumped on Arion and it was a three-minute squash match and bloody as hell! And I thought, 'OK, some of this may be fake, but that guy's real!'"

On the way, Sheik battled both Brazil and his former partner Scicluna in a pair of DC appearances the week before Thanksgiving, then returned to Baltimore for a reprise of the previous month's tag team main event, this time refereed by boxer-turned-wrestler "Two-Ton" Tony Galento,[10] who had been introduced to the grappling game by WWWF president Willie Gilzenberg. The deciding Sheik-Sammartino rubber match finally occurred at Madison Square Garden on December 9 before 10,943 fans rabid for Sheik's blood. And they got it when Sammartino finally got his hands on his rival's infamous pencil and used it against him, repeatedly jabbing him in the arm until the referee called for the bell at just under ten minutes (note that Sheik once again managed to lose without having to be pinned).

That may have been their final MSG main event, but the two men weren't done "popping the territory" just yet. Just five days later, Rudy Miller and Toots Mondt, McMahon's soon-to-be-retiring partner, brought the lucrative act to the Pittsburgh Civic Arena, where Bruno won via DQ. Their scheduled clash at the Philadelphia Arena the week of Christmas was postponed until January 11, when Sheik scored the win via count out. On the following week's Washington TV, Sammartino recruited both Calhoun and Arion to tangle with the heel dream team of Sheik, Scicluna, and Killer Kowalski. Sammartino-Sheik next headlined the Boston Garden on the 20th, followed by a steel cage match five days later to blow off their Philly run.

The Sheik did make one final MSG appearance; it would not be against Bruno, but rather Haystacks Calhoun, who was about twice his size (though advertised as three times). This particular evening would live in infamy thanks to the finish, which saw Sheik get disqualified for grabbing a photographer's camera in typical fashion and smashing it on the ground. As the reviled villain made his way through the crowd to the back, a small riot erupted, resulting in an elderly woman being trampled and severely injured. What happened next is a matter of conjecture, and it's difficult to separate fact from urban legend. Many have claimed that Sheik was banned permanently from Madison Square Garden (some of them also erroneously claim that the riot took place during one of the Sammartino MSG matches). The more likely account is that the relatively strict New York State Athletic Commission, which already had no love for outrageous performers like The Sheik, suspended him from appearing at the Garden (or possibly the entire state of New York) for a period of sixty days. This would be borne out by the fact that the war with Sammartino continued through to the beginning of spring, but would be contested outside the Empire State, specifically with multiple rematches in Boston and Baltimore.[11] As it turned out, The Sheik never again appeared at Madison Square Garden, partly due to his relationship with McMahon becoming somewhat strained in the 1970s—this would add fuel to the inaccurate rumor that he had been banned for life. But banned or not, it was the last time Farhat would work the WWWF territory for any extended period. Nevertheless, he had made his point—the one-time mid-carder and tag team oddity had returned in triumphant fashion, tearing things up with the company's cash cow in every major venue on the circuit.[12] He returned just one final time that year, in June, to battle Bulldog Brower in a heel vs. heel cage match that, along with Sammartino defending the WWWF World title against Killer Kowalski, helped draw fifteen thousand fans to an Abe Ford outdoor mega-show at Boston's Fenway Park.

As for riots like the one that occurred at the Garden, they were a much more common occurrence in the days when many fans truly invested themselves emotionally in the proceedings and gave themselves over to the artifice. Heels especially were often in danger from fan violence—when the heat got too intense, the folks in the crowd might ditch catharsis and look

PRO WRESTLING ILLUSTRATED/KAPPA PUBLISHING

Boston Garden, March 29, 1969: Already banned in New York, The Sheik concludes his legendary feud with Sammartino with a steel cage match that breaks Beantown's indoor sports attendance record.

to do some bloodletting of their own. Consummate shit-talker "Classy" Freddie Blassie was so good at stirring the pot that he famously had fans light his car on fire, had acid thrown at him, and was stabbed many times. In addition to Blassie, other legendary hate-magnets, including Buddy Rogers, Blackjack Mulligan, and "Rowdy" Roddy Piper, found themselves with knives sticking out of them at some point in their careers. And of course, The Sheik being perhaps the most detested character in the history of the ring, found his life in danger on countless occasions, and took serious precautions to protect himself from the rage of those who thought he really was the Devil.

Fans came for The Sheik not only with sharp steel, but much worse: once, in Amarillo, a sixty-one-year-old spectator drew a gun on him and pulled the trigger. Farhat must've thought he was about to meet his maker, only the firearm didn't go off. The story goes that when the gunman was brought down to the police station, his weapon was tested and then worked, firing the bullet that was meant for The Sheik. "He loved Texas because it was such a crazy area," says Jeff Walton, who heard him spin many tales of his days on the road. "He said he never walked to the ring without having a razor blade in his hand, because he said if someone just looked at him sideways, he'd slice them! He had to watch his back. He said, 'I have my blade with me out and exposed at all times, going to and from the ring.'" The anecdotes of The Sheik taping the sharp corners of razor blades to the ends of his fingers, to defend himself if cornered by unruly fans with bad intentions, have been commonly shared over the years and corroborated by many.

"One time in Dayton, my dad's in the ring against Bobo Brazil," remembered Eddie Jr. "The fans are so violent, and so wanting my dad to get killed, that they're willing to do anything. Five people jump in the ring—three have knives, one has a broken bottle, the other one has a chair . . . It was like that everywhere we went in the sixties and seventies. In Cleveland, Ohio, someone picked up these big steps like the ones you go in the ring with . . . and they dropped it right on his head. We thought they were gonna kill him." Lanny Poffo, who came to The Sheik's territory as a green rookie, remembers getting especially close to the mayhem: "One time they had a bit of a riot in one of the towns, where they used to fight outside the ring all the time . . . This fan goes up to him to try to do something, and I go over to help out. He takes a razor blade and he slashes the guy! I thought to myself, he doesn't need my help at all! I think he carried a lot of weapons on him. I don't know how he did it, but I saw him do it so quickly! Just scared the hell out of me, messed me up for a few days."

But pro wrestling is a unique business, in which being extremely hated is just as lucrative as being extremely beloved, if not more so. The last year of the 1960s saw Sheik get to the point where he was so in demand as a touring attraction that he was spending just as much, if not more time outside Big Time Wrestling as he was appearing for his own company. He expanded his operations in Southern California, starting with a return to the area in December 1968, by which point Mike LeBell had rejoined the NWA, renaming his product Hollywood Wrestling. In what was a booking no-brainer, Sheik was paired with Fred Blassie, LeBell's leading heel, top attraction, and a trusted member of the front office. In their first match together at the Olympic, they challenged for the Americas Tag Team Championship against the Mysterious Medics, wrestling's original masked tandem and part of the bizarre phenomenon of villainous masked doctor gimmicks that proliferated throughout the US and Mexico in the 1960s and 1970s.[13]

The Sheik made a total of ten appearances in California during 1969, including a February 21 victory over Bobo Brazil for the Americas

Heavyweight crown, the title that had replaced the old WWA World Heavyweight title. The following month, he was programmed against his former partner Blassie in a feud that would test the limits of just how hated The Sheik really was. On March 21, he lost by count out to the Classy One in a two-out-of-three falls encounter that saw the Americas title held up and vacated. This led to an April 11 rematch in which Blassie captured the belt. Sheik then regained it a mere two weeks later. Along the way, gradually, LA fans began taking a liking to Blassie, a bloodthirsty scoundrel of the ring whose violent ways were alleged to have caused elderly fans in Japan to suffer fatal heart attacks. As arrogant, unsportsmanlike, and obnoxious as Blassie was, at least he wasn't The Sheik—and when they were pitted against each other, the choice of who to support was an easy one for most Los Angelenos. "Blassie never really wanted to go babyface, but he realized times were changing," explains Jeff Walton, who was close to the decision-making process. "He wasn't really a face per se; he was still Blassie, he was a dirty, dirty guy. But the guy he was going against was even dirtier and even more hated."

The Sheik only had two weeks to enjoy his second Americas Championship before stepping into the ring with someone who was arguably an even greater draw in Los Angeles than he was, and inarguably even better at avoiding having to do the job—San Luis Potosí's Aaron Rodriguez Arellano who, using a persona originally crafted for him for a series of Mexican action films, had become lucha libre's first true international crossover star as Mil Mascaras, the Man of a Thousand Masks. Even still, when Sheik dropped the title to Mascaras it was via disqualification, meaning that two of wrestling's most notorious job-avoiders both left the ring without being pinned. He returned on October 3 with an even bigger prize at stake—the NWA World Heavyweight Championship, by then in possession of none other than Dory Funk Jr., whom Sheik had first met in Amarillo six years earlier when he was fresh out of West Texas State. No longer the green rookie being propped up by his dad, Dory Jr. was eight months into a historic four-year reign as world champion; in his first NWA title shot in five years, Sheik took the young titleholder to the limit with a one-hour draw

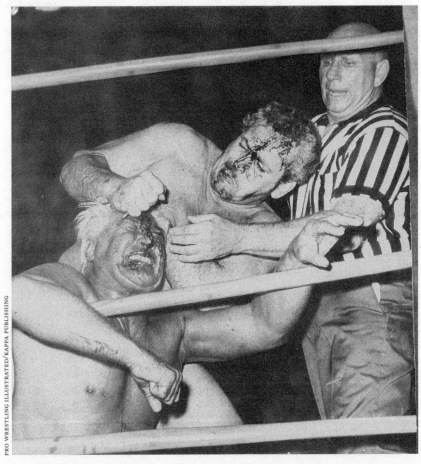

Olympic Auditorium, April 11, 1969: The Sheik on his way to losing the NWA Americas Championship to "Classy" Freddie Blassie via disqualification, as their white-hot feud escalates.

that saw both men score one fall apiece. Obviously, The Sheik could most certainly still go when he needed to.

Even more important than Los Angeles was the pivotal partnership Farhat struck up that year in Toronto with Frank Tunney. The Tunneys had been running shows in the Maple Leaf Gardens for many years with great success, mostly on the back of Bill Potts, a former corner newsboy and the son of an Englishman who had risen to success as Whipper Billy Watson, a superstar so enormous in Toronto that he had even earned the right to keep Lou Thesz's NWA World Championship belt warm for eight months in 1956. But by the late sixties the venerable Ontario territory had grown stale and needed a good shot in the arm. The problem of gate receipts that had been dwindling for years was compounded by mounting tax difficulties. Tunney had been watching Sheik's growing success from across the Great Lakes with great interest, and, despite his conservative reservations, he started to think he might be just that shot in the arm—and so a bargain was struck with the flame-wielding firebrand that would turn out to be somewhat Faustian in nature.

The Sheik had appeared at the Maple Leaf Gardens a dozen times before, but he hadn't been seen there in five years when Tunney agreed to take him on as his partner and booker. Most importantly, he would be making regular appearances in Toronto from now on, as Tunney hoped some of that magic that had been happening for LeBell, McMahon, Funk, and others might also rub off on him. And it did, but at a price—as Jim Freedman described in his seminal 1988 book, *Drawing Heat*:

> For years, Toronto's fans flocked to the Gardens shrieking for The Sheik to lose, to die, to disappear, and the more they came, the more they needed him to return to help clear their bile. Tunney needed him as well, to float his show through troubled waters . . . The power of The Sheik grew steadily in Toronto, until some say The Sheik held the Toronto office hostage . . . The Sheik scared Toronto's fans . . . He scared Tunney, too, showing him what could happen to a territory that began to weaken, that depended on a single talent for too long.

For the next eight years, The Sheik would do in Toronto what he had been doing in Detroit: book himself as the top attraction and the unbeatable heel at the apex of the food chain. And in the beginning, as it had in Detroit, it worked. So much so, that in later years many fans would come to mistakenly believe that Detroit and Toronto were part of a single territory (a perception aided by their sharing of the same TV announcer, Lord Athol Layton).

For the first five of those eight years, The Sheik would enjoy a legendary, infamous undefeated streak, not suffering a loss in 127 consecutive singles matches at the Maple Leaf Gardens during that time. And the names that would be included among those who fell to him reads like a staggering who's who of shining luminaries of the mat. In 1969 alone he beat Watson himself (albeit by DQ) in February; he pinned "Canada's Greatest Athlete" Gene Kiniski, the man who had just lost the NWA World title to Dory Funk Jr. four months prior, in only three minutes in June; the following month, he scored a DQ victory over his old foe, WWWF World Champion Bruno Sammartino, working in Toronto as a favor to Tunney, who had helped him out early in his career; he beat the once-unbeatable Lou Thesz in back-to-back appearances, the former NWA kingpin now stripped of much of his political clout and forced to do business;[14] he upended Quebecois legend Edouard Carpentier in September; and in November, he made short work of a Japanese rookie wrestling under the name Big Saka, who was actually Seiji Sakaguchi, a former All-Japan Judo Champion and rising star of the Japanese Wrestling Association, whose connection with Farhat would help open up a new chapter in The Sheik's career in the years to come. It was all evidence of exactly how much success a wrestler could enjoy—when he was the one deciding who won and lost. In the meantime, under The Sheik's regime, Big Time Wrestling and Maple Leaf Wrestling would come to be unofficial "sister territories."

Added to the list of territories that would taste the blood and fire of The Sheik for the very first time was Hawaii's 50th State Big Time Wrestling, headed by wrestler-surfer Lord James Blears and his partner Ed Francis, the former NWA World Junior Heavyweight Champion whose son Russ, then in high school, would go on to win a Super Bowl as a tight end for the San Francisco 49ers. What was perhaps most significant about The Sheik's initial voyages halfway across the Pacific was who he'd be working with. Pampero Firpo, the Wild Bull of the Pampas, was another of pro wrestling's crazy-eyed and crazy-haired madmen—a 230-pound, five-foot-eight fireplug whose irresistible energy and raucous interview style[15] had transformed him from a monster into one of Hawaii's most unlikely wrestling heroes. Born Juan Kachmanian, he was actually a highly literate and genteel individual who was fluent in eight languages. An Argentine citizen of Armenian extraction, he broke into the business in 1953, but it wasn't until he was working for Ed McLemore in Texas in 1959 that he ran into Jack Dempsey, who came up with the idea for him to bill himself as the son of Luis Firpo, the original Wild Bull of the Pampas, who had famously knocked Dempsey out of the ring in the first round of their 1923 heavyweight title fight in Madison Square Garden.

To Hawaiian fans, Firpo was known as "The Missing Link," and it was under that name that he battled The Sheik on September 24, 1969, in the Honolulu Civic Auditorium, winning by DQ. When they met again three weeks later, Sheik emerged the victor. In the process, a light assuredly went off in Farhat's head—Firpo's look, persona, and histrionics would be perfect for the colorful Detroit Big Time Wrestling troupe. He had encountered Firpo some years before while wrestling in Omaha for Joe Dusek, but that was before Big Time Wrestling; before he had the power to hire him. And although Firpo would remain in Hawaii for the time being, he had made an impression on The Sheik that would pay dividends soon enough.

On the home front, with Farhat's attentions more divided than ever, he felt the need for the first time to bring in someone to help him book his territory. That someone would be Dory Funk's brother-in-law Jack Cain, whom he had met a few years earlier while working in Amarillo. While Sheik still retained total autonomy in the creative direction of his own in-ring programs and angles, for the next five years Cain would be entrusted with essentially making the matches for everyone else on the roster and developing programs and angles for those high enough on the card to be deemed worthy of them. Farhat also began delegating more work to a young man named Bob Finnigan, who had up until then been working strictly as a ring announcer, taking the place of Detroit Tigers PA announcer Joe Gentile, who was unable to travel to all the regional venues outside of Cobo Arena. An aspiring country musician from the Lone Star State, Finnigan was a graduate of West Texas State, the fabled university attended by such wrestling legends as Dusty Rhodes, Stan Hansen, the Funks, Dick Murdoch, and many more. After several gigs in TV and radio, his wrestling connections proved fruitful when he came into the orbit of The Sheik and eventually found his way to Detroit. After a couple of years, he was officially brought on behind the scenes at World Wide Sports and became the producer of Big Time Wrestling's TV programming, among many other front office roles. He would become one of Farhat's most trusted associates and inner circle employees for years to come.

And as if the rigors of the road weren't distracting enough, Farhat was soon faced with the first of several major challenges to his control of the territory. This one came in the form of Bobby Davis, the Al Haft protégé who had pioneered the role of the heel wrestling manager during the 1950s and '60s, but was now looking to make his mark from the promotional end of things. A shrewd businessman with an entrepreneurial spirit, Davis saw himself as the successor to Haft, who had run most of Ohio for decades and had been the official NWA representative there. Sheik's claim to the area was an invalid one in Davis's eyes, as Sheik had purchased the rights from Jim Barnett and Johnny Doyle, whom the NWA considered outlaw promoters anyway.

"I knew The Sheik real well," said the reclusive Davis in a 2020 interview he granted me, one of the first he'd done in decades, and the last before his passing in January 2021. "He was a swell guy, I liked him a lot. He probably didn't like me, because they stole the Michigan and Indiana territory from Bert Ruby and those guys, and they thought they were gonna take Ohio. Well they didn't have any more right to Ohio than I did . . . It was Al Haft's territory I was taking over with his blessing." Davis set up shop in June 1969 under the name Wrestling Show Classics, recruiting for his business partners his longtime friend, former NWA World Champion Buddy Rogers, as well Sheik's good friend and one of the hottest babyface attractions Mark Lewin. Lewin unceremoniously jumping ship in this fashion was part of a pattern that went on during much of Farhat's years as a promoter—some have pointed to his meager payoffs and frustrating booking practices as motivations for many associates to turn against him, but the truth is that business associations in the wrestling industry were always tenuous at best, and guys would always go where the money was, or at least where they thought it was. In the end, they usually came back, and all was forgiven while there was money to be made.

Based out of Haft's old headquarters of Columbus, Wrestling Show Classics quickly moved on Big Time Wrestling, snatching up TV programming spots and running venues throughout much of Ohio, including most notably the Cincinnati Gardens, the Toledo Sports Arena, and Dayton's Hara Arena.[16] Farhat had long considered those "B-towns" compared to Detroit and Cobo Arena, and he would book them accordingly with talent and matches that were not always up to fans' expectations, so some were hungry for something new anyway. Davis's friendship with Lewin led to financial backing from Lewin's friend Ed Blatt, a Cincinnati businessman who was what is sometimes derisively referred to in the business as a "money mark." In addition to Lewin himself, the group snatched up a few more of Sheik's talent, including Killer Karl Kox. They even began taping TV at the Dayton studios of Channel 16 WKTR, bumping Big Time Wrestling out of the building and out of the 5:30 p.m. Thursday night time slot (it was a testament to Sheik's clout that he was able to scramble and get his program back on the air in Dayton a few weeks later, during Saturday afternoons on competing station WKEF Channel 22).

"I was there and went to their shows, and kept a lot of their results," remembers future grappler Jim Lancaster, then still a fan. "I don't know if Sheik was able to prevent them from getting a promoter's license in Michigan or not. Sheik had that kind of power at that time, where he could keep people out." But although they got off to a strong start, Wrestling Show Classics was not destined to last long and had closed up shop altogether by the start of 1970. But for the time being, The Sheik was locked out of Hara Arena and forced to share other buildings, so he began running smaller shows in the surrounding towns and calling in favors from friends, such as "Flying" Fred Curry: "He called me up in Texas, when I was wrestling for Von Erich. He brought me in, and we kicked their ass. They went out of business." Curry also claimed that Sheik wrote Bobby Davis a check for $5,000 just to walk away, which he accepted. Lewin and Rogers had stuck with the promotion until the fall of 1969, but then jumped back over to The Sheik.

Also contributing to the premature demise of the enterprise was an extremely unfortunate and ill-advised incident recalled by Davis: "There was a family that came faithfully every Saturday afternoon when we were televising our shows and interviews. There was a guy that was a member of the family, about forty-three or forty-four years old, that wanted to be in wrestling so bad he could taste it. And he knew how to wrestle, he had wrestled in college. [But] he'd never wrestled professionally. I finally said after three weeks, you be here next week with your trunks and your shoes on, and we'll put you in with somebody. You would've thought I offered him a million dollars. I put him in with Karl Kox, and he had a heart attack and died in the middle of the ring! I could see he wasn't in the best of shape, but I thought, one match, it'd go five minutes, no big deal. But he wasn't ready, and he died." Wrestling Show Classics shut down not long after that, and Bobby Davis, the original pro wrestling heel manager, walked away from the business forever. Although Sheik had technically won back the ground he had lost in central and southern Ohio, he wouldn't get back to running Hara Arena for another couple years.

The promotional wars of that era could be like the wild west, and Farhat knew he had to be on guard at all times. And yet, competition also pushed change and innovation. After losing his locally produced Dayton TV show, he began relying more on a weekly show he had earlier in the year begun producing at an intimate, white-walled television studio located about twenty miles northwest of Detroit in the tiny suburb of Walled Lake, at 100 Decker Road.[17] Aired on WKBD Channel 50, by the middle of 1969 it had become The Sheik's primary TV show, phasing out the tapings that had been going on in Windsor, Ontario, since the Barnett-Doyle days. Although the Walled Lake TV tapings only lasted a couple of years, it is a period still fondly remembered by fans of Big Time Wrestling.

The new decade brought new stars and new promotional alliances to Big Time Wrestling. Added to the roster was Jerry Maiburg, a classic technician from DC who had initially appeared under a mask as Ben Justice, capturing the World Tag Team title with Canadian superstar Rocky Johnson.[18] Justice later unmasked to form a highly successful and even more decorated tandem with Guy Mitchell, aka John Hill, a brawler from Hamilton, Ontario, whom Dick the Bruiser rechristened

"The Stomper."[19] Demonstrating just how isolated the different territories could be in those days, at the same time as he was tag teaming as a babyface in Detroit with Justice, Mitchell was working against The Sheik in Toronto as the masked heel Assassin. Career babyface "Arriba" Luis Martinez had been a dependable upper mid-carder throughout the 1950s and '60s, with long tenures in territories with sizeable Latino populations, including for Mike LeBell and Roy Shire in California, the Funks and Ed McLemore in Texas, Vince McMahon's Capitol Wrestling, and the Arizona territory run by former light-heavyweight contender "Lightning" Rod Fenton. More recent years found him bouncing around Verne Gagne's AWA and Dick the Bruiser's WWA. He and The Sheik had crossed paths in the ring several times over the years, but he had almost twenty ring years under his belt when Sheik brought him into Big Time Wrestling and breathed new life into his career. Starting with his Cobo debut at the end of 1969, a victory over "Beautiful" Bobby Harmon, boyfriend of Sheik's manager Ernie Roth, Martinez became a leading light of Detroit wrestling in the final phase of his career and one of Sheik's chief 1970s adversaries.

In the "new alliances" category, there was the unlikely resurrection of Pedro Martinez's Buffalo-Cleveland circuit, which officially broke away from the NWA and went independent as the National Wrestling Federation in 1970. Taking on Johnny Powers, one of his star performers, as his business partner, Martinez's NWF covered the northern part of New York state where the WWWF didn't penetrate, as well as several other Ohio towns also run by The Sheik, such as Akron and Canton. Theirs was a practical arrangement, born out of survival instinct more than actual amity. Sheik had drawn a lot of money for Martinez years back and was a proven commodity, even if he and Powers never saw eye-to-eye, partly because Powers knew that Sheik would just as soon take all of Ohio for himself. Nevertheless, Sheik made a lot of money for everyone involved by sending Big Time Wrestling talent to the NWF, and so a sort of promotional triumvirate was formed, containing the Detroit, Toronto, and Buffalo promotions, with a free flow of performers moving among them for the next several years. "Martinez didn't run a seven-day-a-week schedule," Dave Meltzer explains. "He only ran a couple days a week. He would use The Sheik's heels, different storylines, but a lot of guys from Michigan-Ohio would work Cleveland-Buffalo at the same time, so they had to be cooperative to a degree."

Thanks to the new cooperation, Farhat was kept busy in 1970 wrestling throughout this three-pronged confederation, including an ongoing feud in Cleveland and Buffalo with Powers, his real-life rival and partner of convenience. Even still, he found time to keep his growing legend alive throughout the country. He showed up back in his old Lubbock-Amarillo stomping grounds in March to tag team with rising star Harley Race, a few years away from the NWA World title. He maintained his relationship with Francis and Blears in Hawaii and began to ponder journeying even farther eastward.

In Los Angeles, the war with Blassie was resumed and taken to a fever pitch. On June 26, they battled to a draw before over ten thousand fans, with Blassie's Americas Heavyweight title on the line. By this point, Blassie had fully transitioned to Southern California's most adored babyface, despite clinging to his violent, roughhouse tactics. In order to rule out the interference of the conniving Abdullah Farouk, the rematch for July 10 was announced as a steel cage match—but not just any steel cage. Whereas cage matches of the past—which were rare to begin with—could be won usually by pinfall or by escaping the cage through the door, this time, a competitor could also win the match by climbing over the top and down to the arena floor. The new structure of metal and wire was dubbed the "Blassie cage" by legendary Los Angeles TV commentator Dick Lane, and the over-the-top rule became standard in the business going forward. Jules Strongbow and Blassie himself booked the finish for the highly anticipated match, which saw Farouk pass what was purported to be a bottle of iodine to The Sheik—as the two men battled furiously atop the cage, jockeying for position, Sheik threw the liquid into Blassie's face, sending him to the mat and allowing Sheik to escape and win the match. Naturally, for the third match in the series, two weeks later, Blassie demanded not only that he and his opponent be sealed inside the cage, but that the weasel Farouk be locked in a shark cage that would be suspended above the ring, eliminating him from the equation. That time, the King of Men finally won the day, as

Maple Leaf Gardens: Abdullah Farouk warns The Sheik's opponent to keep away while he prepares to lay out the carpet for his charge's pre-match prayer ritual.

Farouk howled in disapproval from above (and The Sheik once again avoided being pinned in defeat).

In almost every possible way, The Sheik was at the very top of his game going into the 1970s—as a performer, as a box office attraction, as a businessman. At forty-four years of age, he seemed to be in the prime of his life, and he was. He and Joyce had enjoyed over two decades of marriage; Eddie Jr. had earned his business degree, and his dad began to eye him for a place in the family business; and Tommy, a child of seven, was all the reminder Farhat needed that he had to stay hungry and hold zealously to his spot. As Big Time Wrestling hit its stride, he had just managed to fend off a threat to that spot. But the skirmish with Bobby Davis and Wrestling Show Classics was just a warmup round for the crisis that was coming. Dick the Bruiser and Wilbur Snyder, who had taken Indianapolis by force from Barnett and Doyle, had never been able to wash the taste of their humiliating Detroit defeat out of their mouths. Biding their time to the south for six long years, they decided the moment was right to mount another invasion and strike deep into the heart of the Motor City. This one would be no three-month affair. This time, they were coming to do in business what no one could do in the ring: take The Sheik down. And the years-long struggle that resulted would be remembered by wrestling fans as one of the fiercest promotional battles in the history of the business.

CHAPTER 11

THE BATTLE FOR DETROIT

"We had such a hold on that city.
We could keep fighting them, so let him come and try it."
—EDDIE FARHAT JR.

After a period of so much racial strife, the 1970s was not a good time to live in the Motor City for citizens of all races. The tumultuous season of the late 1960s had borne bitter fruit, and the city was changing for the worse. The riots had led small businesses to close up in droves, and many fled to the suburbs. This left behind a majority African-American population crippled by low income, unable to grow and develop the city thanks in part to decades of housing discrimination, disparity in education, and other severe economic disadvantages. Crime and drugs proliferated, gradually turning the city into a wasteland of urban decay. Compounding the city's problems was the collapse of the auto industry that had been the backbone of Detroit for over half a century. Over the course of the 1960s, most parts suppliers had moved to the South, while major automakers moved their factories outside city limits to avoid paying union wages, then farther away still to Canada and Mexico for tax purposes. By the seventies, those American automakers were also competing with fierce threats from other countries, most notably Japan. A looming oil crisis meant that gas prices were about to skyrocket as well. Jobs dried up, which led to more supporting businesses closing and severe loss of tax revenue, contributing to the nosedive of an American city already in serious decline.

It was ironic, then, that the early 1970s would prove to be the most financially successful period for one of Detroit's most high-profile local

businesses, World Wide Sports, producers of The Sheik's Big Time Wrestling. The years 1972 and 1973 in particular would see business positively on fire, with capacity sellouts at Cobo Arena becoming a regular occurrence and the territory rising to the status of one of the most profitable in the entire country, perhaps second only to the WWWF and at least on par with Hollywood Wrestling. While the city crumbled around them, people came to see The Sheik do battle, bleed, throw fire, and hopefully be defeated.

As with many businesses, in wrestling and elsewhere, spikes had a whole lot to do with competition. To protect his business against an invading force, Ed Farhat had to really step things up, pull out all the stops, and make his product better than it had ever been. When you're not the only show in town anymore, complacency isn't an option. And he wasn't, thanks to the renewed presence of Dick the Bruiser's Championship Wrestling of Indiana, Inc., which did business as the World Wrestling Association. With his junior partner, Wilbur Snyder, Bruiser had attempted a brief coup back in 1965, trying to unify both halves of the old Barnett-Doyle territory, only to be unceremoniously driven back to the Hoosier State in short order. But what would take place from 1971 to 1974 would be a full-on, raging promotional war of the first magnitude. And when the dust cleared, even though Farhat emerged with his business intact, he would eventually find that the end of that heated competition also meant the end of Big Time Wrestling's hot period.

Professional wrestling was a cutthroat business and had had more than its fair share of explosive promotional clashes and territorial squabbles. There was the infamous Texas conflagration of 1953/1954 that pitted Dallas impresario Ed McLemore against Houston king-pin Morris Sigel and partly resulted in the suspected arson destruction

Out of gimmick, Ed Farhat and Ernie Roth—aka The Sheik and Abdullah Farouk—make their way into the building for a night's work.

of the original Dallas Sportatorium. In 1963, a disgruntled Antonino Rocca, jilted by Vince McMahon in favor of Bruno Sammartino, had hooked up with Carolinas promoter Big Jim Crockett in a New York invasion, even running televised cards at the Sunnyside Gardens in Queens on the same nights as McMahon's Madison Square Garden cards across the East River. Not to equate wrestling promoters with thieves, but there was certainly no honor among them, and loyalty was scarce. This would be proven by Sheik and Bruiser's war in Detroit, one of the most intense and long-lasting promotional conflicts the business had seen up to that point.

When comparing the two men who were on a collision course, many similarities and glaring differences emerge. Both were national mat stars made during the 1950s TV wrestling heyday, with the ambition, savvy, and business sense to elevate themselves into successful promoters. Bruiser had done so by brute force, pushing Barnett and Doyle out of Indianapolis. The Sheik had gone the more "honorable" route, buying them out in Detroit—and Barnett would in fact rave for years later how Sheik never missed a payment and treated him fair and square (he had less kind words for Bruiser). Both men were tough as nails, with alpha personalities and a take-no-prisoners attitude that meant neither was anyone you'd want to trifle with. However, William Afflis, alias Dick the Bruiser, was a child of privilege, whose working-class ring persona belied the fact that he had a degree in engineering from the University of Nevada. Ed Farhat, by contrast, had never even been to high school and was a streetwise guy who grew up in an immigrant family that had to scratch and scrape for everything they got. Both were larger than life, but Bruiser, who had always had money, was known for his frugal way with it, saving every penny he could, while Sheik, who had never known wealth before, lived a flashy lifestyle and enjoyed spending what he had. Perhaps Farhat felt he had a little bit too much yet to prove. Perhaps he couldn't bear letting Bruiser do to him what he had done to Barnett and Doyle. Whatever the motivations, they would all play a role in why things shook out the way they did.

Even before the war began, almost as if there was something in the air, The Sheik spent most of 1971 in the comfortable and local triumvirate circuits of his own Big Time Wrestling in Michigan, Maple Leaf Wrestling in Ontario, and the National Wrestling Federation in Ohio and upstate New York. There was far less traveling abroad, which leads one to believe he may have known something was afoot and chose to stay relatively close to home. In the Maple Leaf Gardens, he added to his unbeaten streak with a double count out against NWA World Champion Dory Funk Jr. in June. Earlier in the year, he had collided there with an Indian grappler who had made his name wrestling for Frank Tunney in Toronto and would go on to become one of The Sheik's fiercest in-ring rivals, particularly in that city.

Jagjeet Singh Hans hailed from the tiny Punjabi village of Sujapur, population 1,300, but it wasn't until he arrived in Ontario, Canada, in 1965 with six dollars in his pocket that he started his journey into the business of pro wrestling, earning the ring name Tiger Jeet Singh from his trainer Fred Atkins, who introduced him to Tunney and made him a Maple Leaf Gardens staple. Trading on a similar type of Eastern exoticism that had brough such success to The Sheik as a heel in North America, Singh played up his Indian heritage with elaborate ring entrances and became known for a rough, brawling style that was a perfect match for The Sheik, and it made sense that they would eventually cross paths. Sheik had taken a liking to Singh while working Toronto cards with him, and he recognized that they could make some money together, especially since Singh was the United States Champion as recognized by Maple Leaf Wrestling, and Sheik was the United States Champion as recognized by Big Time Wrestling.

On February 6, 1971, Farhat brought Singh to Detroit for an undercard match at Cobo against a Texan newcomer by the name of Tim Brooks (more on him later). The next night, The Sheik and Tiger Jeet Singh wrestled for the first time in Toronto, US Champion vs. US Champion. The match between the mad Arab and the fierce Indian drew so much attention for its wild action that Farhat booked them to face each other four more times at the Gardens over the next six weeks. Their February 21 encounter drew nearly twenty thousand fans, the largest crowd in forty years of wrestling at the Maple Leaf Gardens. They duplicated the feat for their March 14 encounter. Farhat's intuition about Singh turned out to be right, and Tunney's decision to partner with him was seeming like a most lucrative one. Needless to say, by hook or by crook, The Sheik won all five of those matches.

It was while wrestling for Pedro Martinez and Johnny Powers's NWF in Cleveland that The Sheik shot an angle that was strictly for the regional fans, battling Bulldog Brower to a double count out before 4,423 fans on February 11 at the Cleveland Arena, the home of the Cavaliers basketball team located in the middle of Euclid Avenue, one of Cleveland's busiest downtown districts (similar to the old Madison Square Garden's midtown Manhattan environs). As with many NWF shows in those days, half the card was made up of Big Time Wrestling talent, and Sheik threw them even more of a bone by engineering a finish wherein the United States title would be declared vacant due to the encounter being a lumberjack match in which competitors aren't permitted to leave the ring. Naturally, the controversy was settled at the next Cleveland show the following week, where The Sheik won it back. As was common practice in those days, the phantom title change went unbeknownst to fans back in Detroit, as it wasn't acknowledged on Big Time Wrestling TV.

However, a title change of a more permanent nature took place in Cobo Arena on May 29, 1971, when after years of chasing him, Bobo Brazil took the United States Championship from The Sheik in a steel cage match, with Lord Athol Layton as special referee.[1] Unlike the six-week reign back in '67, this time the switch would stick: The Sheik and his beloved US title belt would be separated for more than a year and a half. Farhat had kept the company's top prize on himself for over six years with only the shortest of interruptions, so he likely felt it was time for a change, and if anyone was going to get it off him, it would be his trusted real-life friend Brazil, who also happened to be the most beloved performer on his roster. If indeed he was aware a promotional war was coming, it's also possible he thought it would be a good idea to change things up by putting his top championship on a wrestler the fans could rally behind, instead of one they detested. Yet to protect himself, the finish of the match involved "biased" babyface referee Layton pulling a fast three-count on The Sheik, allowing him to save face even in defeat.[2] It was considered the second biggest wrestling title change of

1971, behind only Ivan Koloff's shocking upset over Bruno Sammartino for the WWWF title at Madison Square Garden in January.

The 1970s were bringing some new faces to Big Time Wrestling; some truly new to the business, and some journeymen and legends brought in by the promise of good crowds and the hopes that rumors of Sheik's stingy payoffs weren't true. There was the rookie son of Johnny Valentine, whom Sheik would break into the business under the name "Babyface" Nelson, a moniker he hated so much he eventually embraced his famous heritage as Greg "The Hammer" Valentine; Irish Mickey Doyle, a fresh-faced Detroit kid who came out of Lou Klein's gym and became a sentimental favorite despite taking a pounding in his early years from some of Big Time Wrestling's most fearsome heels; the Australian Les Roberts, whose nationality was played up in classic wrestling fashion when Sheik and Jack Cain renamed him Dingo the Sundowner; a brand-new incarnation of the pioneering Australian tag team The Fabulous Kangaroos, put together by Sheik and Cain and consisting of original member Al Costello and former Boston Red Sox recruit "Bulldog" Don Kent, who had an in with Sheik because he had been a protégé of "Leaping" Larry Chene;[3] and Tony Silipini, aka Tony Marino, who, like Luis Martinez, was rescued from wrestling oblivion in the latter part of a long career that had earlier seen him perform to some acclaim as the Battman[4] in Bruno Sammartino's Pittsburgh territory, at a time when Adam West's campy TV series was still all the rage.

Big Time Wrestling's *Body Press* magazine-program was still the envy of the business, and by this point was being pretty much run by Detroit superfan (and future "Supermouth") Dave Burzynski, still a teenager at the time. Contributing most of the photography and the written material, he would be helped along by the wrestling war: "I was writing stories and taking photographs around other territories, too, and submitting stories to *Wrestling Revue*, *Wrestling World*, *Wrestling Monthly*, *The Ring Wrestling*, all the big magazines at the time. But I was a young kid, thirteen or fourteen years old, and I really couldn't crack Cobo, my hometown arena. So, I always took pictures from my seat. I got in the good graces of promoter Les Ruffin in Cincinnati. And there was a time in 1971 that he allowed me to take photographs. The Sheik was on the show that night. Then, during talent raids during the war with Bruiser—I had pix of all the top stars. Joyce Farhat liked what she saw and started letting me shoot ringside. Ed Jr. wanted to buy pictures. It became a weekly, biweekly thing, shooting ringside. My foot in the door." Before long, the young Burzynski had become the closest thing to an official photographer that Big Time Wrestling had.

In the calm before the storm, The Sheik did occasionally spend some time away from his home base, mainly during the summer. He appears to have spent significant time in Hawaii over the summer of '71, presumably as both a vacation getaway and a chance to pick up more dates for Ed Francis and Lord James Blears's 50th State promotion. At the time, he was attempting to take Eddie Jr., then all of twenty-one years of age, a little more inside and show him more about the business; he took him along on that Hawaii trip partially for that purpose (one imagines it was not too difficult to persuade him to come). Chief among his rivals that season was towering powerhouse Ed "Bearcat" Wright Jr., son of a journeyman boxer who had once knocked out Jack Johnson. Just as obstinate about losing as Farhat was, Bearcat had the savvy, as an African-American performer in the mid-twentieth century, to protect his aura and his image; as a result, he was second only to Brazil among prominent Black pro wrestlers, and had in fact become the first Black wrestler to capture a major world heavyweight title when he won Mike LeBell's WWA strap from Fred Blassie in 1963.[5] In addition to his singles clashes with Wright (including an "African death match"), Sheik also opposed Wright in tag matches, teaming with former NWA World Champion Gene Kiniski against Bearcat and a popular young Puerto Rican wrester named Pedro Morales, who had earlier that year been chosen by Vince McMahon to replace Bruno Sammartino as WWWF World Champion after eight long years of relentless title defenses had taken their toll on the Italian Superman.

The day after his African death match with Wright, Farhat hopped on a plane from Honolulu to Los Angeles, where he had been advertised as part of the biggest wrestling event ever staged in the Golden State, to be held August 27 at the massive Los Angeles Memorial Coliseum, home of the LA Rams. For months, Mike LeBell and Jules Strongbow had been carefully putting together a monster card that would make history for several reasons. One of them was that the event would be rebroadcast throughout the area at theaters, auditoriums, and other venues on closed-circuit television, a new technology that LeBell had been toying with of late, and which was a precursor to pay-per-view. The main event was planned as an epic grudge match between Blassie and the man who had notoriously "blinded" him with Monsel's powder (a blood coagulant stolen from the bag of a ringside physician), "The Golden Greek" John Tolos.

However, before the angle to set up the match had been shot for TV, the main attraction for the show as advertised in the weeks leading up to it was the industry's most reliable blood feud, The Sheik vs. Bobo Brazil. It was a no-brainer, as Sheik and Bobo were already both well-established stars in LA, and their bouts had been thrilling fans for years up and down the coast and elsewhere. "They trusted each other, and Sheik really loved Bobo," remembers Jeff Walton. "We built that Coliseum card really with the idea that until we could promote Blassie and Tolos, it was The Sheik and Bobo. Finally, when we busted loose with the angle for Blassie and Tolos, that's when it really started to go. That show took a year and a half to plan. Mike was methodic in planning how everything was gonna go." In the end, The Sheik-Brazil match[6] was the semifinal of an event that attracted a whopping 25,847 fans, setting a California attendance record for professional wrestling that stood for nearly forty-four years before finally being broken in 2015 by WWE's *WrestleMania 31* in Santa Clara (the record for Los Angeles itself still stands). And although the majority of the credit for that crowd must go to Blassie and Tolos, it can't be denied that Sheik and Brazil also played a hand in making a success out of what turned out to be one of the most important wrestling events of the 1970s.

But Farhat did not have long to savor being part of such a groundbreaking event, because Dick the Bruiser was about to strike with his power play. His first maneuver was to make a deal with CKLW-TV in Windsor, Ontario, where The Sheik had previously been doing his weekly TV show before switching to Walled Lake, Michigan. The CKLW broadcast reached nearby Detroit, which was the entire point, since the big goal was to run live shows right in The Sheik's backyard. Exposing the new fan base to the WWA product would be necessary, as would hyping up those cards once they got booked. Key to the deal, and some might even say the main reason it happened, was Lincoln Cavalieri, president of Olympia Stadium, who had been watching with great envy the kind of numbers Farhat was pulling in on a biweekly basis across town, raking in tens of thousands of dollars twice a month in Cobo ticket sales alone. Some believe that Cavalieri may have even contacted Bruiser himself to try to make something happen and bring wrestling back to the Olympia, but regardless of who contacted whom, Bruiser was most definitely very much open to the idea. "Bruiser and his partner Wilbur Snyder wanted a piece of the action," explained Detroit wrestling historian Mark Bujan. "He was running out of Indianapolis but thought there was plenty of money to go around. They booked deals with the Olympia, which wasn't far from Cobo. They thought they could come in and take a piece of the action, which they did."

On the night of Saturday, October 23, 1971, a wrestling fan in Detroit suddenly found himself with not one, but two options. He could go down and grab his usual seat at Cobo Arena for a ten-match card highlighted by Dory Funk Jr. defending the NWA World Heavyweight title against "Big Cat" Ernie Ladd, Bobo Brazil defending the United States title against Wild Bull Curry, Johnny Valentine taking on Rocky Johnson, Gorilla Monsoon tangling with "Crazy" Luke Graham (one half of the inaugural WWWF World Tag Team Champions at the time), former NWA World Champion Pat O'Connor against former Venezuelan boxer Ciclon Negro, Americas Champion Mil Mascaras vs. Fred Blassie in a clash of West Coast legends, and Florida wrestler-promoter Eddie Graham facing Tennessee and Georgia wrestler-promoter Buddy Fuller. Or, he could choose to head over to the Olympia to see: Dick the Bruiser challenge for the WWA World Heavyweight title currently held by Jim Raschke, a highly decorated amateur wrestler who couldn't buy a cup of coffee in the pro ranks until he transformed himself into the nefarious Nazi Baron Von Raschke; Wilbur Snyder and his partner, former physical fitness instructor and 1960 Rookie of the Year Paul Christy defend the WWA World Tag Team title against villainous cowboys Blackjack Lanza and Blackjack Mulligan, managed by twenty-six-year-old "Pretty Boy" Bobby Heenan; and Big Bill Miller collide with Moose Cholak.

If it seems a little one-sided, that's because it was. As a member of the National Wrestling Alliance, Farhat had the ability to defend himself against the invasion by calling on other NWA members to send some of their big guns to help stack the card: Valentine was on loan from Texas promoters Fritz Von Erich and Paul Boesch, Johnson from San Francisco promoter Roy Shire, Mascaras and Blassie from Mike LeBell, Monsoon and Luke Graham from Vince McMahon (whose WWWF had recently rejoined the NWA), and of course Dory Funk as world champion booked by NWA president Sam Muchnick himself. To help add bang to his premiere Olympia show, Bruiser even booked himself to win the WWA World title from Von Raschke that night—but the 4,125 fans who filed into the Olympia didn't know that, and their number was more than doubled by the 8,748 who chose the established Cobo Arena brand instead. It's telling that Sheik himself did not appear in the ring on that first night of the war, and it's reasonable to assume he did so in order to devote his full and undivided attention to running this all-important show from backstage.

This talent-gathering strategy would become a regular one for The Sheik. He stacked his Cobo cards like never before, regularly booking twelve or even fourteen matches for an evening and drawing on a veritable who's who of major attractions from all over the country. It was a great time to be a fan of Big Time Wrestling, and Cobo was really rocking every other weekend—sometimes on consecutive weekends, as Farhat proceeded to throw everything he had at the invading force. During the war, Cobo became arguably the hottest ticket in wrestling, rivaling even Madison Square Garden in terms of star power up and down the card. There weren't a lot of things going right for citizens of Detroit at the time, but there was at least one if you were a wrestling fan.

Bruiser was not without resources, as he was backed by Verne Gagne's AWA out of Minneapolis, a much bigger outlaw promotion that had managed to (mostly) keep the peace with the NWA and ran in territories that were usually not contested by NWA members. Bruiser and Gagne went way back to their days working as top stars for Fred Kohler in

Chicago in the fifties, and at times the WWA would almost be run as a satellite promotion of the AWA. "For some reason, Bruiser and Gagne had it in their minds that they were gonna knock Dad out of the box," recalled Eddie Jr. "Well, excuse me, but you're not gonna do that, especially with a guy that was one of the hottest things going in the country!"

The following seven Cobo Arena cards were similarly opposed by WWA shows at the Olympia on the same night, into February of 1972. It was truly an all-out war unlike anything that had been seen in quite some time, with competing events happening on either end of town, and an embarrassment of riches for fans. And yet still, thanks in part to the steady flow of talent from other territories, The Sheik's Big Time Wrestling maintained a distinct lead in terms of drawing power, sometimes even doubling Bruiser's houses. The first time they even came close was on December 10, 1971, when Big Time Wrestling drew 4,336 for a Cobo show headlined by Bobo Brazil against Chris Tolos (John's brother) and The Sheik against Chief White Owl, while the WWA drew 4,198 for what was a much better card on paper, with Von Raschke defending the WWA title against Snyder, and The Blackjacks defending the tag title against Bruiser and Sailor Art Thomas.

And yet, for the most part, Sheik's houses continued to grow thanks to the stimulation brought on by competition. On February 5, 1972, he drew his first bona fide Cobo Arena sellout of the wrestling war, surpassing twelve thousand fans, dwarfing Bruiser's number—even though Olympia had a seating capacity that exceeded Cobo's by twenty-five percent. Following the trouncing, for the first time Bruiser decided *not* to run directly against the next Cobo show, but rather booked the Olympia for an unopposed weekend. He would still occasionally run directly against The Sheik—thirteen more times over the next two years—but it would no longer be a regular practice. The war was far from over, as Bruiser still had designs on the city, but he had decided to try a different approach to growing his audience.

The Sheik's first unopposed show of the war, on February 19, took things to another level, drawing 12,643 fans, filling Cobo Arena to its absolute capacity, with literal standing room only.[7] It was an all-time Cobo attendance record for wrestling and proof that the promotional battle was actually *increasing* interest in Big Time Wrestling, not diminishing it. It also had a lot to do with the staggering seventeen-match card Sheik and his booker Jack Cain put together, with Bobo Brazil defending the US title against Dingo the Sundowner, Bull Curry taking on Johnny Valentine, and appearances by the massive Ernie Ladd and an even more massive Shohei "Giant" Baba, number-one star of the Japanese Wrestling Association and someone Farhat would be doing a lot more business with in the future.

But the main reason for the colossal sellout was the one-night return of one of The Sheik's hottest rivalries, as former WWWF World Champion Bruno Sammartino had made his way to Cobo Arena for the first time in six years. Bruno had worked Cobo a few times during the early Jim Barnett–Johnny Doyle years before he was champion, and had even been brought in a couple of times by Farhat to defend the WWWF title there,[8] but this was the first (and only) time he would clash with The Sheik on The Sheik's home turf. No longer having the burden of defending the WWWF crown throughout the Northeast on a regular basis, Bruno was finally free (for the time being) to tour the country and the world, appearing in places that had previously seen him mainly in magazines. So, it was only fitting that he would come to Detroit to take on The Sheik, and their raucous one-time-only match lit up the city, ending in a double-disqualification that left both men's egos (though certainly not their foreheads) unscathed.

Nevertheless, Sammartino was less than enamored with his treatment by Farhat. He was already among those who didn't care for him professionally and personally. In addition to not enjoying working with him in the ring, it's even been alleged that, as an ethnic babyface who took pride in glorifying his Italian heritage and had felt the sting of anti-Italian prejudice, that Bruno found The Sheik's persona distasteful for denigrating and negatively stereotyping Arab and Muslim Americans. But when it came down to it, it was Farhat's notorious tightness with money that wound up sabotaging any return business and turned Sammartino off of working for him for good, as is remembered by Dave Burzynski: "Me and Bruno went to dinner that night. He always wanted to go to this great Chinese place, so we went there for dinner after the show, and we got to talking. He said, 'There's supposed to be a return bout in two weeks. Don't say anything, but I ain't showing up. I'm not coming here anymore.' And he told me Sheik had promised him two grand and gave him a check for $800. He didn't show up for that next show, and Sheik didn't know about it at all. In the dressing room it was like, where the hell's Bruno? And I knew, but I wasn't gonna say anything." To save face, and to prevent 9,243 fans from demanding a refund, it was announced that Sammartino's plane had been delayed, and Sheik instead wound up going to a rare one-hour time limit draw with Luis Martinez to try and make up for the disappointment.

It was a glaring example of how Farhat's cheapness could come back to bite him. He didn't always inspire loyalty, and this sometimes made it easier for people to choose to work for his competition. Following this debacle, Sammartino actually crossed lines and began taking dates with Dick the Bruiser's group over at the Olympia, coming in for several shows in 1973 and 1974. Beyond the AWA, Bruiser began to receive infusions of talent from the Rougeaus in the Quebec territory (themselves fighting a scorched-earth promotional war for Montreal) as well as from the Pittsburgh territory now run by Sammartino and his mentor Rudy Miller. Also sending talent to the Bruiser was the eccentric Dave McKigney, who had come to great fame in the 1950s wrestling his trained bear Terrible Ted throughout Canada, and had recently started up his own outlaw company, Big Bear Promotions, in opposition to the Tunneys in Ontario.

The Detroit war had put the NWA in a very tricky position and shed sunlight on some of the backroom politics and crisscrossed loyalties behind the scenes. It was very rare for such a bold, full-scale invasion by an outlaw promotion to be undertaken against an established NWA territory in those days. Although they had worked together over the years, neither Dick the Bruiser nor Verne Gagne were very fond of The Sheik on a personal level, and the feeling was mutual, which had surely only motivated them more to make their move. "If they had liked each other, Dick the Bruiser would've never come in to compete against The Sheik when he did," says photographer Brian Bukantis, who worked for both men at different points of the war and took over production of the *Body Press* in 1974 after Dave Burzynski hit the road as wrestling manager "Supermouth" Dave Drason. "They were both in the wrestling business, they both dealt with each other in previous encounters, but when Bruiser came in and tried to pull people away from The Sheik in Detroit, things really escalated."

Many NWA promoters were also not fans of The Sheik, including president Sam Muchnick, who didn't like The Sheik's violent and sensationalistic act, and had been keeping him out of his own St. Louis promotion for many years. In contrast, Muchnick had been using Dick the Bruiser on his shows, as well as other WWA talent, despite the fact that the WWA was an outlaw promotion—partly because he simply got along better with the Bruiser and respected his real-world sports background. In fact, in the first year of the Detroit war, Muchnick continued to book Dick the Bruiser at the Kiel Auditorium around a dozen times—while simultaneously being compelled to marshal the troops for Farhat at Cobo Arena as he ran *against* the Bruiser. It was a precarious and unsustainable situation, and finally by the fall of 1972, Muchnick was pressured into banning the Bruiser and other WWA talent from St. Louis, at least until the war was settled. It was another example of how Farhat's difficulty in making friends and playing the political game sometimes made things more complicated for him.

Nevertheless, the war was propelling Farhat to the best business he had ever done. Attendance at Cobo, and all throughout the Big Time circuit, was on fire. Creatively, the territory hit its stride in 1972, and that went way beyond just The Sheik as an attraction. To keep his heat going strong, Farhat finally lured the fearsome Pampero Firpo from Hawaii to be his regular tag team partner, forming quite the terrifying and chaotic duo. In another sign of wrestling's isolated nature at the time, Sheik and Firpo were in-ring allies in Big Time Wrestling while battling each other as enemies in Toronto, as The Sheik added the Wild Bull of the Pampas to his ever-growing unbeaten streak at Maple Leaf Gardens. Another strong heel on the rise was Killer Tim Brooks, a cigar-chewing Southern boy who had been broken into the business by his cousin, Waxahachie, Texas's own Dirty Dick Murdoch. Some, like Big Jim Lancaster, go so far as to say that Sheik himself doesn't really deserve the credit for lighting up business at the time: "The Sheik didn't pop the territory. There were two programs: Brooks and Tony Marino working together, and then the Kangaroos working with The Stomper and Ben Justice [for the World Tag Team title] were both happening at the same time, and both had great fan interest. Plus, Brazil had the US title at the time and was working with Johnny Valentine. I never did buy into the idea that The Sheik was the one that popped the territory."

Whatever the causes, The Sheik was living higher than ever. Although he was known to always go home to his family while working the Big Time Wrestling circuit, even if it meant a long drive back from Ohio or Indiana, usually after white-hot Cobo Arena shows, he would join some of his guys for a late dinner in downtown Detroit. His spot of choice

JOHN BRADFORD MCFARLIN

No, this is not a scene from Goodfellas. *It's Sheik and his much-needed bodyguard, police officer Mike Loren, arriving for a show.*

was the legendary Grecian Gardens in Greektown, a roughly four-block stretch on Monroe Street about half a mile from Cobo, where he could hold court and indulge in his beloved Greek food in his own private reserved room. Just a few blocks from there was the historic Sheraton-Cadillac Hotel, a classic skyscraper that had once been frequented by gangsters during Prohibition and was now the place where out-of-town talent would spend the night after the show, and where the parties often continued.

Some of the money was being invested back into the company, with improvements in production including the highly expensive purchase of a mobile TV production truck. An emerging technology at the time, and standard in TV production today, it was a first for a pro wrestling promotion at a time when most shows were either crudely produced or, more often, produced not in-house but by the local TV station crew. Capitalizing on his investment, Farhat began offering the services of the truck under the auspices of his World Wide Sports company beyond his own product, recording and broadcasting college and professional sports like football and basketball, as well as rock concerts for bands performing at Cobo Arena and elsewhere. By 1973, he began using the truck to produce his own TV product, allowing him to move away from studio wrestling and begin recording matches and promos live from Cobo Arena and other venues, to be broadcast later on his weekly TV programs. This practice was decades ahead of its time and foreshadowed what the WWF and WCW would start doing during the Monday Night Wars of the late 1990s. Bob Finnigan was the man in charge production-wise, and he took up more of the announcing duties until he stepped away from the company for a time, starting in 1972 in a failed attempt to start up a roller derby promotion.

The TV presence of Big Time Wrestling in 1972 was the picture of a wrestling company on the rise. In addition to his main weekly show, Sheik added a second weekly show, *World Wide Wrestling*. This maneuver allowed his programming to run on two different stations in the same market, which is what he did in Detroit, running one on WXON Channel 20 on Thursday and Saturday nights, and the other on WKBD Channel 50 on Saturday mornings. The new program first featured Finnigan as host commentator, followed by former ring announcer Chuck Allen, a stocky, genial, and tuxedoed gentleman who looked as if he were put on the Earth to be harassed by angry, shouting wrestlers. Farhat's shows aired on five other TV stations throughout the state of Michigan, as well as ten in Ohio, two in West Virginia, and two in Indiana, including one right in Indianapolis, in retaliation against the Bruiser. With a bold eye toward expansion, he began placing his programming on stations in farther-flung markets where he wasn't even running live events, such as Phoenix, Arizona; Honolulu, Hawaii; and St. Louis, Missouri.

As the unflappable announcer, Bob Finnigan put up with all The Sheik's shenanigans. Behind the scenes, Finnigan was his trusted producer and director.

In his boldest move yet, he even had TV placed in Hartford, Connecticut, in the heart of WWWF territory. This reportedly infuriated Vince McMahon, who himself was having difficulties getting TV clearances in that state, leading Sam Muchnick to intervene and put the kibosh on Sheik's Nutmeg State aspirations in relatively short order. Nevertheless, some have pointed to the Connecticut TV debacle as a source of ongoing heat between The Sheik and the McMahons, partly explaining why he rarely worked for them ever again and also why McMahon would in later years look to annex his NWA partner's territory. Sheik and McMahon also further locked horns at the end of 1972, when a brand-new startup in the emerging realm of cable television, Home Box Office, was on the lookout for some wrestling content to help fill its programming slate. Naturally, McMahon's wrestling from Madison Square Garden was a front-runner, but Finnigan reportedly made a strong effort to pitch HBO on using Big Time Wrestling from Cobo Arena. His negotiations were sabotaged by his own boss when Farhat balked at the steep price HBO was asking, and the WWWF wound up getting the deal, becoming the first regional wrestling group to be broadcast nationally on cable TV.[9]

And it wasn't just in the area of TV that Farhat was ahead of his time. During this boom era, World Wide Sports further diversified into other businesses, including a record label and their own recording studio. In addition to allowing them to produce their own recordings, it gave an opportunity for Bob Finnigan to indulge his rock and country music aspirations,[10] just as it did for Eddie Jr., who in those days was even more interested in music than he was in wrestling. Taking a hint from major sports franchises, Big Time Wrestling began marketing felt pennants featuring the names and likenesses of the promotion's top stars—more than a decade before the WWF would blow the wrestling merchandise business wide open. Before long, Farhat had purchased his own private stretch limousine, with interior walnut wood paneling and exterior trim, and even boasting a telephone—an unheard-of car accessory at the time. This was in addition to his already well-established love of luxury automobiles, with a particular affinity for black Cadillacs and Lincoln Continentals.

But no status symbol would equal the grand structure the Farhats had custom-built in Williamston at 2335 North Williamston Road. Sitting on a gorgeous twenty-six-acre plot of land adjacent to Deer Creek, the four-story structure was designed by noted Michigan architect Howard DeWolfe and constructed at a cost of $438,000 (at a time when the average price of a home in the United States was about $27,000). In addition to Ed, Joyce, Eddie Jr., Tommy, and Paul, Joyce moved her parents in—which was not a problem considering the house boasted eight bedrooms, each with its own deluxe sitting room. Ed and Joyce's primary bedroom featured a Japanese-style stepdown bathtub recessed into the floor. So big was the house, in fact, that it was common for Sheik to put up many of his wrestling talents who were coming in from out of town—sometimes even on a long-term basis, as happened with Greg Valentine, among others. An indoor Olympic-sized swimming pool was situated directly above a gymnasium, with a glass ceiling allowing those working out to see people swimming above them. There was a full-scale library, an elaborate cooking area, and a four-car garage on one side. Containing close to forty rooms in total, the angular, almost Frank Lloyd Wright–esque building was surrounded by beautiful gardens.[11]

"He had all these Arabic statues all over," remembers Fred Curry, who spent many a time there. "I remember Mark Lewin coming there, and he would put a bandage on the heads of all the statues. The place was so intimidating! He had air-conditioning units outside that were bigger than the average person's living room. They had a big waiting room, and you'd have people from the church coming in for donations, and Joyce would be sitting at a big, long table. They really played the part." The sumptuous estate became the new site of regular Farhat family gatherings, fundraisers, and soirees—all bought and paid for by the dollars and cents of those same Big Time Wrestling fans who viciously screamed for The Sheik's blood each and every week, never realizing that he was the man behind the whole show.

While the money rolled in, the war continued. On April 22, 1972, Dick the Bruiser scored his first head-to-head victory, drawing 8,692 fans to the Olympia for a card headlined by Bobby Heenan's Blackjacks defending the WWA World Tag Team title against Bruiser and Wilbur Snyder, and Sailor Art Thomas defending the WWA World Heavyweight title against Ricky Cortez, a Michigan mainstay and former Big Time Wrestling regular who had been one of the first talents to defect to the other side.[12] Meanwhile across town, Big Time Wrestling drew 8,116 fans for a card that featured The Sheik taking on The Stomper, US Champion Bobo Brazil and Wild Bull Curry against world tag champs The Fabulous Kangaroos, and Johnny Valentine battling the ever-popular Cowboy

Bob Ellis, a former army paratrooper and the inventor of the bulldog headlock, who would later defect to the WWA in the coming months. It was the only time that Bruiser would outdraw The Sheik in direct competition in Detroit, although he also turned heads on December 2, when he drew 10,252—his highest number ever at the Olympia—for a titanic main event in which he reunited with his iconic longtime partner "The Crusher" Reggie Lisowski to take on The Blackjacks. The previous week at Cobo, Sheik's troupe had drawn only 6,431, so obviously many fans were saving up their dough to check out Crusher and Bruiser back in action.

Nevertheless, for the most part, The Sheik was maintaining a steady advantage in his hometown, and it appears once he got more comfortable in this position, he started to venture back out on the road more frequently again. On February 8, 1972, he worked Florida for the first time in a dozen years, taking on one of Eddie Graham's most beloved performers, Mr. Wrestling II—a gifted grappler and journeyman competitor who had previously been plain old Johnny Walker, the "Rubber Man," until donning a mask and a mysterious persona had turned his career around and made him a Southeastern icon. Understandably, traveling to Hawaii became a regular thing for The Sheik about every other month or so, and he often brought some of his best friends and trusted employees with him to enjoy the sun and work as either his tag team partner or opponent, including Bull Curry, Bobo Brazil, and Sweet Daddy Siki.[13] He was even given a short run with the Hawaii Heavyweight title, capturing it from Curry in October and holding it three months before losing it in the ring to Hawaii promoter Ed Francis himself.

The Sheik also returned to the Montreal Forum for the first time in four years, and in the process came across the man who would eventually replace Abdullah Farouk as his full-time manager. Eddy "The Brain" Creatchman ran a Quebec scrapyard with his wife, Goldie, and spent his spare time being the most despised wrestling manager in Canada. He had started out in the 1940s and '50s as a wrestler and a referee, but it was when he made the switch to a managerial role in the 1960s that he really hit his stride. Donning giant sunglasses, chomping a huge cigar, and sporting a tackily enormous Star of David around his neck, he played up his Jewish heritage and played into anti-Semitic stereotypes, even taking on an exaggerated combination of a Yiddish and Israeli accent (which would sometimes go in and out). Playing the brash, untrustworthy, greedy Jew to the hilt would've been enough, but paired with his ability to cut loud, grating promos, it gave him the power to turn an otherwise docile crowd into a frothing mass of raging humanity with murder in their eyes.

During his four Montreal appearances in '72, promoter Johnny Rougeau paired The Sheik with Creatchman as his mouthpiece, and it was instantly a heat-seeking dream come true. In one of those appearances, Sheik captured Montreal's International Heavyweight Championship for the second time from charismatic Portuguese superstar Carlos Rocha, raising the ire of Quebecois fans even further. With Creatchman the traitorous Jew gleefully in the corner of the purported Muslim Arab Sheik at a time when Israeli-Palestinian relations were at their volatile worst (the infamous Munich Massacre was just a few months away), it ensured that the duo would be scorned by Jew and Gentile alike. In one of those appearances, Creatchman so fired up the crowd that a riot broke out in the Forum. Other men might have been repulsed by the turn of events—but Farhat was impressed. By the time he lost the International title to Jacques Rougeau Sr. in July, his final Montreal appearance of 1972,[14] he had gotten a solid idea of how well he worked with Creatchman—and how much money they could potentially make together.

He continued his loyal relationship with the Funks, making special appearances in Amarillo and Lubbock—the two Texas towns that had helped make him into a headliner—in August and October, including an encounter with a twenty-eight-year-old Terry Funk, who was just three years away from earning the accolade then held by his older brother, Dory, the NWA World Heavyweight Championship.[15] It would be just the first of many epic in-ring wars between the two over the years. Although he never did return to New York, he did return to Boston, where the memories of the gangbuster business he and Sammartino had done for WWWF promoter and McMahon surrogate Abe Ford still burned bright and apparently overrode any bad blood that may have existed. The day before Halloween, The Sheik made his Beantown reemergence with a match against McMahon's number-two babyface, Chief Jay Strongbow—who was really Joe Scarpa from Nutley, New Jersey, an Italian-American masquerading as a Native American, as many white wrestlers with dark skin and big noses did in those days. Sheik was brought back for the next two Boston Garden shows, for his only two shots against WWWF World Heavyweight Champion Pedro Morales.[16]

The Sheik's fame had spread far beyond North America by this point, and in September 1972 he ventured to a foreign continent for the very first time, setting foot in the island nation of Japan and kicking off an ongoing relationship that opened up a whole new chapter for his career and exposed him to a new audience that would elevate him to near godlike status over the course of the next decade. (For an in-depth exploration of The Sheik in Japan, see the next chapter.)

Far from withering on the vine in the face of Dick the Bruiser's blistering assault, Big Time Wrestling rose to its greatest successes in 1973, which turned out to be the most lucrative year in the history of the promotion. Ed Farhat personally declared over four hundred grand in taxable income that year, and it's believed he made a whole lot more than that. Longtime Detroit fans still talk about the incredible string of sell-outs from December 1972 through April 1973, when Big Time Wrestling filled Cobo Arena to its absolute capacity for five consecutive shows, and six out of seven held during that period. This box office performance blew away the likes of Pink Floyd, Neil Young, Alice Cooper, The Temptations, and Santana, all of whom appeared at Cobo during those months—and it sure as hell put to shame the Detroit Pistons, then plummeting to a .488 season percentage that saw them finish out of the NBA playoffs. Big Time Wrestling was the hottest ticket in the Motor City, and The Sheik was the undisputed King of Cobo.

Part of how he maintained fan interest was through a booking practice known as hot-shotting. He switched the United States title at three straight Cobo Arena shows, first taking it back from Bobo Brazil at the December 30 card (with former heavyweight boxing champion and Detroit legend Joe Louis as special referee), then losing it to Bobo in a steel cage match at the January 13 event, and then finally snagging it once again from Brazil exactly two weeks later. Most promoters shied away from frequent major title changes in those days, fearing it would desensitize fans and devalue the belt—but these were unusual times, and Farhat was willing to pull out all the stops to maintain his advantage and put on a show that kept the name of Dick the Bruiser as far from the minds of fans as possible. On the February 24, 1973, show, Sam Muchnick sent in Dory Funk Jr. to defend the NWA World title against The Sheik, which drew 12,437 fans—while across town, the Bruiser could barely manage half that amount, bringing in just 6,569 fans, despite a stacked card that included Jimmy Valiant vs. Art Thomas, Wilbur Snyder vs. Blackjack Lanza, Cowboy Bob Ellis vs. Blackjack Mulligan, and topped by Baron Von Raschke and Ernie Ladd winning the WWA World Tag Team title from Bruiser and Crusher.

This trend would continue throughout the year, with Bruiser's numbers dwindling while The Sheik's held steady, even if there were no more sellouts. Bruiser's problems in Detroit were compounded by the fact that the much older Olympia Stadium happened to be in a rougher part of town—which was saying a lot for Detroit in the 1970s. The threat of

DAVE BURZYNSKI

Cobo Arena, January 27, 1973: The Sheik on his way to defeating Bobo Brazil for his fourth United States Heavyweight title, just two weeks after losing it to Bobo in a steel cage match. It is the sixth of nine times they would pass the title between them.

crime and harassment of patrons, including rampant car theft, were real concerns and had been driving fans away from all Olympia events. Even the Detroit Red Wings hockey team had to take security measures to reassure worried fans.

It was during the unprecedented sellout streak that The Sheik would lose the services of his longtime manager Abdullah Farouk, aka Ernie Roth. Over their years of making trips together to the Northeast, Roth had managed to make a lot of connections and was well-liked by Vince McMahon, who immediately recognized his uncanny talent and had even used him a bit independently of The Sheik, including a 1971 run managing Blackjack Mulligan. By 1973, McMahon was in the midst of overhauling his rogue's gallery of heel WWWF managers. Wild Red Berry, the former nine-time world light-heavyweight champion who had reinvented himself as the industry's pioneering know-it-all mouthpiece, had tragically lost his priceless gift of gab due to a stroke suffered the year before; Bobby Davis, McMahon's other groundbreaking manager, had left the business after losing his promotional war to The Sheik in 1969; the rotund yet otherwise unremarkable Tony Angelo had migrated to Pedro Martinez's NWF. In their place, McMahon had promoted Louis Albano, a protégé of WWWF president Willie Gilzenberg and formerly one half of the nefarious Sicilians tag team, to the role of fast-talking Captain Lou Albano.[17] He also had his eye on Fred Blassie, winding down his in-ring career due to crippling knee injuries, as a potential full-time manager—and would acquire his services the following year. And to complete his unholy trinity, he hoped to add Ernie Roth full-time.

To sweeten the deal, McMahon even offered Roth and "Beautiful" Bobby Harmon, Roth's partner in both life and business, promotional control of several WWWF venues in Massachusetts, including, most importantly of all, the Boston Garden, where the old regime of Abe Ford and Tony Santos was on its way out. McMahon's plan was to have Roth and Harmon run the Garden with the help of his own son, Vincent Kennedy McMahon, who was coming up in the business at the time, running some towns in Maine while also being the lead WWWF TV announcer. It was an offer Roth simply could not pass up—all that remained was telling The Sheik. "Dad was in the office one day,"

The treacherous Abdullah Farouk was never above passing an illegal foreign object to his man to help him achieve victory—one of the time-honored duties of any nefarious pro wrestling manager.

remembered Eddie Jr., "and Ernie came up to him and said, 'Look, I've got something to talk to you about. I have a chance to go work for Vinny Sr. He wants me to come back to New York to manage a couple of guys. What do you think, do you need me here?' Dad said, 'I will always need you, but I've got Eddy Creatchman and different people I can bring in; it's not a big deal. If you could go to the New York territory and make some good money, God bless you, do it.' Vince McMahon Sr. and my father had been very close friends, and, as a matter of fact, Dad knew Ernie was coming to see him, because Vinny Sr. had already asked him if he could take Ernie for a while, and Dad had already told him yes. But Ernie didn't know this."

McMahon officially brought in Roth for the April 30, 1973, show at Madison Square Garden, where he managed Don Leo Jonathan against WWWF World Champion Pedro Morales. Trading in his fez for a turban and adding some colorful scarves, he rechristened himself "The Grand Wizard of Wrestling" (or just the Grand Wizard for short).[18] He would return to Big Time Wrestling from time to time as Abdullah Farouk, but that was the end of his full-time involvement with The Sheik. Remembering those raucous nights at the Montreal Forum, The Sheik indeed tapped Eddy Creatchman to be Farouk's replacement, and Creatchman would remain at The Sheik's side for the remainder of the Big Time Wrestling years. Louder and much more grating than the snide and eloquent Roth, Creatchman added a new dimension to The Sheik's act, drawing even more heat than before, if that can be imagined. Playing off real-life hostilities in the Middle East, Creatchman claimed to have changed his citizenship from Israeli to Palestinian, generating a kind of loathing that was similar to that of Saul Weingeroff, the Jewish manager of the 1960s who had managed the Von Brauners, a villainous tag team with Nazi German personas.

With Creatchman as his new manager and the United States title once again in his possession, The Sheik led an ever-changing troupe of Big Time Wrestling talent in a full-court press to drive Dick the Bruiser and the WWA out of Detroit. He brought in Chief Jay Strongbow, on fire thanks to his mega-push in the WWWF; as well as the eccentric and outspoken Dr. Jerry Graham, down on his luck and far past his prime, but still able to provoke a crowd and be carried to a decent mid-card match with the right tag team partner; there was three-hundred-pound Peggy Jones, whom Lou Klein had discovered working the counter at an Allen Park bowling alley and brought into the business as Heather Feather, making her name taking on male wrestlers in an attempt to cash in on the growing feminism movement; Farhat even transformed his gardener, John Madincia, into the menacing J.B. Psycho (he had previously held the World Tag Team title as one half of the Skull Brothers tag team).

Big Time Wrestling's TV presence was expanding, with new stations added in Alaska, upstate New York, and western Pennsylvania. Farhat even got his show back on CKLW in Windsor, the same station Bruiser was simultaneously using. To capitalize on the valuable TV exposure, Farhat took a real shot at territorial expansion, eyeing a couple of areas that were considered open because they did not have a local NWA promotion. One of these was Arizona, where longtime promoter Rod Fenton had recently passed away. Farhat ran a series of live events in Phoenix in 1973, bringing along other talent like Bobo Brazil, Luis Martinez, and Killer Brooks, and even booking a few NWA World title defenses from Dory Funk Jr. to help pique interest. He booked a tour of Alaska—about as far as one could get from Detroit without landing in the ocean—putting on shows in the towns where workers were putting in the Alaskan oil pipeline. These were bold moves and indicated the level of Farhat's success and his stature within the NWA hierarchy, no matter how some of his fellow members might begrudge him.

However, the logistics were also very challenging, and it was quite an expensive undertaking, which is partly why the experiment was eventually aborted and Farhat chose to focus his efforts on strengthening the territory he already controlled. After all, he still had a war to win. The hot-shotting of the United States title continued in 1973, with Sheik dropping the belt to Johnny Valentine on July 7, only to win it back in a rematch two weeks later at Cobo, not-so-coincidentally on the first night Bruiser had counter-booked the Olympia against him in four months. He continued to sustain his heat by hooking up with Tim Brooks, another heel on the rise in Big Time Wrestling. Just as he had done in the past with Wild Bull Curry and Pampero Firpo, Sheik recognized Brooks's growing prominence and latched onto it, feeding off it for a time in order to keep his act fresh and using him to take the pinfall if needed. Their first match as a tag team took place in February 19 at the Hara Arena in Dayton, where they took on Bobo Brazil and Tony Marino. "I learned how to be a heel by watching him and listening to him," Brooks remembered in his final interview, in 2019. "I can say to this day there's not a wrestler in this business that can go out there and get heat with the people the way The Sheik did. He could get more heat walking from the dressing room into the ring than most wrestlers could get in a thirty-minute match. Sheik could sometimes have those sumbitches fighting and rioting before he ever got to the ring! He made me his tag team partner a lot, to do what needed to be done. I wrestled with him in a lot of cage matches in Cobo, and in Cleveland in the hockey arena on Euclid Street—some big, big matches there."

As part of the 1973 WFIA Convention, held in Detroit, eighteen-year-old chairman Dave Burzynski presents an uncharacteristically docile Sheik with the Wrestler of the Year trophy. "He had no problem taking the photo because he trusted that it would never be shown," says Dave. "Until now."

Up in Toronto, Sheik's unbeaten streak at the Maple Leaf Gardens continued through '73. Added to the list of those who came up short against the Arabian madman was Chief Jay Strongbow, as well as a colossal newcomer from rural France who tipped the scales at over four hundred pounds and stood about seven feet in height, although in the typically grandiose world of wrestling, he was billed as seven-foot-four. Andre Rousimoff had been turning heads first in Europe, then Canada, then Japan, until in early 1973 he came under the guidance of Vince McMahon, who became his personal booking agent. By the time Frank Tunney brought him into Toronto to face off with The Sheik for the first time on December 30, 1973, Andre the Giant[19] was well on the way to becoming professional wrestling's hottest mainstream crossover star since Gorgeous George. That first encounter ended in a disappointing double-disqualification in under three minutes—such let-down finishes were becoming commonplace in Sheik main events at the Maple Leaf Gardens. It also happened to be the first time Andre had failed to win a singles match anywhere in over a year. Andre also failed to beat The Sheik in a couple of return matches in early 1974, including one in which Sheik actually defeated Andre by count out after throwing fire in his face. When it came to Farhat's booking practices in Toronto, truly no one was above doing the job, and many point to the Andre defeat as the point when fans there started losing their patience with The Sheik's seeming invulnerability, which had stretched the limits of credibility.

While still battling his own promotional rival, The Sheik found himself pulled into another epic territorial dust-up, this one taking place down in Georgia and involving an important figure from his past. After a decade in exile Down Under, during which he turned his World Championship Wrestling promotion into the hottest wrestling company in the history of Australia, Jim Barnett had returned to the United States to take the reins for Paul Jones, the aging promoter who had run Georgia Championship Wrestling for thirty years. Following the shocking death in the ring of Jones's booker and business partner Ray Gunkel in the summer of 1972, Gunkel's beautiful widow, Ann, was further shocked to discover that her husband's shares in the company would not be granted to her after his passing. Not taking the maneuver lying down, she promptly started up her own Georgia promotion, All-South Wrestling Alliance, in opposition to Jones's established NWA group. But Jones couldn't have found a keener wrestling mind than Barnett to help weather the storm. First, he helped get GCW on WTCG-TV, the local Atlanta channel owned and operated by advertising and radio entrepreneur Robert "Ted" Turner, which in a few years would turn into the nationally broadcast cable powerhouse known as TBS. Next, he set out to bring in the hottest talent the NWA had to offer in order to run Ann Gunkel and All-South out of town.

Naturally, high on Barnett's wish list was the man to whom he had sold Big Time Wrestling. The two men had always had a strong working relationship, plus Farhat had never failed to make any of his installment payments on time, which was something Barnett always respected him for. Farhat most certainly knew the desperation of defending one's home turf against an outlaw invader, and so it wasn't a difficult deal to make. On two consecutive Friday night shows in May 1973 at the Omni, Jones and Barnett's primary venue and the so-called "Madison Square Garden of the South," The Sheik and Bobo Brazil descended on Atlanta to wreak their customary havoc, with Sheik winning the first match and then agreeing to an actual pinfall loss to his most trusted rival in the following one, blessing the Omni crowd with a true rarity. The Sheik even made appearances in secondary towns on the GCW circuit like Columbus and Macon, before returning to the Omni one more time on December 7 for a main event pitting him and Robert Fuller, the popular twenty-five-year-old grandson of Alabama and Tennessee promoter Roy Welch, against the duo of "Crazy" Luke Graham and Cowboy Bill Watts, a three-hundred-pound Oklahoman who had given up a contract with the Minnesota Vikings for a career in pro wrestling (which turned out to be a pretty decent decision).[20]

The Sheik was playing his part in helping Paul Jones and Jim Barnett win their promotional war; now all that remained was for him to win his own. There would be one brief detour before that happened, and a historic one in that it would be the last time Farhat would go to work for Vince McMahon, with whom he had spent so much of his early career—and once again, it involved the WWWF World Heavyweight Championship. By 1973, the Pittsburgh territory that had once been run by Bruno Sammartino and Rudy Miller as a satellite promotion of the WWWF had been formally taken over by McMahon. After nearly three years of Pedro Morales as his champion, McMahon had decided to get the belt back on the tried-and-true Bruno. On November 29, he booked Morales to defend the crown against The Sheik at the Pittsburgh Civic Arena, but at the last minute, for reasons unknown, Sheik's opponent was switched to Dominic Denucci, while Morales was sent sixty miles north to a high school gymnasium in New Castle, Pennsylvania, to defend against Fred Blassie instead. It would be Morales's last successful title defense, as two nights later he would lose the championship in the Philadelphia Arena to Stan Stasiak, the Polish-Canadian master of the heart punch, whose entire role was to serve as a brief transitional heel champion and lose the title to Sammartino—which he dutifully did nine days later in Madison Square Garden. Later that week, on December 14, The Sheik returned to Pittsburgh to face Sammartino, who took to the ring in his hometown to make the first defense of his newly regained prize. Sheik got himself disqualified that night in typical fashion, thus ending his in-ring saga with the Living Legend for good and all.[21]

What also had to make things awkward for Farhat was that Sammartino was still taking dates with Dick the Bruiser, who was by that point limping toward the finish line of the once-close Detroit promotional war. Running fewer and fewer Olympia cards in front of smaller and smaller audiences, he finally made the tough decision to extend an olive branch to Farhat. With Big Time Wrestling back on the air in Windsor and beating the WWA in the ratings, and threatening to do so even in Bruiser's Indianapolis stronghold, it was time to cut bait before things got even worse. "Dad got a phone call one day and it was from Bruiser," Eddie Jr. recalled. "He said, 'Sheik, I think we need to talk. I'll get out of Detroit if you pull your TV out of Indianapolis.' Dad said, 'Sure, but you gotta be a man of your word.' And he did, so we did."

On March 30, 1974, Farhat brought Big Time Wrestling to the Olympia Stadium, fulfilling an obligation originally made by Dick the Bruiser, who had backed out as part of his withdrawal from the Motor City. It represented the official end of the three-and-a-half-year Sheik-Bruiser promotional war. That night, Sheik defended the United States title against the Mighty Igor before 10,603 fans—a larger crowd than Dick the Bruiser had been able to draw in that building the entire time he was running it. Even though he had never been able to take a threatening lead in his battle against The Sheik, what characterized Bruiser's effort was the sheer tenacity of it—he stuck with it longer than nearly any other outlaw promotion ever had anywhere in North America, and that was impressive in and of itself.

The smoke had cleared, and Farhat was still standing. His company had not only survived, but thrived, and was positioned at the top of the industry heap. But what Farhat or anyone else couldn't have known on that triumphant Saturday night at the Olympia, was that he would never again experience that level of success—the rivalry had taken his business to unprecedented heights, but now that he had won, what loomed ahead was a slow and steady decline. "After the war was over was when Detroit started going down," explains Dave Meltzer. "Kind of like what happened to the WWF after WCW went down. You get this competition that drives business to record levels, and then when somebody loses, people just get tired of wrestling." The Sheik had reached the mountaintop—now there was nowhere to go but down.

CHAPTER 12

NIHON NO SHEIKU

"If you're a legend in Japan, you stay a legend. And he was."
—DAVE MELTZER

Although developed in the United States, the popularity of professional wrestling was far from confined to the US, or even to North America. In fact, during the second half of the twentieth century, a case could convincingly be made that its American popularity was not only rivaled but exceeded by the cultural cachet it attained in Japan. Ironically, the rise of professional wrestling in Japan coincided with the end of an existential military struggle between the two nations and in a way was directly linked to it. Just as the Second World War had changed the lives of young men like Edward Farhat who were suddenly thrust into a foreign land with rifles in their hands, so, too, did it change the cultural landscape of those foreign lands. And with those changes came opportunities—some of which would arrive much later, as they did over a quarter of a century after the end of the war, when Farhat, now draped in the garb of the vicious Sheik, would find a whole new avenue for success in the Land of the Rising Sun, as many of his North American colleagues were also doing.

If The Sheik was a superstar in the United States and Canada, then the status he would attain in Japan must be described in even more superlative terms—it was there that he became an icon, an almost supernatural force, an evil god of destruction about whom fans had heard whispered tales from across the sea; whose very name and image would take on a power all their own, terrifying children in their beds at night

and causing masses of humanity to part in horror at his very presence. It was a place that provided a platform for him to take his chaos to a whole new level, just at a time when his profile and powers in the West were beginning to wane; it can be argued that just as The Sheik was becoming a major draw in Japan, he was becoming less relevant in North America. In this way, his Japanese exploits helped extend his career as a major player and added strength and momentum to his international legend.

When the forces of the Empire of Japan surrendered to the Allied powers at the end of the summer of 1945, it marked the beginning of a seven-year occupation by American forces. During that time, Americans brought with them more than economic support and food—they also brought *America*, in the form of the latest clothing and hairstyles, entertainment churned out by the Hollywood dream factory, the dulcet tones of Frank Sinatra, Doris Day, and Bing Crosby. There were also American sports, like baseball, which became a cultural obsession in Japan that continues to this day. Straddling the fence between entertainment and sport (although the Japanese approach would always favor the latter) was professional wrestling, which was then experiencing a major boom in America thanks to the advent of television. Already enamored of combat sports and kabuki theatre, it was an easy sell for the Japanese people, who phoneticized it as puroresuringu, or puroresu for short.

In the early 1950s, puroresu got its patron saint thanks to the rise of Mitsuhiro Momota, who had been born Kim Sin-Rak in Japanese Korea but changed his name to avoid discrimination after being adopted by a Japanese sumo trainer-promoter. Training as a sumo wrestler himself, he took on the name Rikidozan ("rugged mountain road"), and he kept that name when he transitioned into the ranks of Japan's burgeoning pro wrestling industry. In short order, he achieved enormous mainstream celebrity status in that country, helped by the explosion of television that had taken place there a few years after it had in America. He used that status to found the Japanese Wrestling Association and built much of his success on the premise of the national babyface taking on dastardly Western heel invaders—a reflection of some of the bitterness engendered by the end of the war and the prolonged occupation.

From the start, the prosperity of the Japanese wrestling business was built in large part on the recruitment of North American talent. Among the first to benefit from this turn of events were Ben and Mike Sharpe, a legit brother tag team from Hamilton, Ontario, that parlayed success in Joe Malcewicz's San Francisco territory into a series of trips across the Pacific; as well as major American performers like NWA World Heavyweight Champion Lou Thesz, "Classy" Freddie Blassie, and Dick "The Destroyer" Beyer, all of whom battled Rikidozan in historic encounters that drew Japanese television ratings figures that dwarf Super Bowl numbers and remain among the highest-rated TV programs in world history. In addition to often (but not always) being portrayed as the bad guys, the Caucasian gaijin performers who were sought after by Japanese promoters usually had qualities that were perceived as alien or other to Japanese viewers—whether it was the bleached-blond hair and bombastic promos of wrestlers like Blassie, the towering physiques of wrestlers like the Sharpes, or the unorthodox ring attire of wrestlers like the masked Destroyer, they brought a color and exoticism with them that made them stand out distinctly from native Japanese competitors, and they were often viewed as stereotypically "American" (even if the wrestlers themselves sometimes were not).

In several ways, The Sheik was an anomaly in Japanese wrestling. Although he was in reality an American wrestler, he was never presented as such, not even in his own country—so there was an extra layer of otherness to him that fascinated Japanese fans, among whom there was an even greater level of suspension of disbelief than their American counterparts. Also, Japanese pro wrestling often tended to eschew the theatrics and histrionics of the American product, focusing on the sports-like element and a type of performance that strove for reality, with the sacredness of kayfabe at a very high premium. The technical wrestling style was prized above all else, which made The Sheik—a performer who threw fire, stabbed people with sharp objects, and whose main offenses often consisted of biting, gouging, kicking, and punching—stand out all the more. He was already pretty unusual on the American pro wrestling scene, but in the world of puroresu, he was like someone from another planet or another realm of existence, which only further enhanced his strange appeal. It was not just that Japanese promoters and fans were willing to overlook his lack of scientific grappling technique and his bizarre rituals and mannerisms; those were the very things that put him in such high demand. "The Sheik was a very unique kind of attraction," explains Japanese wrestling historian Fumi Saito, who grew up as one of those scared kids. "It's hard to compare him to anybody. He seemed like the biggest guy though he wasn't that big or tall. But that crazy look in his eyes. He was very, very special."

Just as happened in his native land, The Sheik became known to wrestling fans in Japan first from magazines—they had seen his crimson-covered visage on the covers of publications for years. The most prominent wrestling magazine in Japan, *Gong*, had started up publication in 1968, at the height of Sheik's superstardom in the US, and The Sheik was one of the few foreign wrestlers to be featured prominently even without ever having appeared there. Meanwhile, Farhat had been taking dates for years for Hawaii's 50th State Big Time Wrestling and Los Angeles's Hollywood Wrestling, both of which were common stopovers for wrestlers going to and from Japan and both companies that had strong contacts in the puroresu business. The LA office in particular had Masaru "Charlie" Iwamoto, a Hawaiian of Japanese descent who had in the years after World War II, to capitalize on anti-Japanese sentiment, taken on the devious persona of Mr. Moto, based on the fictional 1930s secret agent of pulp novels and a series of films starring Peter Lorre. In addition to wrestling, among Moto's other roles was helping American performers get booked in Japan, and it's believed he may have helped The Sheik make his initial contact with the JWA.

But by 1971, the JWA was in ruins. The great Rikidozan had been murdered in December 1963 by a yakuza gangster wielding a knife soaked in pig urine (the motive is still not proven to this day, but the killing may have been either due to a nightclub altercation or retaliation for shoot-wrestling an opponent in the ring). The company's two top stars in the post-Rikidozan era were in the midst of a power struggle that would soon lead both to leave. One was Shohei "Giant" Baba, a nearly-seven-foot-tall former standout pitcher for the Yomiuri Giants who suffered from the same form of gigantism that afflicted Andre the Giant, but had translated it into pro wrestling success after coming under the wing of Rikidozan in 1960 and experiencing breakout stardom in both Japan and the US thanks to his incredible size.[1] The other was Kanji Inoki, the son of an affluent politician, and an overachieving high school athlete who had been living in Brazil when he encountered Rikidozan on a South American tour and came under his tutelage; Inoki was already a star-struck wrestling fan, so making the trip back to Japan to join Rikidozan's dojo was an easy one—as was taking on the first name Antonio, in honor of his idol, Argentinian legend Antonino Rocca.

Originally, Farhat had been scheduled to make his Japanese wrestling debut in September 1971, following his series of appearances in Hawaii and the Los Angeles Coliseum Supershow that summer, but a combination of an injury and the disarray within the JWA at the time put those plans on hold. Finally, one year later, with both Giant Baba and Antonio Inoki gone to start their own independent wrestling companies, The Sheik made his initial appearance in the Land of the Rising Sun—a two-night engagement for the JWA on September 6 and 7, 1972. Typically, foreign wrestlers were brought in for extended tours that covered several weeks, in part to make the most of the extensive travel time to get there and back; but as the owner of his own wrestling promotion in the States, Farhat was not eager to be gone for long, and the JWA was willing to accommodate his schedule in order to finally procure the services of the mysterious and horrifying Sheik.

The two bookings amounted to a back-and-forth with the JWA's top remaining drawing card, Seiji Sakaguchi, who had been added to The Sheik's undefeated streak at the Maple Leaf Gardens three years earlier. This time, Sakaguchi was a much bigger star and on his home turf, holding the United National Championship, a title shared by the JWA and Hollywood Wrestling and defended on both sides of the Pacific. On the first night, before more than six thousand fans at Denen Coliseum, a tennis venue in Tokyo, The Sheik captured the United National title in a three-fall match that lasted less than fifteen minutes. "It was his first night!" marvels Saito. "He won the title in his very first appearance, [and] he was already forty-six. He already had almost twenty-five years on him, he was kind of an old-looking guy . . . but he was a genuinely scary wrestler." The very next night, in the Osaka Prefectural Gymnasium, he lost the title right back to Sakaguchi in two straight falls and just seven and a half minutes of action. Saito was a kid watching on TV from home: "In those days titles really mattered. The previous night Sheik had won in three falls. This time, in the first fall, Sheik got disqualified in four minutes; and three minutes into the second fall, he was suplexed into the ring and Sakaguchi pinned The Sheik, one-two-three. He almost never did that. It's still kind of hard to believe, it's almost surreal."

Clearly, this was a different environment, where Sheik didn't have the kind of political power he did in the States. He also had to respect the pecking order, and as an outsider, a villainous foreign wrestler, he was going to be asked to lose to the popular Japanese hero. Nevertheless, both matches from his initial Japanese appearance were televised, and millions of fans all over the country got to see The Sheik wrestle on their own soil for the first time. But that would be The Sheik's only appearance for the once-dominant JWA, which closed its doors permanently in April 1973 due to dwindling crowds and a lack of domestic star power (both of Sheik's live appearances had only been for half-capacity crowds). In the JWA's place arose All Japan Pro Wrestling, founded by Giant Baba and aired on Nippon TV, Japan's oldest and most well-established television station; and New Japan Pro Wrestling, founded by Antonio Inoki and airing on competitor TV Asahi.[2]

Both former tag team partners and disciples of Rikidozan were now locked in what would be a decades-long struggle for national dominance. Of the two, Baba seemed to be more interested in utilizing major North American stars, possibly due to the much greater success he had experienced in the United States up to that point, having challenged Bruno Sammartino in Madison Square Garden main events a decade earlier and already being a major American draw in many other parts of the country due to his unusual size, whereas Inoki had been treated more as an undercard attraction using such unflattering monikers as "Tokyo Tom." From the beginning, American star power had been a big part of Baba's strategy, and from the beginning of All Japan, The Sheik was high on the list of people he wanted to bring in.

Like many wrestler-promoters including The Sheik himself, Baba was very much about using his own promotion as a platform to put himself over in a big way. He immediately created a brand-new world heavyweight title, the Pacific Wrestling Federation Championship, and then proceeded to book himself to go through a series of gaijin superstar challengers in a gauntlet tournament that included the likes of Bruno Sammartino, Terry Funk, Bobo Brazil, Pat O'Connor, The Destroyer, and Don Leo Jonathan, naturally coming out the other end without a single loss, thus becoming the first PWF World Heavyweight Champion. After surviving such formidable "competition," Baba now needed credible challengers, and thus brought The Sheik to All Japan for the first time in April 1973 for another two-night mini-tour. Their first rowdy main event in Osaka on April 24 was televised as part of All Japan's first-ever Champion Carnival, an annual tournament that would become the longest running anywhere in the world. But Baba vs. Sheik was considered such a huge match that it was held separate from the tournament and resulted in Sheik getting counted out of the ring in just six and a half minutes. They met again the following night in Tokyo at the Nippon University Public Hall, and this time Baba pinned The Sheik in just eight and a half minutes of a one-fall title defense. Two Japan trips, and two pinfall losses for the usually unpinnable Sheik—as with all those other North American main eventers, he had served his purpose of putting over Baba and his new world title.

At the time, business was so hot for Big Time Wrestling that Farhat finally felt he could confidently leave the country for just a few days, with his other talent drumming up enough business and drawing enough fans to justify missing a few shows. Despite, or perhaps because, of the short matches and sometimes chaotic finishes, the fans in Japan were drawn magnetically to him, like moths to a flash-paper flame—whenever he was in the building, they just couldn't look away, and the fear in the room was absolutely palpable. Japanese crowds were known for being quite subdued and respectful, especially compared to American ones, but all that went out the window when The Sheik was in town, and he was known to bring out uncharacteristic reactions from the typically docile Japanese audiences. You could hear screams and shouts from men, women, and children alike, and people would scatter in his path like their lives depended on it. Then sometimes the opposite would occur, owing to a Japanese superstition which dictates that touching something that frightens you will bring good luck. And so, The Sheik would sometimes find himself mobbed with Japanese fans rushing him, quickly tapping him on the arm or the back, and then running away. This famously happened once while Sheik was trying to hide by the curtain one night to check out the crowd and was spotted by a horde of spectators who promptly converged on his location and put *him* on the run—a decided reversal of what he was typically used to. "He told me about having to fight through the crowd," recalls Tommy Dreamer, a longtime colleague and confidant of Sheik's nephew Terry "Sabu" Brunk, who became a trusted family friend. "It was part of their culture, and other wrestlers confirm this. It would be an honor if he hit them, because if he just said 'Out of my way!' then it would be like it wasn't real, so he would show them that it was real. He carried weapons on hand, like homemade shivs in his boots. Because people would try to come after him, and there were sometimes riots."

Farhat waited a year and a half before coming back to Japan, and this time he would controversially work out a deal with Baba's rival Inoki to come in for a two-week tour with New Japan, his first time working for the other group. For a couple of reasons, it would turn out to be his only one. With his promotional war with Dick the Bruiser behind him,

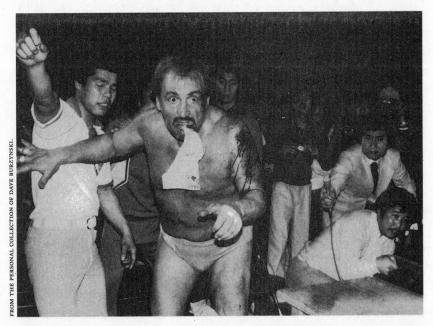

The Sheik arguably caused more chaos and hysteria in Japan than he did anywhere else.

FROM THE PERSONAL COLLECTION OF DAVE BURZYNSKI.

it seemed like the perfect opportunity to return to Japan safely, without having to worry about dividing his attention. What he didn't realize was that he was about to face his third and final coup attempt—and this time, the parties involved were waiting for him to leave the country in order to make their move. The week of November 3, 1974, after overseeing a Sunday night show at the Maple Leaf Gardens that saw him defeat Tiger Jeet Singh in a steel cage main event, Farhat came home to Williamston, then hopped on a plane for a New Japan tour that was set to begin on Friday, November 8, with a match against Seiji Sakaguchi at the intimate Korakuen Hall in Tokyo's Bunkyo ward. Immediately after he left the US, a secret cabal of Big Time Wrestling personnel, including Killer Brooks and Tony Marino, then locked in a money feud for the company; Ben Justice, who was red-hot after turning heel on his longtime tag team partner The Stomper; ring announcer and TV commentator Terry Sullivan; and most notably Farhat's own booker and right-hand man, Jack Cain, who had spearheaded the whole maneuver, officially left the Farhat promotion and started running shows under their own company banner, International Wrestling. They managed to attract several more of Farhat's people, even including photographer and front office employee Dave Burzynski.

"That was a big blow at the time," says Lou Klein trainee Big Jim Lancaster. "Why did they jump ship? It was my understanding that he would hold guys down. [But] the payoffs were the number-one thing. If the houses were good, some of the top guys would do OK. I was a Klein's Gym guy, brand-new in the business. I worked a sellout that drew $62,000, and I got fifty dollars. It was that kind of stuff. A lot of the guys grew weary of having those bad payoffs. Plus they could never get over. He would never allow another heel to get as hot as he was." It was a shocking betrayal, and an indicator of Farhat's difficulty at times in inspiring loyalty in those who worked for him. Blindsided by the defections, instead of the two weeks he had been booked for, he stayed for only one, highlighted by an infamous lumberjack match with Inoki that ended in forfeiture when The Sheik left the ring and refused to return. By Friday, November 15, Farhat was back in Michigan to try to get his house in order. Inoki is believed to have been less than enthused by the situation, compounded by the fact that apparently Farhat was in breach of the exclusivity agreement he had made with Baba's All Japan. Not only did Farhat never work for Inoki again, but the International Wrestling debacle made him so afraid of leaving the country that he didn't return to Japan for three years.

When he finally did return, in December 1977, it would be his first proper two-week tour, as part of All Japan's original Open Tag League, a round-robin tag team tournament that drew on talent from around the world and became a major annual tradition that continues to this day. It would also be The Sheik's most legendary Japanese tour, cementing his iconic status in that country—a status that still held water some fifteen years later when he returned there in the twilight of his career. Much had changed since Farhat's last Japanese trip. His company, World Wide Sports, was in a tailspin. Attendance and TV ratings for Big Time Wrestling were drying up and revenue had slowed significantly from the salad days of the early seventies. In short, Farhat was in greater need of cash to help keep his company afloat, and he needed Japan—and its hefty paydays for American stars—more than ever.

His partner in the tag team tournament would be an individual who would figure prominently in the second half of The Sheik's career; someone whose ferocity, unpredictability, and sheer violence in the ring were arguably rivaled only by The Sheik himself, from whom he had borrowed quite liberally, truth be told. Larry Shreve was a dirt-poor kid from Windsor, Ontario, the son of a Blackfoot Native American father and an African-American mother, who had seen The Sheik during his early years wrestling for promoters like Harry Light and Bert Ruby, and later Jim Barnett and Johnny Doyle in the original Big Time Wrestling. A master of karate and judo from a young age, he was recruited by Montreal wrestling promoter Jack Britton (a former assistant of Light) in 1958 at the age of seventeen. After toying with a few different gimmicks, Shreve first came to work for The Sheik in Big Time Wrestling in 1965 as opening match guy Zelis Amara. Just two years later, while working for Rod Fenton in the British Columbia territory, he took on the persona that would take him to wrestling immortality over the next forty years: Abdullah the Butcher, the Madman from the Sudan. Wearing the head-scarf and pointed boots, refusing to speak on promos, and utilizing an ultra-violent and almost completely wrestling-hold-free style that included assaulting his opponents with sharp objects and bleeding profusely, Shreve made it obvious where his inspiration had come from—even if he did incorporate martial arts elements like the wearing of judo pants and the use of hand-thrusts to change things up a bit.

By the time they teamed together in Japan for the first time, The Sheik and Abdullah the Butcher were already well-acquainted. The Butcher had been working Big Time Wrestling undercards as early as 1969 and was given a World Tag Team title reign with Killer Tim Brooks in 1974 and a two-month US title reign in 1975.[3] Later that year, seeing the obvious potential in such a crazed pairing, The Sheik had elevated him to the latest in an ongoing string of monster heel tag team partners for himself. In addition to the Big Time circuit, they had been teaming as well as opposing each other all over North America in places like Montreal, Toronto, Georgia Championship Wrestling, Nick Gulas's Tennessee-Alabama territory, and in Texas on both the Dallas and Amarillo circuits. They made a formidable duo, whether as partners or opponents, with the younger and (somewhat) spryer Abdullah only further accentuating The Sheik's already intense and demonic aura. "I think Abby would try to be at a greater level than The Sheik, and he couldn't quite make it," explains Terry Funk, who would play an integral part in that 1977 All Japan tour as well. "But Abby was one hell of a heel too. I'm not underselling him either; two of the greatest heels in the country at that time."

The tour consisted of a grueling thirteen matches over fourteen days in twelve different cities including Yokohama, Osaka, Hiroshima, and Nagoya, with opening and closing matches in Tokyo. Aside from the tag team tournament, The Sheik was matched in singles encounters against several notable performers from all over the world: They included distinguished British catch wrestler Billy Robinson, a proponent of the feared Wigan style and a product of Billy Riley's infamous "Snake Pit" training school, who was considered one of the most dangerous legitimate grapplers in the world; Dory Funk Jr., who along with his brother Terry had become enormously popular among Japanese fans, who were enthralled by American performers who played the cowboy role; Masao Kimura, on loan from All Japan competitor International Wrestling Alliance, where he was in the midst of his third reign as IWA World Heavyweight Champion; Baba protégé Tommy "Jumbo" Tsuruta, who had represented Japan in the Munich Summer Olympics five years prior; and of course, All Japan kingpin Baba himself. The fact that The Sheik lost each of those matches by either disqualification or count out in less than ten minutes speaks volumes about their chaotic nature, as well as about the nature of The Sheik as a performer by the late 1970s. Still, the Japanese couldn't get enough of it.

But the meat of the tour was in the thirteen-day Open Tag League tournament itself. The Sheik and Abdullah the Butcher mowed through seven different teams, scoring six victories and one draw, leading to a final confrontation with the team of Dory and Terry Funk on December 15 before twelve thousand fans in Tokyo's Sumo Hall. By that point in their careers, both of the Funk brothers had enjoyed reigns as NWA World Champion, with Terry having just passed the title to Harley Race in a classic encounter some ten months prior at the Maple Leaf Gardens.[4] The Funks also knew Farhat very well, having practically grown up around him all through the years he had spent working for their father, who had died tragically four years earlier after suffering a heart attack while demonstrating a wrestling hold on a friend. Terry and Dory Jr. were now in charge of the Amarillo territory their father had left behind, which was suffering a similar slow death to what was happening to Farhat's territory.

The explosion of bloodshed and unhinged violence produced by these four men when they clashed that final night in Tokyo is evidence that you don't necessarily need wrestling holds and scientific technique to put together a hellaciously thrilling wrestling match. It was unlike anything the Japanese audience was used to seeing, and while watching the match you can sense the horror and panic in the crowd. The madness begins from the outset, with the Funks blindsiding The Sheik before he even gets a chance to go into his pre-match ritual, drawing first blood (quite literally) from their insane opponents. What follows is fifteen tense minutes of biting, kicking, choking, and rending of flesh. Midway through, Sheik and Abdullah begin mercilessly jabbing Terry's right arm with Abby's trademark fork (Terry obliges with a rare arm blade job), as the referee conveniently misses the relentless transgressions. Finally, the fork is spotted and removed, and Dory finally gets the tag from his beleaguered brother, storming the ring with righteous rage to the adulation of the fans. As Terry's bleeding arm is bandaged at ringside, The Sheik brandishes his weapon of choice, the pencil, against Dory. When Dory gets his own hands on the implement, the crowd comes unglued—a common babyface spot in America, but one that was brand-new to the virgin Japanese crowd. In the end, The Sheik's pencil chicanery is spotted by the selectively sighted ref, who calls for the disqualification, giving the match and the Open Tag League trophy to the Funk brothers. But the havoc doesn't end there, as Sheik assaults the ref and a wild pull-apart ensues when the ring is filled by the "young boys," greenhorn wrestlers who customarily lurk around the ringside area to assist in any way needed.

"Oh my God, what a match, what a moment!" marvels Saito. "[The Funks] were like famous cowboys in Japan. That match made Abby and Sheik bigger heels, because the Funks were so loved by the crowd out of the American teams. Abby's scary, Sheik's scary, and there's no language barrier about it." The match was burned into the psyche of Japanese fans, the older of whom still talk about it to this day. From that point on, the name of The Sheik (and Abdullah the Butcher, for that matter), was inscribed among the all-time great foreign wrestlers in the history of puroresu. So notorious and revered was the matchup that it was revisited three times: in their 1978 Tag League tournament rematch, the pull-apart brawl after the match lasted a full eight minutes and spilled all over the building; the following summer featured perhaps their wildest brawl of all, a savage gutter fight ruled a no-contest after twenty-one minutes of chair-throwing and pencil stabbing, with all four men reduced to bloody messes fighting through the crowd for another eight minutes; their final blood-drenched clash, in the 1979 Tag League tournament, saw the Funks score a decisive victory at last when Dory pinned The Sheik after Abdullah accidentally laid out his own partner. This resulted in the inevitable falling-out of the team, with The Sheik blasting the Butcher with not one but two fireballs as he was rushed from the ring. These matches are not for the faint of heart, not even by modern-day standards; they are among the seminal bouts that set the bar for what would become hardcore wrestling—a bar that some would say has never been cleared.

For a man in his early fifties, for whom the rigors of the ring had taken their toll, these tours could be quite demanding. Eddie Jr. put it best when asked to recall his father's reactions to those Japanese trips: "They were tough, hard, cold, wet, long, and boring. He couldn't wait to get home. He said they were just very tough tours. People thought it was glamorous, like you're like a movie star, but your means of getting to different cities in that area are very hard. By the time he got home, he had to rest for two weeks just to recuperate." But they also paid very well, and as World Wide Sports circled the drain at the end of the 1970s, they were among the only things enabling the Farhats to fend off bankruptcy—or, at the very least, postpone it. In his 2003 book, *Chokehold*, Jim Wilson claimed that Farhat's standard Japanese deal was for $5,000 per match, paid in cash before he even stepped in the ring—not a bad deal for what would often amount to ten minutes of work—and it was said that he would come back from his Japanese trips with his wrestling boots literally filled with money. Farhat was also using his new connections in Japan to get more of his talent booked over there as well. This included Killer Tim Brooks, whom he helped get started over there beginning in the fall of 1977, leading to a long-running relationship between Brooks and All Japan that continued for years after Big Time Wrestling folded.

In addition to the big Funks tag team rematch, the 1978 Tag League tour was a nine-day affair that saw Sheik square off with some familiar opponents like Baba and Tsuruta, as well as Nick Bockwinkel, the golden-haired second-generation superstar from St. Louis whom Sheik had first faced in Chicago's International Amphitheatre back in 1956, when Bockwinkel was a twenty-one-year-old rookie, and who now wore the AWA World Heavyweight Championship—a title he had held for the past three years. As Eddie Jr. described, after Farhat returned home on December 10, he took most of the rest of the month off, working only three matches on the Big Time Wrestling circuit, including a defense of the US title against Bobo Brazil in Toledo on

Christmas Day. Without as much creative control over the pace and style of his matches as he had at home, those Japanese tours were getting tougher and tougher on his aging body.

By the summer of 1979, Big Time Wrestling was a shadow of its former glory, running only a couple of shows per month. And The Sheik's schedule was nothing like it had been. In June, he is only known to have had six matches—a couple for Nick Gulas in Tennessee, a couple for Dave McKigney in Ontario, and two shows at Cobo Arena (one of which was a chain match against the Mighty Igor that lasted less than a minute). In July, he took more dates in Japan than he did in North America, with Big Time Wrestling running only two shows the entire month. Not only was his business failing, but so was his working ability—Japan once again offered him a chance to make up for the former, and to get around the latter. Sheik may have been slipping out of the mainstream of American wrestling, but he was just as much an icon in Japan as ever.

Similarly, at the end of the year, after having worked just two Cobo dates and one Toledo Arena date in November, Farhat headed back to Japan for his third All Japan Tag League tournament, where he and Abdullah would finish in third place behind only the Funks and the team of Giant Baba and Jumbo Tsuruta. On December 2 in Hokkaido, on day three of the two-week tour, The Sheik battled another international superstar, Mil Mascaras—and true to form, both men once again avoided having to job to the other, ending their match in a double count out. When one week later, Abdullah and The Sheik battled Mascaras and his similarly masked brother Dos Caras, the result was unsurprisingly another double count out. The tour concluded on December 13, after which The Sheik made one stopover in Hawaii to work a date for Peter Maivia, a real-life Samoan high chief who had been a major star for Ed Francis and Lord James Blears before buying the Hawaiian territory from them earlier that year. After arriving home in time for the holidays as usual, he worked very few dates for the next few weeks, taking his typical post-Japan break. It was the first year in which he had worked multiple overseas tours, owing in part to the fact that he was needed less and less on the home front.

Multiple tours would become the norm for The Sheik going forward, as he began relying more on taking dates wherever he could get them, with his own promotion folding. In late April and early May of 1980, he was brought in to All Japan for a week as part of the Champion Carnival. However, possibly to avoid needing to ask him to do any jobs, The Sheik was kept out of the tournament itself, being used instead as a special attraction, Japanese audiences now having grown a bit accustomed to his act through repeated visits. Among the highlights of the 1980 Champion Carnival tour was his April 24 match against one of the industry's new young lions, a twenty-six-year-old product of West Texas State University named Ted Dibiase, the adopted son of Iron Mike Dibiase, who had died of a heart attack in the ring at the Fair Park Coliseum in Lubbock in 1969. The week built up to May 2 and The Sheik's first Japanese match against Abdullah the Butcher—the death match payoff to their falling out the previous December. Although technically just three and a half minutes bell-to-bell, the two men brutalized each other for much longer than that, with a brawl throughout the arena that lasted longer than the match itself. Not even TV announcer Takao Kuramochi was safe—he wound up a bloody mess as well. The hyper-violent bout was deemed so disturbing by Nippon-TV that they refused to air it.[5] Most telling of all was that the crazed Abdullah the Butcher was positioned as the babyface, proving that fans would choose to cheer for literally anyone over The Sheik. But it was also a sign of the changing of the guard—Abdullah's star in Japan was on the rise as he became more of a central gaijin figure, while The Sheik's was gradually waning.

The very next day, The Sheik was bandaged up and back in Cobo Arena in Detroit, reclaiming his United States Championship from the Mighty Igor. Only three more matches in the Michigan-Ontario area would follow that month. By the fall of 1980, Big Time Wrestling had effectively closed up shop, and Farhat was getting used to promoting much smaller independent shows around the Michigan-Ohio area, as well as becoming much more itinerant, taking bookings wherever he could get them. In November, after a week spent in sunny Florida wrestling for Eddie Graham's promotion, Farhat came home for Thanksgiving, and then was promptly back on a plane to Japan to take part in his fourth World Tag League tournament.

This time, his selected tag team partner would be an interesting and slightly controversial choice, particularly from Farhat's point of view. Frankie Cain of Columbus, Ohio, was a twenty-year veteran who had gotten his start working for the Nick Gulas–Roy Welch contingent down south and got his first taste of success teaming with fellow Gulas-Welch regular Rocky Smith as the groundbreaking masked Infernos tag team, known to terrorize Southern rings with their manager, J.C. Dykes, in the late 1960s. The Infernos were also known to throw fire, something The Sheik had already been doing for years by that point—and Cain would take the fire gimmick with him when he left the tag team in 1969 to strike out on his own as The Great Mephisto. The persona was probably the most successful of all The Sheik knockoffs of the era,[6] but it was still a knockoff—or, at least, that's how Farhat saw it. And with the beard, robes, kaffiyeh, and camel trunks, it would be hard to disagree, even if The Great Mephisto did cut his own promos. All through the seventies, Cain had taken the gimmick on the road to places like Florida, Texas, and Northern California—all places where Farhat had worked before.

One story has it that Farhat walked right up to Cain when he got off the plane in Tokyo, slapped him in the face, and said, "That's for stealing my gimmick." "I asked Frankie Cain about that," offers Scott Teal, who worked with Cain on his autobiography. "He said he never had any problems with Sheik over gimmick infringement. Never had any words about it." If there was any heat, it certainly was minimal and quickly dispersed—especially since the two men had to work together on a fourteen-day, twelve-city tour. The Sheik and The Great Mephisto faced off against teams like the Funks, now-former AWA World Champion Nick Bockwinkel and Jim Brunzell (one half of the AWA's top babyface tag team along with Verne Gagne's son Greg), Baba and Tsuruta, as well as Abdullah and his new partner Tor Kamata (another Hawaiian working as Japanese).

In singles appearances, Sheik also rekindled his one-on-one war with the Butcher, battling him in another gruesome affair in Sapporo on December 1 in which Farhat took the blade to both his head and his arm to horrifying effect. The match ended in disqualification for The Sheik when Great Mephisto interfered on his behalf, followed by Tor Kamata, who joined Abdullah to run the heels off. Eight days later in Osaka, Sheik crossed paths with another promising young star of the new generation, twenty-seven-year-old Rick Steamboat, who had been one of Jim Crockett Jr.'s top babyfaces in the Carolinas for the past three years and was in fact then the reigning Mid-Atlantic Heavyweight Champion. Watching Steamboat's explosive, aerial offense against Sheik's then largely immobile working style is jarring to say the least (Sheik even takes an extremely rare dropkick bump for Steamboat), but before long the match devolves into the usual stabbing, chair-throwing, and brawling around the arena—after The Sheik is inevitably disqualified, he wanders through the crowd absolutely covered in blood, seeming to take pleasure from sending the Japanese spectators fleeing in terror in his path.

The year 1981 would be the last Farhat would come to work for Giant Baba, but he made the most of it with three separate tours: one in January right after the new year, one in late spring, and one at the end of the year for his final World Tag League appearance. A renegade outlaw from the NWA by that point, a man without a company, he was still shown loyalty by Baba despite Baba's prominent NWA membership.[7] On January 3, 1981, less than four weeks after having left, The Sheik was back in Tokyo, taking on Abdullah the Butcher in Korakuen Hall for the Butcher's United National title, the same title Sheik had briefly held during his first Japan visit, back in '72. It would be the last time the two men would face off on Japanese soil. After only a five-day run filled with the expected five-minute disqualifications and count outs, Farhat was back home catching his breath before hitting Florida for a one-week engagement for Eddie Graham.

At the time The Sheik returned to Japan in late May, he hadn't worked anywhere for nearly a month. With more free time on his hands, he was able to devote three weeks to the tour, making it the longest of his All Japan runs. This extended tour included his final singles matches with Baba himself, taking place on June 1 and June 6 (Sheik never did get that elusive win over the Giant). But just as had been happening in the States, it had become apparent in Japan that The Sheik was really at his best at this point with a tag team partner—someone younger and more mobile to take the bumps, and to take the falls if need be. On this tour, two red-hot young heel performers were chosen. One was thirty-five-year-old Michael Davis, who had begun wrestling for Vince McMahon's Capitol Wrestling in 1961 at the tender age of fifteen, but who really started picking up steam some fourteen years later, when McMahon christened him Bugsy McGraw. McGraw had had some previous success as a gaijin wrestler for All Japan—at the time he worked with The Sheik, he was coming off several prosperous years in Florida and was on the verge of going to Dallas to become a superstar for Fritz Von Erich. Sheik's other tag team partner on the spring '81 tour was Fijian former bodybuilder and ten-year wrestling veteran James Reiher, who had broken into the business in the Pacific Northwest as Jimmy Snuka and was now a leading heel for Crockett, best known for popularizing top-rope maneuvers.

After capping off the three-week tour with a rematch against Steamboat, Sheik returned to the States for another three-week break before heading back down to the Sunshine State, by that point one of the only American territories that was still using him. Much of his time in those days was spent working for the "Bear Man" Dave McKigney in Ontario, which is where he spent most of the summer and early autumn of 1981. His partner for his last All Japan World Tag League tournament in late November and early December was someone with whom he was well acquainted—Mark Lewin, now working a maniacal heel gimmick after decades as a white-meat babyface.

And speaking of maniacs, this last tour helped Farhat get to know someone who represented the future of gaijin wrestling in All Japan, and with whom he shared a lot of traits both in and out of the ring. Frank Goodish had been a San Antonio sportswriter before his six-foot-eight, three-hundred-pound frame and impressive football background nudged him into the world of professional wrestling in 1973. Three years later the ball really got rolling on his career when Vince McMahon brought him into the WWWF for a run against Bruno Sammartino and gave him the name Bruiser Brody. With a long scraggly beard, a black mane of hair, and a head full of scars, he made a name for himself as an uncontrollable wild man of the squared circle, a master of the brawling style who delighted in taking opponents apart with a throaty bellow and a crazed look in his eye. He had been turning heads in Japan ever since his first tour there in 1979, checking a lot of gaijin boxes for Japanese fans as he did. He was also quickly gaining a reputation as a man of very strong opinions, who would go to great lengths to protect his best interests. It was rare to see in a worker, most of whom just did whatever promoters told them, fearing for their livelihoods. Brody had no such fear, and the best way to describe him depended on who you asked. For many fellow workers who revered him, he was a champion of the boys, who refused to be taken advantage of. To most promoters, he was a difficult pain in the ass whom they tolerated because he drew money like water from a well. Like The Sheik, he very often refused to do jobs and would sometimes even refuse to sell for an opponent he didn't respect. By all accounts, they had very similar attitudes toward the business, being both as independent-minded as they were. "Sheik really respected Bruiser Brody for looking out for himself and not allowing promoters to screw him over," explains historian and writer Scott Teal. In short, they both knew their worth and the value of protecting their marketability, and they recognized in each other men who could keep their heads above the bullshit of the business.

Brody and The Sheik faced each other twice on that tour: once in a tag team match with Snuka and Lewin as their respective partners, and once in a singles match that saw Brody win by disqualification. They had run into each other before in the spring of '77 while working in Dallas, but this time was different. This was a changing-of-the-guard moment. Following his last date of the tour, a December 13 tag team match with Lewin against the legendary reunited tandem of Harley Race and Larry "The Axe" Hennig,[8] The Sheik returned home to Michigan, never to return to All Japan Pro Wrestling. Brody, meanwhile, went on to become one of the major American faces of the new era of All Japan, along with the likes of Stan "The Lariat" Hansen, Terry "Bam Bam" Gordy, and "Dr. Death" Steve Williams. The era of The Sheik was over. "He just stopped," remembers Fumi Saito. "He didn't come back. It was very symbolic, because 1981 was the only time Sheik made three tours. And there was Jimmy Snuka, Ricky Steamboat, and the Von Erichs, on tour with Sheik—the up-and-coming superstars. It was like handing the torch. That was the last time."

The Sheik's withdrawal from Japan was part of a larger development. At fifty-five years of age, his in-ring career was clearly winding down, and probably several years later than it should have. His schedule was slowing down more and more into part-time territory, and by September 1982 he had effectively gone into semi-retirement. His personal and professional lives were in shambles, and his body was starting to disobey him, typified by his aging hips, severely compromised from years of ring rigors and badly in need of surgery. Japanese promoters and fans had been willing to overlook his age and obviously limited style, and after a time the legend of The Sheik was all that was keeping it going, overshadowing the actual man who had created it. But there was only so far that could go, and eventually it was time to draw the curtain. Those years in Japan had given his career a new lease at a time when American audiences were moving away from him. Still, reality eventually caught up with him, even across the sea.

But the legend of The Sheik, much like the man himself, was a difficult thing to destroy and proved to have staying power long after most presumed it dead. The Sheik would do very little wrestling anywhere in the 1980s, but the day would come—almost exactly a decade after he had left it behind—that the Land of the Rising Sun would once again bear witness to the fearsome visage of The Noble Sheik. He would be a very different man by that point, bowed with age and ill health; the wrestling business would be a very different business; and the company he would work for would be about as different from Baba's All Japan as you could get. But the name value he had worked so hard to build in that country would serve him well, and Japan would one day come into the picture once again, just when The Sheik needed it more than ever.

*The Good Times:
Sheik and Joyce
in a rare personal
photo from the
1960s; quite the
striking couple
away from the
ring.*

*Madison Square Garden, October 21, 1968: Bruno Sammartino defends the WWWF
World title against The Sheik for the first time. Referee Danny Bartfield attempts to
control the madman's illegal tactics, to little avail, as Sheik would win the bout via
count out.*

A firm believer in the "when you've got it, flaunt it" philosophy, The Sheik was known for his jewelry, expensive suits, and outrageously groovy attire.

The blood was one of his trademarks—something that could be expected in just about every Sheik match. And contrary to some speculation at the time, it was very, very real.

Most of The Sheik's TV studio appearances were one-sided squashes against pitiable enhancement talent who invariably wound up in the camel clutch.

Farhat arrives at the arena in his civvies, all business as he prepares to don the robe and headpiece for another night of mayhem as The Sheik.

Cobo Arena, 1972: Wrestling The Sheik was never pretty, as Tony Marino found out more often than most.

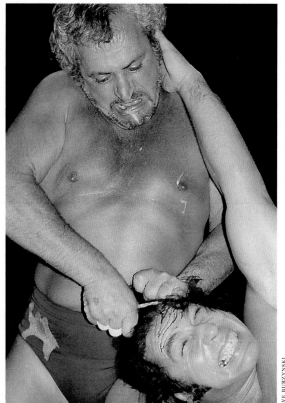

DAVE BURZYNSKI

DAVE BURZYNSKI

May 17, 1974: The Sheik dances with his mother-in-law, Ellen Fleser, at the wedding of his elder son. Eddie Jr. and his new bride, Kathy, can be seen mingling with guests in the background.

Market Square Arena, September 21, 1974: Their promotional war outside the ring over, Dick the Bruiser and The Sheik do battle inside the ring on Bruiser's home turf of Indianapolis.

Late 1970s: Andre the Giant uses The Sheik's own medicine against him. In their more than two dozen singles matches between 1973 and 1981, neither man ever scored a single pinfall over the other.

West Texas, 1977: The Sheik met his match in the equally sadistic and bloodthirsty Abdullah the Butcher. A mentor to Abdullah away from the ring, The Sheik shared a ring with the Butcher scores of times, as both an opponent and a tag team partner.

The Sheik is flanked by his two notorious handlers—Eddy Creatchman, his manager from 1973–1980, on the left, and Ernie Roth (aka Abdullah Farouk), his manager from 1967–1973, on the right.

A sure-fire heat-getter, The Sheik performs his ceremonial prayer ritual, here wearing the late-1970s version of his United States Heavyweight title belt.

Even after moving to the WWWF full-time, Abdullah Farouk was known to make the occasional trip back west to return to the side of his noble Sheik, such as this appearance at the WGPR studio in downtown Detroit, circa 1975.

Miami Beach Convention Center, October 15, 1980: Three days after the last Big Time Wrestling show at Cobo Arena, his own promotion now gone, The Sheik makes his first post-BTW appearance, taking on Dusty Rhodes in Florida.

*Hollywood Sportatorium,
November 21, 1980: The Sheik
finishes up a week of dates back
in Florida, shedding blood with
The American Dream inside a
cage. Dusty is joined in the match
by manager Oliver Humperdink,
and Sheik by his manager for the
Florida stint, Lord Alfred Hayes.*

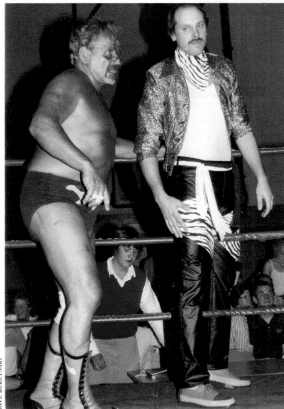

*Mid-1980s: The
last manager of The
Sheik, "Supermouth"
Dave Drason made
appearances with the
legend throughout
Ontario, Michigan,
and Ohio. Along the
way, his childhood idol
became a trusted friend
and confidante.*

Just Like Old Times: In the twilight of their lengthy careers, The Sheik and old foe Luis Martinez clashed in a series of matches throughout Ontario for indie promoter Dave "Bear Man" McKigney in the early 1980s.

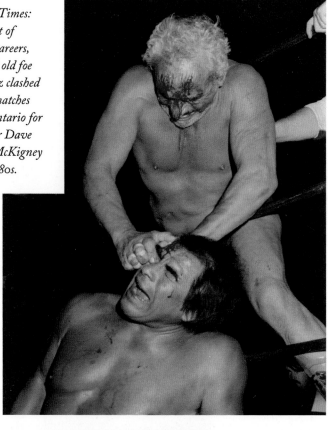

JOHN BRADFORD MCFARLIN

FROM THE PERSONAL COLLECTION OF DAVE BURZYNSKI.

Japan, early 1990s: Near the end in FMW, The Sheik was both feared and beloved, and he wasn't above spoofing himself, as his nephew Sabu took on the unlikely role of handler.

The gravestone of Edward and Joyce Farhat in Williamston, Michigan. For a decade prior to Joyce's passing in 2013, only a flat military plaque had marked the site of The Sheik's burial.

Wearing an asbestos mask to protect his face from being burnt from The Sheik's fire, Bull Curry engraves his initials into his opponent's forehead, probably with a #2 pencil he found laying around ringside that had been dropped by mistake.

Dave "Drason" Burzynski cherishes his Sheik memorabilia collection, which includes this actual blood-encrusted pencil that Wild Bull Curry—famously donning an "asbestos mask" to protect himself from The Sheik's fire—used to brutalize his nemesis in a 1973 Cobo encounter.

Possibly the first magazine to feature The Sheik (of Araby) on the cover. He and Gypsy Joe (far left), Fred Kohler's Midwest Tag Team Champions, pose with referee and former world heavyweight boxing champion Jack Dempsey (second from right) and an unidentified woman.

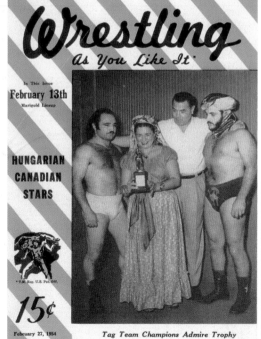

After the demise of Wrestling As You Like It, *editor Dick Axman started up* Wrestling Life, *here heralding the emergence of The Sheik's new fire gimmick, as he cemented his role as a top villain of the mat.*

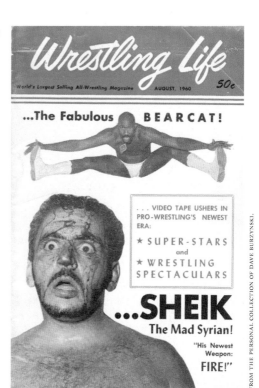

In a pre-internet, kayfabe age, Lou Sahadi's Wrestling Confidential *purported to rip the lid off the business. Still, The Sheik remained as inscrutable as ever.*

One of the most memorable *Sheik covers of them all, from* Wrestling Revue, *the premier wrestling magazine of the 1960s and '70s.*

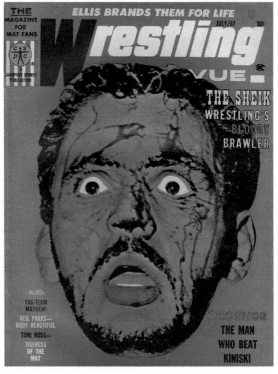

The local Baltimore Civic Center program advertises the upcoming rematch between Sheik and WWWF World Champion Bruno Sammartino—the first steel cage match ever held in that city, and the second-to-last match of their epic 1968–69 feud.

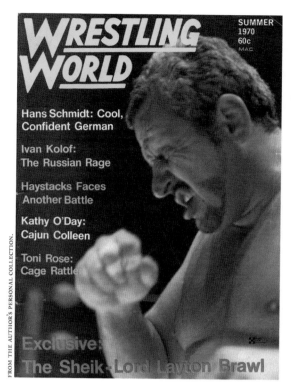

Lou Sahadi, a fellow Lebanese-American, made sure that his good friend The Sheik was featured prominently and often on the cover and in the pages of Wrestling World.

A Los Angeles arena program advertises an explosive heel vs. heel encounter between The Sheik and L.A.'s most hated scourge, John Tolos. This was Sheik's first appearance on the West Coast since the massive L.A. Coliseum Supershow the previous summer.

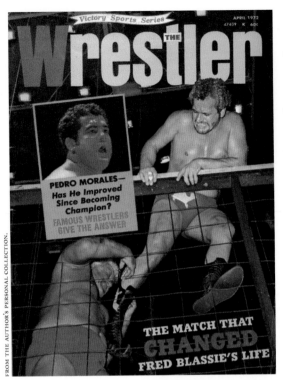

The 1970 feud with Sheik that finally turned Fred Blassie babyface in California had an impact that continued to be felt for years to come.

One of the finest wrestling programs in the business, Body Press *was the official publication of Big Time Wrestling, and back issues are cherished by collectors to this day.*

CHAPTER 13

I LIKE TO HURT PEOPLE

"It's a three-ring circus; a Roman arena. The men in the ring are gladiators, and the crowd, the common folk, are getting their chance. Their chance to act against authority figures that they cannot be aggressive toward in their own real lives. Their chance to beat the men around that they feel have been beating them."
—DETROIT REPORTER AND PSYCHOLOGIST DR. SONYA FRIEDMAN,
RINGSIDE AT COBO, APRIL 16, 1977

It was the best of times—but it wouldn't be too long until it was the worst of times. The spring of 1974 was a great time to be a fan of Big Time Wrestling. It was an even greater time to be the owner of Big Time Wrestling. The territorial war with the WWA was over. Faced with dwindling attendance and potential threats to his TV markets, Dick the Bruiser took his proverbial ball and went home, ceding uncontested control over Detroit back to Ed Farhat, The Sheik (who had never truly lost it in the first place). Farhat even got control of more territory in Bruiser's home state of Indiana as a result of the peace accord. But being good men of business, the two grizzled pros would very quickly turn an eye toward collaboration and transforming that real-life struggle into a scripted one for TV screens and arenas throughout the Michigan-Ohio-Indiana area, thus proving that no matter how bad grudges may get in the wrestling industry, there's no such thing as leaving money on the table.

Sheik and Joyce held court at their palatial Williamston estate, the site of regular family gatherings and industry parties, and money was no object. The Lansing boy who grew up during the Great Depression and dreamed of bigger things had achieved them, and it seemed like it

WRESTLING 8PM
AUG 31
BRUISER vs THE SHEIK
SEPT 8   EVEL KNIEVEL   4 PM
MARVIN GAYE   SEPT 7
SEPT 10 TO 15   DISNEY ON PARADE
ELVIS
NO PARKING

would never end. The family even began to grow, as on May 17, 1974, at St. Mary's Church in Williamston, Eddie Jr. married the beautiful young Kathy LaRue, who had been a teenage crush one year behind him in high school and later part of the nursing program at Michigan State while Eddie Jr. was there pursuing his business degree.[1] The new couple lived on the Farhat compound, and on Christmas Eve of the following year, Kathy gave birth to their first child, daughter Jennifer—making The

Sheik a grandfather at age forty-nine, and while his own younger son Tommy, now an uncle, was still only a boy of twelve.

The Sheik was living the dream, but what he didn't realize was that the dream's days were numbered. It didn't look like it in the spring of '74, but he and his company had just reached their peak and were about to begin tilting in the other direction. The shift would be gradual, but in just six and a half years' time, World Wide Sports and Big Time Wrestling would be no more. The heated competition with the Bruiser had propelled him to new heights and forced him to fight for his survival, attaining record business numbers in the process. But once that competition was gone, as often happens not just in the world of entertainment but in the world of business in general, a malaise began to set in. Interest wouldn't dry up overnight, but the crowds and level of popularity just would never again reach the levels they did in the early seventies. Most would also argue that Farhat simply wasn't motivated to try as hard as he had before. He had, as the old-timers liked to say, gotten the wrinkles out of his belly.

Some of it was simply the inevitable march of time. Farhat was now fast approaching fifty years of age and was still fully active in the ring. His once jet-black hair had taken on a salt-and-pepper gray that would soon turn to silver. His age was becoming apparent not just in his appearance, but also in his work. More and more, The Sheik came to rely on his persona and his gimmick to lighten the load. In his matches, fans had come to expect that anything that would typically be described as wrestling would be at a minimum; the holds he had employed in his youth were all but gone, replaced by brawling and roughhousing tactics that started immediately from the opening bell. While the style fit with The Sheik's wild and rule-breaking character, it also was a lot easier on his aging body—a body that had now been thrown around hard rings for close to three decades. Blood was almost a certainty in every Sheik match, from his opponent but even more reliably from himself, and the blading scars on his forehead grew thicker and more numerous—to the point where he didn't even always need an actual blade to get the job done, as a forceful rake of the finger would sometimes be enough to open up the brittle skin. And the use of fire, once a special occurrence to be seen maybe once a year in any given territory, was becoming more commonplace as well, as The Sheik used it to get that reliable pop from the crowd and maintain the aura of ever-present danger that was necessary to preserve his mystique. The elaborate flint magician's fingertip device was replaced with a plain old disposable butane lighter, of the kind introduced by the Bic Corporation in 1973.

The mid-1970s was a time of transition for Farhat and Big Time Wrestling, as well as for the entire National Wrestling Alliance. At the twenty-eighth annual NWA convention, held in New Orleans the first week of August 1975, Sam Muchnick finally, and much to his own relief, stepped down as NWA president, the position he had held for twenty-four of the twenty-eight years the Alliance had existed, and was replaced by Jack Adkisson (aka Fritz Von Erich) of the Dallas terri-tory. Jim Barnett, now firmly in control of Georgia Championship Wrestling and on the verge of bringing it to national cable television via Ted Turner's TBS network, was voted first vice president and placed in charge of booking the world heavyweight champion, a responsibility also previously held by Muchnick. Farhat's pal Mike LeBell became second VP, a modified version of his lofty ambitions within the organi-zation. But Muchnick had for a generation been the glue holding the NWA together, and with his withdrawal from power, the organization began to show signs of strain. The infighting would get worse without the "soul" of the Alliance to keep everyone in check, and the camarade-rie and support—forced though it may have been—that had long been among the major boons to joining the group began to erode. Under Barnett, the NWA World title began to be treated less like a protected object of prestige that was elevated by the pedigrees of those who held it and more like a prop used to elevate its holders, with title changes becoming more common and champions being booked not so much as respected sports figures but more as heelish invaders sent in to make the local hero look good. In short, in the next few years it became a little less "all in this together," and a little more "every man for himself"—ironically, just when Farhat needed it most.

Yet one of the other ironic things about this transitional period for Big Time Wrestling was that just when things were trending downward, the company would come up on the radar of a group of filmmakers who would help capture it for posterity, in the process making a difficult-to-describe hybrid of a mockumentary that eventually—after several years on a shelf—became one of the unlikeliest of cult classic B-movies at a time when Big Time Wrestling itself had already become a relic of the past. As such, the film would become something of a melancholy time capsule, displaying a moment in the heyday of territorial wrestling and in the tenuous final years of one of its most important and once-dominant bastions.

In the wake of the end of the promotional war, which was a stretch where red-hot talent was circulating through the Detroit area on a regular basis, the supply of new stars began to slow just a bit in the mid-1970s. In addition to Abdullah the Butcher becoming a new breakout star in the area, there was "Big Money" Hank James, the flamboyant babyface who had previously been a star for the Funks in western Texas and was marketed as the half-brother of Bobo Brazil; the rookie tag team of Samoan brothers Afa and Sika Anoa'i,[2] who had broken into the business in the Stampede and Vancouver promotions up in Canada as The Wild Samoans but were brought into Big Time Wrestling as The Islanders; Lou Thesz, the legendary world-beating heavyweight champion and former standard-bearer of the NWA, in need of money and humbling himself on the mid-card while pushing sixty; even Michael Thomas Farhat, youngest son of Sheik's oldest brother, Lewie, back from the recently concluded Vietnam War, who wrestled as Mike Thomas to keep the family name kayfabed.

During his time on the Big Time circuit, The Sheik paired up his nephew in the ring with another green newcomer destined to one day become just as big a star as Sheik himself, if not more so. Randy Poffo was a second-generation wrestler from Zanesville, Ohio (a spot show town on the Big Time circuit), who had spent his first four years out of high school playing minor league baseball in Florida for the farm systems of the St. Louis Cardinals and the Cincinnati Reds. While down in the Southeast, he dabbled in the family trade first for Ann Gunkel's outlaw All-South Wrestling Alliance in Georgia, where his older brother, Lanny, had just broken in a few months prior, and then in Eddie Graham's Championship Wrestling from Florida. He had been performing under a mask, first as The

Executioner and then The Spider, until he finally put his baseball career behind him when he got cut from the Chicago White Sox organization, and embraced pro wrestling full-time, coming to Big Time Wrestling in March 1975 under his real name. He joined Lanny and their father, Angelo, who had known and worked with The Sheik since the fifties and whom Sheik had procured from Barnett in Georgia. Randy spent the first fifteen months of his full-time wrestling career working for The Sheik and would feel forever indebted to him for the break.

"The Sheik loved my dad, and my dad loved The Sheik," Lanny recalls warmly. "My dad went to The Sheik and told him Randy got released from baseball and wants to become a wrestler. Sheik would always say the same thing: I'll take care of him. That was his code word. Randy owed it all to The Sheik. He thought The Sheik was amazing, he would study him." Later, when his career began to take off as Randy "Macho Man" Savage, he employed much of the ring psychology he learned from The Sheik, and he even incorporated his wife, Elizabeth, into the act, mistreating and bullying her as a means to get heel heat, just as The Sheik had done with Joyce in her Princess Salima days.

Lanny's memories of The Sheik from those days are fond and specific. They help to shed light on Ed Farhat the human being, who by the mid-1970s had spent so many years successfully hiding his true self from the world that there is no known public footage of him out of character or even speaking in his own voice. Outside of those close to him, the character had almost literally become the man, but Lanny got to see the other side. "He was a very, very well-dressed man," he remembers. "He'd wear these crazy suits that you'd never see anyplace. Everything was tailor-made. This was in the days of the musk cologne, and he used to wear a heavy amount of it, so I always knew when he was coming. He was a close talker. He had these piercing eyes, and this horrible forehead, and he'd come right up to you with his eyes. He talked like a guy who had lost a few fights, like a boxer that had hit the canvas a few times. Very enthusiastic, but not perfect diction."

Farhat continued to book himself as Big Time Wrestling's top star and main attraction, which by that point had been going on for a full decade. As Big Jim Lancaster and others have noted, if any heel began to get more heat than he did, he would usually turn them babyface, feud with them, and eventually defeat them, thereby cooling off their heat and preserving his own. He did this very thing with his former tag team partner Pampero Firpo, whom he turned on at the end of 1973 and entered into a main event program with that stretched into 1974. He took a brief break from the United States title in late winter, dropping it to Tony Marino on March 2 at Cobo and then regaining it at the next show two weeks later—a typical method of keeping interest in the title, which he had used several times already by this point. Despite the end of the promotional war, The Sheik still stayed pretty close to home for most of the first half of 1974, with notable exceptions being his monthly forays to the Montreal Forum for Johnny Rougeau's International Wrestling, then locked in battle with cross-town rival Grand Prix Wrestling, run by rugged Quebecois brothers Maurice "Mad Dog" Vachon and Paul "Butcher" Vachon, one of the most successful tag teams of the 1960s, who had now turned their eyes toward tag teaming in the promotional

Cobo Arena, December 15, 1973: After two years of teaming in the Detroit territory, The Sheik turns on Pampero Firpo with a fireball to the face. Unbeknownst to Motor City fans, the two had already been warring with each other for most of that time in the nearby Toronto territory.

end of the business. While there, he battled Montreal legends like Don Leo Jonathan and Edouard Carpentier, and he even enjoyed a final brief reign as IWA International Champion, defeating amateur standout Michel Dubois,[3] a Carpentier protégé. The Montreal Athletic Commission stripped him of the gold in July, citing "violent behavior"—an amusing sign of how much the athletic commissions still held sway over professional wrestling in those days and how little they understood the business they were supervising.

On April 20 in the Cincinnati Gardens, he wrestled Wild Bull Curry for the final time—after a monumental four decades in the ring, the Wild One was finally winding down his full-time career, although he would continue to make occasional appearances for Big Time Wrestling over the next couple of years. Meanwhile on the other end of Ohio, Farhat stumbled into what looked like a plum opportunity for expansion when Pedro Martinez and Johnny Powers's National Wrestling Federation closed up shop in the summer of '74. Farhat had already been sending his talent regularly to work the NWF circuit, so it seemed like something of a formality, albeit an expensive one, as Farhat chose to do business the respectable way, buying the territory from Martinez and Powers the same way he had bought Big Time Wrestling from Barnett and Doyle. This gave Farhat control over northwestern Ohio towns like Cleveland, as well as spots in western Pennsylvania and upstate New York, including NWF strongholds like Rochester, Syracuse, and Buffalo. That upstate area was given to TV and ring announcer Buzz Benson to run, and it would turn out to be more trouble than it was worth—the TV contracts alone were very expensive, and now Sheik's wrestlers would have to travel much farther as the circuit expanded. The combination of increased overhead and growing dissatisfaction among the workers put a strain on the promotion and, some would say, hastened its decline.

By this point, Farhat and Dick "The Bruiser" Afflis were in talks to iron out the details needed for a mind-blowing cross-promotion that they hoped would light up business for both their organizations. Fans had been following the promotional war for years and were well acquainted with the real-life bad blood between Big Time Wrestling and the WWA—it was a no-brainer to make a deal that would see Sheik

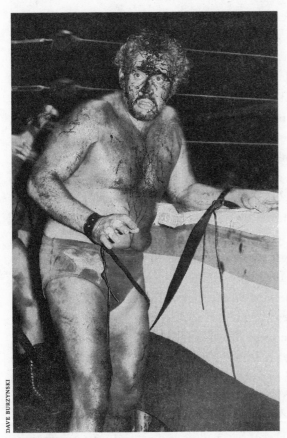

Cobo Arena, March 16, 1974: Renewing their epic feud of 1972, Sheik and Tony Marino traded the US title back and forth. Here, the mad Syrian regains the gold from Marino in a blood-soaked Italian Death match that saw them strapped together at the wrists.

and Bruiser meet in the ring and allow other talent from both groups to intermingle. As the deal was worked out, Farhat felt more comfortable roaming abroad again. On July 15, 1974, he made his career debut in the wrestling hotbed of Memphis, then still a bulwark of the Nick Gulas–Roy Welch Mid-America territory that dominated the South. Wrestling was religion there, and the white-domed Mid-South Coliseum was its cathedral. There, before a capacity crowd of 11,700, The Sheik headlined against former disc-jockey and illustrator-turned-wrestler Jerry Lawler, a three-year pro and native son of Memphis who was then in possession of the Southern Heavyweight title, the ultimate prize in the territory, which he had just won the previous week for the fourth time from the city's top babyface and number-one star, "Wildman" Jackie Fargo.[4] The feud with Fargo, Lawler's real-life mentor, was in the midst of elevating Lawler into the spot of the new top man in town, and by the end of the month, he'd be crowned "King of Wrestling," a moniker he still proudly holds to this day. But a few days before that happened, he had to go through The Sheik—a literal baptism of fire, as Sheik blasted him with flame during an encounter that was ruled a no-contest. Backstage, Lawler was so impressed with the trick that he had Farhat teach it to him, and thus the fireball became a part of Lawler's repertoire from that point forward as well—making him perhaps the only man to use it with The Sheik's blessing.[5] Following the Lawler match, Sheik returned to Gulas territory several times throughout 1974 for monthly shots, mainly taking on Fargo for a series of wicked brawls in places like Nashville, Louisville, and Birmingham that are probably what The Sheik is most remembered for in the Tennessee-Kentucky-Alabama area to this day.

Immediately after helping elevate Jerry "The King" Lawler to greatness at a pivotal moment in his career, The Sheik made history again five days later, when he went to work for his former bitter rival Dick the Bruiser for the first time since before the promotional war. On July 20, The Sheik appeared in Indianapolis for the WWA, defeating Sailor Art Thomas, although the match was fourth from the top—perhaps a psychological tactic designed to humble the man who had driven the Bruiser out of Detroit. Farhat had had no such agenda just two months earlier, when he had brought the Bruiser to Cobo Arena for his first appearance there since 1963—a full year before Farhat had even started running the place. The Sheik wasted no time in giving the people what they really wanted to see, only first in tag team form. Sheik would have to work heel, of course, so he'd have to bury his ego and bring in Bruiser as the babyface, joining him with the beloved Mighty Igor to seal the deal against himself and Killer Tim Brooks, who had become the newest recurring ally for Sheik after turning Firpo face. However, the highly anticipated match broke into complete chaos, ending in a double-disqualification, with Brooks taking the brunt of the babyface assault, as was his role in protecting The Sheik. The disappointing outcome was one of the first signs of mishandling in what should have been a dream feud and a sign of bigger booking issues at the top in Big Time Wrestling.

With two alpha males in the wrestling business, and two men who guarded their images and marketability fiercely, it was going to be a difficult balance to keep from the beginning, and the trajectory of their ongoing two-territory program throughout that first year bears that out. Tag team matches and non-finishes abound, with neither man wanting to be the one to do a clean job to the other—and since they were both bosses in their respective domains, there was no one to challenge them on that thinking. The end results:

- **Detroit, July 13:** The Sheik and Killer Brooks defeat Dick the Bruiser and Ernie Ladd.
- **Detroit, July 27:** Bruiser and Bobo Brazil defeat Sheik and Brooks in a cage match that lasts only a minute.
- **Indianapolis, August 10:** Sheik and Sgt. Jacques Goulet defeat Bruiser and Art Thomas via count out.
- **Detroit, August 31:** Their long-awaited first one-on-one encounter comes to Olympia Stadium and ends in a no-contest, with no winner declared. Despite being held in the larger capacity Olympia rather than Cobo, the match draws only 8,253, far short of a sellout.
- **Chicago, September 7:** On an AWA super-show at Comiskey Park for Bruiser's partner, Verne Gagne, Sheik and Bobby Heenan beat Bruiser and Brazil when Sheik pins Brazil.[6]
- **Detroit, September 14:** Their first Cobo one-on-one match—another double-disqualification.
- **Indianapolis, September 21:** Their first Indy singles match produces another no-contest.
- **Detroit, September 28:** Sheik is the first to score a singles victory—but by disqualification.
- **Detroit, October 5:** Sheik beats Bruiser in a steel cage match—no pinfall.
- **Indianapolis, October 12:** Bruiser and Brazil beat Sheik and Heenan. Heenan takes the fall.
- **Detroit, October 20:** Bruiser and Luis Martinez defeat Sheik and Ben Justice by DQ.

- **Chicago, November 23:** Yet another one-on-one no-contest, this time for the AWA at the International Amphitheatre.
- **Cleveland, November 25:** Sheik vs. Bruiser ends in a double count out.
- **Indianapolis, November 29:** Sheik wins by DQ in a chain match.
- **Detroit, December 7:** Sheik and manager Eddy Creatchman beat Bruiser and Pampero Firpo.

Cobo Arena, October 5, 1974: The first steel cage encounter of the Sheik/Bruiser feud sees Sheik emerge victorious through dubious means.

Regardless of their refusal to put each other over, The Sheik and Dick the Bruiser were now playing nice, which made the NWA powers-that-be very happy, especially president and chief peacemaker Sam Muchnick, then in his final year in office. No longer an outlaw, the Bruiser was now welcome to return to the NWA capital of St. Louis. And perhaps in a show of solidarity, and also since Farhat had been sending Big Time Wrestling tapes to broadcast on St. Louis TV during his customary summer off-season, Muchnick even invited Sheik against his better judgment, a move he would immediately regret. On August 9, one day after battling Central States Heavyweight Champion and perennial Kansas City headliner Bob Brown to a double-disqualification for Central States promoter Bob Geigel, The Sheik traveled to the nearby Kiel Auditorium, Muchnick's home base, to take on former NWA World Heavyweight Champion and consummate wrestler's wrestler Pat O'Connor—their first meeting in eight years. The optimistic and perhaps naïve Muchnick asked Farhat to keep the match in the ring and to put over local favorite O'Connor. St. Louis was a squeaky-clean territory, and Muchnick wanted his shows to be respectable athletic events to impress all his sportswriter friends. But The Sheik had other plans and was clearly there that night to go into business for himself. What he actually did when he hit the ring couldn't have been further from what Muchnick had asked—jumping to the outside, throwing chairs at the startled O'Connor, and generally wreaking absolute havoc until the referee had no choice but to call an audible and disqualify The Sheik, which gave O'Connor the duke, just not how Muchnick intended. Both Muchnick and O'Connor were beyond incensed, but Farhat was just remaining true to his character. Farhat had one more commitment for Muchnick just two weeks later, which was turned into a two-minute undercard squash match over journeyman Devoy Brunson, on a card that featured both Bobo Brazil and Dick the Bruiser in the main event—a political snub if ever there was one. That would be the last time The Sheik was ever invited to St. Louis.

The Sheik's travel plans had been seriously crimped all throughout the promotional war, and he had only come out to California, one of his favorite spots, a handful of times in the past three years. That changed in late 1974, as Farhat felt safe enough to begin going out to LA to work for Mike LeBell—and shop on Rodeo Drive—again. He worked four different dates at the Olympic Auditorium in late summer and early fall, mainly working with Pampero Firpo and Mighty Igor, two talents with whom he was quite familiar, both of whom had recently left the Detroit area to settle on the West Coast for a bit. His first of these, an August

30 match against Firpo, was made infamous by his blasting of beloved referee Johnny "Red Shoes" Dugan with a fireball. After the match, some photos were staged for acclaimed Olympic boxing and wrestling photographer Theo Ehret that purported to reveal Dugan's scorched face—legend has it the effect was achieved using sandpaper—and when the image appeared in print in *The Wrestler* magazine and other places, it only helped lend further credence to The Sheik's long-held position as the most feared man in wrestling.

Meanwhile, the real Ed Farhat was busy living it up with LeBell. And not just in LA; sometimes they would take a little detour and make the one-hour flight over to Vegas, another of Farhat's favorite playgrounds. "He liked going there and spending three days, taking a break," remembers Eddie Jr. "Playing craps, seeing some shows. It was a good time . . . From 8 a.m. to 6 p.m., he would be out at the pool taking the sun. Then at night, he would come in and have dinner and go shoot some craps. He loved the sun. Always out in the sun, every day." Eddie Jr. still came out sometimes with his dad, although in his youth he was more interested in what LA might have to offer in the music world rather than the wrestling one. "Eddie wanted to start a rock band—he asked me if I could hook him up with record companies," remembers LeBell front office man Jeff Walton. "I couldn't help; it wasn't my world—I didn't know anybody . . . At that time, Sheik was trying to help him as much as he could. But Junior didn't know what he wanted. He didn't have the drive for the business his father did. When I took him around and was showing him the sights, I said, 'Why don't you get in the business? You're a pretty big guy.' He said, 'No, I'm not interested. I've got a band I'm gonna try to push, and my dad's paying for a bunch of stuff.' His heart wasn't in the wrestling business at the time."

Meanwhile up north in The Sheik's stronghold of Toronto, 1974 saw the end of the undefeated streak that had begun five years earlier and had seen Farhat go 127 singles matches at the Maple Leaf Gardens without a loss. Many felt that he had finally gone too far in February when he booked himself to go over Andre the Giant via count out, and it was perhaps a reaction to that when the two men met again in the Gardens on August 11 before more than ten thousand fans that he actually permitted Andre to have the victory—and even then, not by pinfall, but via disqualification. Of course, the very next month he was back to his old tricks again when he stepped into the ring in Toronto against NWA World Heavyweight Champion Jack Brisco, the handsome and soft-spoken Native American from Blackwell, Oklahoma, who had captured the NCAA national heavyweight wrestling title in his senior year at Oklahoma State and was now in the midst of a two-and-a-half year reign at the top of the pro wrestling mountain. This was the first of two shots The Sheik received against Brisco,[7] the fifth NWA World titleholder he had challenged thus far in his career. Any Torontonians expecting a scientific clinic that evening were surely disappointed by the four-minute double disqualification brawl they were given. Brisco, with his "real sports" pedigree, was somewhat embarrassed to wrestle The Sheik, and a match like that only reinforced that feeling—needless to say, his opinion of Farhat as a worker was far from glowing.

The year would close with a bang, namely Farhat's betrayal by his booker Jack Cain while away in Japan in November. Cain was joined by an alarming number of defecting Big Time Wrestling talent, including the likes of Luis Martinez, Killer Tim Brooks, Tony Marino, Al Costello, Ben Justice, and even J.B. Psycho, The Sheik's gardener. Adding insult to injury, Farhat had just helped Brooks get booked with Giant Baba in Japan earlier that month. The group formulated their plan while Sheik was overseas working for Antonio Inoki. Among them was also announcer Terry Sullivan and photographer and front office man Dave Burzynski. "I was called by Terry Sullivan and Killer Brooks," remembers Burzynski. "They said, 'Yeah, there's going to be a show this Saturday coming up at Cobo.[8] Brooks, Marino, Ben Justice, and Dr. Beach,[9] we're not going to be there. Neither is Terry Sullivan and Jack Cain." As soon as he high-tailed it back from Japan, Farhat saw to it that there was no way Cain's group could run the major venues in Detroit—his war with Bruiser had taught him that much—and so they mainly confined themselves to the lesser Ohio spots like Canton and Toledo and some even smaller towns in that area. But this was not an operation anywhere near the level of the WWA—their TV exposure was extremely limited, with only a brief stint on the air in Toledo, using footage shot at the University of Windsor. With Farhat exerting all his political might, it was doomed to fail from the start, and the group only lasted in the area for about a year, by the end of which they were running an ice-skating rink in Toronto.

There's also reason to believe Farhat may have exerted a little more than just political might. "Jack Cain went back to Williamston because he had his house there," Burzynski recalls. "It was said that somebody came to The Sheik and said, 'Hey, Jack Cain's at this bar or restaurant.' And I guess Sheik went there and confronted him, and Jack Cain didn't last long in that town anymore." One by one, the big names scattered, some never to return to Big Time again: Brooks headed for more familiar environs in Texas, Costello went into retirement, Justice headed to Bruiser's camp before quitting the business. Psycho saw the writing on the wall earlier than the rest and was welcomed back by Farhat for a bit before finishing out his career not long after. Martinez and Marino, however, jumped ship to yet another outlaw that had taken shape in 1975—and not just any outlaw, but the mother of all 1970s outlaw promotions.

Eddie Einhorn of Paterson, New Jersey, had gotten his start in sports as a hot dog vendor in Comiskey Park in 1959 and 1960,[10] but was now fast becoming one of the hottest names in televised sports, a true pioneer who had established the first syndicated TV sports network and helped popularize televised college basketball in the 1960s. In 1974, his TVS Television Network backed short-lived NFL competitor the World Football League, and now he was looking to cause the same kind of disruption in pro wrestling. Einhorn happened to be a good friend of Ron Martinez, who happened to be the son of former NWF outlaw promoter and Sheik associate Pedro Martinez. Ron introduced Einhorn to his dad, and the two men hatched an idea to create the industry's first true nationwide wrestling promotion, the International Wrestling Association. Based out of Martinez's old headquarters in Cleveland as well as offices on Madison Avenue in Manhattan, they planned to take on the NWA, the WWWF, and anyone else who might stand in the way. Using Einhorn's TV connections, they were able to get clearances in several key markets, including New York City, where they got on the air for nationally syndicated WOR-TV Channel 9, which had long been the home of Vince McMahon and the WWWF—now relegated to area UHF Channel 47 WNJU. Martinez's connections in the wrestling world helped them steal away major talent like Mil Mascaras (who became their headliner and world champion), Cowboy Bob Ellis, Ernie Ladd, Bulldog Brower, Mighty Igor, and Oreal Perras, the son of an Ontario dairy farmer who was much better known to wrestling fans as former WWWF World Heavyweight Champion and Soviet scourge "The Russian Bear" Ivan Koloff.

Einhorn and Martinez were out to compete with not just one territory but all of them, and to make their IWA the pro wrestling equivalent of the NBA, NFL, NHL, and Major League Baseball. And according to the son of The Sheik, if they had their way, added to that list of major talent, as well as promotional partners, would have been The Sheik. In his 2009 radio interview with Gary Cubeta, Eddie Jr. claimed that the group came to his father early in the venture and made him a partnership offer. "Eddie Einhorn went to my father about five months before the move happened, gave him a briefcase of a million dollars," remembered Eddie Jr. "He said, 'I'll give you this, plus fifty percent of the territory, you run the whole thing, and we take the whole country by storm.' He turned them down." Although Farhat, like many other promoters, had tried their share of invasions and expansions over the years, this was something on a whole other level. Joining with the IWA would've meant turning on all of his friends and colleagues and going against everything that the old gentlemen's agreement that had defined the wrestling business for decades was all about. Strained as many of those relationships may have been much of the time, it's easy to see how Farhat was not willing to blow them up entirely.[11] And ultimately, his wisdom proved sound. By the end of the year, the venture had hemorrhaged enough money to provoke Einhorn to cut bait and return to what he knew best, which later included starting up the SportsChannel cable service, becoming head of CBS Sports, and eventually an executive for the Chicago Bulls and Chicago White Sox. Martinez's old partner Johnny Powers joined him in Einhorn's place, but the much scaled-down IWA was no match for the established promotions, and they were totally out of business by 1978.

At the time of the IWA's launch, Farhat would've had little trouble turning down their alleged offer, partially due to the fact that he was still holding his own relatively well in 1975. Putting grudges of the past behind him, Mark Lewin had returned to the Big Time Wrestling fold hotter than ever, with Farhat using Lewin's Jewish heritage to turn their ongoing in-ring feud into something of an exploitative social commentary on deteriorating Israeli-Arab relations during the 1970s, made even more pointed by The Sheik's Jewish turncoat manager Eddy Creatchman. In June, when The Sheik made his first-ever appearance for Stu Hart, the raspy-voiced shooter who had grown up in a tent on the prairies of Alberta and whose Calgary-based Stampede Wrestling covered most of Western Canada, he took Lewin with him, bringing their feud to the Ogden Legion Hall for one night. Lewin even enjoyed a couple of United States Championship reigns at the expense of The Sheik and of "Bulldog" Don Kent, who, along with Abdullah the Butcher, had become one of The Sheik's regular tag team partners following the departure of Killer Brooks.[12] In the wake of the loss of Jack Cain, Farhat took on as his new booker Tom Renesto, a thirty-year veteran of the wrestling business who had risen to fame as one half of the internationally famous masked Assassins tag team along with former amateur boxer Jody Hamilton, before retiring from the ring and taking on a booking role for Ann Gunkel's All-South Wrestling in Georgia until its 1974 demise. The beloved Lord Athol Layton had begun to reduce his announcing duties, accepting a job as goodwill ambassador for Bacardi Rum—a role to which his regal bearing and sophistication were appropriately suited. This left the returned Bob Finnigan, as well as Chuck Allen and the also-returned Terry Sullivan, back from Cain's outlaw outfit, to take on the lion's share of TV announcing duties.

Although fans were wearying of The Sheik's routine and his repetitive booking philosophies were showing signs of strain, he remained among the top heels in the business. In Toronto, despite the end of his undefeated streak, he continued to book himself at the top. In February 1975, in two villain vs. villain dream matches at the Maple Leaf Gardens, he took on another of the greatest heels to ever draw breath, Killer Kowalski, who had been his occasional tag team partner back in the Capitol Wrestling and Barnett-Doyle days, but whom he had never

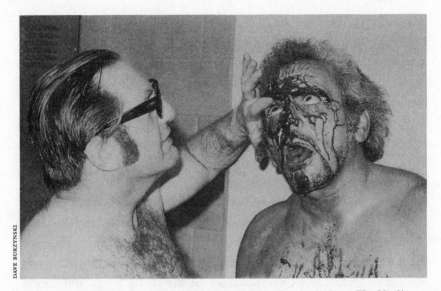

Crimson Mask: A concerned Eddy "The Brain" Creatchman checks on The Sheik's grisly wounds after a match.

faced before as an opponent. The Sheik-Bruiser dual-territory feud was officially blown off at Indianapolis's Market Square Arena on Valentine's Day of all days, with the Bruiser defeating Sheik in a cage match—and for those keeping score, no, neither man ever pinned the other during the entire program, ensuring both of their outsized egos remained dutifully preserved. But make no mistake, The Sheik's ability to draw major heel heat was still there and could be seen firsthand in the way fans tried to get their hands on him, such as in this Eddie Jr. anecdote from a show at the Cincinnati Gardens in the mid-1970s: "Dad was wrestling Bobo. We always left our limo in back of the building, police always watched it. That night when the show was over, it was my dad and myself, we went to go in the car, and this little kid yelled out, 'Sheik, better look under your car!' So our driver peeked underneath there and said, 'You're not gonna believe this, but you better get the hell away from the car.' Somebody had planted a stick of dynamite! From that day on, he would always put the car inside the building."

Still, as time went on, the numbers were starting to slip. During this period, Big Time Wrestling was running both Cobo Arena and the

Olympia Stadium, so part of the problem was clearly that they were spreading themselves too thin. The April 6, 1975, show at the Olympia, headlined by Abdullah the Butcher defending the US title against Pampero Firpo and the father-and-son team of Angelo and Lanny Poffo battling the team of Bobo Brazil and Hank James, was a bit of a sobering wake-up call, with the stadium seats left two-thirds empty. Farhat tried to amp up the violence and mayhem in an attempt to drive ticket sales by having Abdullah the Butcher and The Sheik turn on each other in a series of brutal yet wrestling-free matches, but it did little to help, and their May 30 Cobo main event duplicated the one-third crowd capacity, only this time at Big Time Wrestling's hallowed home base. By the latter months of the year, less-than-half-capacity crowds at Cobo had become the norm, with not even The Sheik-Lewin feud bringing any improvement. The October 25 Olympia show headlined by Sheik and Lewin drew a mere 3,234 to the fifteen-thousand-seat building. There was no doubt about it at this point—the territory was cooling down.

In addition to Detroit, The Sheik and Abdullah also brought their blood feud up north to the Maple Leaf Gardens, as well as down south for a series of wild matches at the Atlanta Omni for Jim Barnett's Georgia Championship Wrestling, which was heating up rapidly just as Big Time Wrestling was losing steam. It was part of a new growing partnership between Farhat and his old associate, which led to Sheik doing a series of appearances in the Peach State just as GCW was set to rock the wrestling industry by getting beamed across the country via the new cable and satellite network TBS in 1976. Barnett and his booker Harley Race—who hadn't forgotten Farhat's kindness to him early in his career—were gung-ho about bringing in a slew of big names to help his company make as big a splash as possible as it became the first promotion to have national TV penetration since the old Marigold Arena days of his former boss Fred Kohler in the fifties. And even though the viewership of TBS in the seventies was a far cry from the monster audience of the DuMont Network in the fifties, it was enough to ruffle the feathers of other regional promoters unused to having to compete for TV attention in their own fiefdoms. They were now the second company that could be seen on national cable, with the WWWF

Madison Square Garden cards still being broadcast on HBO, although in '76 the broadcast was "demoted" to the New York–based Madison Square Garden Network. Attempting to get in on the act, Bob Finnigan even moved to work out a deal to have Cobo Arena cards broadcast on competing subscription cable network Showtime as part of its original slate of programming in the Bicentennial summer of '76, but was reportedly vetoed again by Farhat, who balked at the hefty price Showtime was asking. The conflict appears to have been a source of frustration for Finnigan, who was trying to reverse the increasingly negative momentum of Big Time Wrestling and throw their hat into the growing ring for national expansion, another move for which Farhat was hesitant, as was evidenced by the IWA situation.

The signs of strain were showing not just in Detroit, but also up north in The Sheik's other stronghold, Toronto, where his relationship with promoter Frank Tunney was on the wane; the blockbuster numbers Sheik used to bring in were shrinking, and Tunney began to seriously question Farhat's need to keep himself booked at the top of the card. Not long after his undefeated streak at the Maple Leaf Gardens ended, Farhat also began taking dates with another Ontario promoter, one who had long worked in the shadows of Tunney's major NWA-affiliated operation and who had been somehow surviving for years with his much smaller piece of the Ontario wrestling pie. Dave McKigney had first come to prominence in Canada in the 1950s using the more French-Canadian-friendly name Gene Dubois,[13] and was known throughout the territories as the trainer of Terrible Ted, a six-hundred-pound black bear with whom he—and whatever unfortunates could also be persuaded—would stage exhibition matches of man vs. beast. Eventually, he grew out his hair and beard to prodigious length and starting going by "The Bear Man" (or alternately, "The Wildman") Dave McKigney. Based out of McKigney's ramshackle cabin on a hill in the woods in Central Ontario, Big Bear Promotions had a love-hate relationship with Tunney's Maple Leaf Wrestling—sometimes they shared towns and Tunney would tolerate him, other times he was viewed as an annoying outlaw operating on the periphery. But McKigney typically ran smaller towns that Tunney rarely or never got to, and most importantly did not have television, and so Tunney never saw him as a serious threat. Farhat started working McKigney shows in April of 1975—perhaps a sign of his deteriorated relationship with Tunney, or perhaps simply because he needed the money at a time when his own business was starting to decline. For a couple of years, Farhat was even able to pull off the impressive political feat of working for both McKigney and Tunney simultaneously—but it definitely was something he wouldn't have done back when things at Maple Leaf Gardens were riding high.

As he approached fifty years of age while maintaining a full-time wrestling schedule, Farhat finally had to make a concession to his own body when he began experiencing serious abdominal pain that was linked to gallbladder disease. No doubt his prodigious love of fried foods, red meat, and sweets did little to help the worsening issue, and likely contributed to it—but in his defense, this was still a fairly common problem in people and even athletes of his generation, at a time when the dangers of trans fats hadn't yet been fully outlined and the health food craze was still some time away. Unfortunately, minimally invasive laparoscopic surgery was also about a decade away, and so the only option to remove the failing gallbladder was through the more archaic cholecystectomy, or open surgery requiring a large incision and hours of general anesthesia. It was a procedure that could be quite the ordeal, took time to recover from, and unfortunately in hindsight seems to have had long-term effects on Farhat's life and career that would be nothing short of disastrous, and much of his future woes could be linked in some way to it.

The weekend of February 13, 1976, The Sheik had a trio of matches against archrival Mark Lewin. On Friday, he defeated him in Canton, Ohio, to win the United States Championship, and then the following night he duplicated the feat in Cobo Arena[14] in a "loser leaves town" match. He defeated him a final time in the Maple Leaf Gardens on Sunday, and then the following day, February 16, went in for his gallbladder surgery. He knew he'd be out of action for nearly three months, and so Big Time Wrestling's United States Championship was vacated (it would later be awarded to Bobo Brazil for the twelfth time). Tellingly, Farhat did not give up the Toronto version of the United States title, which he also held—instead, Tunney had to go five Maple Leaf Gardens events without his US Champion and headliner. Tunney couldn't have been too happy about the turn of events, but he made up for it by having his close ally Vince McMahon send up WWWF World Champion Bruno Sammartino for title defenses at each of those five cards.

It was the longest The Sheik had been away from the ring since the earliest years of his career, when he wasn't yet full-time. While he was recovering from his surgery, Farhat relied on headliners like Bobo Brazil, Hank James, and Bert Ruby's old pupil George "The Animal" Steele, now a major star, to continue drawing crowds throughout the circuit, as well as the feud between Chief Jay Strongbow and Don Kent, which headlined most of the Big Time Wrestling shows during his absence. For one Cobo show, he brought in Killer Kowalski for the main event; another featured an all-star tournament for the vacant United States title. Finally, The Sheik returned to the ring on April 23, not in Detroit, but in the Atlanta Omni, taking on his old associate Thunderbolt Patterson, now a beloved top-flight babyface in GCW. He went back down to the Omni a week later for a tag team encounter, and then the following day, May 1, he made his triumphant return to Cobo Arena to pick up right where he left off, resuming his feud with the also-returning Mark Lewin. Two weeks later at the next Cobo show, he reclaimed the US title Bobo had been keeping warm for him, and the following day he completed the comeback by jumping right back into the main event at the Maple Leaf Gardens (and, predictably, Sammartino was nowhere to be found, after having spent the past three months as Tunney's headliner).

Although Farhat had stayed out of the ring even longer than the typical recovery time usually required for his surgery, his day job was far from an easy, low-impact one, and it seems that he still could have benefited from more time away to heal (some would certainly argue it might have even been a sign to retire and stick to running his business from outside the ring). For a time after his return, he wrestled with a large bandage taped right in the middle of his abdomen to cover the incision, and once removed it revealed a permanent, snaking scar that resembled a vicious stab wound. There was also a lot of pain involved in his recovery, which was common following that procedure, and which also was good reason to have considered stepping away from the ring for good, since in order to perform, like many pro wrestlers who struggle with chronic injury, Farhat required painkillers to a greater degree than those who didn't make a living smashing their bodies into other people and inanimate objects. It was a predicament that did not bode well for his future.

But for the time being, he was still experiencing the last gasp of his prominence within the business. His return to action came just in time for him to take part in an inter-promotional event that was about to take the business by storm and cross over directly into mainstream pop culture consciousness. Muhammad Ali, undisputed heavyweight boxing champion of the world, was on a collision course with none other than Antonio Inoki, after Inoki and New Japan Pro Wrestling offered the champ $6 million to try to settle the eternal debate of what discipline was superior, boxing or wrestling.[15] The bout was signed in March 1976 and set to take place at Tokyo's Budokan Hall on June 26, with plans to broadcast it on closed-circuit television all over the world. Vince McMahon was designated the promotional liaison in North America, as the WWWF then had a strong working relationship with New Japan, but McMahon was working closely with promoters in other parts of the country in order to coordinate and properly hype the various regional closed-circuit broadcasts, including Eddie Graham in Tallahassee, Jim Barnett in Atlanta, Stu Hart in Calgary, Verne Gagne in Chicago, Roy Shire in San Francisco, Fritz Von Erich in Dallas, Paul Boesch in Houston, Mike LeBell in Los Angeles, Dick the Bruiser in Indianapolis, and The Sheik in Detroit.

In addition to being a promotional partner, The Sheik was given the auspicious role of Ali's wrestling trainer, helping to prepare the Greatest for what he might expect when stepping in the ring with a wrestler.[16] This was feasible in large part because Ali happened to have recently purchased a sprawling ranch near the Michigan village of Berrien Springs, about two hundred miles west of Detroit. Farhat was invited there on several occasions in the spring of '76, posing with Ali for the news photographers and making a show of giving the legendary boxer some tips on the finer points of grappling—the irony of which was not lost on the sportswriters covering the "training camp." In an amusing piece for the May 8, 1976, *Detroit Free Press* ("The Sphinx to Train the Mouth"), Jim Benagh wrote, "His publicity people say The Sheik doesn't speak English, which is not quite true because he spoke a lot of it at Ali's Berrien Springs farm when there was some money at stake." Benagh also describes Ali and The Sheik locking up in the front yard, only to have Ali's concerned cook, a wrestling fan well aware of The Sheik's proclivities, break up the scuffle with a broom, warning Sheik, "Don't hurt my little boy!" Big Time Wrestling announcer Chuck Allen, on hand as The Sheik's spokesman, even alluded to Sheik's real-life friction with Inoki from his ill-fated 1974 New Japan tour, citing it as Sheik's motivation for training Ali. All the ballyhoo was right up Farhat's alley as a consummate showman, and he would cherish the Ali experience for the rest of his life.

The Ali-Inoki fight was carried at over 150 closed-circuit locations across the United States, including nine locations within The Sheik's territory. At Olympia Stadium, Farhat presented a live four-match card headlined by Sheik vs. Pampero Firpo for the United States title, followed by a closed-circuit broadcast of Andre the Giant taking on heavyweight boxing contender Chuck Wepner live from a show being simultaneously presented in New York's Shea Stadium by Vince McMahon, as well as the broadcast of the Ali-Inoki fight itself. The Ali-Inoki bout and the Andre-Wepner bout were broadcast to all closed-circuit locations, with other regional promoters also putting on accompanying live events like Farhat and McMahon did.[17] As for the match itself, it was a bit of a debacle, with Inoki staying prone on the mat for most of the fight to avoid Ali's explosive punching power, delivering vicious kicks to the champ's legs that landed him in the hospital after a tedious fifteen-round draw. The bout itself may have been a critical bust, but it was a success in demonstrating what wrestling promoters could actually still accomplish when they worked together.

With the Ali-Inoki whirlwind now behind him, Farhat was focusing on two new developments in the closing months of 1976, aside from trying to figure out how to reverse his dwindling business. He worked out a deal that would bring him back to East Texas for the first time since the Ed McLemore days of the 1950s. This involved working with two of his fellow NWA brethren: Fritz Von Erich, who ran Dallas–Fort Worth, Corpus Christi, and San Antonio and had taken over from McLemore after he died of a heart attack in 1969;[18] and Paul Boesch, the former Long Island lifeguard with the industry's most infamous cauliflower ears, who had gone down south and taken over Houston after the death of Morris Sigel in 1966. Starting with an October 4, 1976, appearance in the Will Rogers Memorial Center in Fort Worth to take on Rocky Johnson, The Sheik began making multiple shots per month for Von Erich and Boesch all the way through the middle of 1977, also battling the likes of Andre the Giant, Dory Funk Jr., Von Erich himself in a battle of aging wrestler-promoters who insisted on keeping themselves on top, and including a January 22, 1977, challenge in the Sam Houston Coliseum of world heavyweight champion Terry Funk, the second Funk brother to wear the NWA crown.[19]

It was in Dallas in the spring of '77 that The Sheik had his first encounters with Bruiser Brody, starting with a Sportatorium match on April 5, featuring fellow hardcore pioneer and good friend Bull Curry as referee, and ending on May 10 with one of the earliest examples of a Triple Threat match, featuring Sheik, Brody, and Von Erich. Meanwhile in Houston, The Sheik was setting the town on fire with Virgil Riley Runnels, a Texan who had swiftly become one of the hottest attractions in the country, the proverbial plumber's son with the heart and charisma of a Baptist preacher, who went by the name Dusty Rhodes. Farhat had mentored Rhodes early in his career, giving The Texas Outlaws, his formative tag team with Dick Murdoch, a shot in Big Time Wrestling. Rhodes had also learned a thing or two from The Sheik about the value of blading and seemed to be trying his best to catch up to him in terms of scarring up his body. By the time they met in the ring in Houston, they were equals as far as being top draws, and Farhat was so impressed with how far Dusty had come that he brought him in around the same time for some memorable main events at Cobo Arena.

What was also occupying Farhat at the time was something that for a while didn't look like it was going to happen—preparing Eddie Jr. for the ring. After years of focusing on a possible music career, Farhat's older son, now twenty-six years old and married with a baby girl at home, had decided to give the family business a try. Part of the reason for this was that Farhat had plans to install his son as the new booker for Big Time Wrestling. Tom Renesto's tenure had been a short one, as he took an offer to book for Nick Gulas's Memphis-Nashville circuit. Dory Funk Jr. had briefly stepped in to help out, but it seemed Farhat was ready to impart the job to someone he knew wasn't going anywhere, as was sometimes the practice among wrestling promoters, who were an untrusting bunch by nature. Not long after Eddie Jr. got the book, he started learning the ropes with Lou Klein as well as his dad and others. "Two weeks before I was going to get in the ring," remembered Eddie Jr., "We were home and I was joking with Dad and I said, 'It's too bad you can't wrestle.' And he laughed at me, and we went to the gym, we got into the ring, and he almost killed me. He knew everything! I said, 'Oh my God! You can do all this?' He said, 'Yeah, it's just not my style.'"

Early 1970s: Eddie Jr. watches his father head out to the ring for another battle. Pampero Firpo stands in the background on the far left.

For Eddie Jr., it was important that, just like almost all bookers in the wrestling business, he got a taste of what it was actually like to go through the ropes and take the bumps: "When I started and I was just booking cities, I was a little bit of an ass, because I was a kid. Then I realized you have to be a good businessman. Just because your dad's The Sheik and you own the company, you can't treat people like shit. One thing that helped me respect these guys is getting in the ring myself. I wanted to know what they were going through." Because The Sheik's persona still had to be protected at all costs, Eddie Jr. was not presented publicly as his son, but rather as Captain Ed George, a working-class, blue-collar hero. He debuted in January 1977, and one of his first matches was a tag team encounter in Toledo pitting him and fan favorite Tony Marino against Don Kent and Ed's own father, the dreaded Sheik. "I was thinking, 'What the hell am I doing?'" remembered Eddie. "But it was too late! I thought, 'OK, it's cool, I can do this.' Then here comes Dad, and I began regretting it . . . I could see the look in his eyes—he was not my dad, he became that badass . . . So the bell rings, I got the hot tag and hit the ring like a runaway train . . . [I thought] 'Oh God, here he comes!' I hit Dad again and again, and out he goes. I tag my partner, he does his thing, and about ten minutes later we finish. Kent gets me close to Dad and he cracks me with his taped pencil. Hurt like a bitch! I get rolled up, one-two-three. While I'm on my back, I'm thanking God it's over . . . I walk in the dressing room and here comes a chair flying at me, then my bag and clothes. Dad says, 'What was wrong with you? You were hitting so hard you broke a tooth!' About a week went by . . . Dad said, 'Why do you want to wrestle?' I said, 'When I talk to the talent and I tell them the finish and a few things I need in their match, I want them to know I would never ask them to do anything I have not done.'" [20]

And yet to many, the appointment of the inexperienced Eddie Jr. as booker was another sign of darker times ahead for Big Time Wrestling. Nevertheless, one of the greatest ironies in the history of the company was that just as things were turning sour, Detroit wrestling was to be targeted as subject matter for the most unlikely and unusual of motion pictures. Two aspiring filmmakers who had grown up in the area, and were familiar with The Sheik and his decades of destruction, decided they wanted to capture him, his troupe of colorful characters, and their hyper-violent, offbeat brand of wrestling for posterity. The end result, though not finished for nearly a decade, would be an unforgettable time capsule of pro wrestling in the territorial era that would come to be known as *I Like to Hurt People*—but back then at the beginning, it wasn't really determined what it was going to be called, or even what the specific nature of the project would be. All that Donald G. Jackson and Bryan Greenberg knew was that professional wrestling, specifically the professional wrestling to be found in their part of the country, was a fascinating phenomenon worthy of their B-movie sensibilities. Besides, it was conveniently close by and required a fraction of the production work usual for a movie.

Jackson had grown up in Adrian, Michigan, just an hour southwest of the Motor City, and had been working, like so many, including Farhat, in an automobile factory while dreaming of making movies. When a friend of his got injured in an accident at the plant, they used the settlement money he got to fund Jackson's first attempt at directing, a low-budget horror flick called *The Demon Lover*, the cast of which included Gunnar Hansen (Leatherface of *Texas Chainsaw Massacre* fame) and Val Mayerik (creator of comic book character Howard the Duck). Detroit native Greenberg worked as an assistant cameraman and editor on that film, immediately after having broken into the business on *Northville Cemetery Massacre*, helmed by future *Harry and the Hendersons* and *Angels in the Outfield* director Bill Dear. Having gotten their feet wet in the horror genre, Jackson and Greenberg initially envisioned their next project to be along those lines. But first, they needed a way into a notoriously closed business. That way turned out to be Bob Finnigan, to whom they were introduced by a mutual friend, and who was always on the lookout for ways to expand Big Time Wrestling's presence.[21]

What Jackson and Greenberg initially pitched to Finnigan was a movie called *Ringside in Hell*, which would feature The Sheik as a wrestler possessed by the Devil, and would use actual ring footage in addition to scripted segments. In order to help introduce them to everyone, Finnigan helped get Jackson and Greenberg invited to Sheik and Joyce's big New Year's Eve party at the Farhat estate. "It was really interesting to be at a party where you had people from state government and professional wrestlers mingling around," Greenberg muses. "They were pretty well off. Their home was like a small hotel."[22] At first, Farhat was predictably skeptical of the whole concept, but he reluctantly agreed to let Jackson, Greenberg, and the rest of their crew take a shot at it and see what would happen. On New Year's Day 1977, he flew to Atlanta for an Omni match against Thunderbolt Patterson, followed by a week-long Texas run. Meanwhile, the crew was given the green light.

It started with granting access to live events. This began not at a Big Time Wrestling show, but rather at a WWA card in Indianapolis on February 12, where The Sheik was taking on Dick the Bruiser in a steel cage match. From the very start, it quickly became apparent to Jackson this his initial horror film concept was going to be impossible. "We realized there was no way we'd ever be able to control the wrestlers," admits Greenberg, who served as chief cameraman on the project. "So, we decided to make it more of a quasi-documentary and found out that worked really well. Everything fit together after that, and that was the birth of *I Like to Hurt People*."[23] Beginning in April 1977, Jackson, Greenberg, and the crew became semi-regular fixtures backstage at Cobo Arena for nearly a year, gradually winning over the suspicious talent and getting them to let their guard down. Most importantly of all, of course, was winning the trust of The Sheik himself.

"It came down to getting him to really communicate with us," explains Greenberg. "The more we hung out with him, the more of a bond it became. The Sheik was a really good business guy, really easy to talk to, pretty sharp. He also had a good sense of humor, and we just hit it off. He never questioned what we were doing; he really trusted us, and saw we were having fun doing it. We would come to his house, shoot interviews at his office. At the end of the day we'd be in the kitchen hanging out eating hot dogs. We weren't a threat. We weren't going to reveal their trade secrets, and we weren't asking for them. [At first] I was really apprehensive. Are these guys half-crazed? But they turned out to be the nicest people ever. They really loved each other. It was a club. Once we got inside the club, it was really great because everybody treated us well and enjoyed having us around. Once The Sheik gave his blessing to us, it didn't matter who came to town, they were gonna be in the film. We felt privileged that we got through that door. They never really revealed anything to us, and we didn't really care."

The crew was given access almost everywhere, recording matches—many of which would not have otherwise been filmed—as well as backstage and ringside promos, and even conducting interviews of their own. On some occasions, they were allowed to script and orchestrate segments of their own, such as a memorable parking lot encounter between two young men and Andre the Giant, who emerges from a cramped Jeep to intone his first scripted line on film ("Are you talking to Andre?");[24] as well as a tongue-in-cheek backstage confrontation between Dusty Rhodes and New York Raymond, a colorful and eccentric character on the Michigan-Ohio wrestling scene known to hawk souvenirs at events and who had ingratiated himself to the Farhat family. It certainly didn't hurt that talent was paid for their work, and also that Finnigan continued to be a liaison through the whole process.

But even as the film crew was documenting Big Time Wrestling, the signs of decline continued, both in the promotion and in The Sheik's own career. Mike LeBell brought him in for one date in March, but it was his first West Coast appearance in three years, and his last for another three. Gulas kept using him for his wild-and-woolly Tennessee shows, where matches with Bobo Brazil and his ongoing feud with Jackie Fargo continued to please the mayhem-loving Southern crowds. The outside bookings were growing fewer, and Sheik's status as a bona fide national touring attraction was slipping. Also slipping was the Big Time Wrestling talent pool, and Farhat's eye for new prospects. In January, he brought in Gino Hernandez, a handsome young Paul Boesch discovery spotted while working the East Texas circuit, and he even put the United States title on the rookie with a win over Don Kent. Hernandez was destined for big things in the business, and it seemed like a rare sign that Farhat was seriously interested in grooming new young stars—but he only took the gold from Hernandez and put it back on himself a mere three months later, returning to business as usual. It was a disheartening move that many point to as emblematic of a systemic problem within the company and in Farhat's booking philosophies.

Meanwhile, television problems were brewing as well. Cincinnati promoter and front man Les Ruffin's retirement caused Farhat to lose his TV contacts in that city, and his programming wound up being dropped in one of his major markets (he continued running the Cincinnati Gardens nonetheless). It is also suspected that a particularly gory studio squash match between The Sheik and enhancement talent Denny Alberts, which also happened to be captured on film for *I Like to Hurt People*, may have helped precipitate the cancellation. Up north in Ontario, former Sheik ally George Cannon had picked up the pieces of the failed Jack Cain insurrection and the IWA and started up Superstars of Wrestling, competing directly with Big Time Wrestling's Southern Ontario shows, as well as Tunney's operation, and even succeeded in getting television across Canada, which could be seen on UHF in nearby Detroit. Cannon went so far as to buy commercial time during Big Time Wrestling broadcasts, an extra slap in the face.[25]

The buzzards were already beginning to circle, and it was certainly a far cry from the halcyon days of consecutive sellouts at Cobo Arena and main events all over the country. Nature was beginning to catch up with the once seemingly immortal Exalted Sheik, now in his fifties, and his dream was dimming in the face of grim reality. And yet as tough as things were looking, they were about to get a whole lot more dire. Big Time Wrestling was spiraling toward oblivion faster than anyone could've anticipated, and Farhat's place among the business's elite figures was fading away. As glorious as his rise had been, his fall would be equally catastrophic. The man who threw fire was going down in flames.

CHAPTER 14

THE DEATH OF BIG TIME WRESTLING

*"He lived an image of himself. He viewed his life inside a plot featuring
The Sheik as the unlikely hero, an Arab immigrant with a dream and an
insistent charm, slippery and dispassionate as a con man, invincible, and with
the fickle power of a king to give favors to his friends ... Safe inside this plot,
this image of himself, he was immortal. His mythology, for that's what it was,
supported tons of dreams, and many of them came true. He had collected a
modest fortune in his life ... The only hitch lay in the fact that being fiction,
the plot would sometime have to face real life. He'd get older."*
—JIM FREEDMAN, *DRAWING HEAT*

What went down in Detroit at the end of the 1970s is one of
the absolute tragedies of the history of territorial wrestling,
and a cautionary tale about how no company, no matter how
prosperous, is immune to the dangers of poor decision-making and the
vicissitudes of the economy. It was certainly one of the greatest disappointments of Ed Farhat's life, and a sad turn of events for the many
associates and fans who remembered the glory days that weren't very far
in the past at all. In a handful of years, Big Time Wrestling went from
drawing regular sellouts at the 12,500-seat capacity Cobo Arena, to little
more than two thousand fans by the time they finally shut their doors
in 1980. One by one, the TV deals would disappear, and the talent pool
evaporated, leaving behind a motley crew of local guys and some long-
in-the-tooth Sheik loyalists. For a brief moment, Farhat's company had
been one of the hottest anywhere in the world—but those days might
as well have been an eternity ago. Big Time Wrestling had set the Great
Lakes region on fire during the Lyndon Johnson and Richard Nixon

FROM THE PERSONAL COLLECTION OF DAVE BURZYNSKI.

administrations. By the time Ronald Reagan was elected, it had faded without a trace, and all that was left for anyone who loved it were the memories.

As with the downfall of any wrestling organization, there are many theories as to what exactly went wrong and many who have their own versions of why it all happened. Some of the reasons were connected to Farhat himself, but some were out of his control. "As much as I admired him, he couldn't step away," admits Kevin Sullivan of his idol. "And when you own a territory, eventually you have to step away. Look back at the territories that succeeded for a long time. Eddie Graham was a young man, and he stepped away. Bill Watts was a big star all over the country, but he stepped away. Look at Verne Gagne's territory—he didn't step away. Sheik didn't step away. Any place where the promoter was the top guy and didn't step away—things went bad. It's hard to wear both those hats, and he wore them for a long time. He had a gimmick where he could've lost and got his heat back. He had to know when things were going down, what to do to make it right. But he said no, I wanna be in that position. As great as he and Bobo were, how many times can you see the same guys wrestle?"

Year after year, Farhat had continued to keep himself on top, and it had come back to haunt him. Owning his own company gave him the perfect vehicle to keep himself relevant as long as he wanted to be—plus, he was hesitant to trust anyone else with that top spot, never knowing when they might jump ship on him. In Ed Farhat's mind, the only person that could be trusted in that position was Ed Farhat. This went hand-in-hand with his refusal to put anyone over in any decisive way. His heelish ways had worked in spades, in that fans desperately wanted to see him get beaten and were willing to get behind anyone who could do it. But in the end, The Sheik was never beaten, at least not convincingly and conclusively—he just kept going on, either winning or finding some other way to survive and fight another day. Eventually, the fans just gave up hope that any of their heroes would prevail. And then they stopped caring. "His matches in the late seventies were five minutes," says Dave Burzynski. "Go in, draw some blood, throw some fire, fight outside the ring, and that was it. Every week. And the other talent that he had around him just wasn't strong at all, not enough to draw people in." The same thing was going on in Toronto, where The Sheik went undefeated for years, as in Detroit. "Most promoters, the smart ones, moved aside and tried to bring in new talent," said Scott Teal. "But there were many that couldn't let it go. They wanted that main event payoff, and also what they made from the promotion."

Most other promotions had a rotating roster of stars, with new ones being made all the time—it was necessary for the long-term health of any territory. And to be sure, that did happen in Big Time, just not to the same degree as it did in other places, especially after the early seventies. Most heels who got major heat that could threaten The Sheik's top heel position wound up turned babyface, and most babyfaces that made it to The Sheik's level would be beaten and lose their momentum, usually moving on to greener pastures. Eventually, the fans caught on. Perhaps owing to Farhat's mistrustfulness, or perhaps owing to his reputation for poor payoffs, he also tended to rely repeatedly on the same circle of talent, more than most other territories did. Fans saw many of the same stars, the same feuds and the same matches time after time, nothing that could sustain interest for that long. "One of the last matches I went to was in 1978," remembers ardent Big Time Wrestling fan Alan Haugabook, who later worked with The Sheik as referee A.T. Huck. "The main event was Sheik and Firpo. Match lasted all of two or three minutes, I was so disappointed. A lot of his matches later on were simply so short like that. A lot of people say he didn't groom anybody to take his spot, but I remember Mark Lewin being champ for a while, Randy Savage was here, Terry Funk, Austin Idol. But too little too late, because none of them really got a push at the top . . . His son Eddie Jr. started pushing himself, too, as Captain Ed George. If they had run with Savage or Idol or Funk on top and given them a chance, maybe it would've survived."

There was no question that Eddie Jr. could be a polarizing figure, and The Sheik placing him in an authority position did not seem to help matters, either creatively or in terms of locker room morale. It also didn't help with the goodwill of the fans, most of whom had no idea he was The Sheik's son but still didn't seem to take to him as a performer, made worse by how hard he was being pushed—at one point even being given the hastily manufactured "World Wide Sports Heavyweight Championship" as a way to further his legitimacy. Promoters giving unwarranted pushes to their sons was nothing new in the wrestling business, and it usually didn't come to any good—not everyone would have the kind of blockbuster success Fritz Von Erich had marketing his sons in Dallas in the eighties, for example. For many longtime fans of Big Time Wrestling, the rise of Capt. Ed George is seen as something of a "jump the shark" moment. "Boy, nobody liked him," remarks the characteristically blunt Big Jim Lancaster. "He was one of those guys—my daddy's the boss, and he put me in charge of the dressing room. He tried to be a bully, especially with us younger guys, because we just wanted to be in the business ... The old-timers didn't have any respect for him and very seldom listened to him. He gave out finishes and told us what some of our matches were gonna be and what they were trying to accomplish. But he was not well-liked at all."

One often-heard story from this period comes from Terry and Dory Funk Jr., longtime associates and supporters of The Sheik. When Sheik's promotion was in trouble, the Funks were among those who felt a duty to try and help out, and they came up north to work a few shows and try to pop some houses. On one occasion, they recalled being in the locker room at Cobo Arena on a night when Sheik was out of town and had left his son in charge;[1] as they waited for their payoff at the end of the night, suddenly Eddie Jr. ran in and tried to claim that the cashbox had been stolen. It's worth mentioning that they are not the only ones to have told such a story. There was desperation in the air, and this points to another harsh reality of his downfall: The Sheik was running out of money. "He had money problems, and I'll tell you why," explains Fred Curry, a close family friend. "Later on, when he started losing his TV, and when the economy started dying in Detroit, this guy would never give up what he had. He would still play the gimmick, he loved to gamble, and when things started getting bad, it was because he always played the gimmick. He was down and out, and a lot of the top guys he had working for him left him. He had a lot of competition come in; he had a lot of people who worked for him going to work for the competition. He started losing and he never would quit. Joyce told me, 'He won't freakin' quit. He's draining all our money.' He always carried a wad of cash around, quite a bit. He always had twenty-five credit cards. He played the part, and he'd spend the money. He always had his gold rings, his alligator shoes, nothing but the best. But that was all from when he was making a lot of money at Cobo. When we went to Vegas, he was a wild guy, he would blow money there that people would take a year to make, and it was nothing to him, he'd laugh about it."

Depleting funds meant that people were not going to get paid. In the past, talent had complained of poor payoffs, and they certainly got

Cobo Arena, July 9, 1977: Out of loyalty to The Sheik, Terry Funk was one of the last major national stars to keep coming into Big Time Wrestling even in its waning days.

BRIAN BUKANTIS

a lot worse in the late seventies, but now it was more than just the boys getting short-changed. "I heard rumors that he stopped paying bills," explains Al Snow, who crossed paths with Sheik on the Michigan-Ohio wrestling scene not long after Big Time Wrestling's demise. "Where I lived, in Lima, Ohio, Sheik's TV had been off the air for a long time [before he went under]. A large part of that was because he left bills unpaid. TV stations didn't wanna do business for a long time locally with wrestling, because Sheik had left behind a lot of buildings and TV stations he had burned by not paying them." Jim Lancaster confirms this from firsthand experience as well: "When his promotions closed, he still owed plenty of TV stations money throughout Michigan and Ohio. I tried to get wrestling on Channel 35 in Lima, and the station manager laid an old bill in front of me for $450 that Sheik owed. He said, 'Here's

my experience with wrestling. You make good on that, and we'll talk.'"
The promotion was hemorrhaging money, and Farhat tried to stop or at
least slow the bleeding by using his own personal savings, which were
diminishing as well.

Even the NWA didn't have quite the power or united front that it
once did, and promoters like Farhat who found themselves in trouble
were also finding out that they were more and more on their own. It
was also not lost on him that the brotherhood that he had been loyal
to all those years was beginning to fail him when he needed it most.
And whatever shows of loyalty and support there may have been smelled
of opportunism, as the vultures began to circle. Jim Barnett's return to
prominence within the NWA, both as the booker for the world heavyweight champion and the man behind the nationally broadcast Georgia
Championship Wrestling, should've been a boon to Farhat given their
history, but Farhat began to suspect his old associate had treachery on his
mind and was out to take back the territory he had sold to him years ago.
The Sheik had been making appearances for Barnett on TBS and at the
Omni, and in exchange was getting precious access to Barnett's nationally recognized superstars for his own shows—only he started to notice
that GCW talent that he had advertised in good faith was beginning to
no-show his events, something The Sheik believed Barnett was orches-
trating to sabotage him so Barnett could move in and pick up the pieces.
And there was some truth to the belief that Barnett was trying to capitalize on national cable television by expanding GCW's physical presence,
as he would eventually begin running shows in places like Tennessee
and Alabama (formerly strongholds of the also-weakening Nick Gulas),
as well as Sheik towns like Columbus, Ohio, and Huntington, West
Virginia.[2] "After a while we gave up and decided to just use our own
guys from the area," said Eddie Jr. "I think it was a bit of a plan to do bad
to my dad. There were a few stars I can't mention, big names, and they
would come in and wrestle on the show, but things they would do and say
behind the scenes did a job on us."

But even if he had avoided bad booking decisions and threats from
other promoters, Farhat would still have had to contend with the realities
of running a Detroit-based business in the 1970s. The demise of the auto

industry that had once been the backbone of the Motor City had hit people hard, as did the after-effects of the oil crisis from the first half of the seventies; by the end of the decade, the city and its citizens were near broke. Leisure time was at a premium, as was the money to spend on it: professional wrestling, like other forms of entertainment, was a luxury many simply couldn't afford. The city bad become desolate, depressed, and crime-infested, and as the heart of Big Time Wrestling, once that dried up, so followed the surrounding towns. "The United Auto Workers union was fighting for a living wage," explains Poffo. "Then Chrysler and GM and Ford, they upped the salaries and passed the expenses on by charging more for the cars. Finally, Germany and Japan are making better cars, and then next thing you know Chrysler, GM, and Ford are going down the drain. Toledo made the glass. When the car business goes down, they don't need glass for the windshields. So, Toledo was depressed, Detroit was depressed, Flint, etc. The car business dictated the wrestling business. When they went sour, so did we."

It must also be pointed out that contrary to his larger-than-life persona, Ed Farhat was a human being, and human beings are prey to weaknesses. He also happened to work in a business that notoriously amplifies and encourages those weaknesses, and many are the performers and promoters, past and present, who have succumbed to the attractive lure of vice in its largely unsupervised and shadowy world. No accurate telling of Farhat's life would be complete without pointing out that these personal failings did undeniably contribute to the downfall of his company and to the difficult years that followed. Farhat's love of gambling and high-living, which had been a cause for unheeded criticism from those around him for years, was becoming a real issue, as his life savings and company funds were frittered away on frivolous expenses and failed attempts at winning back what was lost. There was also a harsh reality that was becoming the whispered talk of the wrestling industry— that substance abuse had been rearing its ugly head. Since his gallbladder surgery, Farhat had been working through a great deal of pain, and many believe that the need to dull this pain may have been what led him down the path beyond prescription medication to harder, illicit drugs, including, eventually, cocaine and heroin. This tragic progression was far from uncommon in the wrestling industry, but usually only afflicted workers, not promoters. In Farhat's case, because he continued to push himself as an in-ring talent, he exposed himself to the perils they face as they get older and their bodies break down, and this did not bode well for someone who owned a major pro wrestling operation and was responsible for important decision-making on a regular basis.

Even more rampant than drug use in the industry was marital infidelity, with the attractions of life on the road overcoming all but the most austere individuals. Farhat was not immune to this either, and he was one of the many who paradoxically played the parts of both family man and ladies' man simultaneously. A surprisingly handsome man when not in character, Farhat was known for a kind of gallantry that would sometimes catch women off guard, such as in a story told by Bill Apter of bringing his new wife backstage at the Maple Leaf Gardens during a working honeymoon in Toronto: "We walked into the office, and there was The Sheik. He knew I was smart to the business. But he looked at her and he approached us . . . he looked at me kinda weird like he knew who I was, and then he took her hand, in a king-like manner, and he kissed her hand, and walked away. Just like that. A great moment." Jim Freedman describes a similar moment in *Drawing Heat*, in which Farhat became enamored with a young woman they encountered in a shopping mall near Cochrane, Ontario: "He declared to her she was the most beautiful woman he had ever seen, and he meant it, so help me, so much so that he brought her hand to his lips. Her whole body blushed. I looked at the conviction in his face as he lingered with her hand in his, and at the eyes of the attractive teenager, terrified and touched by the senior man's painful expression of the heart." Unfortunately, the influence of substance abuse seems to have turned this somewhat romanticized aspect of Farhat's personality into something much more dangerous and harmful to his career and even more importantly, his home life, as he still happened to be married to a woman who had sacrificed everything to help him become the man he was, and who loved him dearly through all of it.

These harmful aspects of Farhat's life during this period have understandably been touchy subjects rarely discussed over the years and remain so today, and thus the whole and specific truth can be difficult to reliably ascertain. But with the passage of so much time, there are some willing to offer thoughts, including Fred Curry, who was close to all of it as it was happening: "Joyce was a terrific gal, I had a lot of respect for her. It was a happy marriage at the beginning, but later he started going out with this flighty-looking waitress. At the end, their marriage kind of went down the tubes, but she always stood by him . . . She was a terrific, terrific woman. I never saw big affection, though. I was walking through Cobo Hall one time, and he and Joyce were walking in front of me, and he had his hand on her hip. It was the only time I ever saw any affection between them. He blasted her a couple times toward the end, and I was shocked. How could he talk to Joyce like that? Things changed. He started doing his own little thing, going out. And she was always true blue." Dave Burzynski, who had departed the territory by that point but still kept in touch with the goings-on back in his beloved Detroit, recalls a similar story: "I was hearing from other guys that Sheik had a girl-friend and was heavy into gambling and drugs . . . And it was basically catching up to him at that time."[3]

It was a time of contradiction, to be sure. While Farhat's hold on his business was slipping, Don Jackson and Bryan Greenberg were continu-ing to shoot footage for their pseudo-documentary film. Meanwhile, the product was noticeably contracting. Financial difficulties began emerg-ing as early as 1974, when the vaunted production truck was repossessed and sold off to a local televangelist, which led to a move away from on-location arena matches on TV and back to studio wrestling in down-town Detroit at the WGPR facilities, a definite step backward. And when the stations made the decision to start charging directly for airtime rather than banking on making their money from advertising, the cash-strapped Farhat was forced to accept a cheaper late-night time slot that shrank his audience even further. This more limited reach in turn meant a handicapped ability to draw viewers to attend live events, thus feed-ing into what was becoming a self-perpetuating cycle of decline. And yet even in these final years of Big Time Wrestling, when the flow of new talent had slowed to a trickle, Farhat was able to rely to a smaller degree on the relationships he had spent years in the business building to bring in a handful of notable names to help shake things up. These included the towering master of the heart punch, Douglas "Ox" Baker of idyllic Waterloo, Iowa, known for his shaved head and prodigious facial hair, who managed to keep the United States title away from The Sheik for a few weeks in the fall of '77; former WWWF World Heavyweight Champion Stan "The Man" Stasiak, from whom Baker had co-opted the heart punch; and the young and handsome Raymond Rougeau, eldest son of Montreal promoter Jacques Rougeau, on loan from Jim Barnett in Atlanta.

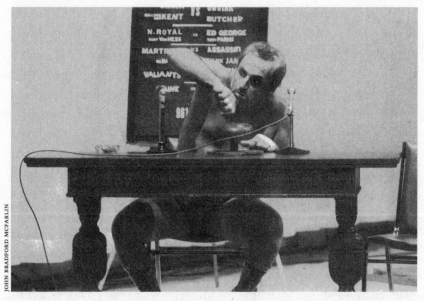

October 1977: The Sheik takes over the timekeeper's table at a Big Time Wrestling TV taping. Note the sign behind him, advertising the matches for the next Cobo Arena card.

Farhat was also getting a bit of what seemed like help from his former boss Vince McMahon, with whom he began something of a working relationship that involved the WWWF sending in talent to Cobo Arena like they had during the promotional war earlier in the decade. It began Thanksgiving weekend of 1977, when the muscle-bound and tie-dyed Superstar Billy Graham, the newest McMahon sensation, who had ended Bruno Sammartino's final world title reign the previous April in Baltimore, came in to defend his championship against New Zealand's Tony Garea, recently one half of the WWWF World Tag Team Champions.[4] Also on the card was another WWWF import, "High Chief" Peter Maivia, who faced The Sheik himself the following month at Cobo when the WWWF crew returned once more (that time, Graham defended the world title against Big Time Wrestling's most beloved babyface, Bobo Brazil). Yet the contrast between the two companies by this point was stark: earlier in November, Graham had been performing in Madison Square Garden in front of eighteen thousand people—at Cobo, that number was a mere two thousand.

Farhat's troubles extended to Toronto as well, where his eight-year partnership with Frank Tunney was about to come crashing down. Attendance had been dwindling at the Maple Leaf Gardens, and Tunney blamed this in large part on The Sheik continuing to book himself as the top attraction and being unable to deliver more than repetitive, short and violent matches. Meanwhile, Tunney was being threatened by the growing popularity of George Cannon's Superstars of Wrestling, which was running all over Ontario and had even managed to book a major show at the Canadian National Exhibition Stadium in his own backyard the year before. When Cannon threatened to run the CNE Stadium again in the summer of '77, Tunney responded by booking it for three consecutive monthly events, effectively locking him out. He relied on Farhat to book those shows, which produced disastrous results that proved to be the final nail in the coffin of their relationship. The events were notoriously plagued by no-shows, including the mega-popular Dusty Rhodes, a close friend of The Sheik's who nevertheless skipped all three events for which he was heavily advertised. For the main event of the first show in June, Farhat booked himself in a five-minute disqualification against longtime opponent Tiger Jeet Singh. For the second show in July, he challenged new NWA World Heavyweight Champion Harley Race for the first time and also booked Superstar Graham vs. Chief Jay Strongbow for the WWWF World title. Nevertheless, the shows all drew in the ten-to-fifteen-thousand range, which wouldn't have been too bad for Maple Leaf Gardens but were huge disappointments for the seventy-five-thousand-seat-capacity CNE Stadium.

With Tunney and Farhat already squabbling over money and Farhat's share of the promotion, this was the straw that broke the camel's back. The Sheik never appeared for Tunney again, and going forward Maple Leaf Wrestling would instead enter into very lucrative partnerships with the WWWF, AWA, and Jim Crockett Promotions, arguably the three hottest companies in North America at the time. Needless to say, Tunney never looked back. As for Farhat, he had lost the territory that was second only to Detroit in terms of importance to him, having burned out the fan base there just as he had in his own home base. Going forward, he would maintain his presence in Ontario by working more often with "Bear Man" Dave McKigney on his independent cards—a far cry from the NWA-affiliated, big-money Tunney promotion. This partnership produced the short-lived effort known as Canadian Big Time Wrestling, which even managed a few TV tapings, but for the most part was a small-town house show operation.

Dates on the Big Time circuit were growing fewer, especially beyond Cobo Arena, and when it came to outside bookings, The Sheik was finding himself in Japan more than he was in his own country. There was talk of additional TV stations dropping his programming, and a cursory look at the TV product of this era leaves little doubt as to why. "The shows were not [airing] in order," recalled Eddie Jr. "It came to a point they started filming and not even really caring which segments were right. They were just throwing together shows and putting them out. Nineteen seventy-seven and 1978 were when things started getting rocky. They were just getting shows out to keep from losing their TV. They lost control of what was supposed to go where. We did our editing at a local TV station in Detroit." Whatever domestic outside bookings Farhat was taking by this time were with those who had been most loyal to him over the years, which included the Funks, whose Amarillo-Lubbock territory was dying on the vine much like his was. He spent much of the latter months of 1977 shuttling back and forth from Michigan down south to Texas as well as to the Alabama-Tennessee-Kentucky circuits run by Nick Gulas and the Welch-Fuller family. In addition to his long-standing relationship with Gulas, he was also motivated by his son's continued musical aspirations, since Gulas's home base was in Nashville, the capital of the country music industry. Eddie Jr. was keen on making some connections and becoming a crossover success, not just for his own sake but for that of his family—which grew on April 4, 1978, with the birth of The Sheik's first (and only) grandson, Edward George Farhat III.

As things worsened, the film crew continued to make appearances at Cobo Arena, shooting footage for what would become *I Like to Hurt People*. By early 1978, it had been over a year since Jackson and Greenberg had begun filming, as they were running into their own financial backing difficulties that had slowed production down. They took a particular liking to female wrestler Heather Feather and her feminist angle of wanting to compete against men, and footage they shot of her being interviewed backstage, as well as fulfilling her goal in the ring, would be some of the most endearing and memorable material in the finished product.[5] They also managed to capture a truly rare and unforgettable moment as Eddy Creatchman, having turned on The Sheik after causing him to lose the US title to Ox Baker by throwing the towel in, was confronted by none other than Ernie "Abdullah Farouk" Roth, making a brief return from McMahon-land to manage his old charge as he attempted to regain the title from the Ox, now managed by Creatchman. "It was priceless," recalls Greenberg. "Being in the room was incredible. We kept the cameras rolling, and it's the only time we ever caught these guys out of character, and unfortunately, I can't find the footage for the life of me! They were rolling on the floor laughing. The craziest thing is about two hours before that, Sheik was yelling at Ox Baker. You didn't wanna mess with The Sheik. Apparently, Ox Baker did, and got an earful."

By the end of winter, shooting had finally wrapped and it was time to go through the footage. Jackson and his team spent the next few months trying to edit something together, but it was during that time that the project just petered out—there was no more money, and the folks involved were being beckoned to other projects. The footage wound up going with Jackson in a move to California, where it would be put on the shelf, both literally and figuratively. It looked like all the work had been for nothing, and it was definitely disappointing, but Farhat had other things to worry about at the time.

He was willing to try just about anything to increase fan interest except removing himself from the top position, and this included the unthinkable: taking inspiration from the heel vs. heel feud with Baker and Creatchman in which The Sheik had begun to hear some sentimental cheers from the familiar crowd, Farhat actually turned himself babyface in June, using the betrayal of his former tag team partner Don Kent as the catalyst. For the first time since he had transformed himself into the vicious Arabian madman in the late 1940s, The Sheik, once the most feared and despised man in professional wrestling, was one of the good guys. In addition to Kent and Baker, he feuded with Stan Stasiak, Abdullah the Butcher, and a heel Terry Funk, from whom he regained the United States title in October. He got the opportunity to tag team with his son for the first time, as well as the most unlikely of all tag team partners, Bobo Brazil, with whom he joined forces twice at Cobo Arena over the summer.

But perhaps in retrospect, the most interesting thing to come out of the brief "babyface Sheik" era was the feud that took place against the returning Randy Poffo, a rookie no longer, who was quickly making himself into a superstar as Randy "Macho Man" Savage. Farhat had encountered Savage again while working down south for Gulas, where he was distinguishing himself as Mid-America Heavyweight Champion, and he was sufficiently impressed to bring Randy back to Big Time Wrestling, this time without his brother and father. This resulted in two back-to-back main events for the United States title at Cobo Arena in February and March of 1979, which can now be looked back on as a true changing-of-the-guard moment (even though Sheik won them both, of course). Within six years, Randy Savage would be one of the hottest wrestlers in the country, and in less than a decade, the world, as one of the most recognizable faces of a whole new era in the business. And yet during this nascent period, Sheik and his son both had him do jobs to them. By the end of spring, he was off to better things and back on the path to pro wrestling immortality.

The Sheik's face turn is not fondly remembered by fans—unlike some other face turns by longtime heels like Fred Blassie, Fritz Von Erich, and Gorilla Monsoon for example, it simply did not take. After three decades of unbridled mayhem and evil, people simply were not willing

Cobo Arena, March 10, 1979:
Just two years after christening
himself "Randy Savage"
in Georgia Championship
Wrestling, a grateful Macho
Man did the honors in Detroit
for the man who gave him his
first break in the business.

BRIAN BUKANTIS

to accept him in this form, despite the fact that by this time his persona had already devolved into something of a caricature, losing a lot of its edge. The Sheik was a paradoxically endearing figure by this point in his career, but fans still were not comfortable being overtly pushed to cheer for him. They even tried it in Dick the Bruiser's Indiana territory—where he continued to be a regular attraction—after several months of trying to rekindle the legendary Sheik-Bruiser feud in Indianapolis and Fort Wayne, and even in Chicago for Bruiser's pal Verne Gagne. By the end of 1978, fans were given the ultimate reversal of fortunes as The Sheik and Dick the Bruiser, who had previously battled each other both in business and in the ring, actually teamed up at Cobo to face the Funks. But despite this historic teaming, a mere 3,197 fans turned up to see it. All told, the babyface experiment lasted about ten months, after which The Sheik reverted back to his diabolical ways, for good.

And regardless of that experiment, it never extended to The Sheik's other appearances throughout the South, which continued through 1978 and were just about the only trips he made besides Japan. The Funks had finally sold off their family's western Texas territory to Blackjack Mulligan and Dick Murdoch, who kept bringing Sheik in as they attempted to keep the dying region alive for the next two years—but the glory days of Lubbock sellouts in the 1960s were a distant memory.

Gulas, meanwhile, was fighting a losing battle for survival against upstart outlaw promoter Jerry Jarrett, who had started out selling programs for Gulas with his mom as a kid before eventually working his way up to being Gulas's assistant. After their falling out, Jarrett started up the Continental Wrestling Association and took top star Jerry "The King" Lawler with him, together turning Memphis into one of the nation's hottest wrestling towns. By 1980, Gulas would be out of business, but in the meantime Sheik did what he could to help him draw some houses, which often included working with some of his promising new talent.

One of these was twenty-year-old rookie Bobby Eaton, whose unassuming demeanor belied his extraordinary talent. Gulas thought so highly of Eaton's ability that he quickly paired him with his less-than-extraordinary son George, whom he was desperate to get over, and also matched him against The Sheik in a couple of matches in Eaton's hometown of Huntsville, Alabama,[6] in the summer of '78—five years before Eaton began his legendary run as one half of The Midnight Express. Gulas had also recently paired up two other youngsters destined for greatness: fast-talking twenty-year-old newcomer Michael Hayes of Pensacola, Florida, and Chattanooga's own Terry Gordy, a thick and powerful eighteen-year-old who had already been five years in the business. In May and June of 1979, with only half a year of full-time teaming under their belts, Hayes and Gordy tangled with The Sheik and his former booker Tom Renesto in a series of clashes in Nashville and Chattanooga that were the epitome of the grizzled old guard versus wrestling's new school. Within a couple of years, Hayes and Gordy would be setting the world on fire as The Fabulous Freebirds, but on those Tennessee nights they were just a couple of fresh-faced kids battling wrestling's thirty-year scourge.

Strained as it may have become, Farhat's working relationship with Jim Barnett remained a vital lifeline for him. Barnett's pull in the NWA helped bring some top talent to Cobo Arena in 1978, like Mil Mascaras, whom The Sheik faced for the first time in nine years on the April 1 card, and Harley Race, once the broken-legged rookie Farhat had kept afloat, now the NWA World Heavyweight Champion, who came in to defend the title against The Sheik at the March 18 show, the first time the NWA title had come to Cobo since the Dory Funk Jr. days at the height of the Bruiser war. In return, while his own company remained (just barely) in operation, The Sheik continued to appear for Barnett in Atlanta, as well as other Georgia towns like Augusta, Rome, and Columbus. Sheik worked with the likes of his pal Abdullah the Butcher, who continued to be a major GCW draw, as well as with other Georgia stars like former three-time Mr. USA bodybuilding champion Tony White, aka Tony Atlas, and former New York Jets linebacker Edward "Wahoo" McDaniel, the Native American superstar whose rugged, take-no-prisoners style had made him a legend to Southern fans. As Barnett's company began using their national cable presence to expand, Barnett began working with Farhat in co-promoting shows in towns like Columbus, Ohio, and Huntington, West Virginia, which fell within Farhat's domain. Although it may have seemed like friendly cooperation, the message was

Cobo Arena, March 18, 1978: The Sheik receives his last shot at the NWA World Heavyweight title when Harley Race comes to Cobo for the only time as champion.

clear: Barnett was interested in taking back these towns and was only playing nice with Farhat (for the moment) as a gesture of respect for their history together. But make no mistake—Farhat was being gradually pushed out, and he knew it.

As if his personal and business problems weren't enough, tragedy struck the Farhat family on December 12, 1978, when Michael Farhat, son of The Sheik's eldest brother, Lewie, and his wife, Agnes, was killed with a shotgun during a domestic dispute with his wife, Linda, at their mobile home in the Chateau Estates trailer park in Howell, about forty miles outside of Lansing, in the presence of their one-year-old child. Just twenty-seven years of age, Michael had been a sergeant in Vietnam and later wrestled for his uncle in the mid-seventies as the masked Patriot and Michael Thomas, even getting booked in an opening match with Killer Kowalski at Cobo Arena during The Sheik's gallbladder hiatus, but he'd been out of the business for a couple years by the time of his death. Nevertheless, it was Michael's famous uncle who was summoned to McPherson Community Health Center that night to identify the body.

As the decade reached its end, business difficulties were leading to tax and legal problems that were all coming to a head. Farhat was cutting whatever corners he could to keep his business solvent, but the unpaid bills were piling up, and the money was drying up. He was shortchanging everyone—building fees weren't being met, and the buildings were starting to notice. On January 12, 1979, Big Time Wrestling held its final card at the Cincinnati Gardens, arguably Farhat's second-most important venue, with a main event Cincinnati fans had seen countless times for more than a decade: The Sheik vs. Bobo Brazil (this time with Karolyn Rose, wife of Cincinnati Reds hit king Pete Rose, as a special referee).[7] On April 23, the company took its final bow at Hara Arena in Dayton. They held on to the Toledo Sports Arena all the way till March 27, 1980, with a final card that featured The Sheik against Georgia journeyman Jerry Oates[8] and an appearance by Ginger the wrestling bear. The loss of venues was in conjunction with the litany of local TV stations dropping Farhat's programming after many months of declining viewership and unpaid bills. Unpaid taxes and other expenses, including one from an electrical contracting company that had done work on the Farhats' palatial Williamston estate, resulted in liens being put on the house, and there was talk of possible foreclosure in the air.

Even his old friends the Poffos had targeted him in an anti-trust lawsuit in August 1979 that took aim at a host of NWA promoters that also included Barnett, Gulas, Jarrett, Lawler, Bruiser, Wilbur Snyder, Verne Gagne, Eddie Graham, Bob Geigel, and Buddy Fuller. Earlier in the year, Angelo and his sons, Lanny and Randy, had started up their own independent company, International Championship Wrestling, based in Knoxville, Tennessee, and encroaching into towns in Kentucky, Missouri, Illinois, and West Virginia. Naturally, this put them on the radar as an outlaw promotion, and they came to know the detrimental effects of pro wrestling's monopolistic practices as promoters who felt they "owned" certain territories refused to share talent with ICW and even began blacklisting those who did work with them. Farhat, being the brazen contrarian that he was, tried to stay loyal to the Poffos and had agreed to work some dates for ICW (besides, the extra money wouldn't hurt). But in the end, he bowed to pressure from Barnett, Gulas, and the others to turn down the offer, which wound up getting him lumped in the lawsuit with the rest of the defendants.[9]

With fewer venues to run, Big Time Wrestling was only putting on a handful of shows per month, sometimes as few as two or three, with the mighty Cobo Arena holding on by a thread. A concerted effort was made to use Capt. Ed George as a headliner for shows where The Sheik was not appearing, which was less than helpful. Attempting to buck the lowered expectations of what he was capable of doing in the ring, the fifty-two-year-old Sheik amazingly battled Ox Baker to a one-hour draw on March 31 at the Detroit State Fairgrounds. In a then-rare example of spotlighting a hot new talent on the way to doing great things, when former powerlifter Dennis McCord reinvented himself as the bleached-blond "Universal Heartthrob" Austin Idol, Big Time Wrestling was one of the first places he was allowed to shine before moving on to stardom as part of Jarrett and Lawler's Memphis circuit. But for the most part, near the end, the Big Time Wrestling roster was filled out by local guys like preliminary wrestler John Bonello of Ontario, who received a push large enough to propel him to two tag team title reigns in 1980, and Detroit's

Malcolm Monroe, who went by the nickname "Sweet Daddy" in tribute to an African-American pioneer of the previous generation, Reginald Siki. Most of these were talents who had not and would not work extensively in other areas and certainly did not pack anywhere near the star power of the international legends that fans had grown accustomed to seeing at Cobo Arena. "He used a lot of local guys toward the end, because they were cheap," recalls Les Thatcher, who by that point was working as a TV producer-announcer for Ron Fuller's Knoxville-based Southeastern Championship Wrestling. "Even the greatest workers in the world were only good for so long in a territory. Sheik just burned himself out, and the babyfaces he worked with. I see the value of blood. But someone was almost always bleeding. He kept doing the same basic formula in the same towns, and the only face that changed was the babyface on the other side of ring."

Beyond Big Time Wrestling, many other territories had also burned out on The Sheik, and he had to look farther abroad in some cases to find places where his act would still be fresh. In addition to Japan, this included Puerto Rico. It was there that Puerto Rican mid-carders Victor Jovica and Carlos Colon, who had experienced some success in Stampede Wrestling and the WWWF respectively, had cornered the market on their native island by founding the World Wrestling Council, predictably making themselves overnight world-beating superstars in the process. From the beginning, the WWC traded in wanton bloodshed and threshold-pushing violence, which meant it was tailor-made for The Sheik, as well as Abdullah the Butcher. In fact, for his Puerto Rican debut on January 6, 1979, The Sheik teamed with Abdullah, then the WWC Puerto Rican Champion, to take on Colon and his former WWC World and North American Tag Team Championship partner Jose Rivera at San Juan's Roberto Clemente Coliseum, then the largest indoor event facility on the island.[10]

In July 1979, The Sheik wrestled only one match for Big Time Wrestling (a draw with Mark Lewin at Cobo) and spent half the month working for Giant Baba in Japan. After he returned, he renewed his working relationship with Vincent J. McMahon, who by then was working very closely with his enterprising son Vincent K. McMahon—commonly known within the business at the time as Vince Jr.—in running the group whose name his son had persuaded him to shorten to the World Wrestling Federation, or WWF. For the August 25 Cobo event, the McMahons sent their current WWF World Heavyweight Champion: squeaky-clean, red-haired and freckled Bob Backlund of Princeton, Minnesota, a former Division II NCAA Champion who was the absolute antithesis of Superstar Billy Graham, the man he had upended for the title at Madison Square Garden a year and a half earlier. The Sheik put his US title against Backlund's world title in a true clash of styles that night, as well as at the October 28 Cobo card,[11] and he also took on another imported McMahon talent at the September 8 Cobo show—burly Croatian Josip Peruzovic, who used his animosity for his Soviet oppressors as the impetus to become the Russian caricature Nikolai Volkoff.

Big Time Wrestling, and the vaunted Sheik–Dick the Bruiser feud had its last feeble gasp of relevance in the fall of 1979, a time when album-rock radio stations across the country, including Detroit's 101.1 WRIF-FM, waged a now-baffling cultural war against the rise of disco music. The war was not without its racist and homophobic overtones, and profiting from those was certainly not something the pro wrestling business had ever been above, so it perhaps was less than surprising that The Sheik and the Bruiser would agree to a cross-promotion with WRIF—a symbolic clash in which Dick the Bruiser would fight on behalf of rock n' roll, and the evil Sheik would paradoxically fight on behalf of disco (maybe some folks had gotten a look at Farhat's decidedly funky attire away from the ring). The bout was heavily hyped in the Detroit area as part of WRIF's "Disco Sucks" campaign, and it's worth noting that not even this promotion was enough to convince Farhat to do the job, as he counter-intuitively won the match via count out. Predictably, despite all the hype, the match did little to alter Farhat's fortunes and, if anything, only further highlighted what a parody of his once-fearsome self he was in danger of becoming.

In the old days, there was an expression in the wrestling business—"lifting the spike"—that came from the carnival days and meant that a promoter was closing the show. Although he didn't want to, 1980 was the year Ed Farhat lifted the spike for Big Time Wrestling. By then, the choice was really out of his hands. Even loyalists like Bob Finnigan and Lord Layton had abandoned him—Finnigan to pursue his music career full-time rather than continue butting heads with his boss, and Layton to throw all his effort into being a Bacardi spokesman after seeing that the operation he had enjoyed working with for nearly two decades was a shadow of its former self, as was the man running it. Even Eddie Jr. made the decision to step away from the ring as the bookings grew fewer and farther between, performing as Capt. Ed George for the last time on the January 19 Cobo Arena show with a win over his old foe Don Kent: "I had come to terms with it. I had realized that it was over, and you had to move on. I think it was harder on my parents because it was really their territory and they put a lot of heart and soul into it, especially my father. I know it tore him up, and I know it made him sad, but he was sick, and there was nothing he could do about it."[12]

In addition to the maneuverings of his promotional "partners" Barnett and the McMahons, Farhat was fielding offers from expansion-minded promoters looking to buy the territory outright, including Ron Fuller, Jim Crockett Jr., and Bill Watts, whose brand-new Mid-South Wrestling Association had just muscled Leroy McGuirk out of Louisiana, Mississippi, and Arkansas. The word had spread throughout the business that Sheik's territory was extremely vulnerable and that Detroit in particular was a dying city—in wrestling, just as it was otherwise. Some promoters who had been happy to book him in years past were avoiding him, most notably Mike LeBell, who brought him to Los Angeles for two shots in April 1980—one a tag team match pitting him and Pampero Firpo against legendary masked luchador Blue Demon and second-generation main-eventer Chavo Guerrero,[13] and then a singles encounter with Guerrero the following week for Guerrero's Americas Championship. These would be the final times that The Sheik would appear in the state of California, once one of his favorite and most lucrative stops.

Inevitably, the time came when even the shows at Cobo Arena were in danger. Perhaps knowing that his time there was limited, Farhat began to gradually shift his main operations to the Canton Memorial Civic Center, one of the last major arenas he was still running, as well as the humble Lincoln Park Community Center, twelve miles south of

Detroit on I-75. On April 22, it was to Canton and not Cobo that Farhat brought in Bob Backlund for a world title defense against top WWF challenger Cowboy Bobby Duncum (an old West Texas State buddy of Bob Finnigan's).[14] For his June 28 Cobo Arena event, Farhat pulled out all the stops and called in a whole bunch of favors, drawing talent from everywhere for a one-night tournament for the vacant North American Tag Team title. On hand were Giant Baba and Jumbo Tsuruta from All Japan, as well as tried-and-true names from Big Time Wrestling's past like "Flying" Fred Curry, "Big Cat" Ernie Ladd, and Sheik's old tag team partners Abdullah the Butcher and Killer Brooks.

Even that didn't prevent Farhat from losing television in Detroit—the very lifeblood of his organization. For the first time since Barnett and Doyle had first put it on the air in 1959, Big Time Wrestling was off the air in the Motor City. Naturally, this crushing blow made it next to impossible to attract crowds to whatever live events were left. Farhat was scrambling, relying even more on his arrangement with Barnett and Georgia Championship Wrestling, and even taping some TV for secondary markets out of West Virginia, where he and Barnett were co-promoting often. He took on more dates for Dave McKigney, with whom he was also doing a little co-promoting in Ontario. In most of the summer and fall, the Canton Memorial Civic Center became the equivalent of what Cobo Arena had been, and it was there that The Sheik once again faced Bob Backlund in a couple of blood-soaked encounters in September—the second being a steel cage match won by Backlund, who nevertheless was deprived of the United States title on a technicality (specifically being that Farhat had no intention of letting him abscond with it to the WWF).[15]

The McMahons were clearly feeling out the territory and hoping to stake their claim, seeing as Michigan and especially Ohio were so close to their home base in the Northeast. There was no love lost between them and Farhat by that point, but Farhat needed all the help he could get, even if it was coming from those looking to supplant him. Expansion was on their mind, egged on no doubt by the younger McMahon, whose lofty ambitions were then only beginning and were still held in check by his father's old-school sensibilities. Perhaps with their assistance, Farhat managed a brief return to Cobo Arena in October with two consecutive weekend events, the first pitting himself against ever-loyal Dory Funk Jr. in a gory "nail-board match" main event, and the second turning into something of a showcase for the company that was looking to get their talent over and move in.

It's difficult to pinpoint the exact date that a wrestling promotion essentially closes up shop, but for most who analyze such things, the closest thing to the death date of Big Time Wrestling would be Sunday, October 12, 1980, just two nights after the Pistons season opener against the Washington Bullets, when Ed Farhat brought his brand of entertainment to beautiful, air-conditioned Cobo Arena for the very last time. Outside of the usual band of local Detroit talent, the only past Big Time greats who made it were Mighty Igor, who came in from Puerto Rico, and Farhat's one-time right-hand man Don Kent, who had begun taking dates with George Cannon's Superstars of Wrestling after Farhat lost his TV. The Sheik did not appear in the main event, as the two top spots on the card were occupied by WWF talent: World Champion Bob Backlund teamed with McMahon's top touring attraction Andre the Giant to take on Wild Samoans Afa and Sika, once Farhat's longest-reigning World Tag Team Champions, now holders of the WWF World Tag Team title; then, Backlund performed double duty, defending his crown against Olympic strongman Ken Patera. In the third match from the top, Sheik had booked a sentimental farewell match against his legendary archrival Bobo Brazil, whom he had just wrestled in a couple of steel cage matches for the Bear Man in Ontario three months earlier but who hadn't appeared at Cobo in a year and a half. It was meant to be a fitting coda to their legacy in Detroit. However, in one of the most telling examples of how badly Farhat had been burning bridges, the man who had been his dearest friend in the business, whom Farhat had even put up in his home during his messy divorce less than three years earlier, no-showed The Sheik's final bow at Cobo Arena, forcing him to defend his US title against non-descript mid-carder Bob White. Brazil chose to remain in Springfield, Illinois, where he had wrestled the night before—for Dick the Bruiser's WWA. He then took the week off.

The tenuous Farhat-McMahon alliance collapsed after that night, and The Sheik finally lost Cobo Arena—the equivalent to McMahon losing Madison Square Garden, Barnett losing the Omni, or Tunney losing Maple Leaf Gardens. For all intents and purposes, World Wide Sports, and Big Time Wrestling, was no more. "We just had to let it go," Eddie Jr. recalled. "It just got worn out. We didn't change. We kept going with the same people and thinking it was gonna get better. He was a great card and drew millions of people, but sometimes you have to know when not to be in the main event. When to take a rest. What happened with Dad was he didn't trust anybody to take that top spot . . . It just came to the point where there were personal things in his life, things happen and there was nothing we could do about it. He had his run, and that's it."

Farhat would continue attempting to promote independently in the area, and Lord knows he would continue to wrestle, but the days of his running his own territory were over, and the days of his being an NWA member in good standing would be ending not long after. For sixteen years, he had ruled the eastern Midwest with an iron fist, but in doing so, he had also ground it into dust. For a handful of those years, his promotion could even make a claim to having been the hottest in the country, but those days had receded into wrestling's smoky past, and in a few more years, with the landscape of the industry altered beyond recognition, it would almost seem to newer fans as if it had never happened at all.

CHAPTER 15

WANDERER IN THE WILDERNESS

"This business sucks. And Sheik never knew when to get out."
—JOYCE FARHAT, AS TOLD TO "FLYING" FRED CURRY

C oming out of the doom and gloom of the 1970s, the 1980s was a decade of excess, of booming business and a cautious return to optimism (at least for those for whom business was booming). The charge was led by the baby boom generation, which had once epitomized the counterculture and now had become the culture. And in the professional wrestling business, that generation would be embodied by Vincent Kennedy McMahon, who had spent his childhood in a trailer park in North Carolina before being taken in by his rich and powerful father in his teens, eventually rising in the ranks in his family's company, on a mission to become richer and more powerful than his father could've ever dreamed. Thanks to this new Vince McMahon, in the 1980s the pro wrestling industry would see more drastic, violent, and lasting change than at any other point in its history, before or since. And yet one man who would be almost completely left out in the cold during this period of transformation and mainstream success was The Sheik, for whom it turned out to be just about the lowest point of his professional and personal life. Just as wrestling was about to explode into the pop culture zeitgeist in a way it hadn't in decades, the man who had been one of its most feared and respected power brokers and most memorable superstars found himself relegated to the periphery, on the outside looking in.

On the morning of June 6, 1982, at the luxurious Warwick Hotel in midtown Manhattan, the younger Vince McMahon sat down with his

father and his father's partners, Bob "Gorilla Monsoon" Marella, Arnold Skaaland, and Phil Zacko, and made a deal to purchase the Capitol Wrestling Corporation and absorb the World Wrestling Federation name and brand into his own Titan Sports, Inc. What the sellers didn't fully understand at that meeting was that the junior McMahon intended to take the Northeastern-based wrestling company national, which was going to upset a whole lot of people his father had spent many years doing business with in relatively peaceable fashion. Many of the old-guard territorial promoters, men like Verne Gagne, Jim Crockett Jr., Bill Watts, Mike LeBell, Paul Boesch, Frank Tunney,[1] Bob Geigel, and Jim Barnett, would soon find themselves in the direct path of his naked ambition, forced to deal with the WWF expansion by either going to war or selling out. But Ed Farhat would be spared this decision, as years before McMahon's plans were being set in motion, he had already gone out of business, leaving Michigan and Ohio as largely "open" territories, although Farhat himself would dispute that claim.

To be sure, Farhat was not the only promoter who had already gone belly-up by the time of the WWF mass invasion. The Amarillo territory once run by the Funks was long gone, as was Roy Shire's San Francisco fiefdom, and the venerable St. Louis Wrestling Club, once the vital heart of the NWA, was on life support. The NWA's territorial system was in tatters, and the independent promotions they termed outlaw were proliferating. Farhat had never been too popular within the old boys club as it was, and now that he and his position had been gravely weakened, most of them were all too happy to write him off and move in for the kill. His paranoia toward the end of Big Time Wrestling had been largely justified, as can be seen by looking at what happened in Ohio and Michigan, his two remaining strongholds, in the immediate months and years after his company closed up shop, before the WWF even came into the picture. In January 1981, Jim Crockett Promotions began running the Cincinnati Gardens and did so until November 1982, when Barnett's Georgia Championship Wrestling (now calling itself World Championship Wrestling) took over. The same thing happened at Hara Arena in Dayton. Barnett also took Columbus, Springfield, and Canton. A small upstart indie group featuring a bunch of Big Time cast-offs, backed by George Cannon's Superstars of Wrestling out of Ontario, ran the Toledo Sports Arena for a bit before Barnett moved in there as well. By 1983, Barnett had added Akron and Cleveland to his Ohio circuit. Even Joe Blanchard, whose Southwest Championship Wrestling was based in San Antonio, Texas, took a shot at running some smaller Ohio towns on the strength of his national cable deal on USA Network.

In the immediate wake of the Sheik's departure, Cobo Arena in the heart of Detroit remained pretty silent in terms of wrestling, although

Cannon did make a concerted effort to resurrect Detroit wrestling in March 1981 and January 1982, joining forces with Tunney's Maple Leaf Wrestling to run Cobo, with decidedly lackluster results. And while not even Barnett could get his hands on the Motor City itself, he moved into Michigan in a big way, taking Lansing, Grand Rapids, Saginaw, Port Huron, Muskegon, Battle Creek, Flint, and other towns over the course of 1982. Helping him expand the organization and running many of these shows for him was his partner and booker Alan Rogowski, better known in the ring as Ole Anderson, member of the vaunted Anderson wrestling "family." The gruff Anderson was far more intimidating than the diminutive and effete Barnett, which might have been the point, but that didn't stop Farhat from squawking about the way things were going. In his mind, he still owned the territory—after all, he had bought it from Doyle and Barnett himself once upon a time, and no one had bought him out for it. Farhat demanded his cut from Anderson, which he agreed to at first, to try to placate him. But once it was clear that Farhat no longer had any leverage to make these demands, the payoffs stopped. "They didn't take it from him, because he had killed it," offers Kevin Sullivan, who first met Sheik in those dying days while wrestling for Barnett. "There were still lines you couldn't cross, but the respect was gone by then."

There's no denying that by the beginning of the 1980s, Farhat's reputation within the industry had suffered greatly, and that was in significant part his own doing. Many no longer wished to do business or be associated with him. Rumors of his substance abuse had spread, as had stories of his marriage with Joyce being on the rocks and his taking up with a girlfriend. In the wake of their separation, the grand estate that had symbolized the Sheik's impressive wealth through the previous decade had been vacated and fallen into disrepair. Eventually, it would be sold at auction. Bankruptcy soon followed. "It became like business didn't really matter [to him]," recalls Jeff Walton, who watched as Farhat's once-tight relationship with Los Angeles promoter Mike LeBell fell apart. "He wasn't making the kind of money he had been making. He met a young gal, about twenty-seven years old when he met her. He had an affair with her, and he left Joyce. The girl wasn't really much. She was just younger than Joyce. And when you have a midlife crisis, a lot of times it turns to someone younger. That's what happens. Nobody wanted to work with him because he was really unreliable. It got to the point where even Mike LeBell refused to see him when he came into town. Mike would say, 'Jeff, get on the phone with Sheik and tell him that I'm out of town.' And I found out later that the Sheik was borrowing money from Mike; of course, he needed it for whatever addiction he had. It was also because of this gal. It got to the point where he had no money. He wanted to borrow a big sum of money from Mike to try and get his business going again, but Mike had heard such bad stuff about him, that he was going around to a lot of promoters and borrowing money, and it went up in the drugs and with this girl."

Farhat had not worked more than two matches in the past five years in Southern California, once arguably his strongest territory outside of his own home base, and never would again, no matter how hard he tried to rekindle the old days. It was a telling sign of which way the wind was blowing and reflected what was going on in some other places as well. "Pretty much the whole wrestling industry knew about it, and they were avoiding him," Walton confirms. "He was so deep into it at one point and was refusing any kind of help . . . Eddie would come into the office because he just flew in in the morning and wanted to see Mike, but Mike didn't wanna give him anything, because Eddie wasn't paying him back. And I think that was happening with a few promoters that Sheik really knew and could talk to. I asked Eddie if he needed to go to Beverly Hills or go to Rodeo Drive, and he'd say, 'No, no, I just stopped by to see how Mike was.' And this happened more than once. By the second time, he knew Mike was just avoiding him. He said, 'Tell Mike thanks for nothing.' That was one of the last times I saw him. I felt very bad for Ed. He had helped us out when we needed help a few times on cards, and then you turn your back on the guy? But see, by then I knew what the business was like. It's cutthroat, and when you're not in it, it's 'out of sight, out of mind.'"

The Sheik reserved a special level of resentment and bitterness for Barnett, whom he blamed thereafter for much of his business troubles. He wanted a bit of revenge against the man he felt had turned on him, which is largely why in the spring of 1981 he threw his lot in with the International Wrestling League, a bold outlaw group going head-to-head with Barnett in Atlanta. He partnered with two men who also had axes to grind with Barnett: Thunderbolt Patterson, who had felt the pinch of racial prejudice in Georgia among many other places, and Big Jim Wilson, a former offensive lineman for the San Francisco 49ers, Atlanta Falcons, and LA Rams, who claimed Barnett had blackballed him for refusing his sexual advances. But Barnett had the full force of the NWA and Turner Broadcasting behind him, which gave him a decided advantage. He also blatantly used his power as the booker of the NWA World Champion to his advantage, booking a quick title switch between Harley Race and handsome young heartthrob Tommy "Wildfire" Rich, his top babyface at the time, the same week Wilson, Patterson, and Sheik were planning to run the Omni with a troupe of outlaw wrestlers headlined by Patterson vs. Sheik for the US Championship (which Sheik still held, continuing to bill himself as champion for years after the demise of Big Time Wrestling). Clearly, Barnett was trying to juice his business in the face of direct competition, but there were also persistent rumors that in order to earn his brief title reign, Rich had been less resistant than Wilson when it came to Barnett's advances. Farhat was more than happy to feed into these rumors, even claiming to have walked in on Barnett and Rich during a party at Barnett's house, but that was more than likely just sour grapes on Farhat's part.

The outlaw show at the Omni was a disaster for Wilson and Patterson, but especially for The Sheik. For years, he had brazenly taken up with outlaw promoters, and his feelings of being betrayed by Barnett and the NWA only made him more brazen in that regard. But going head-to-head against Barnett in Atlanta was a bridge too far, and at the NWA's annual meeting on October 12, 1981—one year to the day after his last show at Cobo Arena—it was decided that Farhat would be kicked out of the organization for good, his long-standing membership revoked. He was also blackballed by the group, although they never would've admitted that much under oath. This was a crushing blow to his already devastated career—in the wake of Big Time Wrestling's closure, there had still been a couple of NWA promoters willing to use him, most notably Eddie Graham in Florida and Giant Baba in Japan, but after his NWA banishment, even those opportunities disappeared.

From then on, The Sheik was a true outlaw himself—a renegade who barnstormed the territories, taking work wherever he could get it. He completed his turn on the NWA by choosing to switch sides in the Poffo anti-trust lawsuit and testify against the NWA, helping to expose it for the monopoly it was. He continued to promote small shows at humbler venues throughout Michigan, Ohio, and Southern Ontario under the Farhat Enterprises umbrella, but they were now independent shows, without the backing of the NWA.[2] He freely worked for other independents, including Dave McKigney's Big Bear Promotions, with which he already had a healthy relationship. McKigney even reportedly cut him in as a partner for a time, and The Sheik spent much of the early 1980s touring little Ontario towns like Simcoe, Kingston, Guelph, and Sarnia with other fading stars of the area—a far cry from the days of sellouts at Cobo and the Maple Leaf Gardens. Nevertheless, it did yield some memorable results, such as the renewal of his feud with old rival Luis Martinez as well as revisiting other classic rivalries with the likes of Tiger Jeet Singh, Andre the Giant, and, of course, Bobo Brazil. Thanks to his history with the Poffo family and his decision to help them in their lawsuit, he also found a home in their Kentucky-based ICW, where his United States title was now officially recognized.

Houston promoter Paul Boesch, who was having his own issues with the NWA thanks to a couple of high-profile no-shows by world champion Harley Race, entered into promotional partnerships with the AWA and Blanchard's SCW and put together a tournament in the Sam Houston Coliseum in September 1981 to crown his own world champion, utilizing lots of non-NWA talent, including The Sheik, who battled Ernie Ladd and Gino Hernandez over two nights of the tournament, which was eventually won by Wahoo McDaniel. But bookings like this were becoming the exception to the rule, and by 1982 things had really dried up, with The Sheik working mainly for McKigney and the Poffos.[3] He did himself no favors by continuing to be resistant to losing matches, insisting on being recognized as United States Champion, and demanding payoffs that may have been reflective of his value in years gone by but certainly weren't anymore. In addition to the addiction issues that concerned promoters, there were other health issues, as Farhat's body was simply breaking down due to the natural wear and tear of being in the ring for thirty-five years and being in his mid-fifties. His knees were shot, as were his hips, which were known to occasionally pop out of place during a match. As his mobility decreased, he relied even more on the blood and the fire—razor blades and Mycitracin antibiotic ointment were indispensable tools of the trade that he brought with him wherever he went, as he did the Kleenex tissues he would use to dab the brittle scars on his forehead that were known to randomly rupture throughout the course of the day.

After spending most of the beginning of '82 in Kentucky, he returned to the Bear Man circuit at the end of winter, and this time he had by his side a new manager, the last he would use regularly in his career. Eddy Creatchman had gone back to Quebec when Big Time Wrestling went down the tubes, and so Farhat turned to someone he already knew quite well and who had worked for him before—his former photographer, magazine editor, and front office employee Dave Burzynski, who had been spending the years since he left Farhat's employ honing his skills as a performer on the independent circuit, including a stint with George Cannon's Superstars of Wrestling, as "Supermouth" Dave Drason. Burzynski had learned from some of the best: timing from Cannon; mic skills from Ernie "Abdullah Farouk" Roth, perhaps the greatest talking manager of all time; bumping from Bobby Heenan, perhaps the greatest bumping manager of all time. Plus, Burzynski had grown up idolizing The Sheik and the two were already well-acquainted, so it was a natural fit. Unlike his predecessors Farouk and Creatchman, Drason didn't have the benefit of appearing on TV with The Sheik as there was no more TV. He also didn't venture with Sheik beyond the Michigan-Ohio-Ontario area, but then again, Sheik himself wasn't often straying beyond that territory by that point either. "Still, it was a great thrill for me," says Burzynski. "I knew what the fans wanted to see, because I was one of them at one time. But when I was managing The Sheik, it was a whole different ballgame . . . I always described it as the two longest walks in your career. The first one is that walk to the ring and the second one, after he wins, is trying to get back to the locker room. That always scared me. I can't tell you how many times I was punched, kicked, or had stuff thrown at me. At the end of every Sheik match, I'd always sacrifice myself to the babyface and take bumps into the corner or the top rope." As Drason, Burzynski would remain by The Sheik's side for local appearances for the next two or three years.

DAVE BURZYNSKI

"Supermouth" Dave Drason imparts some sage advice as Sheik wards off the pesky paparazzi.

It looks to be shortly after Farhat's return to his home area in the early spring of 1982 that he was involved in a car accident while riding with his son Eddie Jr., daughter-in-law Kathy, and six-year-old grand-daughter Jennifer. Despite his noted reputation as a speed demon behind the wheel,[4] Farhat was not to blame, but it is possible that the accident contributed to the growing health problems he was suffering by this time.[5] By the end of the summer, Farhat finally made the no doubt difficult decision to go into a sort of semi-retirement, and it would be the last time he would ever sustain anything even resembling a full-time schedule in North America. After a final Bear Man date, a steel cage match against Tiger Jeet Singh on September 5, 1982, at the Lakeshore Lions Arena, an ice hockey rink that served as a practice facility for the Toronto Maple Leafs, The Sheik did not step into a ring again for eight months. Existing records from this era are sparse, but it would appear as though he didn't wrestle more than a handful of matches per year for the remainder of the decade, totaling fewer than forty known appearances between 1983 and 1988—practically retired by wrestling standards.

This "lost period" of Farhat's life and career wasn't all dark, but it did see him fade away from the mainstream of major league professional wrestling. He was at his most vulnerable point financially, but it is believed that he did get some help from family members, as he was fortunate to also have many successful siblings, such as his brother Edmund, an influential lobbyist and business consultant, and Topper, a highly placed Michigan state official. The Sheik may have been more famous than they were, but in the end, the field in which he had attained his enormous notoriety was far more volatile and uncertain than the more conventional and less visible avenues they had chosen. Their assistance, combined with whatever sporadic bookings he was able to land for his asking price, seems to have helped keep him afloat during those slim times in the mid-1980s. Family support came in other ways, too, such as his becoming a grandfather for the third time when twenty-year-old Tommy and his wife, Kari, brought their first child, Susan, into the world on March 9, 1983.[6]

As for Joyce, it was no doubt a frustrating time. Predictably, The Sheik's dalliances were short-lived, and there were periods of reconciliation with his wife—but it is easy to imagine the heartbreak and anger of a woman who had devoted her life to helping her husband live his dream, and who had helped him build an empire, only to be betrayed in such a fashion. It had to be difficult, but their history together, and no doubt their continued connection to one another, is what kept her open to taking him back, although their troubles were far from over.

In the spring of '83, Farhat began again taking a handful of dates with the Poffos and McKigney. Meanwhile, Vince McMahon was testing the waters of his grand plan to expand the WWF into a national enterprise. He had already spread north from his metropolitan New York City stronghold into upstate New York areas like Buffalo and Rochester, which The Sheik had given up on years prior after snatching them up from the retiring Pedro Martinez in the mid-seventies. Now he was working his way into some smaller Ohio towns like Copley, Warren, and Struthers, still relatively under the radar compared to the bigger cities Barnett and Anderson had grabbed.

That summer, Farhat took the first step into a relationship with someone who would be linked with him for the rest of his professional life—someone he had known since birth, but to whom he would soon become closer than ever before. He was a nephew, but he may as well have been a son. For all intents and purposes, he was. Terry Michael Brunk was the youngest of seven children born to The Sheik's baby sister, Genevieve. Of all the many kids of his generation of the Farhat family, he was the one who had the greatest fascination, from a very young age, with what his famous uncle did for a living and would watch him on TV during the heyday of Big Time Wrestling. His parents had divorced when he was only three, and his relationship with his stepfather was severely strained at best. For as long as he could remember, Terry looked up to his uncle as a surrogate father figure, whom he would see regularly at the family's huge Sunday dinners at the Sheik compound. From the age of seven, Terry worked with his mom at Rocky's Teakwood Lounge, the restaurant on Kalamazoo Street in Lansing owned by his cousin Philip "Rocky" Farhat.[7] But as a teenager, without a strong authority figure at home, he began to get into trouble with shoplifting and other forms of larceny. Still interested in wrestling, he got it into his head that he wanted to give it a try, and he started pestering his uncle to train him. But it was a very closed business in those days, and The Sheik had quite a bit on his mind as it was, with his company having just collapsed, so he kept turning him down.

That changed in the summer of 1983, when eighteen-year-old Terry's associations with the wrong kind of people came to a head at a friend's high school graduation party, where he was shot point blank in the face during a drunken brawl. He miraculously survived, and while recovering from the injury, made the decision that he wasn't going to take no for an answer. He wanted no part of the road he was heading down, and his uncle finally agreed to help him on a different path. As soon as he got out of the hospital and was fully recovered, he began training his body, putting on muscle weight, and reading all he could about wrestling technique. Within a year after the injury, he had moved in with his uncle in Williamston full time[8] and kicked off in earnest his journey to becoming the true protégé of The Sheik and the inheritor of his mantle in many ways. Far more than Eddie Jr., it was Terry who would eventually carry on the family legacy in the ring. "His son never loved wrestling," explains Fumi Saito, who had the honor of interviewing both The Sheik and his nephew over the years. "He always wanted to quit. I've heard that he asked his father if he could. And then his nephew became like a surrogate son to him. Because everybody in the family said no to him—don't be a wrestler, it's not a very good business—but he insisted he wanted to do it. Sheik's sons didn't really understand the business like he did, and so he could be hard on them. Sometimes you just want to get away so you're not always in your father's shadow and do something else."

Shortly after agreeing to train his nephew, Farhat did something he rarely did anymore in those days—he got on a plane for some bookings far outside his typical domain. In this case, it was somewhere he had never appeared before and where his legend was likely still intact: the island of Trinidad,[9] where he wrestled two matches in Port of Spain— one against his old adversary, the equally crazed Bulldog Brower, in one of the last matches of the Bulldog's twenty-five-year career. But while he was over there, someone else had just debuted for the WWF that would impact his career and legacy in indirect ways, and with whom his name would remain permanently entangled, much to his chagrin.

Hossein Khosrow Ali Vaziri was a standout amateur grappler from Tehran, Iran, who had spent time as a bodyguard for Shah Mohammad Reza Pahlavi before trying out for his country's Olympic Greco-Roman wrestling team in 1968. He moved to the United States to compete in the AAU, winning a gold medal in 1971. The next year he became a coach for the US Greco-Roman team at the Munich Summer Games. Known for his formidable real wrestling skills, he caught the attention of fellow former Olympic wrestling hopeful Verne Gagne, always on the lookout for "legitimate" talent for his AWA roster. Vaziri pulled double duty as both a performer and a trainer for AWA greenhorns in now-legendary training camps that included the likes of Ken Patera, Ricky Steamboat, Jim Brunzell, and a chubby kid from Minnesota named Richard Fliehr. Having no love for Ed Farhat, who was by the mid-1970s already losing influence in the business anyway, Gagne eventually bestowed on Vaziri the persona of The Iron Sheik[10]—complete with kaffiyeh headpiece, pointed boots, and a variation of the camel clutch as a finisher, as well as a clean-shaven head and handlebar mustache reminiscent of Ali Baba, the 1930s Armenian superstar who had taken Detroit by storm back when Farhat was a boy. Still, when Vaziri initially traveled to territories where Farhat had appeared extensively, he would use alternate names, such as in Texas, where he was Muhammad Farouk, or during his original 1979 WWWF run, when he was known as Hossein Arab.

However, by the time Vaziri returned to the Northeast in August 1983, Vince Jr. was in charge, and he had none of his father's professional history with Farhat—who was by then already considered a relic of the past in the "what have you done for me lately?" world of wrestling. Vaziri was reintroduced to the WWF as The Iron Sheik, along with manager "Ayatollah" Fred Blassie, and immediately began attracting nuclear crowd heat thanks to the still-fresh wounds of the Iranian hostage crisis only a couple years in the past as well as the hyper-jingoism of Reagan-era America in general. The Iron Sheik played into American Islamophobia in an even more direct way than Farhat ever had. Unlike the Midwestern-born Farhat, Vaziri seemed more the genuine article, speaking Farsi during interviews, and when he did speak English, denigrating the United States and praising his beloved homeland of Iran.

The Iron Sheik had been brought to the WWF to fulfill an essential role in McMahon's larger plan. To truly make his company into a mainstream powerhouse, he needed a larger-than-life superhero to be the face of the whole operation—someone the media would adore, someone who would make a great action figure, someone kids across America would worship. And the vanilla, soft-spoken Bob Backlund, then five years into his reign as WWF World Champion, simply wasn't going to cut it. McMahon wanted desperately to get the belt off Backlund and onto the man he'd hand-picked for the role: six-foot-six, three-hundred-pound bodybuilder and bass player from Tampa, Florida, Terry Gene Bollea. Coming fresh off his breakout film role as Thunderlips alongside Sylvester Stallone in *Rocky III*, Bollea had originally been brought into the business by Jack Brisco and Eddie Graham in Florida, and in his original WWF run in the early eighties, McMahon's father had christened him Hulk Hogan. He was still calling himself that in Gagne's AWA, where his popularity skyrocketed just before McMahon poached him as part of the cherry-picking talent recruitment he was doing in order to make his roster a who's who of territorial wrestling superstars.

In those days, it was unheard of to have two babyfaces go at it for the title, and so a transitional heel champion was needed to take the gold from Backlund and promptly lose it to Hogan, and The Iron Sheik, who had very quickly become the most hated wrestler on the roster, was just the guy for the job. On Christmas 1983, Farhat made his return to the Atlanta Omni after a four-year absence, his final appearance for Barnett, to take on the unpredictable fireplug Buzz Sawyer[11]—the threat of McMahon's growing power making strange bedfellows, indeed. The very next night, Vaziri trapped Backlund in the camel clutch in the center of the ring at Madison Square Garden to take the WWF title.[12] And although he spent less than a month as WWF World Champion, The Iron Sheik became part of the massive WWF explosion that occurred once Hogan captured the championship on January 23, 1984, and the company's national conquest kicked into full gear. The Iron Sheik was one of a pantheon of legitimate pop culture sensations that also included Jimmy "Superfly" Snuka, Andre the Giant, "Rowdy" Roddy Piper, Nikolai Volkoff, Ricky "The Dragon" Steamboat, Randy "Macho Man" Savage, and many more. Thanks to McMahon's merchandizing and licensing vision, The Iron Sheik's likeness could be found in Saturday morning cartoons, on lunchboxes, in toy form, and even on ice cream bars. It was, as Burzynski would describe it, the "nail in the coffin" as far as Farhat's relevance in the business. From then on, the persona of The Iron Sheik would completely overshadow Farhat in the eyes of the general public, to the point where Farhat began billing himself as The Original Sheik in order to avoid confusion. To this day, mention the name Sheik in a wrestling context to ninety percent of the general public under the age of fifty, and the first—and likely only—person that comes to mind is Hossein Vaziri, not Ed Farhat.

Farhat's feelings on this development appear to have evolved over time, but he certainly wasn't thrilled about it in the beginning. "People who found out that I managed The Sheik would assume it was The Iron Sheik, and it would piss me off to no end," remembers Burzynski. "I would tell him about it, and he would just shake his head and say he was just a goddamn jabroni." Lanny Poffo, who remained friends with Farhat even after he and his brother had also joined McMahon's troupe, saw it differently: "He respected him because he was legitimately old school. He was from the old country. Sheik didn't mind that." And Rudy Hill, who spent time with Farhat at the end of his life, describes a man who seems to have come to terms with what many consider the ultimate gimmick infringement: "The first time I talked to him about it was at a dinner we had in Fort Wayne, Indiana. And his words were, 'Fuck him! Fuck him! He ain't shit.' Then, the last time I spoke to him, we talked, and I mentioned The Iron Sheik, and he said, 'He's doing good for himself, good for him.' I asked him what he thought of his gimmick, and he said 'It's not really my gimmick, it's the Middle East gimmick, isn't it?' I wasn't really expecting that!"

And yet, while The Iron Sheik became something of a cultural icon thanks to the WWF marketing machine, coming along at a time when McMahon's product had conquered the American zeitgeist and became something more than wrestling, it must be pointed out that to those who follow the history of the industry, there is really no comparison between him and The Sheik. Thanks to the national WWF expansion, The Iron Sheik would be seen simultaneously by millions of fans across the country, something The Sheik, whose heyday took place in the territorial era, hadn't really experienced, at least not since the DuMont days in the fifties. Nevertheless, The Iron Sheik was nowhere near the powerhouse main event heel draw that The Sheik had been, and certainly not for anything near the sustained number of years that he was. The Iron Sheik was a supporting player in a cast, while The Sheik held the starring role, and some would say was the whole show. And although his name carries a greater level of cultural cachet these days among casual fans, The Iron Sheik, in the grand scheme of things, was a figure of much lesser significance than The Sheik, not to mention power behind the scenes. The Sheik is on the short list of all-time legendary wrestling villains alongside people like Gorgeous George, Buddy Rogers, Killer Kowalski, Ray Stevens, Fred Blassie, Harley Race, and Ric Flair—an echelon The Iron Sheik simply can't lay claim to.

But it was during The Iron Sheik's world title reign that McMahon finally achieved something he had long been planning—the invasion of Detroit. He had already moved into Cincinnati and Dayton a few months prior, but the Motor City was a major urban center he knew he'd need, and one he very much wanted to add to a growing collection that already included San Diego, Los Angeles, and St. Louis—all towns whose local promotions had either lost significant power or closed up altogether. McMahon cared nothing for the NWA's traditional boundaries—he had withdrawn the WWF from the organization that year—and in a testament to how far The Sheik had fallen off the map by that time, in negotiating for control of Detroit, McMahon came calling not to Farhat, but to George Cannon, whose Superstars of Wrestling group had been the major presence in the area since Big Time Wrestling closed up shop. McMahon flew Cannon out to New York and worked out a deal that would make him the WWF's official Detroit promoter for $60,000 per year. Cannon also had two other things McMahon coveted and got as part of the deal: an impressive syndicated TV network that covered much of Canada and the Midwestern US, and the rights to the Superstars of Wrestling name, which McMahon wanted both for his flagship TV show and to help him rebrand his pro wrestlers with the proprietary label of "Superstars."

All the while, Farhat watched helplessly as other men bought and sold the city he had helped build with the literal blood and sweat from his brow. On December 30, 1983, Vince McMahon set foot in the hallowed Cobo Arena for the first time, co-presenting with Cannon a WWF card headlined by Jimmy Snuka, Andre the Giant, and Rocky Johnson taking on The Wild Samoans, no strangers to the building. The show was rounded out by some of Cannon's local talent in subordinate positions, like The Great Wojo and Chris Carter, and little people Farmer Pete and Ivan the Terrible. Although he was his world champion at the time, not even Vince McMahon had the nerve to bring The Iron Sheik to Cobo Arena for that first show (he was sent to Maryland to defend the title on the same day).[13] But Detroit was scorched earth as far as wrestling went, and not even the mighty WWF could resurrect it overnight, as the evening's paltry crowd of 2,300 would demonstrate.

That first WWF card at Cobo was allegedly the site of one of wrestling history's most debated urban legends, and it has directly to do with The Sheik. One version, as told to me by Jerry Jaffee, a former Sheik wrestler then working for the WWF as Dr. Jerry Graham Jr., who claimed to have heard it from former Big Time Wrestling talent and then–WWF star George Steele, has it that Vince McMahon granted Farhat a special audience that night out of deference to how he had selflessly helped his father out back in the late 1960s by coming in for his blockbuster feud with Bruno Sammartino. At this meeting, McMahon offered Farhat a spot on the WWF crew, with a significant salary.[14] "But The Sheik wouldn't go because he couldn't be on top and be the champion," recounts Jaffe. "I heard Sheik told Vince that Detroit was his town. He wanted to work with him, but he wanted to keep the town. He wanted to be the boss in Detroit, and pay Vince a booking fee to use his men . . . [But] The Sheik was just getting too old. I felt bad for him because that gimmick was his whole life." The other, less complimentary, and frankly less likely version of the story goes that McMahon arranged the meeting in order to humiliate Farhat, to have him beg for a job and then turn him down, as payback for either negative things Farhat had been saying about him or perceived slights dating back to whatever heat there may have been between Farhat and his father in the seventies. Whether this supposed meeting ever even happened is a matter of conjecture to this day. Either way, The Sheik was out in the cold.

Over the next few months, as Ohio came pretty much under WWF control with the conquest of Akron, Columbus, Toledo, and Cleveland,

McMahon and Cannon continued to run Cobo on a regular basis, with similarly uninspired results. Still, with the loss of serious ground to McMahon, and having spread himself a little too thin in his own attempt to go national, even Barnett was on the ropes, and in July 1984, he and his business partners Jack and Jerry Brisco sold their majority interests in Georgia Championship Wrestling to McMahon and also went to work for him (forcing out an incensed Ole Anderson in the process). Barnett became a valuable consultant to McMahon in those early expansion years, using his own TV connections to the WWF's advantage and bringing his decades of accumulated wrestling business savvy to bear.

While all this was going on, and the WWF was bursting onto the public consciousness thanks to the involvement of popular entertainers like Cyndi Lauper and Mr. T, as McMahon gradually spread his product to TV markets across North America and snatched up major talent from all his competitors, decimating the NWA's territorial system in the process, Farhat was relatively quiet, and The Sheik made few appearances, even in his shrinking corner of the wrestling world. His rancor toward McMahon only grew, and many who knew him during that time recall he had nothing nice to say about the WWF impresario—it was believed that the feeling was mutual. Even though in the past he had had his own issues with the boys club that ran wrestling, he was not happy with the way McMahon had gone about dismantling the old system and gradually putting all his former colleagues out of business—and once Vince McMahon the elder passed away on May 24, 1984, from the pancreatic cancer he had been hiding from his family and friends for as long as he could, it really opened the floodgates for his son to do whatever he wanted with impunity.

By the middle of 1984, Farhat was focusing much of his energy on preparing his nephew Terry for the ring. In his autobiography, Terry describes a grueling process not uncommon in the days of pro wrestling as a tightly protected society, with his uncle testing his mettle by subjecting him to endless, seemingly menial, and exhausting tasks like chopping wood and assembling then deconstructing the ring repeatedly. If The Sheik was envisioning that Terry might quit and run screaming back to his mom, then he was greatly mistaken. The twenty-year-old took everything his uncle dished out, and when the actual in-ring training began in earnest, he took to it like a natural, just as he began traveling to The Sheik's bookings and getting a good look behind the curtain—although his old-school uncle did little to nothing to "smarten up" the kid to the true nature of the business, at least not yet. Insisting that he would have no easy breaks or special treatment, Farhat made sure that everyone treated him just as they would any newcomer. In fact, in those early formative years, Terry served as a combination assistant-chauffeur for The Sheik, carrying his bags and driving him around in the vintage 1972 limousine he still had from the Big Time Wrestling glory days. It was all part of the process, even if there were times he could be very hard on the young man.

Meanwhile, what Farhat didn't realize was that another by-product of the WWF-driven mid-eighties wrestling renaissance would be the resurrection of a project from his own past that seemed long dead and gone. After shooting all the footage for their pseudo-documentary in the late seventies, filmmakers Bryan Greenberg and Don Jackson had gone their separate ways—Greenberg to Carmel, California, to work for a production company headed by Michael Nesmith, former guitarist for The Monkees, directing short clips for *Saturday Night Live* and music videos for the likes of Prince and Steve Miller Band,[15] and Jackson to Hollywood to try to break into big-time producing, taking on random special effects and cinematography gigs along the way that included work on James Cameron's *The Terminator*. While working in the effects division for the B-movie production and distribution company New World Pictures, Jackson got wind of a new home video division that had just been started up.[16] Likely inspired by the new mainstream pro wrestling craze, Jackson felt the division would be the perfect outlet to finally release his shelved Detroit wrestling project, and he brought it to the attention of his superiors, who agreed and bankrolled the completion of the picture. "My career was moving forward, so I really wasn't thinking about it anymore," Greenberg remembers. "So Don made his deal and called me up and told me by the way, we just sold this to New World. I never saw anything financially at all, but I'm glad he was just able to finally get it out. I never had any animosity toward Don for making the deal without me."

The film was not yet in releasable form, and extra footage was required in order to hold together all the now-vintage wrestling material they had shot some six to seven years prior. To give the movie more of a "story," a whole new subplot was added involving a "Stop The Sheik" movement that opposes the Arabian madman's heinous actions, with new footage scripted and shot around Detroit to later be edited into the finished product. Of the many matches shot at Cobo, certain gems were selected for inclusion, such as The Sheik vs. Dusty Rhodes and a star-studded battle royal from April 16, 1977; Captain Ed George vs. Don Kent from October 15, 1977; The Sheik vs. Terry Funk from July 23, 1977; Abdullah the Butcher and The Sheik vs. The Funks from September 3, 1977; and The Sheik vs. Dick the Bruiser in a steel cage from February 12, 1977, in Indianapolis, in addition to classic promos from Rhodes, the Funks, the Bruiser, Bobo Brazil, Ox Baker, and others.

The original songs for the movie had been written and recorded in the seventies by Bob Finnigan—by that point reinventing himself as country music recording artist R.C. Finnigan—as well as a local band he worked with called The Woolies, fronted by brothers Bob and Jeff Baldori. In the end, when it looked like the movie was really going to happen, Finnigan and the Baldoris (spearheaded by Bob, whose day job was a law practice specializing in artist representation), asked for a prohibitive amount of money, and so only one of their songs made the final cut—the one which lent its name to the new title of the picture, inspired by a line spoken in the film by Eddie Jr.: "I Like to Hurt People." In the end, Jackson tapped his friend Sam Mann—an actor-musician he had worked with on some previous projects—to help flesh out the final soundtrack with some new songs, and also reached out to local musicians Jesse Hawkins and Mark Boone, with whom he had become acquainted earlier in the project through Finnigan.[17]

Once the whole thing was finished, only one piece of the puzzle remained before it could be released: The Sheik's permission. Jackson had contacted Farhat as soon as he worked out the New World deal—in fact, in the only instance I have ever found of Ed Farhat being quoted in public out of character, he told the *Lansing State Journal* on the occasion of the movie's eventual release on July 16, 1985: "All of a sudden,

they called back and said they'd sold it. I said, 'Fine, send the money.'"
And send it they did: seeking a release of any claims of ownership by
Farhat, Jackson sent him a new contract and a check for ten grand, to
be delivered by Mark Boone, a longtime fan who happened to know
Farhat's exact whereabouts. "Don didn't know where The Sheik was,"
Boone explains. "By then, he had filed for bankruptcy, lost his mansion.
We heard he was wrestling at some high school in East Detroit. Don
said we gotta get these papers to him and make him an offer for this
movie. I guess they figured The Sheik owned it. They overnighted an
envelope to us, and we went down to this high school on a Friday
night . . . We knocked on the dressing room door, and this guy named
Pat Chene answered it. He was a gofer for The Sheik. Playing hard-
ass like he's somebody important. 'We'd like to talk to the Sheik . . .'
He's sizing us up, scruffy-looking rock musicians. We said we had a
contract from New World Pictures for the movie. He goes back in the
dressing room, and out comes Sheik's wife, Joyce. We talked to her
for a minute. She goes back in the dressing room. Next thing I know,
out comes The Sheik. I'm used to this guy I saw beat the shit out of
Johnny Valentine and Bobo Brazil. All of a sudden, I'm looking at an
old man! [But] I'm still marking out cause it's the fuckin' Sheik. He
tears open the FedEx tab on the envelope and reads it, says something
to his wife. She gives him a pair of women's reading glasses! Here's The
Sheik, who I idolized since I was a kid, in his wife's reading glasses
looking at this contract. He read the dollar amount . . . It was a smile
I can't even describe. You had to be there. He's excited, patting me on
the back and everything. Takes us back in the dressing room, and here's
Bobo Brazil, older than dirt, and Luis Martinez, Crusher Cortez, and
a lot of younger guys playing cards. Sheik starts boasting and bragging,
showing off his contract. All these guys were past the big money years
by that point. We hung out in the dressing room for a while, everyone
was very cordial with us. We stayed and watched the show."

With the wrestling craze at full tilt following the WWF's partnership
with MTV and the presentation of the first *WrestleMania* spectacular
live from Madison Square Garden, the time was ripe for *I Like to Hurt
People* to finally be released to VHS and laserdisc. In its finished form,

the film is a quirky yet reverent time capsule of a period in wrestling long gone, swept away by the very company whose fame was the catalyst for its release. It might not have captured Big Time Wrestling at its peak, but it stands as a rare testament to an era in wrestling of which precious little high-quality film footage survives. The irony was that by the time it finally hit the market, The Sheik and his whole outfit had been cast aside by the business, making it even more of a unique relic than it started out as. Despite the timing of the release, *I Like to Hurt People* came and went with little to no fanfare, failing to reach even a fraction of its target audience. However, as time went on, as happens on occasion with bizarre projects such as this one, it did find a sizeable cult following—a combination of old-school wrestling fans and connoisseurs of strange cinema—and today stands, unexpectedly enough, as the single greatest permanent record of Big Time Wrestling that exists.

But Farhat's daily life was touched little by any of this in 1985. It was a year in which he was faced with the death of his older sister Olga and of his father-in-law and former business partner, Francis Fleser, who had been the public face of World Wide Sports and Big Time Wrestling. It was also the year he unleashed his nephew on the unsuspecting wrestling world, starting in May 1985 at a tiny show in a town six miles north of Detroit with the unlikely name of Hamtramck, put on by Big Jim Lancaster, who had gone from a Big Time Wrestling journeyman and product of Lou Klein's gym to a promoter and trainer in his own right. When Terry arrived at the venue that day, he discovered that his new ring name would be Terry S.R. (sometimes "Essar")—when he pressed his uncle on the meaning, he wouldn't reveal it, but many (including Terry himself) believe it stood for Sheik's Revenge, an appropriate name for the kid Farhat believed could carry on his fearsome legacy in the business that had done him wrong. That night, Terry S.R. went to a ten-minute draw with a local talent calling himself The Canadian Road Warrior, a very bare-bones match with little razzle-dazzle, just basic old-school wrestling. The competition would get better. The ring style would change. And so would the name, eventually.

Shortly after making his official debut, Terry traveled with his uncle on a tour of the South Pacific that included Singapore, Malaysia, and

Indonesia.[18] While Farhat was focusing on traveling with his nephew, the WWF made deeper inroads in Detroit. Before long, the partnership with George Cannon went predictably by the wayside, as McMahon discarded him when he no longer needed him (Cannon would later describe the partnership as the worst business decision he ever made).[19] There would be no more local talent at Cobo, just the homogenized WWF product every other town was getting. In August 1985, after a year and a half of trying, McMahon scored his first sellout in the Motor City, only not at the quarter-century-old Cobo Arena, but at the much newer and larger arena that had recently been built right next door and named after one of Detroit's *other* great sports legends, world heavyweight boxing champion Joe Louis.[20] Nearly twenty-one thousand fans were drawn that night, and over thirty thousand just five days later to the Michigan State Fairgrounds to see Hulk Hogan defend the WWF World title against Farhat protégé Greg "The Hammer" Valentine. Less than three months after that, the WWF drew the first wrestling sellout Cobo Arena had seen in a dozen years. Although they would still occasionally run Cobo, the Joe Louis Arena would become the Detroit venue of choice for the WWF, with the older Cobo, abandoned by both the Pistons and the Red Wings, reduced to a venue mainly for rock concerts and auto shows. If it had been tenuous in the beginning, it was no longer: Detroit belonged to Vince McMahon. The crowds were finally coming back, only this time for a dramatically different brand of wrestling that largely appealed to a new breed of fan, many of whom were too young to even remember the heyday of The Sheik, Bobo Brazil, and the rest.

It was humble Bear Man shows in Ontario all the way for the increasingly unsteady Sheik, who defeated Ricky Johnson (Rocky's brother) in a steel cage match in the Toronto suburb of Scarborough one day after his sixtieth birthday. Two months later, in August 1986, he managed to land an important booking in one of the only American territories still standing, albeit barely. Hawaii's Polynesian Pacific Wrestling was the last vestige of the once-mighty territory of Lord James Blears and Ed Francis, now run by Lia Maivia, the widow of Peter Maivia, who had suffered an untimely death in 1982. The company had already been struggling when Vince McMahon finally turned his attention to the island chain after having conquered most of the continental US.[21] The WWF rolled into Honolulu for the first time on July 10, 1986, selling five of eight thousand seats at the Blaisdell Arena for a card headlined by Ruby trainee George "The Animal" Steele against ornery second-generation Kansas City grappler Cowboy Bob Orton Jr. With a second show scheduled for September, it worried Maivia and her booker Lars Anderson enough that they booked a blockbuster show at the eighty-thousand-seat Aloha Stadium featuring as much unaffiliated outside star talent as they could find. There was Antonio Inoki, who also brought with him a contingent of New Japan wrestlers including Kengo Kimura, Seiji Sakaguchi, Tatsumi Fujinami, and the rookie Keiji Muto. Jerry Lawler came, representing the Memphis territory (then battling its own WWF invasion) as he took on Steve Rickard, a performer-promoter who was New Zealand's wrestling kingpin.

The Sheik, who had enjoyed several Hawaii bookings the year before thanks to then-booker Kevin Sullivan, was chosen this time to take part in the show's main event angle, violently interrupting the $22,000 Bodyslam Challenge being undertaken by fellow loose cannon Bruiser Brody (on loan from Fritz Von Erich's World Class Wrestling Association in Dallas) and local talent Grizzly Smith,[22] leading to an "impromptu" six-man tag team barbed wire match in the main event. The match reunited Sheik and his longtime foe Mark Lewin—who had by then taken on an equally deranged heel persona since coming under the "evil influence" of Sullivan in Championship Wrestling from Florida—as they teamed with the mammoth Prince Kamalamala[23] to take on Brody, powerlifting champion Jeff Magruder, and Keith Hart, the third son of Stampede Wrestling's Stu Hart.[24] But despite The Sheik and everyone else's efforts, the outdoor show was an unmitigated disaster, plagued by no-shows and a driving rainstorm, and drawing a mere nineteen hundred fans to the cavernous stadium (advertised as ten thousand), barely earning enough to cover the rental fee for the building. Owing partly to the complete failure of the event, within two years Maivia was out of business entirely, and her weekly Honolulu cards would be replaced by semi-annual appearances from the WWF's touring troupe. The Aloha Stadium show would turn out to be The Sheik's final televised match in the United States.

Terry continued to gain experience working McKigney's shows with his uncle, even facing off against him in the ring for the only known occasion on December 28, 1986, in Windsor. He also worked the small Michigan and Ohio independent shows his uncle continued to promote in towns like Warren and Akron. Farhat tried to take his nephew with him everywhere he went, but as his health and influence weakened, those opportunities were becoming increasingly rare. On January 12, 1987, The Sheik made his final appearance in the ailing Montreal territory, then run by Gino Brito and his protégé and longtime tag team partner Dino Bravo, working a thirty-second opening match on a card headlined by Abdullah the Butcher vs. Bruiser Brody. By that point, Bravo and Brito's International Wrestling had a sporadic "working agreement" with Vince McMahon, and it's very telling that The Sheik was not used on the WWF co-promoted event at the Montreal Forum just three days prior. Five months later, International Wrestling would be out of business, with Bravo and others scooped up by McMahon.

Last on The Sheik's farewell tour of the dying territories was a two-week stint back down in Florida in February and March 1987. He hadn't worked there in years, and much had changed: longtime promoter Eddie Graham had killed himself two years prior, reportedly despondent over steep financial losses from high-living, questionable real estate investments, and the encroaching WWF machine. Now running the show were former tag team partners and top Graham attractions Duke Keomuka and Hiro Matsuda, with help from booker Kevin Sullivan, a longtime admirer of The Sheik who used his influence to help get his idol booked—just as he had done while booking for Lia Maivia in Hawaii in early 1985. "We became very close friends," remembers Sullivan. "He would come down and visit in Florida ... He would pay for everything, drinks, food . . . He was very, very good to me. He was a big deal. By that time, things had started turning around for him, and he was well-heeled again, money-wise. His brother had helped him, he was well-to-do, a mover and shaker in the political realm ... I remember in Hawaii, Sheik had a bag full of money and was running around giving it out to people!" During his last Florida run, The Sheik worked some dates as part of the War of the Worlds series

Windsor Arena, December 28, 1986: Giving new meaning to the term "tough love," The Sheik steps in the ring for the first and only time against his young nephew and student Terry, the future Sabu.

BRIAN BUKANTIS

of supercards, which included two wild double count out brawls with Bruiser Brody in Fort Lauderdale and Miami.

As Sullivan attests, by 1987 Farhat had somewhat rehabilitated himself financially, but there is also evidence that he could be all too quick to return to his old ways—radio host Gary Cubeta, for example, recalls the bizarre experience that same year of spotting The Sheik, in full gimmick and surrounded by a crowd of onlookers, having a run of bad luck at the craps tables in Bally's casino in Las Vegas. And while he was figuring out new ways to run through whatever money he did have coming in, Vince McMahon was busy putting the final piece into place to cement his national domination, and it would occur right in The Sheik's backyard on March 29, at the colossal Pontiac Silverdome, just thirty miles north of Detroit. There, the WWF packed in more than seventy-eight thousand fans,[25] a new North American record for wrestling, to witness *WrestleMania III*, with a main event for the ages pitting WWF World Champion Hulk Hogan against Andre the Giant. In addition to the live crowd, the event drew nearly a half million buys in the new medium of pay-per-view television, grossing in the vicinity of $10 million, and signaling in so many ways the symbolic victory of McMahon in his relentless quest to take over the wrestling business.

Farhat, now a grandfather four times over with the birth of Tom and Kari's daughter Kelli in June, continued plugging away on the local independent scene on a part-time basis. With no television exposure whatsoever, he became a purely live attraction, roaming the backwaters of the pro wrestling landscape, a legend of the past who could only be seen by those who came out and bought a ticket. In cramped halls, high school gymnasiums, and community centers, he brought however much of that Sheik magic he could still muster—an urban myth of the business come to life, ambling to the ring on his busted hips and knees, in obvious pain and still in the thrall of the substances he used to keep that pain at bay, throwing fire and blading everyone in sight in matches that rarely lasted more than a minute or two. Some of the unsuspecting folks who bought those tickets still got a glimpse of wrestling history now and then, such as on January 15, 1988, when The Sheik went one-on-one with that other hard-headed barnstormer Bruiser Brody for the last time, on an indie show in suburban Michigan. History was made again five months later, when Brody returned to the area for an indie card at the Packard Music Hall in Warren, Ohio, joining "Exotic" Adrian Street, a hard-nosed son of Welsh coal-miners who had achieved cult status playing against type as a flamboyantly effeminate homosexual, opposed on the other side of the ring by The Iron Sheik and The Original Sheik—the only time that Vaziri and Farhat ever worked together. Just thirty-three days after that match, Brody would be stabbed to death in the locker room showers of Loubriel Stadium in Bayamón, Puerto Rico, by disgruntled WWC booker Jose Gonzalez, angered by Brody's self-advocacy and jealous of the fact that the perceived outsider was outdrawing him and everyone else on the full-time roster.[26]

It was one of several grievous losses to Farhat's trusted circle that followed one after another that year. He had just lost his older brother and benefactor Joseph (aka Topper) in February. Twelve days prior to Brody's murder, on the Fourth of July, "Bear Man" Dave McKigney met a tragic end when the minivan he was riding in while on a tour of Newfoundland swerved to avoid a moose on the Trans-Canada Highway thirty-seven miles outside of the town of Gander and plunged off a bridge a hundred feet into the brook below, killing him instantly and mortally wounding Keith Franke, a former WWF superstar who, as "Adorable" Adrian Adonis, had wrestled "Rowdy" Roddy Piper in the Pontiac Silverdome the previous year.[27]

Just eleven days after Brody's murder, in the early morning hours of July 27, Farhat suffered the greatest loss of all when his thirty-five-year-old nephew Paul Ritchie, whom he had raised as his own son since the age of twelve, was murdered in the basement of his home on the east side of Lansing. Ritchie was known to pick up men from the seedy section of Michigan Avenue, some of whom his roommate found to be pretty sketchy. That's apparently what he did the night of July 26, when he was seen leaving popular gay bar Joe Covello's Lounge with thirty-year-old Brian Merriman. An altercation broke out between the two once they arrived at Ritchie's home, resulting in Merriman stabbing Ritchie twenty-five times and fleeing the scene. Merriman would remain at large for a year and a half before detectives tracked him down in Iowa. He was convicted of second-degree murder in 1990, and sentenced to forty to sixty years in prison.

Despite these losses, Farhat would give himself very little time to mourn. Just four days after Paul's murder, The Sheik would be in the center of the ring in the one place no one ever expected to see him again: Cobo Arena. It would be the last major league pro wrestling match he would ever have in the United States. And just like in Hawaii and Florida, it would all be thanks to Kevin Sullivan. By that point, the company Sullivan had been working for, Championship Wrestling from Florida, had basically been swallowed up by the only territorial company that had been giving the WWF anything close to a run for their money, the Carolinas-based Jim Crockett Promotions. The last major vestige of the NWA, Crockett Promotions had purchased the national TBS time slot from Vince McMahon after McMahon's northern product was rejected by Southern fans used to seeing Georgia Championship Wrestling. Starting in 1985, Jim Crockett Jr. found himself with a national cable platform, and he used it to push beyond his traditional boundaries in response to the WWF, absorbing other territories like the Central States promotion out of Kansas City and Bill Watts's UWF (formerly Mid-South Wrestling), and competing directly against the WWF in many TV and live event markets across the country. Crockett had moved into Ohio alongside the WWF in 1985, as well as Michigan towns like Lansing, Saginaw, and Grand Rapids, and had begun running Cobo Arena by the fall of 1987, not long after the WWF had abandoned it for the Joe Louis Arena.[28]

By the summer of 1988, Crockett Promotions was bleeding money but trying to stay in the fight. They embarked on their third annual Great American Bash tour, a series of thirty-eight televised and non-televised house shows across the US, designed to show the company's national reach. When Sullivan learned that the thirty-fourth stop on the tour was set to hit Detroit, he saw it as the perfect opportunity to unleash The Sheik on Cobo once again and worked to convince Crockett and his booker Dusty Rhodes, no stranger to The Sheik or Cobo Arena. "It was completely my idea," Sullivan explains. "Jimmy Crockett said to me, he won't draw. And I bet Dusty $500 that we'd draw over $100,000. They hadn't had a $100,000 house there in years." The main event was booked as a steel cage match pitting Rhodes and The Sheik against Sullivan and Rhodes's old Texas Outlaws partner, Dick Murdoch.

It was the first time Farhat had set foot in Cobo in eight years, and he intended to make the very most of it. Jim Cornette, manager that evening of the NWA United States Tag Team Champions The Midnight Express and a wrestling fan since childhood, has told the story of watching in awe as The Sheik intentionally arrived at the arena while the opening match of the card was in progress, his stretch limousine entering the giant back door of Cobo Arena, as the crowd of over seven thousand—the majority of them with fond memories of the wars he had had in that very building—stopped watching the match and craned their necks to see

The Sheik emerge from the limo in a three-piece suit, his hair dyed the same jet-black color it had once been, attendants carrying his bags as he deliberately made his way through the locker room door. The place was positively buzzing. The Sheik started the match as a de facto babyface alongside Dusty, the sentimental favorite of the enthusiastic crowd—he may have been a monster, but he was *their* monster. However, that didn't last long, as the four-minute match was booked to have a suitably shocking finish, with The Sheik turning on his partner. "It was the strangest match I've ever been in," recalls Sullivan of the main event that night. "It was the only time in my career I've been involved in a double switch. The match ended up with me and The Sheik against Dusty and Dicky. It was a cage match, all four of us in the ring. [The double switch was] Dusty's idea, because he and The Sheik had had a long feud too."

Sullivan won the bet that night, as the show drew in excess of a hundred grand and proved to be one of the biggest crowds and largest gates of the entire 1988 Great American Bash tour. It was also the largest Cobo Arena crowd The Sheik had performed for in eleven years. It was a glorious moment for fans of Big Time Wrestling, watching The Sheik return to his home turf one more time after all those years. A return match was scheduled for September, building off the double switch, that was to have had The Sheik and Sullivan going against the reunited Texas Outlaws, Rhodes and Murdoch—former Big Time Wresting World Tag Team Champions who had defended the title at Cobo Arena nine times in 1970. But Farhat and Crockett got into a money dispute that killed the deal—recognizing himself as a big reason for the crowd they had drawn, Farhat demanded his usual ten percent cut of the gate, just as he had always taken from the Cobo Arena shows of old. When Crockett balked at paying him $10,000, Farhat no-showed the return match and had to be replaced at the last minute.[29] It was the last time The Sheik would ever work for a major American promotion. As for Crockett, just four months after the Cobo show, on the verge of bankruptcy after spreading himself too thin in the battle with the WWF, he sold his family business to Ted Turner, whose company Turner Broadcasting owned TBS. Turner changed the name of the company to World Championship Wrestling, or WCW. Half a year later, Dusty Rhodes was in polka-dot tights, working for Vince McMahon.

By the end of the 1980s, the pro wrestling business in North America had been transformed beyond recognition. The territorial system had been utterly laid waste, with ninety percent of regional companies out of business. The NWA had been reduced to a relic, a handful of independent promotions hanging on to an affiliation with WCW that would only last a couple more years before the big-time Turner organization lost patience with it. The WWF had become literally synonymous with wrestling in the US and was poised to go international in the coming decade. With nowhere to work, and health issues dragging him down, Farhat finally made time for the double hip replacement he so desperately needed. There are no records of any Sheik matches between mid-1988 and mid-1990, and for any other human being it would've been the perfect opportunity to allow the body to heal and to ride off at least semi-gracefully into the sunset of retirement.

But Farhat was no ordinary human being, and his life was far from simple. Adding insult to injury, he was sued by the WWF's parent company, Titan Sports Inc., in December 1988 for trademark infringement. Details of the case are sparse, but the timeframe of the accused infringement was the late 1970s, and the *Body Press* magazine is mentioned directly, seeming to indicate that it may have had something to do with WWWF photography being used without permission, perhaps during the period when WWWF stars like Superstar Billy Graham and Bob Backlund were being brought into Big Time Wrestling. This was also part of a larger campaign the WWF was undertaking at the time—a war on outside wrestling magazines and an attempt to establish what it considered its own intellectual property. Nevertheless, the timing of the case is alarming, as was the $42,701.16 that Farhat was ordered to pay when the court ruled in Titan's favor.

Joyce had taken her husband back, but things were far from rosy. The specter of addiction had never gone away, and some close to him at the time recall that going into the 1990s, Farhat's substance abuse problem had become worse than ever as his chronic pain had only increased with age and continued physical exertion. "I never saw his drug use, but I did see its effects," recalls Dave Burzynski. "Pain in his face, the inability to get into the ring, his lack of movement, and no longer caring what he did in the ring that the fans might see through. Also, just being careless around fans and people, not like his old self." Living arrangements from this era are less than clear, as the Farhats are listed as being in possession of their original home at 3275 East Grand River Avenue in Williamston as well as another residence around the corner at 3750 Webberville Road, indicating they could possibly have been living apart yet very close by for part of that time. Money was getting tight again, and the old Grand River Avenue home was in danger of foreclosure, just as the larger estate had been a few years earlier.[30]

For these reasons, not to mention his continued drive and need to prove himself at the only thing he knew how to do, Farhat remained open to taking up the mantle of The Sheik again, if only someone was willing to give him the opportunity. When that opportunity eventually came, he would be mentally ready, although far from physically, as his repaired body was still nowhere near ring shape and never would be again. But he'd take the chance, not only for his own career, but just as importantly for the burgeoning career of his nephew, who stood to benefit by being in his orbit. Despite the protestations and persuasions of family and close friends to the contrary, The Sheik would rise again, in his mid-sixties, for one last run—not in the United States, but in Japan, where a decade of absence had only amplified his legend among fans who had not been privy to his public decline. The most unlikely of comebacks was about to become a reality.

CHAPTER 16

ONCE MORE INTO THE FIRE

*"We said to him, 'Why are you still doing this?' And he would just say, 'I
have to. I want to. I'm OK. And mind your own business.' That's just the
way Dad was. He knew what he wanted, and that's all there was to it."*
—EDDIE FARHAT JR.

Т he glory days of the 1950s and pro wrestling's first TV golden age
were only a few decades in the past by the start of the 1990s, but they
may as well have been several lifetimes ago. The larger-than-life
superstars who had come into Americans' living rooms on those circu-
lar, black-and-white twelve-inch screens, and who had become national
celebrities and household names had, along the journey from Truman and
Eisenhower to Bush and Clinton, receded into shadowy memories of a
bygone age, and even less than that for a younger generation of fans, in
a business notorious for neglecting its own history in favor of the next big
show. In a time before the internet and YouTube, the legends of the fifties
may as well have been medieval troubadours—remembered by the faithful, but as far removed from the current scene as possible.

"Gorgeous" George Wagner, the Toast of the Coast who had once
hobnobbed with Bob Hope and Burt Lancaster, and who was wrestling's
first bona fide genius performer, died penniless of a heart attack the day
after Christmas 1963 at age forty-eight, his friends raising the money to
buy him a gravestone.[1] The high-flying Antonino Rocca, after years of
drinking himself into an early grave, finally achieved the goal in 1977,
dying in New York's Roosevelt Hospital of a urinary infection at age
fifty-five. The massive Haystacks Calhoun, broke and living in a double-
wide trailer, died of diabetes in 1989 at age fifty-five, having lost his leg to
the disease three years earlier. Farhat's great promotional rival, Dick the

Bruiser, watched his Indianapolis promotion shrink to nothingness by 1989 in the wake of the WWF expansion and went to work as a WCW road agent—just two years later, the sixty-two-year-old died of a ruptured blood vessel suffered while lifting weights. His longtime tag team partner, Reggie "The Crusher" Lisowski, had left his AWA home to take a part-time deal popping some Midwest houses for Vince McMahon before retiring to South Milwaukee. Killer Kowalski had retired in 1977 at age fifty, opening a wrestling school in Malden, Massachusetts, that would produce some of the greats of a later generation. Verne Gagne's AWA floundered on life support, running Las Vegas casinos until going belly-up in 1991, landing the former Olympic hopeful in bankruptcy court. The graceful Ricki Starr got out early, taking bookings in Europe starting in 1973 and then retiring and taking up permanent residence there shortly after, living in relative anonymity. "Mr. America" Gene Stanlee got out even earlier, retiring in 1968 and parlaying his impressive physique and health-conscious lifestyle into a career selling nutritional supplements and coaching Hollywood big-shots like Tom Cruise and Tom Hanks. The original Nature Boy, Buddy Rogers, had been mounting a comeback for Philadelphia promoter Joel Goodhart in 1992 at age seventy-one shortly before he fell and broke his arm in a supermarket and subsequently died in a Fort Lauderdale hospital after a series of strokes possibly due to a congenital heart defect.

And yet, even into the 1990s, there was one national star of those far-off DuMont Network days who could still be found plying his trade—an anachronism approaching seventy years of age, still hitting the road, lacing the boots, and pulling on the trunks, not really because he wanted to, but because in certain ways, both ephemeral and concrete, he had to. In an earlier time, he had been the raven-haired, sharp-eyed, exotic Sheik of Araby, but these days he was simply The Sheik. The hair had grayed long ago; the eyes were still sharp as ever, though little else was, aside from the razor blades that he still used to do one of the only things he still could: bleed. The once-flourishing territorial system of which he had been a part was now replaced with an "independent circuit" of small-time operators, running humble venues with little to no TV, in the lengthy shadows of the WWF and its would-be adversary, WCW.

In these shadows moved The Sheik, still making appearances for anyone who could afford his ten percent of the gate. But even more than the domestic business, it would be the Japanese business that would beckon him for one last run. It wasn't the Giant Baba scene of old, to be sure, but it was still a culture that remembered and revered him, and most importantly, it was a money offer that was simply too good to pass up. And so, against the advice of concerned family and friends, Farhat would return to the closest thing to a full-time schedule he had attempted in nearly a decade, and in an environment riskier and more dangerous even than what he had experienced in his prime. It would almost kill him— not once, but twice. But like everything else he'd encountered so far, it didn't. He was still The Sheik after all, and this is just what he did.

But first, he had to get back on his feet again—quite literally. At the start of the 1990s, Farhat was still recovering from his double hip replacement, and he began focusing on training some young new prospects who dreamed of one day entering the ring, just as he had been doing for his nephew Terry, who now had a couple of years' experience under his belt and would assist his uncle in the more hands-on aspects of teaching. The Sheik would never open up a formal wrestling school the way others like Kowalski had done in Massachusetts and longtime journeyman "Pretty Boy" Larry Sharpe had done in New Jersey with his lauded Monster Factory. But he did squeeze half of a wrestling ring into the back of his son Tommy's autobody shop, charging hopefuls a $2,000 fee to take from his learning tree. Every little bit helped in those days, but Farhat was far from pushy about money with his trainees, unlike some less scrupulous ex-wrestlers known to fleece naïve rookies. It was more important to him to give back to the business that had given him so much, and it also helped keep him busy and around the thing he loved.

His initial group was just a handful of students, with one among them a kid from Battle Creek, Michigan, who would go on to achieve worldwide success and a legendary career that would begin inside that half-ring in Tommy's shop. Rob Szatkowski had been a little too young to watch Big Time Wrestling, but as a teenager he became a fan of the WWF, which had just invaded the area. At sixteen years of age, Rob had been among the seventy-eight thousand in attendance for

WrestleMania III at the Pontiac Silverdome, and when the WWF rolled into his hometown three months later, he even got selected to appear in the ring with Ted Dibiase, newly arrived to the WWF as the repackaged "Million-Dollar Man," in a skit in which the rich and evil Dibiase paid him a hundred bucks to kiss his feet. After graduating high school, he decided to give wrestling a try, but in an era when the business was still quite closed, he didn't really know where to go. He was thinking of giving Kowalski's school a try, but while bagging groceries at a local supermarket, he ran into one of Farhat's trainees, Tom Bennett, who informed him that there was another wrestling legend training pupils right in their own backyard.[2]

Bennett first brought Szatkowski to see The Sheik in December 1989, and Joyce, who even then was handling the business end of her husband's operation, signed him to a student contract. Rob informed him that he had a kickboxing background, and Farhat told him to hit the ring and show him what he could do. "And so I did some cartwheels," Rob remembers. "Sheik said, 'What else do you know?' So I did some somersaults and backflips, and he said, 'What else?' I did some splits and some jumping spin-kicks. 'What else?' I ran out of stuff to do! And then eventually he put his nephew Terry in the ring with me, and I had no idea what to expect. Afterwards, not having any clue if I was impressing anybody or not, I was waiting for every word that came out of his mouth. At the end of the day he said, 'OK, come back next week and bring me some money.'"

Unlike most of the prospective trainees that came through those doors, Rob actually did keep coming back week after week. He began making small installment payments, whatever he could afford, sometimes as little as thirty or forty dollars. But Farhat never complained—he obviously saw something in Rob early on and wanted to nurture it. He trained Rob and the other trainees in his old-school fashion, having Terry really work with them in the ring, but never afraid to shout pointers and reprimands from ringside. Occasionally, when he thought they were going too easy on each other and had seen all he could stand, he would make his way into the ring and stretch them, demonstrating more wrestling knowledge than he ever actually showed in his matches. He was especially tough on Rob, tying him in knots and making sure he never forgot that once he stepped between those ropes, he wasn't putting on a show—first and foremost, he was trying to win. There was no "smartening up"—that would happen naturally, through regular exposure to the business, just as it had for Farhat himself.

Once the weather warmed up, they took the half-ring from Tommy's shop and brought it outside to The Sheik's backyard, where the training continued. "We'd be in the ring, and he would be usually in a chair," Rob remembers. "He put all this oil on himself and he's sitting there getting sun while he's watching us. He was always about the basics. He never wanted to see us flipping and jumping around unless we could fit it in. It was always about headlock-go-behind-takedown and try and pin them. That old-school foundation. If somebody was lying on their back and we didn't dive in, we would get yelled at. And we couldn't be stiff enough with each other for him either. Every once in a while, he would step into the ring, and it was something that we didn't really want, because he would really crank it up to show us what he was talking about. He would choke us and bite our nose. He would give it one hundred percent, and he never one time ever smartened us up to anything about it being a work. We knew, but he never once said, 'Here's how to get a guy without hurting him,' or 'Here's how to land.' But the ironic thing about him teaching that way is that I'm sure obviously he learned the fundamentals when he was breaking into the business, but basically for the last thirty years of his career, he wasn't known for doing any of that stuff. He would have these little five-minute matches where he was stabbing a guy with a pencil for most of the time. He didn't really have to do it anymore."

Rob recalls that even though he spent a lot of time around Farhat in those days, The Sheik still clung to kayfabe and to preserving his mystique and his persona. Very often, especially in the beginning, he would still be in character for much of the time, breaking now and then to offer advice during training and during candid moments relaxing by the pool between sessions, when he would share stories from his remarkable forty-year career. "Everything that he did was so people believed everything he did," Rob explains. "People thought that he didn't even speak English. I was scared of him, even in my first year or two of being in the business. He very rarely broke character, even around us." Still, Rob remembers a poolside incident or two which may have seemed playful enough at the time, but in hindsight, shed light on the highly strained nature of the Farhats' marriage: "He rode Joyce so hard in front of us. She would make hot dogs for all of us, and he'd go, "What the fuck? Hot dogs? What are we, twelve years old?' I was only nineteen and I felt bad for her. She'd say, 'Don't listen to him, Robbie, he's just joking.' And he'd say, 'She's been saying that for years, I'm not joking!' She would go, 'Oh, stop it,' and he would say, 'I've been saying this for years . . . "How long you gonna be here, when you gonna get outta here? When you gonna leave me?" She thinks I'm joking!' It was really awkward for us because we were so young, we didn't know how to take it. But we trusted that she knew that he was joking. I think he was, but I don't know. At the time we weren't sure."

As it turns out, there was more to things than just the playful ribbing of a cantankerous older couple. On June 7, 1990, appearing to have had all she could stand from her husband for a wide array of reasons, the beleaguered Joyce finally filed for divorce. Financial hardship was rearing its ugly head again, as the threat of another foreclosure loomed, this time over the East Grand River Avenue house. But the training and the allure of the wrestling business carried on, this time with greater economic urgency. Besides, it was all he had ever done and knew how to do well—going back to the auto assembly line was certainly not on the table. That summer, Farhat put together what would be the final show he would ever personally promote, resurrecting the Big Time Wrestling banner one last time and calling in favors from the likes of "Flying" Fred Curry, Abdullah the Butcher, and Ken Patera for an event at the Toledo Speedway. Farhat also used the show to give some exposure to some of his young trainees, and Szatkowski was given his first official match, a kickboxing exhibition in which he used the shortened ring name "Rob Szat." In the main event, The Sheik battled Abdullah the Butcher for the first time in nearly a decade.

For the occasion, Farhat also bestowed upon his nephew Terry the persona that would stick with him, in one form or another, for the rest of his career. The rumor had already gotten out that Terry S.R. was actually the nephew of The Sheik, so Farhat decided it would be alright to reinvent his nephew a bit by capitalizing on that knowledge and making him into a variation of himself. Wrapping an Indian headdress around his head that was similar to the ones he himself used to wear very early in his career, Farhat informed Terry that he was now Sabu the Elephant Boy—taking inspiration from the classic adventure film that had first made such an impact on him back when he was just a boy of eleven.[3] Although the 1937 Sabu who inspired Farhat was the hero of the movie, Farhat envisioned his nephew as the kind of exotic heel he had been. On that day in Toledo, Farhat's old friend Fred Curry did the honors for the youngster, giving Sabu the Elephant Boy a notch in the win column for his first night as the new character.

Still looking for revenue streams and things to monetize as divorce proceedings carried on, Farhat looked to the library of Big Time Wrestling video footage he had amassed from his years running the territory. Although far from complete, due to the common practice in those days of taping over old shows and reusing tapes in an era when promoters (and TV producers in general) didn't have the foresight to imagine the old footage would ever be of value, what tapes existed had been sitting in Farhat's garage for years. Although what he had was not in the best shape, the VCR and home video boom of the 1980s had made lots of old pop culture ephemera—including old-school wrestling TV—suddenly valuable, and at the start of 1991, Farhat took out the backseat of his Cadillac and filled it with Big Time Wrestling master videotapes, which he then drove down to Tampa, Florida, where his former colleague and longtime Buffalo promoter Pedro Martinez, along with his son Ron, had set up a home video distribution business, PM Film and Videotape, in the wake of the collapse of the IWA.[4] In that "wild west" era of home video distribution, the Martinezes had been amassing—and in many cases bootlegging—classic TV footage, including wrestling footage from their own IWA as well as stuff from the old Chicago Kohler promotion, the Hollywood Legion Stadium, the Gulf Coast territories, and even some 1960s WWWF stuff, among other things. The classic Detroit footage would certainly make a welcome addition to that collection, and so they apparently purchased the collection from Farhat, later putting it out as part of their low-budget line of vintage VHS releases in the 1990s. It's believed that whatever Big Time footage is still available for public consumption today comes from that original PM Video footage archive.[5]

Farhat became something of a booking agent for his nephew and Szatkowski, taking them along with him, helping to get them work, and making sure they were booked whenever he was. This included a seemingly humble yet momentous event at the Azteca Hall in Detroit on February 23, 1991, put on by veteran Detroit journeyman Malcolm Monroe's local independent promotion, Midwest Championship Wrestling, which turned out to be the last known time The Sheik would ever wrestle in the Motor City, as well as his final encounter with the greatest in-ring rival of his career. Along with The Sheik himself, Bobo Brazil was probably the only other superstar of the late-forties, early-fifties TV wrestling boom still roaming the backwaters and making his living between the ropes. On that night, the two men, both in their mid-sixties, took their epic feud into its fifth and final decade—nearly thirty-five years after their first match at the Benton Harbor Naval Reserve Armory on May 11, 1956. "It was my first night as a referee," remembers Alan Haugabook, aka A.T. Huck, the third man in the ring that night. "I wanted Sheik to throw fire at me. So they're working out the match, and they tell me, Sheik is gonna get me—so I'm thinking he's gonna throw fire. But Bobo gave me a headbutt, and before I knew it The Sheik was on top of me and just kind of whisked across my forehead, and I felt this cold sensation. Come to find out I was bleeding. I thought they used blood capsules; they didn't smarten me up at all. Then I realized, no, my head was cut. So I rolled out of the ring, somebody covered my head with a towel, blood was all over the floor . . . I have a scar on my forehead today, the only time I ever got color. I didn't complain about it or anything, and The Sheik liked me from that point on. After the match, both of us were sitting on the bench together, both bleeding. My first night as a referee!" The headbutt drew a disqualification for Brazil, giving the final victory in wrestling's longest running feud to The Sheik. The war that had spanned a continent had at last come to an end, before a few hundred people at a catering hall.

The following month, The Sheik found himself booked in Philadelphia for the first time since his wars with Bruno Sammartino in the late sixties.

But this time, it wasn't for the WWWF but for an upstart indepen-dent promotion called the Tri-States Wrestling Alliance, established by former insurance salesman and rabid wrestling fan Joel Goodhart as an attempt to appeal to a certain segment of the hardcore wrestling fan base throughout New Jersey and Pennsylvania who felt a bit disenfranchised by the WWF's sanitized, kid-friendly product. Goodhart had deep pock-ets and a respect for the industry's proven stars from the past and present who weren't being used by McMahon. For his TWA Winter Challenge II on March 2, 1991, he booked a main event rekindling the Memphis feud between Terry Funk and Jerry Lawler, and the card also included such talent as Ivan Koloff, and Stan Lane, formerly of The Midnight Express. Their Toledo Speedway match still fresh in their memory, The Sheik and Abdullah the Butcher brought their inimitable brand of unbridled chaos to the City of Brotherly Love, to the great appreciation of the notoriously bloodthirsty Philly faithful, many of whom had only heard secondhand tales of their mayhem from days of yore.

"Goodhart was spending all kinds of crazy money on talent," remem-bers producer and TV-radio host Evan Ginzburg, a lifelong wrestling fan who was there that night. "These were loaded shows. He was selling out these small buildings, but still losing money. So he brings in The Sheik against Abdullah . . . I'm backstage, [with] various wrestling media there. We're all chatting and amiable and excited because it's a loaded show. We were really too young to see The Sheik back in the sixties when he was last here. All of a sudden, The Sheik walks into the dressing room, and everything goes silent. You could hear a pin drop. The guy has so much charisma and gravitas, and he was just scary. Everybody just watched him walk in, and it was this surreal moment. It was like, holy shit, that's The Sheik! Later, we're sitting out in the stands watching as fans, and The Sheik comes out and these so-called smart fans look *scared*. He was lunging at various people as he was walking to the ring, and they would reflexively move back as if he was attacking them. There was this whole crazy atmo-sphere, between respect and awe. He and Abdullah came out and they had a great match! Time stood still for that match. They were brawling, they were blading, they were bleeding, they were rampaging around the build-ing. It was exactly what you'd hope it would've been."

Terry, who by that point had shortened his name to just Sabu, also appeared on the card in a battle royal, taking his first bow in a town where he'd make his name. The response to the first Sheik-Abby match was very positive, their drawing power contributing to a crowd of 1,735 and a gate of $32,000—the largest of either in the history of Goodhart's promotion. When Goodhart brought them back in the fall, he put them in the main event, inside a steel cage.[6] By that time, things had improved a bit in Farhat's personal life—just eleven days after the first TWA match, Joyce officially withdrew her divorce filing, and the forty-two-years-married couple officially reconciled. Whether this was due to a true commitment to improving their relationship, simple force of habit, or if it had anything to do with the sizeable jackpot that Joyce, an avid lottery player, had won that same year is hard to determine, but the fact remains they were willing to give it another try and remained together from that point on. It is reasonable to assume that one of Joyce's conditions would be that she would have to be the only woman in her husband's life—a status she had more than earned. Meanwhile, Farhat was continuing to help Sabu and Rob, this time using his relationship with Jerry Lawler and Jerry Jarrett to get them booked for a Memphis run in the spring and summer of '91 (Rob continuing to work under his unwieldy birth name, and Sabu temporarily having his name adjusted to Samu).[7]

No amount of indie bookings or jackpot winnings could dig the Farhats out of the financial hole in which they found themselves like the phone call they were about to receive from a Japanese wrestling promoter dead set on disrupting the tried-and-true industry that had been ruled for twenty years by Antonio Inoki and Giant Baba. Long before he had become a promoter, Atsushi Onita could trace his relationship with The Sheik back to the mid-1970s, when he had dropped out of high school to go to work for Giant Baba in All Japan Pro Wrestling. In addition to learning the ropes as a worker, Onita, as was and is typical in the Japanese pro wrestling business, took on a very subservient role as a rookie wrestler or "young boy," meaning he became part manservant, part gofer, part ring attendant to the veteran performers—and in the case of Onita, that happened to be Baba himself, for whom he became a personal attendant. In such a position, the young Onita had access to the upper-echelon talent during All Japan's initial heyday, and one of the gaijin attractions he never forgot was The Sheik, standing in awe of his mystique and his power over crowds. In the years immediately following the end of The Sheik's relationship with All Japan in 1981, Onita had made a name for himself as one of the company's premier junior heavyweights, but injuries halted his promising career by the middle of the decade. After taking a few years off to recuperate and heal, in 1989 he got into the promotional game himself, starting up something entirely new on the Japanese scene: a pro wrestling company built around his fascination with two distinct combat sport genres. One was martial arts, his own expertise in which he had been perfecting since his youth; the other was the breed of hyper-violent "death matches" he had witnessed while spending time in the Memphis territory in 1981. He called his new enterprise Frontier Martial-Arts Wrestling, or FMW.

Far from the heights of All Japan and New Japan, FMW took shape as one of Japan's earliest successful independent promotions, providing something of an underground alternative to the Big Two—a grittier, smaller group that began generating buzz despite no weekly television presence. And within its first couple of years of existence, the martial arts aspect began to take a backseat to the violence, as FMW became an early pioneer in popularizing what would soon come to be known as hardcore wrestling, or as it was often known in those days, garbage wrestling—a term that could be used both affectionately or derisively. "FMW was very much against Giant Baba's school of wrestling," explains Japanese wrestling historian Fumi Saito. "They had this mentality that it was like a flipside of everything major league in Japan. Still the same method, but Onita did everything garbage." As part of putting his new promotion on the map, in addition to establishing new stars, Onita was also searching for some big names from both the Japanese and American scenes— talents that his audience would recognize from years past, whose stars maybe had dimmed a bit and were ripe for a return. They also needed to have a style that would be a good fit for the edgier, more violent FMW product. Before long, Onita turned his attentions toward locating the man he had watched send Japanese fans screaming from their seats once upon a time.

"There was a middle person who was looking for him," Saito recalls. "Is Sheik still around? Can he work in the ring? Can he really go on tour? Many people didn't even know Sheik was still active." Once Onita finally found him, Farhat discovered that one thing FMW was not lacking in was money: a deal was made whereby The Sheik would be paid $10,000 per appearance—exactly double what his All Japan rate had been a decade earlier. Needless to say, this was a deal that was simply too good to pass up, despite his advanced age and poor health. In fact, it was just the lifesaver he needed. FMW wanted him, the Japanese fans wanted him, and they were going to get him. Another condition of the deal was that The Sheik would be bringing Sabu with him, as Farhat was also eager to use the new arrangement to help further his nephew's waxing career. In fact, on the plane over to Japan for their first three-week FMW engagement, Farhat had a momentous conversation with his nephew that changed the course of his career. Up till then, Sabu had been wrestling the conservative style demanded by his uncle, but he was capable of so much more. Behind closed doors, he had perfected a more thrilling, more dangerous, high-flying daredevil style that was totally different from anything his uncle had done. Up to then, it had only been in private, but Farhat let him know it was time to unleash his true potential. He had big plans for Sabu's Japanese debut, and told him to let out all the stops. Needless to say, it was music to Sabu's ears.

Rob Szatkowski, meanwhile, did not join The Sheik and Sabu on their Japanese sojourn. He parted ways with his mentor and comrade for the time being, ready to begin spreading his wings and flying on his own. One week before Sheik and Sabu landed in Japan, Rob began working for a Tampa, Florida, indie called the International Championship Wrestling Alliance. While there, taking cues from both his love of kickboxing and his passing resemblance to the world's most famous kickboxing movie star celebrity, he changed his ring name to Rob Van Dam. The rest was history.

The Sheik and Sabu made their FMW debut on Wednesday night, November 20, 1991, at the Osaka Prefectural Gym, where nineteen years earlier Sheik had lost the United National title to Seiji Sakaguchi.[8] The encounter, part of the World's Strongest Tag Team tournament, pitted them against the duo of young British grappler Mark Starr and Horace

Boulder, whose uncle happened to be WWF World Heavyweight Champion Hulk Hogan. At age sixty-five, it was clear that this wasn't quite The Sheik Japanese fans may have remembered, but the allure was still there, and Sabu's breathtaking new style certainly made up for his uncle's clear limitations. "It was the same gimmick people loved," says Saito. "People accepted him almost as an instant babyface. The real Sheik, the guy you grew up watching, you know? We were excited. Also, Sabu was accepted by Japanese fans right away because this is The Sheik's legitimate nephew."

From the beginning, the formula was simple: Sabu would dazzle the crowd and do the heavy lifting, while The Sheik would be The Sheik, which by that point was more than enough. The lion's share of his FMW matches would be tag team affairs with his nephew, and in fact out of the seventeen matches on that first tour, only two were singles matches, one of which was against Onita himself—a dream come true for the wrestler-promoter in which The Sheik actually agreed to drop his fabled United States Championship to him, an almost mythical moment for longtime Japanese fans. His work in FMW would allow Farhat to go back to the closest thing to a full-time schedule he had done since the early 1980s. The extreme violence of FMW, while suited to The Sheik's persona, was more of a physical danger to him at that age, which is why Sabu's involvement was all the more crucial to making it work. For example, right out of the gate, their first tour included a couple of falls-count-anywhere street fights, which seemed appropriate for a wrestler who spent so much time outside the ring during his matches anyway. "In the tag team tournament Sabu was in the ring about ninety percent of the time," admits Saito. "The Sheik would walk outside the ring and scare people. An old man, but the aura was the same, and even more believable than he was twenty years back. He got even scarier, that's the funny thing about it. He's doing the same act, but people kind of took him as the babyface because they loved him. The older wrestling fans had a real fond memory."

Farhat and his nephew came home for the holidays, making one brief stopover in Lowell, Massachusetts, for an ill-fated pilot TV taping for the American Wrestling Federation, an extremely short-lived start-up put together by twenty-one-year-old legal librarian Gordon Scozzari, sinking the $100,000 he had inherited from his parents into the abortive affair.[9] But for the most part, for the next three and a half years, The Sheik would appear almost exclusively in Japan, for FMW. In 1992 alone, there would be six different trips to Japan, generally ranging from a week to two weeks in duration, between the beginning of January and the middle of August, totaling fifty appearances that year alone. Generally, these were matches of about five minutes or less, and at a rate of $10,000 a pop, it's hard to argue with Farhat's determination to keep at it, in spite of the risks, as the work was single-handedly lifting him out of financial duress and helping to ensure that his golden years (insofar as the term could be applied) were funded. He got to tag team with Kevin Sullivan, a very friendly face from the States who helped Sabu look after him during the time he was there. He got to work with other up-and-coming talent destined for great things in the years after FMW, including Mike Alfonso, a cousin of Horace Boulder's then known as The Gladiator, who would later achieve fame on both sides of the Pacific as Mike Awesome; Rick Bognar, then known as Big Titan, but later infamous for his role in the WWF as the "imposter" Razor Ramon in the late 1990s; and former WWF enhancement talent Louie Spicolli, who wrestled there under a few monikers, including The Bodysnatcher and Mercenario #3.

But it also quickly became clear that the dangers involved in working at his age, particularly working in this style of promotion, were very real and could have catastrophic results. On January 10, 1992, The Sheik faced Onita in his first barbed wire death match, a no-disqualification affair in which the ropes of the ring are replaced with barbed wire—a grisly innovation of Onita's that quickly made his promotion both infamous and legendary. During the match, a bleeding Sheik, with help from Sabu, wrapped Onita in some of the barbed wire, only to have the promoter turn the tables and, while still wrapped in barbed wire, slap on a half Boston crab leg hold that actually caused The Sheik to submit—a finish that would have been literally unheard of in the Arabian madman's heyday.

But nothing prepared Farhat—or anyone else involved, for that matter—for what occurred on Wednesday, May 6, 1992, in a parking lot in the city of Sanda, twenty-five miles northwest of Osaka. Onita, inspired by things he had seen in Carlos Colon's brutal Puerto Rican promotion, decided to take the barbed wire death match to a grim new level by having the wires wrapped in kerosene-soaked cloth and lit on fire. It would be the world's first "Ring of Fire" barbed wire death match, and it would also be The Sheik's first brush with actual death in FMW. With Onita and his usual partner, Tarzan Goto, defending their Martial Arts Tag Team title against Sheik and Sabu, the match came off the rails almost immediately, as the ring attendants ignited the wrapped wire, and high outdoor winds caused the flames to spread to the ring apron. Within a couple of minutes, the four combatants and the referee were surrounded by fire. The heat inside the ring quickly became unbearable; so intense, in fact, that the barbed wire began to glow red. A sense of real terror set in, and a panicked Onita waved off the match; fearing for their lives, everyone made a hasty exit from the ring—everyone, that is, except the sixty-five-year-old Sheik, who had had a hard enough time climbing into the ring to begin with, let alone getting out.

After leaping through the barbed wire ropes with his customary agility, a horrified Sabu looked back to discover that his uncle was still in the ring, the flames closing in as he struggled to maneuver his way out. A gaggle of FMW "young boys" began spraying the ring with fire extinguishers and tossing buckets of water—futile gestures toward putting out a blaze that was now totally out of control, but it provided just enough of an opening for Farhat to crawl from the ring, as the area was cleared of the 5,011 spectators who had paid to watch the debacle. Before arriving firefighters could get the blaze under control, the entire ring was literally reduced to a pile of cinders and twisted metal. While Farhat had escaped the ring, he hadn't escaped injury, as in exiting through the wire he suffered horrible burns across his back. Still, he stayed in character even after exiting the ring, hurling flash paper fireballs at his opponents even as the flesh on his cooked back screamed in searing pain. He was eventually rushed to a nearby hospital, where he was treated for the burns as well as for smoke inhalation. Some reports have it that he slipped into a coma for a time. The terrifying accident was a wake-up call for a man already in questionable health for anything even resembling an athletic endeavor, and who, in most other lines of work, would be ready to retire and go on social security. It made national headlines in both Japanese and American wrestling media, drawing worldwide attention to the aging Sheik, a name most fans hadn't heard in years, but for all the wrong reasons. The irony that the man who had spent his career wielding fireballs was nearly incinerated in a flaming ring was lost on no one.

The very next day, Sabu was back in the ring for a barbed wire death match (no fire) against Onita and Goto, with Horace Boulder as his replacement partner, winning the Martial Arts Tag Team title in Tokyo. Farhat remained in the hospital recovering from his injuries, but just eighteen days later, he was back in the ring for one more match of the tour, before returning home with his nephew for three weeks. For any other performer, perhaps that would have been the end—but Farhat's relentless perseverance, in addition to the exorbitant money still being offered, kept him coming back. When he returned in the summer, perhaps as a sign of gratitude and maybe a little remorse, Onita did the honors for The Sheik, dropping his company's top title, the Martial Arts Heavyweight Championship, to him in Sapporo. Still, gratitude and remorse only went so far, as the bout was contested as a barbed wire cage death match. It would be the last championship The Sheik would ever win. While champion, he was paired up with another aging gaijin legend, Tiger Jeet Singh, with whom he hadn't shared a ring in nearly a decade—only this time they met not as enemies but as tag team partners. When accumulating injuries and the general wear and tear became too much for Farhat to bear, he made the decision to drop out of the tour in mid-August, relinquishing his Martial Arts title to Singh and going home. Sabu continued on for most of the year in FMW, often taking his uncle's place in big matches and moving up the card as a result. He began taking center stage, his wild, unpredictable, and death-defying ring techniques swiftly turning him into a bona fide sensation. But the endless barbed wire matches were also taking their toll on the envelope-pushing young wrestler, whose body before long became a map of lengthy scars that would become something of a personal trademark and a testament to how far he was willing to go to sacrifice his body for the sake of his career.

After five months off, not only did Farhat return to FMW in 1993, but he made more wrestling appearances that year—the same year his oldest grandchild graduated high school—than he had in any single year since 1981. With sixty-four matches spread out over six different tours, it represented the height of his FMW involvement, as he continued cheating the inevitable march of time a little longer.[10] He also used his position as an elder statesman of the business to pull back the curtain on his persona just a bit to share some of his wisdom with the younger talent, as Saito recounts: "They all traveled around Japan on the same bus. And Sheik really had a good time talking to the younger guys and telling these old wrestling tales, it was really educational. A real legend is on the bus, and everybody's listening to him. So Sheik almost became a real person, and it was his time to tell all the tricks of the trade and secrets of the business and to pass the torch to the boys." Traveling through Japan with The Sheik could have other advantages as well, as the legend was well-regarded amongst the yakuza and other big-shots with a lot of money to spend. Luxurious dinners and even more luxurious gifts were not uncommon from those who considered The Sheik a man worthy of their utmost respect, and he often came home with jewelry and other expensive items in addition to the mountains of cash he was being paid.

Not only rekindling his feud with Singh in 1993 one last time, The Sheik even got the chance to step in the ring with Singh's son, Tiger Jeet Singh Jr., who just three years later would sign a big contract with the WWF to appear as Tiger Ali Singh. And there was one more legendary Japanese gaijin feud that Onita brought back, as he signed the "middle-aged and crazy" Terry Funk to come in for a series of matches in the summer, including an August tag match pitting Funk and Tarzan Goto against Sheik and Sabu, and a singles match between the two hardcore wrestling icons the following week at Tokyo's Korakuen Hall, where a dozen years prior Terry and his older brother had taken on Sheik and Great Mephisto as part of All Japan's Real World Tag League tournament. Things were quite far removed from those glory days of the late seventies and early eighties, but it was still another way Onita was able to appeal to some older Japanese fans who still remembered. Funk also got to have his first matches with Sabu, which became an extension of the long-running feud with his uncle, and in many ways the new feud came to be regarded with as much reverence if not more, as it helped make Sabu as much as anything that happened in FMW, and eventually carried over into the United States.

The place where it did carry over would have a long-standing impact on Sabu's career, on the development of hardcore wrestling, and on the entire American pro wrestling landscape in general. The previous year, with the Pennsylvania-based Tri-States Wrestling promotion on its last legs due to excessive spending, Joel Goodhart had sold his interest in the company to his business partner, third-generation Philadelphia jeweler and pawnbroker Tod Gordon, who reorganized it as Eastern Championship Wrestling. Based out of a South Philly bingo hall on the corner of Swanson and Ritner Streets that Gordon termed the ECW Arena, the reinvented company had gotten on local late-night TV on both Philadelphia and New York cable, gradually attracting a cult fan base for its growingly edgy and "smart" product designed to appeal to the more mature fan fed up with the mainstream American wrestling epitomized by the WWF. Gordon's booker was the fast-talking and charismatic Bronx native Paul Heyman, who had been mesmerized by the wrestling business ever since he finagled his way backstage at Madison Square Garden as a photographer while still a teenager in the early eighties. A natural born carny, Heyman's career had taken him from a slick promoter for New York's notorious Studio 54 nightclub before age thirty, to an obnoxious onscreen manager in the dying days of the territories in places like Florida, Memphis, and the AWA, and he had taken the job with Gordon after just having been fired from his four-year WCW run as Paul E. Dangerously, the cellphone-wielding "Psycho Yuppie."

In the fall of 1993, Heyman was just putting his creative vision for ECW in place and had taken notice of what FMW had been doing in Japan. In part wanting to replicate their gritty, underground, alternative position in the United States, he took an interest in some of their talent, most notably Sabu, whom he felt strongly about building ECW around as its unique attraction. Sabu and his uncle had taken a break from Japan and returned to the States, and Heyman used it as the perfect opportunity to book Sabu for the first time. By this point clad in a head-scarf and flowing robe, he looked for all the world like a more toned and scarred version of The Sheik in his prime—until the bell rang. His high-flying, devil-may-care style, which typically involved putting himself and his opponents through ringside tables—a tactic rarely seen in those days—made him an instant hit with the ECW Arena faithful, earning him the nickname "The Homicidal, Suicidal, Genocidal, Death-Defying Maniac," and on his second night in the company, he won the ECW Heavyweight title from Pittsburgh's Shane Douglas, a trainee of longtime Sheik opponent Dominic Denucci.

The time back home also gave Farhat the opportunity to do something that would have once seemed unthinkable: appear at a wrestling fan convention. Understandably, his persona and strict belief in preserving kayfabe meant that he had always been largely invisible to fans aside from when he was in the ring, and certainly direct interaction with them had been off-limits in order to preserve his carefully guarded mystique. But times were changing, and part of those changes meant that fans would get their first chance ever to mingle with and get autographs signed by The Sheik, and it would be a legendary moment fondly remembered by all who got to be a part of it. The event was the third annual installment of the Weekend of Champions, a groundbreaking convention put together by the well-connected John Arezzi, a man equally popular with both fans and talent. Arezzi had already turned heads starting in 1991, when he brought in both Nature Boys, Buddy Rogers and Ric Flair, for their first convention appearances. The following year, he publicly "reunited" Bruno Sammartino and his pupil Larry Zbyszko, who had engaged in one of wrestling's hottest feuds a dozen years earlier. This time, he wanted to up the stakes by making history with The Sheik. "I was promoting shows and working pretty closely with Sabu, and really close friends with Kevin Sullivan," Arezzi remembers. "I had an idea, not knowing he'd ever accept, that I wanted to bring The Sheik in as the headliner for the 1993 convention. I reached out to Kevin Sullivan, and he came back and said, surprisingly, he would do it! I remember negotiating the fee, it was $2,500. I didn't speak to Ed; I negotiated with his wife. He showed up at the convention, and it was a big deal because he had never done anything like this before and he never did it after. I wish I could tell you I had a lot of interaction with him, because I always was fascinated by him. He was one of the only performers that, even into my days as a talk show host and promoter, the suspension of disbelief really never left me. Even when I met him and shook his hand, even when I paid him, I paid his wife, and I didn't engage in any conversation with him."

But just because he was appearing and signing autographs, that didn't mean he wouldn't be completely in character. For both days of the convention, those in attendance got The Sheik in all his glory, taking pictures with cautious, intimidated fans in his three-piece zip-up suit while shouting gibberish and brandishing a giant sword. "He'd have the sword, and if he saw a fan who looked a little intimidated, he would bang it on the table to try to scare them away," Arezzi recalls. "People would laugh nervously and then get their autograph. It was almost like going to a haunted house, where you didn't know what was gonna happen." As bizarre as it was, it represented the only time that rank-and-file fans had ever gotten that close to the most feared and reviled villain in the history of the ring, and the memorable happening made it Arezzi's most well-regarded Weekend of Champions of them all. In addition to his autograph signings, The Sheik also accompanied Sabu to the ring for his match against high-flying lucha libre sensation Konnan on the live card that accompanied the convention.

Just the week before, Sabu had gotten an early experience of how his relationship with his uncle could have unintentionally negative effects on the trajectory of his career. Shortly after he won the ECW Heavyweight title, a much bigger opportunity showed itself. He got a call from James J. Dillon—a former wrestler who had gotten his first big break in The Sheik's territory back in the 1960s and now ran the WWF's Talent Relations department—to come in for a tryout. After Sabu's recent success in Japan and in Philadelphia, Vince McMahon was interested in seeing what he could do.[11] He was booked for back-to-back nights in upstate New York, first a TV taping in the Mid-Hudson Civic Center in Poughkeepsie for *Monday Night Raw*, the WWF's new flagship prime-time USA Network show, in which he faced prelimi-nary wrestler Scott Taylor;[12] and the next night a taping in the Glens

Falls Civic Center for the syndicated *Wrestling Challenge* program, in which he traded high-flying maneuvers with the dazzling Owen Hart, youngest son of former Calgary promoter Stu Hart. Many were impressed, including Owen's older brother, top WWF attraction Bret "Hit Man" Hart, as well as McMahon, who offered him a job. The catch was that Sabu would have to be repackaged as a new character that the WWF could own and monetize. His uncle had ingrained in him the importance of protecting kayfabe, protecting his established persona, and never speaking publicly, just like he had done.[13] McMahon was willing to accommodate him, proposing a variation of the tried-and-true Sheik persona: The Sultan, a masked and turbaned heel who used a manager to do the talking for him. Sabu was already leery of bending to the WWF's will, but the deal-breaker came when McMahon told him that the manager they had in mind for him was The Iron Sheik. Knowing this would truly break his uncle's heart, Sabu turned down the flabbergasted McMahon's $250,000 dream offer, and decided to stick with working for ECW and FMW.[14]

Regardless of his decision, Sabu's career was still doing well as he made a name for himself in both his companies of choice and began stepping out from beyond his uncle's formidable shadow. To Heyman he became something of a pet project and a foundational talent on which he and Gordon could build the company that was quickly becoming the talk of the wrestling business. His matches with Terry Funk from that era made a mark with ECW fans that never left and contributed more than anything to the growth of his legend. Farhat, meanwhile, took no bookings for the remainder of 1993, even as his nephew continued working in Japan. He buried his eldest brother, Lewie, who passed on November 6 at the age of seventy-eight, and he gave his own body whatever chance he could to heal, or at least recover from what he had been putting it through overseas. By that point, even he had to realize that he would not be able to keep up the façade for very much longer, and it's possible that his plan at the time may have been to not return to Japan at all, especially now that his mission to make Sabu into a sensation had started paying off. It was Sabu who was quickly becoming the new face of hardcore wrestling—the style pioneered by The Sheik himself. The nephew he had ridden pretty hard during those formative years was now filling him with great pride, and, for the first time, he was letting him know.

Sabu got a rare opportunity to return the favor on February 5, 1994, when he actually brought The Sheik, who had first made a name for himself in the Marigold Arena some forty years before, to the ECW Arena—the cutting-edge epicenter of 1990s wrestling—for a show suitably called "The Night the Line Was Crossed." It was a rare clash of eras that took place in part because of Sabu's growing profile within the company as well as the influence of Kevin Sullivan—the man who had previously helped get The Sheik booked in Florida, Hawaii, and on The Great American Bash—who also happened to be working at the time for Gordon and Heyman, both great Sheik admirers going way back. Tommy Laughlin, a twenty-three-year-old kid from Yonkers who had been making a name for himself on the Northeastern independent circuit and had broken into ECW at the same exact time as Sabu under the name Tommy Dreamer, remembers that night well: "When he first walked in, he was wearing the kaffiyeh. Right away, he had the presence of The Sheik, in a three-piece, tailor-made pinstripe suit. He looked like a bad man, full of class. Sabu was carrying his bag, and they had a referee carrying the other bags, like a young boy train. I remember being intimidated by his presence. I'd fight anybody, but when The Sheik walked in, the whole locker room got quiet and stood up for him . . . This is ECW—insane wrestling guys. But that guy could kill us. And meanwhile, he was probably like our grandfathers."

And true to form, The Sheik wasn't just there to take a bow or watch his nephew's match (a marathon three-way encounter in which Sabu and Shane Douglas challenged Terry Funk for the ECW Heavyweight crown). He came to wrestle, and he was paired with Hawaiian grappler Pat Tanaka (whose father, Duke Keomuka, he had teamed with in Texas in the 1950s) against the tandem of Sullivan and another member of ECW's newest crop of future stars, a former judo champion from the Red Hook section of Brooklyn, New York, named Pete Senerchia, who wrestled as the savage Tazmaniac.[15] It was the only appearance by the innovator of hardcore wrestling for the company that was in the midst of inventing the term, but sadly it happened about twenty years too late. After making a completely crazed entrance in which he knocks over the entire ring entrance set, The Sheik, unable to even enter the ring due to the absence of ring steps, opts instead to brawl with an obliging Sullivan through the crowd, rendering each other bloody messes as Tanaka and Tazmaniac go at it between the ropes. Unable to get through the locked barricades and get close enough to the ring, Sheik fumbles with his flash paper and gets off a fireball through the ropes within the reasonable vicinity of the Tazmaniac, who sells it like a champ as Tanaka scores the pin for his team. The Sheik then lets off another less-than-accurate fire blast in Sullivan's direction as they battle to the back. Faint chants of "Sheik" can be heard from the ECW Arena faithful, a notoriously tough crowd that was understandably a bit let down by the rare appearance from the godfather of hardcore.

Farhat was keenly aware of the disappointment, as is evidenced by Dreamer's recollection of being driven back to the hotel that night with Sheik and Sabu, by a critical fan who got more than he bargained for: "We're going over the bridge by where the Eagles play, over the

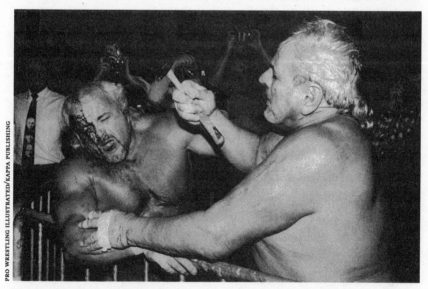

ECW Arena, February 5, 1994: A 67-year-old Sheik attacks Kevin Sullivan with the timekeeper's bell hammer in his one and only appearance at the world's most famous South Philly bingo hall.

Schuylkill River. The guy who's driving the car says to The Sheik, 'Such an honor to see you live. It sucks that you missed the first fireball, but you got it the second time.' The car goes silent. Sabu tells the guy to shut up because he sees Sheik getting mad. And then Sheik threw a fireball at the guy while he's driving and goes, 'Did I miss now?'"

By the middle of the next month, The Sheik and Sabu were back in Japan for another three-week tour. They returned for a second 1994 run at the end of April that culminated in what many consider the last major match of The Sheik's career. Each year, FMW held its huge anniversary show at the venerable Kawasaki Stadium, and for the fifth annual extravaganza, on May 5, The Sheik was booked to face his old archrival Terry Funk. With more than fifty-two thousand fans looking on—the largest crowd by far of Farhat's entire career at that point[16]—the two warhorses battled for six blood-soaked and flame-seared minutes, summoning up the spirit of the 1970s one last time. Five weeks later, on June 11, back in the United States, The Sheik returned to the Lincoln Park Community Center to work for Malcolm Monroe in his first Michigan match in over three years. He had been booked to wrestle Abdullah the Butcher, but when Abdullah no-showed with a flimsy excuse,[17] Monroe himself stepped up to take his place. The fans on hand, some of whom had seen The Sheik appear at Cobo Arena in his heyday, likely had a tough time recognizing the nearly immobile sixty-eight-year-old man struggling to get in the ring that night. Nevertheless, they can take solace in being part of history, as it would be The Sheik's final match in the United States.

It seemed that finally, and prudently, The Sheik was winding down. The fall of 1994 saw the last of his full engagements with FMW in the form of two more two-week tours. However, at this point it was clear that he was mainly there to support Sabu. Gone were the death matches, and several of his appearances saw his role relegated strictly to being in his nephew's corner. Sabu's star had risen to such a degree that he had even been trying his hand at his own promotion in the Michigan-Ohio area, based out of the Lincoln Park Community Center. The once-mighty National Wrestling Alliance had, in the wake of the brutal territorial wars of the 1980s, been reduced by the mid-1990s to a loosely affiliated collection of low-profile independent promotions, and NWA president Dennis Coralluzzo, along with Detroit-area wrestling historian and promoter Mark Bujan, banked on the star power of The Sheik's nephew to help establish the local promotion, called "NWA Sabu." However, the new group was doomed early on when, in August 1994, Tod Gordon and Paul Heyman pulled off one of pro wrestling's most notorious double-crosses. ECW had been a member of the NWA and had agreed to hold a tournament in the ECW Arena to crown a new NWA World Heavyweight Champion, in what was supposed to be a crucial step on the road to rebuilding the organization. However, Gordon and Heyman instead used the moment as an opportunity to put their own company on the map at the expense of the venerable Alliance. When Shane Douglas emerged victorious in the tournament, he unceremoniously threw the iconic NWA title belt to the ground, on orders from Gordon and Heyman, and, to the shock and dismay of Coralluzzo and longtime NWA promoter Jim Crockett, declared that the NWA was dead and that, going forward, the ECW Championship itself would be recognized as a world title. He also announced that Eastern Championship Wrestling would now be known as Extreme Championship Wrestling—a name they had been more than living up to.

Sabu was a crucial element in the exploding ECW revolution, and his success had carried over into Japan as well. In December, he faced the difficult task of informing both Onita and his uncle that had been offered a job by none other than Antonio Inoki, owner of the country's top wrestling company, New Japan Pro Wrestling. Owing to their past difficult relationship, this was not a place where The Sheik would be following his nephew. However, Farhat understood the business and the incredible opportunity that was being afforded Terry—which was also partly the culmination of his own hard work in grooming him. Much to Terry's relief, Farhat gave his blessing to his nephew's new endeavor. The Sheik made two more appearances for Onita right before Christmas— conspicuously absent from his side was Sabu, who started for Inoki on Christmas Eve.

With Sabu no longer needing his help, and having made well over $1 million working for FMW, Farhat was likely weighing the continued health risks when he opted to remain in the United States as 1995 began. Old age, and everything that came with it, was clearly upon him. In March, he mourned the loss of the sixth of his ten siblings, his brother Amal, who died at age seventy-two. Nevertheless, the allure of the ring, and of the associated paydays, remained too attractive to ignore for long. Onita persuaded Farhat to return to Japan one more time, coinciding with FMW's big sixth-anniversary show at Kawasaki Stadium. Sabu was over there for a series of engagements for Inoki and had agreed to meet up with his uncle to return home after his brief two-night appearance. It seems likely, looking back, that Farhat would have literally never stopped pursuing work if the choice had been his own. However, this time the choice would be made for him thanks to a second near-fatal catastrophe, this one something that everyone involved had to see coming sooner or later. It was only a matter of time before Farhat's body would let him know that it had taken all it was capable of taking, and that finally happened after the sixth-anniversary show.

The date was Friday, May 5, 1995. The crowd that night was FMW's greatest ever, at 58,250 strong. It was the largest crowd to ever witness The Sheik perform live, and, as it turned out, the last. But that fact was yet unknown to anyone on hand that day, including Farhat himself. His opponent was Tijuana's Leonardo Carrera Gomez, a thirteen-year veteran luchadore who had been performing under a mask with a gimmick inspired by the Japanese superhero TV series *Ultraman* until Onita had traded in his mask for face paint and reinvented him as the sinister Damian 666, this time taking inspiration from the 1976 horror film *The Omen*. He had been an on-again, off-again ally of Sheik and Sabu during their time in FMW, but on this night did the honors for the Arabian madman. Just like in the old days, the fans scattered in The Sheik's path as he made his way through the crowd with a giant flaming torch. After a minute and a half of wanton torch-waving and stabbing, The Sheik, unable to even get down on the mat, scored the pin by dropping to one knee on his opponent while still holding on to the top rope for balance. A career spanning forty-eight years, without question one of the longest in the history of the ring, thus came to a halt. What had begun at Lansing's Prudden Auditorium before a few hundred spectators on January 14, 1947, at a time when Harry Truman occupied the White House, Betty Grable was Hollywood's hottest starlet, and Nat King Cole's "I Love You for Sentimental Reasons" topped the pop charts, ended that day in Kawasaki Stadium, at a time when Truman and Grable had been replaced by Bill Clinton and Meg Ryan, and America's number-one song was Montell Jordan's "This Is How We Do It."

Whether Farhat intended for it to be his last match is a moot question. The following day, as he stepped inside a taxi that was supposed to take him to Sabu's hotel to prepare for the long trip home together, Farhat suddenly felt his left arm go numb. Crushing chest pains ensued, and after a few minutes, he was being taken from the taxi and put into an ambulance for the trip to a local hospital. His nephew, still on a high from having just won New Japan's prestigious IWGP Junior Heavyweight title before forty-eight thousand fans at the Fukuoka Dome, became concerned when Sheik never showed up, and he was soon informed of the terrible news of his uncle's heart attack by Onita. By the time he rushed over to the hospital, doctors were already performing open heart surgery, and Farhat had been hooked up to a ventilator. Terry then contacted his aunt Joyce, who arrived in Japan the next day to join him at Farhat's bedside. After a few scary days, he finally regained consciousness. The power of speech returned not long after.

By the grace of God, he eventually pulled through. But the looming and inevitable fact he had been evading for so long was finally staring him, his wife, and his nephew firmly in the face—unless he wanted to lose his life in the not-too-distant future inside the ring to which he had already given so much, it was time for The Sheik to finally succumb to the unrelenting passage of time, to hang up the pointed boots, the camel trunks, and the kaffiyeh and retire. This time, it would be for good. His health, already on the brink, would never be the same after the experience. But as much as wrestling had been destroying his body, in some strangely symbiotic way it had also been keeping him going. By the time he stepped away, so long after he should have, it would be tragically difficult for him to enjoy the retirement he had so richly earned.

CHAPTER 17

THE LAST DAYS OF THE SHEIK

"I want people to know that this was a real human being. This was not a robot.
This was not a piece of steel like he portrayed to everyone . . . This was a man who
had emotions and feelings. And I was one of the lucky ones to get to see that."
—"RUDE BOY" RUDY HILL

The professional wrestling business that Ed Farhat left behind was as unrecognizable from what it had been in his heyday as the man himself was. The National Wrestling Alliance had been relegated to the obscure periphery of the business, its territorial system a distant memory. Vince McMahon's World Wrestling Federation and Ted Turner's World Championship Wrestling (on the verge of a corporate buyout by Time-Warner that would set in motion its eventual demise) battled for national supremacy in the form of a brand-new "Monday Night War" between its two directly competing flagship TV programs, *WWF Monday Night Raw* and *WCW Monday Nitro*. The South Philly juggernaut Extreme Championship Wrestling, though smaller in scope, was now under the complete control of Paul Heyman, who had bought out his partner Tod Gordon and was innovating with fresh ideas and edgy concepts that would eventually be co-opted by both of the Big Two. Detroit's Cobo Arena, abandoned by the WWF for Joe Louis Arena next door, had become the exclusive home of WCW, which had been drawing lackluster crowds of one to three thousand there for years.[1]

The episode in Kawasaki had been the ultimate reality check for Farhat. His family had been begging him to walk away from the business for years, and now that he had, walking itself was becoming next to impossible. He had built a notorious reputation as one of the longest-tenured performers, if not *the* longest-tenured performer, in the history of the business, and now that it was finally, truly over, he had paid the price. He would never fully recover from that heart attack, which only further aggravated his worsening health issues, related to years of abuse to his body in the ring, not to mention years of substance abuse at such an advanced age. His remaining time in retirement, which encompassed less than a decade, would be characterized by a physical condition that was declining at an alarming rate. But through it all, right to the very end, he remained in character whenever interacting with anyone outside his close family and friends. No matter what, he was true to the act, and was always still The Sheik when in public, never speaking, never letting down the kayfabe façade that had become his greatest trademark. Even his grand-children, who were the light of his life, called him Grandpa Sheik.[2]

"The match in Japan was his final hurrah and it satisfied him," remembered Eddie Jr. "He came to terms with himself. He realized he had done it all in his life. He lived a full life. Whatever he was looking for or searching for, he must've found it. And he was ready to just relax and try to feel better and get healthier. And that's when he started getting really sick."

In the new three-company landscape of pro wrestling, Sabu's star had continued to rise. ECW was growing in power and influence, and Sabu had been a part of that—there was even talk of his old running buddy Rob Van Dam coming in to join him, after having followed in The Sheik's footsteps and making a major name for himself working for Giant Baba in Japan. Sabu, meanwhile, had been making the best money of his career so far working for Baba's rival, Antonio Inoki. His commitment to Inoki had in fact led to a falling-out with Heyman in mid-1995 that eventually led to Sabu getting an opportunity with WCW at the end of the summer. Eric Bischoff, a former landscaper, veterinary assistant, and butcher from Detroit who had gotten his first break in the business working in the TV sales department of Verne Gagne's AWA back in the eighties, was now running WCW for Turner Broadcasting, and on a mission to overtake the WWF. To that end, he was busy scooping up talent from not just the WWF, but also Japan, Mexico, and ECW.

At the urging of longtime Farhat family booster Kevin Sullivan, who was head WCW booker at the time, Bischoff brought Sabu in for a few TV tapings in August, September, and October, leading up to a big appearance at WCW's *Halloween Havoc* pay-per-view event, scheduled to take place right in the heart of Detroit at the Joe Louis Arena.[3] Things seemed to be taking off for Sabu, and as a way of returning the favor to his uncle, who lived right down the road anyway, he convinced the reluctant WCW brass to allow him to use The Sheik as his manager for his pay-per-view match against the masked Mr. J.L. (fellow ECW original Jerry Lynn). No major American company had touched him in seven years, but it seemed harmless enough, and so on October 29, 1995, before thirteen thousand fans—the largest North American crowd to see him in eighteen years[4] and the first time he'd been on national TV since the DuMont Network days of the 1950s—The Sheik took one last bow for the Detroit faithful. Unfortunately, it turned into a disaster, as in the early moments of the match, Sabu executed a moonsault from the top rope to the outside of the ring, wiping out not only his opponent, but also his sixty-nine-year-old uncle, who suffered a broken leg. Still, Sheik managed to stay upright at ringside, urging on his nephew and periodically swiping at Mr. J.L. with his saber. Following Sabu's victory, J.L. also gained the unique distinction of being the last person to ever get a fireball to the face from The Sheik. Unfortunately, The Sheik had gone into business for himself—the stunt had not been approved by a horrified WCW management, who decided the legend's services would no longer be required in Sabu's corner. Of course, that turned out to be a moot point anyway, as Sabu only worked one more date for WCW before being abruptly fired after asking for more money.

Farhat was now at the point where even a brief public appearance could put him in peril, and after Sabu patched things up and went back to work for ECW at the end of the year, The Sheik kept a very low profile, fading into retirement as he had intended. He focused on his beloved family, spent time on his love of painting and gardening, and watched lots of golf on TV. He continued following the exploits of both his nephew and Rob Van Dam in ECW and would still see them whenever they happened to be passing through the Michigan area, which would be more often as Heyman's company made the move to pay-per-view and began to expand beyond its Northeast boundaries. "I remember the last time I stopped in to see him when I was in town," says Van Dam. "He said that he was proud of me, and for some reason I didn't know that he was following me, because it wasn't like I was on *Monday Night Raw*. But he was like, 'Yeah, of course! I know how good you got, I'm proud of you and glad that you're doing very well.' That made me feel really good." Sabu even got his one and only chance to wrestle at Cobo Arena in February 1997 on an episode of *Monday Night Raw*, thanks to a cooperative arrangement between the WWF and ECW.[5]

On one of those ECW runs through the Midwest in the first week of 1998, when the group was running a couple of shows in nearby Inkster, Michigan, and at the fabled Tyndall Armory—once one of Dick the Bruiser's main venues, back in the WWA days—The Sheik and Joyce were treated to a visit from not only Sabu, but also Heyman, Tommy Dreamer, and his girlfriend at the time, Trisa Hayes, a former backup dancer for Prince who had been working for ECW under the name Beulah McGillicutty. The ECW crew had driven together in a Winnebago just to take advantage of the chance to spend some time with Sabu's legendary uncle. "He was one of the nicest guys," recalls Dreamer of the visit. "I just sat under the learning tree as he told stories. I thought when I'd show up at his house he'd be like a crazy man and have a sword in his mouth with a pencil, but he just was telling me about the business. I remember staring at his forehead like, 'My God, look at the wars this man has been through.' We had such a nice time; it was just one of those special days where we were just being wrestling fans. I was thinking, 'How did I just have lunch with The Sheik at his home?' He was a really, really awesome individual and I could see why Sabu loved him so much."

Just as Joyce had taken care of all his financial affairs through his career and been a true partner, she now had to take greater and greater care of the man himself, who by age seventy-two had gotten to the point where he could no longer walk unassisted. His vulnerable condition understandably seemed to be bringing them closer together than they had been in a very long time. They had come through great difficulty and the near-breakup of their marriage, but ironically were still together, even as Eddie Jr. and Kathy's marriage was coming to an end after twenty-four years. In June 1998, Sheik lost his older brother Edmund, the one so many reporters, researchers, and historians had commonly mistaken him for, and it was beginning to look like he might be joining him sooner rather than later. In recognition of his failing health, and the prospect of one day being unable to make the trip at all, he finally agreed to having an official retirement ceremony, courtesy of Atsushi Onita and FMW, the company that had given him his last shot at the business he loved. It was a symbolic decision that made it very clear that Farhat had finally internalized and accepted that he would never be competing in a wrestling ring again.

The ceremony was held on December 11, 1998, as part of the ECW-FMW Supershow, a weekend of events held at Tokyo's Korakuen Hall and co-promoted by the two hardcore wrestling groups from two different continents. Joyce and Sabu would be coming along, as well as Sabu's new bride, Hitomi, whom he had married in the US the previous year but with whom he'd planned a traditional Japanese ceremony for her family and friends. Several other ECW talents were sent over the weekend, including Dreamer, Van Dam (ECW World Television Champion), ECW World Heavyweight Champion Shane Douglas, and ECW World Tag Team Champions The Dudley Boyz, Buh-Buh Ray and D-Von (aka Long Island's Mark LoMonaco and Devon Hughes).

Perhaps if it were any other wrestling legend, this would've been the moment to drop the act, to come before the people at last as a real, genuine human being, separate from the character that had entertained them all those years. But this was The Sheik—a man for whom the persona and the human being had become one and the same long, long ago. This was no character. This was a part of who he was, what he had vehemently clung to for half a century, and he was not about to abandon it, not even for the most solemn of public occasions. To watch the retirement ceremony now is to witness a strangely moving, one-of-a-kind blending of kayfabe and reality that serves as the ultimate culmination of the career of the Arabian madman. There had been concern that he would not be able to even walk to the ring unassisted, but once the moment of truth arrived, he somehow flipped the switch, kicked into another level, and transformed himself one last time. Accompanied by a dapperly attired Sabu, The Sheik ambles delicately to ringside, resplendent in his flowing robe and head-scarf, hurling fireballs as if by force of habit, and chasing away fans with a scimitar. With the aid of Sabu and others, he must practically crawl between the ropes to get in the ring, and he does his best approximation of his camel walk once inside. Several dignitaries and journalists cautiously approach him to bestow gifts and tokens of appreciation, which he hesitantly accepts while shouting gibberish at them and waving his weapon in their direction. This builds to Onita himself presenting a custom-made championship belt, which Sheik throws to the mat, after which the two men embrace. As the promoter walks away from the old man whose bags he used to carry when he was a teenager, wiping tears from his eyes, The Sheik does something remarkable: He grabs the microphone and shouts, "Onita, ichiban!" He then bows to the audience and, as if to demonstrate his respect for them the only way he will allow himself to, he shouts, "Allah! Japanese!" The lights dim and a ten-bell salute is rung as he continues to stare menacingly and shout. Then, as he carefully makes his way through the ropes and down to the floor with copious assistance from Sabu and others, he waves to the crowd and yells, "Allah! Bye-bye!" before making his way to the back as Sabu holds the belt high. A fleeting moment of whimsy from the man who had once haunted the nightmares of the Japanese fans and now brought a twinkle of warm nostalgia to their eyes, as he briefly thanked them with the gift of his true self. It would be his final public appearance.

The next afternoon, Sheik and Joyce attended Sabu's wedding ceremony, held at the thirteen-hundred-year-old Asakusa Senso-ji, the oldest Buddhist temple in all of Tokyo. On the final day of the Supershow weekend, Sabu received a special wedding gift when he and RVD captured the ECW World Tag Team title from The Dudley Boyz, then everyone headed over to an after-party-cum-wedding-reception at Tokyo's Hitotsubashi Hall, where The Sheik held court one more time over the awestruck ECW and FMW talent. "Remember the movie *The Godfather*, how everyone went up and paid their respects to him?" explains Dreamer. "There was not one person there who didn't do that for The Sheik. I remember the close-to-four-hundred-pound Buh-Buh Ray Dudley being humbled by him, as was everyone. We all sat at the table together. In that setting, he still commanded that presence, but it was different. He was smiling, he'd be happy—but you would still feel like he may take this fork and stab someone with it. And you'd be OK with it because you were at a wedding with The Sheik." Following the reception, Sabu and the rest of the ECW crew spent the night at Roppongi's Hard Rock Cafe, while Sheik and Joyce retired to the hotel. The next morning, everyone went their separate ways—Sheik and Joyce on a twenty-hour flight back home to Williamston, while Sabu, RVD, and the others had a weekend of ECW Pennsylvania shows ahead of them. It had been a great experience, and a great chance for Farhat to say what he had to know was a final goodbye to Japan.

Wrestling had been all Farhat had known for so long that it was positively in his blood. Once he was no longer a part of it in any way, his deterioration increased exponentially, as if his attachment to the ring had been somehow holding him together. By the turn of the new century, he had completely dropped off the radar, unseen by anyone except those very close to him. Sabu, meanwhile, had gotten a new chance at WCW when he was again approached by Kevin Sullivan, this time joined by fellow Sheik-ally J.J. Dillon, who had jumped from WWF to WCW Talent Relations head, and offered a deal in excess of $400,000. It would have been a life- and career-altering moment, if not for the combination of his mother suffering a heart attack, which delayed his signing, and the political maneuverings of Paul Heyman, who insisted Sabu was still under contract to ECW. It was a disappointment from which Sabu would really never recover—a lost opportunity to make his ailing uncle proud, and to follow his footsteps into wrestling immortality. One wonders if Farhat had been more vital and still involved in the business, whether his influence could have made a difference. "It's very hard to be a son—and that's what he was, a surrogate son of a legend," Sullivan says, looking back regretfully. "Sabu always respected the shit out of The Sheik. He wanted to please Sheik all the time. It was very hard on him. The Sheik was very good to him, but very hard on him, harder than he was on his own kids. I admire Sabu very much and like him very much, but I think he was trying to impress The Sheik so much, that he has massacred his body. He had some bad luck. I got him into WCW, and he was going to sign for a three-year-deal, but our legal department terminated his contract before he signed it. His life would've been completely different if that lawsuit thing didn't block him."

The vying for Sabu had been part of a larger struggle, as both ECW and WCW were fighting for their very survival at that time. By the start of 2001, both companies had gone completely out of business, with the WWF eventually buying out all their assets. After nearly twenty years, Vince McMahon's mad dream had finally come true. His truly was the only show in town—or in any town—and for the first time in history, the pro wrestling business in North America had only one "major league," with not just a national but a global presence. Rob Van Dam, less concerned with money than with enjoying his career on his terms, had been a Heyman loyalist to the end, but by the summer of 2001, he had seen the writing on the wall and finally made the long sought-after jump to the WWF, where he would become an overnight main event sensation and a household name. The kid who had started out in Farhat's half-ring had made good, and then some.

Almost at the exact moment that his pupil had crossed over into the big time, Farhat's health took a serious blow from which it would never recover, when he was diagnosed with multiple myeloma, a form of plasma cancer which festers in the marrow of the bones. The disease has the added effects of blocking the blood's production of antibodies, thus making the sufferer vulnerable to a whole host of other illnesses and infections, as well as rendering the bones brittle and prone to injury. It's quite likely that he had been suffering from the disease for years before the official diagnosis, as it would explain his marked decrease in mobility, as well as the leg fracture he suffered at *Halloween Havoc* from a relatively harmless fall. In April 2001, the Farhats had no choice but to declare bankruptcy once again, as medical bills were no doubt piling up, with going back to work no longer an option. He lost his older sister Julia just four months later at the age of eighty-four, by which point he had been confined to a hospital bed in his home. Before long, rumors began to spread throughout the industry among those who knew and remembered him well: The Sheik was dying.

Eddie Jr. had been living with his parents during his father's last years and, almost as a tribute to his father, had begun getting his feet wet in the wrestling promotions business himself with some independent shows in the Michigan area. "I'd come home from a show, and he was so bad and so sick," he recalled. "He was in and out of the hospital, but he'd say, 'How'd it go?' I'd talk to him for a few minutes, but then he was just gone, in another world. But you could tell the love and the emotions he had for the business were still there. He missed it." Some came to visit, like former tag team partner "Killer" Tim Brooks, and retired manager Al "Percival" Friend, who had gotten some of his earliest breaks working for Farhat back in the sixties. In a 2009 radio interview,[6] Friend recalled his last time seeing him in the summer of 2002: "He was in a hospital bed for the last year and a half of his life . . . He had lost so much weight. I was very shocked. I also had never seen him without a big smile, so full of life. As I looked at him, he was dozing in and out of sleep. He had just got through with a physical therapist that had come by at his estate, and he was very happy that I was there, but he just kept going in and out of sleep. I knew that it wouldn't be too long that I would be getting a call, and it wasn't."

Eventually, Farhat's mind, or what was left of it, became preoccupied mainly with his seemingly endless progression of worsening symptoms. As is common with his form of cancer, organ failures inevitably followed. Those close to him recall swelling in different parts of the body, likely related to kidney failure, a common side effect. Exploratory surgeries provided little benefit. He eventually developed osteomyelitis, a staph infection of the bones, which his body was unable to effectively fight. By the end of 2002, financial woes had caused him to finally sell the East Grand River home he had owned since the 1960s. His health worsened, as he developed restrictive lung disease, meaning that even breathing and speaking became laborious tasks. More and more, he was slipping in and out of lucidity, and his granddaughter Jen recalled in her retrospective for the locally published *Jack Detroit* magazine that there would be times he would have difficulty remembering who he was, or more accurately, who he had been.

And yet there were other times he could still remember quite clearly, as is evidenced by a remarkable anecdote from Farhat's final days recalled by "The Rude Boy" Rudy Hill, a Midwest indie wrestler best known at the time for his close association with Insane Clown Posse, a Detroit-based hip-hip duo that had also made waves in the pro wrestling world thanks to their past association with WWF, WCW, and ECW, as well as their own indie promotion. Hill had been a fan of The Sheik as a kid and had gotten to know him on the indie scene in the 1990s. At the very beginning of 2003, when it was clear that Farhat was on his deathbed, he summoned Hill to his home for a visit: "I remember John 'Pee Wee' Mohr, the referee, came to my place of business and was like, 'Listen, Sheik wants you to come by today.' I said, 'I get out at nine tonight, and by the time I drive all the way out there, it's gonna be eleven.' He said, 'Sheik wants you to come.' So of course, I did." Hill wound up spending hours talking with Farhat into the early morning.

When he arrived at the house, he noted that still sitting there in the backyard was the fabled purple Lincoln Continental Mark III with white interior, complete with car phone, now more than thirty years old. Joyce answered the door and led him to the plush bedroom where The Sheik lay bedridden, covered in lavish quilts, almost like a true Sheik from tales of old, only smaller, meeker, and weakened, his days of majesty now behind him. On his nightstand sat a framed photo of himself with Muhammad Ali, from their days preparing for the Inoki fight in '76. And on the wall, overlooking the bed, was a giant framed photo from the heyday of Cobo Arena, looking down on a sold-out crowd, with The Sheik and Bobo Brazil waging war in the center of the ring. Hill sat by the bedside, looking up at the picture of the man in his prime, and down at the image of the man as he now was, so very fragile, yet still with those deep scars and that intense look in his eye. He had known him for close to fifteen years, and yet, somewhere deep in his core, Hill was frightened. The Sheik was still that man he remembered.

Sheik had recently suffered a stroke, and his words were slurred, but Hill remembers maybe asking three questions that long night. The rest of it was The Sheik doing exactly what he was the least known for doing—talking and talking and talking, eulogizing his late friend Bruiser Brody, absolving The Iron Sheik for his gimmick infringement, and telling stories of his career, as Hill absorbed as much of the knowledge as he could. It was a much calmer and humbler man than Hill had known before—a man who knew his fate was at hand. "He just wanted someone to talk to," Rudy remembers fondly. "I loved the man. My whole back is tattooed with him. And I knew I was saying goodbye to him. If he had the chance, he would've mended a lot of burned bridges. He didn't treat me like shit, but I watched him treat people like shit. I've seen him go off on some people. The way he was stern with his students. He didn't give a damn who was around. He just wanted people to learn the right way."

Joyce, the long-suffering wife who had been with him through the very good and the very bad, would come into the room and sit with him, holding his hand while he told his stories to Rudy, in between bringing tea as the two men conversed into the night. Like many others close to the couple, Rudy had heard the stories of how he had strayed, of her anger and feelings of betrayal, of the near-divorce. But here, at the end, he could see the love between these two people, that no matter what the ups and downs were, they were still there, holding one another, together in the end, the mistakes of the past behind them. The hand that had reached out to so many opponents in violence now holding tight to the woman he loved, who loved him and always had. "That was the human side that I got to see," says Rudy. "That is when I realized, this is Eddie Farhat I'm knowing right here. This is when I found out that The Sheik was a human being." By the time they were through talking, it was nearly four in the morning, and Rudy was getting ready to leave.

"Everyone forgot about me, kid," said the frail and tired old man in the bed.

"What do you mean, sir?"

"You see that phone? It hasn't rung in two years."

"Well, I haven't forgotten about you."

"I'm happy you haven't."

With fragile hands, Farhat weakly scribbled down his new phone number and asked Rudy to please keep in touch. He asked his young admirer and friend to stay a while longer. Joyce was preparing hummus and coffee for breakfast. But the responsibilities of life beckoned, and Rudy politely excused himself. On the way out, he passed Eddie Jr., whom he had remembered as Capt. Ed George, coming out of the basement; then, longtime family friend and former employee Ray Selby, better known to fans as New York Raymond, another house guest at the time, standing in the kitchen archway. Awestruck with disbelief, glowing with overwhelming childhood nostalgia come to life and a memory to last forever, he got in his car and drove to tell his father, who used to take him to see The Sheik wrestle, of the unforgettable experience.

Just a few days later, both his kidneys and liver failing, and down to only 121 pounds—roughly half the weight he was billed at during his career—Farhat was brought to Sparrow Hospital on the east side of Lansing. There, in the early morning hours of Saturday, January 18, 2003, he told Joyce that it was time, and asked to be taken off his respirator. At 3:10 a.m., surrounded by his wife and sons, Edward George Farhat, known to all but a very select few as The Noble and Exalted Sheik, who had spent his entire career avoiding defeat at every turn, laid down for the one opponent that always goes over in the end. His passing at the age of seventy-six occurred just two days short of the fifth anniversary of the death of his greatest foe, Bobo Brazil, who had passed from a stroke just a couple of hours west in St. Joseph, Michigan, in 1998.

Sabu was in Japan preparing to wrestle Junior Heavyweight Champion Kendo KaShin before forty-five thousand at All Japan's *2nd Wrestle-1* live on pay-per-view from the Tokyo Dome when he heard the news from other wrestlers buzzing about it in the locker room.[7] Minutes before he came out for his match, he called his mother back home to confirm. In tribute, he wrote "Sheik" across his chest and his armband before walking down to the ring to wrestle. Abdullah the Butcher, also at the show, announced The Sheik's passing to the live audience and the many more Japanese fans watching at home. That same day, Rob Van Dam was on the other side of the world, wrestling for Vince McMahon (whose company had recently changed its name to World Wrestling Entertainment, both as an acknowledgement of the evolving nature of its product and due to losing a trademark lawsuit with the World Wildlife Fund) at the *Royal Rumble*, his second-biggest show of the year, also live on pay-per-view from Boston's FleetCenter.

Neither man would be able to attend the funeral services scheduled for Tuesday, January 21—Sabu unable to secure a flight home from Japan in time, and Van Dam prevented by his obligations to McMahon, who, ironically enough, had him booked on a WWE tour of South Korea and Japan later that week and wouldn't grant him the time off. In fact, Dave Burzynski remembers that although there were hundreds of family and friends in attendance, he was the only person from the pro wrestling business who came to pay their respects, something that bothers him to this day. Calling in sick to his day job at AT&T, Burzynski arrived that bitterly cold morning at Gorsline Runciman Funeral Home, directly across the street from Sparrow Hospital, to find the viewing taking place in the hall, with Farhat's World War II medals on proud display: "I walked up to the casket. And, oh my God—he was unrecognizable . . . Just this little person in this casket. The only thing that I really recognized was his beard, he still had that saber kind of beard. And the forehead." Dave paid his respects to the family and recalls how relieved Joyce seemed that the whole ordeal was finally over. A Catholic funeral mass was held down the road at St. Mary Church in Williamston at

The funeral card of Edward George Farhat.

Edward Farhat
"The Sheik"
Williamston, Michigan

BORN
June 9, 1926
Lansing, Michigan

DIED
January 18, 2003
Lansing, Michigan

SERVICE
St. Mary Catholic Church
Williamston, Michigan
Tuesday, January 21, 2003 at 11:00 a.m.

OFFICIATING
Rev. Karl Pung
St. Agnes Catholic Church
Fowlerville, Michigan

INTERMENT
Mt. Calvary Catholic Cemetery
Williamston, Michigan

CASKET BEARERS
Steven Ording, Edward Farhat III, Dan Fleser,
Ernie Dennis, Ronald Farhat, David Farhat

11 a.m. sharp, and those on hand that day remember that aside from one reference to "Edward" early in the service, even the priest referred to him as "Sheik"—which all would agree would've been exactly as he wanted. He was given a soldier's burial later that day at Mt. Calvary, a small Catholic cemetery in Williamston, with a standard military placard to mark the grave.

The relative ambivalence of the wrestling industry to the death of one of its all-time greatest performers and attractions carried over in the days that followed. Despite having one of his greatest students on its roster, WWE made no mention whatsoever on either of its TV programs that week of the man who had once headlined sellouts at Madison Square Garden against their greatest world champion, and who had been a peer of the company's founder. All Japan Pro Wrestling, by that time operated by Motoko Baba — widow of the Giant, who had passed in 1999 — showed more reverence than any American company, announcing that its next show, on February 8 at Korakuen Hall, would be in tribute to one of its greatest gaijin stars, The Sheik. Longtime fans in the Detroit and Toronto areas noted the relatively slim coverage his death received in the major newspapers in those towns, where his name had once drawn more money than any other athlete or entertainer. The *New York Times* did mark the event with a substantial obituary, and Farhat's local paper, the *Lansing State Journal*, obtained a memorable quote from one of The Sheik's few remaining loyalists and colleagues in the business, former NWA World Heavyweight Champion Dory Funk Jr.: "He became the best and hottest drawing card. When we got together, it was always a packed house. I feel like I lost a very close friend of mine."

No one would ever accuse the professional wrestling business of having an overabundant appreciation of its history or of the stars and pioneers who helped build it. But to the fans who were there for the great times, and who remembered, it was a palpable loss of a man who seemed so much more than a man—who seemed like someone who was somehow beyond things like mortality. But, as Rudy Hill discovered, Ed Farhat was indeed a human being, whose days in this world were numbered just the same as anyone else's. Not even the most protected persona in the history of the industry could protect him from that. But even though he himself couldn't cheat death in the end, what Farhat left behind—the memories, the matches, the sublime terror, the flaming trail of blood and destruction in major cities around the globe, would indeed live on. In that way, it could be said that although Ed Farhat was gone, The Sheik would never die.

CHAPTER 18

A LEGACY WRITTEN IN BLOOD

"Since the dawn of time, there have been tens of thousands of men who can call themselves professional wrestlers. Of them, not one was more hated. And because of the changing nature of the business, probably no one ever will be."
—DAVE MELTZER, WRESTLING OBSERVER NEWSLETTER,
JANUARY 27, 2003

T he truth of the matter is that for as many people as there were in the business who loved and admired Ed Farhat, there were just as many, if not a little bit more, who didn't. The man burned his share of bridges and made his share of enemies, there's no denying it. Dave Burzynski came face-to-face with this harsh reality in the months following The Sheik's death, including at the annual Cauliflower Alley Club reunion for retired wrestlers and industry professionals in Las Vegas,[1] where he got into a conversation with former NCAA and NWA champion Jack Brisco about the passing of his former mentor and idol, and Brisco—who famously considered wrestling The Sheik to be "beneath" him—callously remarked, "It couldn't happen to a nicer guy." Or later at a reunion of Toronto wrestlers, where longtime Sheik promotional rival-partner Johnny Powers had a similarly flippant reaction to the news. "It pisses me off to this day," says Burzynski. "I'm sure there are tons of guys out there who hated his guts or couldn't care less. But there were also a number of us who thought he was the greatest thing in the world."

Those in the latter group were certainly pleased when, perhaps in part to make up for having snubbed him at the time of his death, WWE in 2007 announced that The Sheik would be inducted into its Hall of Fame at a special ceremony held at Detroit's historic Fox Theatre, last of the lavishly ornate 1920s movie palaces. Vince McMahon and company had rolled into town for an entire week of events in the Motor City, culminating in *WrestleMania 23* at Ford Field, new home of the Detroit Lions, and it certainly seemed like the perfect opportunity to honor the greatest wrestling star in the history of that city, not to mention the man who had once run it. In my capacity as senior editor of *WWE Magazine* at the time, I had the honor of attending the ceremony live and witnessing the packed house pay posthumous tribute to a legend whose name still held awe for the thousands in attendance, which that night also included members of the Farhat family, most notably Joyce, who accepted the accolade for her late husband.

The Sheik joined a Hall of Fame class that included his former rivals Dusty Rhodes and Jerry Lawler, as well as his former World Tag Team Champions, The Wild Samoans. And although he hadn't set foot in a McMahon ring for almost thirty-five years, it was fitting that WWE, which had now established itself (whether everyone approved or not) as the last company standing and the primary caretakers of the history of the business, should honor the man whose legacy as one of the biggest stars to ever lace up a pair of boots transcended any one company and put him on anyone's list of all-time greats. Naturally, it was Rob Van Dam and Sabu who were chosen to induct him. Sabu had by that point joined Van Dam as a contracted WWE talent, with the company attempting to revive the ECW brand, which it now owned,[2] and with which Sabu was more associated than practically anyone. In his autobiography *Scars, Silence, & Superglue*, he recalls incurring McMahon's wrath that night by refusing to break character and break his code of silence—instead, he allowed RVD to deliver a heartfelt speech, while he stood alongside and nodded his approval, an occasional wistful smile crossing his face. Even at his uncle's Hall of Fame induction, the values Sheik had instilled in his nephew towered above all else. "I felt very honored to be inducting Sheik and even representing him," Rob remembers of that night. "I think that I realized at that time that Sabu and I were pretty much the only official products of Sheik that were in the industry, and we were doing really well too."

Joyce fought back tears as she looked out at the crowd there to honor the husband she had only lost four years prior, and she spoke fondly of the affection he had for the fans, in spite of how much they always rooted passionately against him. The following night, she took to the stage with the other inductees to take a bow before the 80,103 fans in attendance at *WrestleMania 23*, the largest crowd to ever witness pro wrestling in the city of Detroit.[3] The WWE Hall of Fame sometimes takes criticism for being predominantly a WWE marketing tool rather than a genuine place of tribute, but there is no question it is the industry's most high-profile hall of fame, the one most known to the mainstream public and the casual fans, and to be named in it is still widely considered an honor, not least of all by those chosen for inclusion. It also brings with it the WWE's coveted "Legends contract," which includes monetary compensation that no doubt came in handy for Joyce, whose financial woes had only worsened since the loss of her husband.

More recognition followed. In his lifetime, The Sheik had already been inducted in the 1996 inaugural class of Dave Meltzer's *Wrestling Observer Newsletter* Hall of Fame, often looked upon by insiders and purists as the most legitimate. Three years after his WWE induction, the National Wrestling Alliance inducted him into its hall of fame alongside the likes of longtime promotional associate Nick Gulas, as well as former NWA World Champions Buddy Rogers, and—ironically enough—Jack Brisco. The vindicating move served as recognition for his crucial role in the organization for so many years, as well as symbolic forgiveness for his 1980 blacklisting. In 2011, one of his greatest living adversaries and friends, Mark Lewin, was chosen to induct him to the Pro Wrestling Hall of Fame in Amsterdam, New York—which, unlike the WWE, NWA, and *Observer* halls of fame, boasted an actual physical building, like the nearby halls of fame for baseball and boxing.[4]

Sabu's involvement with WWE did not last much longer beyond that hall of fame induction evening in 2007. The company had been intent not only on using him, but on giving him a major push and making him into the face of its new ECW "brand." However, his reluctance to stray from what his uncle had taught him—most particularly refusing to speak on camera in spite of McMahon's insistence that this would be required of someone he was grooming to be one of his top stars— did not serve him well. His clashes with management over money and the creative direction of his character led to the permanent dissolution of WWE's relationship with him and the last of his several chances with the company. Although he would experience some success in other companies in later years, he never attained the heights that his prodigious talents should have guaranteed him, and he has expressed regret over perhaps heeding his uncle's advice a little too closely and being a bit too difficult. To some critics, the influence of The Sheik became less an advantage and more an albatross around Sabu's neck over the years, as he still dutifully adhered to the sanctity of kayfabe, becoming one of the only major talents to still refuse to publicly break character in an era when such attitudes had long ago been abandoned, and retaining the deep suspicion and cynicism that had once served his uncle well in another time, when he had much more leverage and power behind the scenes than his nephew ever enjoyed.[5] Nevertheless, to this day, Sabu is recognized by those in the know as one of the single most influential and important performers in the evolution of pro wrestling over the past thirty years, and he is cited by countless top-level talents as one of their greatest inspirations. Perhaps chief among these is Rob Van Dam himself, a much more easygoing person by nature, who did achieve tremendous success in WWE, spending six years there in the 2000s as a main event attraction and capturing nearly every title available, including the world championship once held by the likes of Bruno Sammartino, Pedro Morales, Bob Backlund, and Hulk Hogan. In 2021, he even joined his mentor as a member of the WWE Hall of Fame.

There would be one last hall of fame induction Joyce would attend for her husband—perhaps the most ironic one of all. On July 25, 2013, The Sheik was inducted to the Greater Lansing Sports Hall of Fame—an honor typically reserved for so-called legitimate sports legends, but in this case, the magnitude of the man no doubt encouraged a break from tradition. One last time, he would be confused with his older brother Edmund, as the organization sought to somehow justify the inclusion of such an outrageous entertainer by bringing up his supposed athletic accomplishments at St. Mary's High School and the University of Michigan. Four months after the induction dinner, having spent over a decade without her husband, Joyce Fleser Farhat lost her own bout with cancer at the age of eighty-three. At her passing, a new custom-made gravestone was added to the site of Edward's military marker. As a nod to their unique marriage and life together, the new stone featured a camel on Edward's side, and a butterfly on Joyce's, The Sheik and his Princess reunited again. It was the end of an era. The last of the eleven Farhat siblings, Sheik's younger sister, Eva (Sabu's mother), and his older brother Moses, had already passed away in 2011 at age eighty-two and 2012 at age ninety-two, respectively. But the family would continue: before her death, Joyce got to enjoy three great-grandchildren that her husband had never known. After her own passing, two more would be added to the fourth generation of the Farhat family to be born in the United States.

Sadly, by the time of her death, the opulent days of grandeur that she had been used to living with her husband were long gone, never to return. In place of the sprawling, twenty-six-acre Williamston estate that she had once affectionately named Tahraf (Farhat backwards) was a trailer that she shared with Eddie Jr. As for the estate itself, it had long ago been bought by a family friend and transformed into a popular bed and breakfast—where two of the Farhats' granddaughters were reportedly married—and remains so to this day, bringing in countless guests each year who likely have absolutely no idea of the identity of its legendary former owner or of the many luminaries and memorable gatherings once housed under its roof. Eddie Jr., in the years following the loss of his father, continued his attempts to resurrect the glories of Detroit wrestling with his independent promotion, the All World Wrestling League, with little success. During the 2020 COVID-19 pandemic lockdown, he instead regrouped and chose to focus on his original love, country music. His younger brother, Tom, had long assisted him with the AWWL, working to keep their father's memory alive, while also owning and operating Thomas Auto Body & Parts in Williamston for many years. After a lengthy struggle with kidney cancer, Tom died on October 1, 2020 at age fifty-seven. Despite finally beginning to experience some success with his music, Eddie Jr. became understandably disconsolate after the loss of his brother, compounded with his own ongoing struggles with kidney disease. In his weakened condition, he had been a vocal advocate of the importance of observing safety precautions during the pandemic, but he unfortunately contracted the disease and lost his life to it in the morning hours of Monday, March 22, 2021, less than six months after Tommy's passing, four days shy of his seventy-first birthday, and on the same day I finished the manuscript for this book.

Since the death of The Sheik, the venerable building once known as Cobo Hall has hosted pro wrestling on only four occasions, with the first two being a 2004 edition of *WWE Monday Night Raw* and the 2006 return after a fourteen-year hiatus of WWE's *Saturday Night's Main Event*, which drew only seven thousand fans—a slow night back in the Big Time Wrestling salad days. In 2010, the arena portion of the convention hall, which had been the home to Detroit wrestling for more than half a century, the space where The Sheik, Bobo Brazil, Mighty Igor, The Hell's Angels, Tony Marino, Mark Lewin, Sweet Daddy Siki, Ben Justice and The Stomper, the Funks, Abdullah the Butcher, The Fabulous Kangaroos, Luis Martinez, and so many others had done battle before a transfixed public for decades, was unceremoniously shut down, gutted, and converted to a forty-thousand-square-foot ballroom, a renovation completed in 2015. Two years later, the hall presented a two-part event put on by Xtreme Intense Championship Wrestling, a local group owned and run by Malcolm Monroe Jr., son of the late Big Time Wrestling regular, who had died in 2004. In the main event that night, he teamed with his own son, Malcolm Monroe III, for the historic occasion. The following year, XICW returned one more time for a show that featured a battle royal to crown the first holder of the XICW United States title belt, a replica of The Sheik's classic original Big Time Wrestling US belt of the 1960s, which was won by prolific Canadian independent wrestler Michael Elgin.

Shortly thereafter, partly to honor the fiftieth anniversary of the infamous Detroit race riots, the name and likeness of Mayor Albert Cobo, whose record on race relations in the Motor City was highly questionable, was removed entirely from the facility, with corporate naming rights sold to TCF Bank.[6] Although it still stands on the banks of the Detroit River, the building once known as Cobo Hall, The House that Sheik Built, is almost completely unrecognizable today as the location where so many indelible memories were once made. Even the Joe Louis Arena was shut down in 2017 after thirty-eight years of dutiful service. Today, when WWE rolls into town once or twice a year, they run a new arena, named after the fast-food pizza chain Little Caesars.

As with anything, time marches on, even for The Sheik and everything he built. It can be argued that Ed Farhat was responsible for drawing in more revenue for the city of Detroit than any other athlete, entertainer, or promoter during his time at the helm of Big Time Wrestling, with regular sellouts and near-sellouts at both Cobo Arena and the Olympia Stadium that outshone any local major league sports teams or nationally touring musical acts that came through during that period. Yet there isn't a statue or even a plaque to commemorate him anywhere in that city, or anywhere else for that matter. But fans of a certain age will never forget, even as the memory of the general public fades as it always does. "He's remembered very well if you're over age forty," said Mark Bujan, who was long among the most active and passionate of those fans of a certain age before his untimely death in April 2021. "A lot of the younger fans, if you mention 'The Sheik,' they think Iron Sheik. Young kids today don't have a clue of what they missed. They don't get it. We're a dying breed. I'm dedicated till the day I die to keep the memories alive." Adds Alan Haugabook, who knew the man from both sides of the ring ropes: "The younger generation knows of The Sheik because we talk about him so much. But I don't think that they really know the magnitude. That was forty-plus years ago!"

And what was that magnitude, exactly? Simply put, The Sheik was the greatest money-drawing heel in the history of the pro wrestling business and, by all accounts, the most passionately reviled by fans—as crucial a metric as there is for villains of the squared circle. And in an era when a sizeable portion of the audience truly believed what they were watching, and the rest chose to willingly suspend their disbelief in the pursuit of a good time, that really meant something, and will never be duplicated. "There was a guy that was probably between two hundred and two-ten, yet he scared the hell out of everybody," recalls a seventy-six-year-old Terry Funk from his home in Amarillo, Texas, the rigors of his own fifty-year career now finally behind him, as well. "He scared the shit out of me every time I got in the ring with him. I didn't know what the hell that goofy bastard was gonna do. People say that wrestling isn't real. Well, somebody forgot to tell that son of a bitch! He didn't know a wrestling hold, but he knew that goddamn violence. He played that persona better than anybody. And I don't even know if it *was* a persona. He might've been that goddamn nuts."

Sheik's dedication to kayfabe, as demonstrated here by the continued awe of even one of his greatest rivals and colleagues, was without match in the annals of a business built on artifice. He came up in an era when you protected your persona—"gimmick" is far too small a word—because by doing so, you protected your livelihood. And yet nobody protected it like The Sheik, who carried on the act, both inside the ring and out, right to the grave. His career stands as the most extreme example of protecting the business and of keeping its secrets and its mystique alive, as he kept people guessing for his entire public life. The persona and the man, in the view of the world at large, and maybe to a certain extent in his own mind, became one and the same, in a way that is unparalleled among pro wrestlers and puts him in a class with pop culture icons and enigmas like Mae West, Liberace, Mr. T, Vampira, Andy Kaufman, and Leon Redbone, who maintained their persona to the point where the real human being underneath became all but unknowable to any but a very tiny, trusted circle. "That was what made him an attraction, that's what sold tickets—his persona, who he was," explains Ohio fan turned modern legend Al Snow. "It wasn't his wrestling—he was not an exceptional wrestler. It was his personality and the fact that you could believe in him. All the crazy stuff that he did, you could still believe who he was. And that's probably one of the most important things. He wasn't huge, he wasn't a big, imposing figure of a man, but you treated him as such." In an industry which has largely abandoned its secretive philosophy over the past twenty to thirty years in favor of the more open approach taken by other forms of entertainment, no longer desperate to maintain its authenticity in the face of a general public that's in on the secret, the very notion of what The Sheik built his career on is now quite alien and impossible to reproduce. His act today would more likely provoke snarky, ironic chuckles rather than gasps of shock and terror. And in that, we've lost something valuable.

Beyond the chuckles, The Sheik today might provoke horror of a very different kind, as it's also fairly certain that such a character could not even be attempted now. Ed Farhat, a Catholic American man, not only portraying a Muslim and Arabian-born performer, but doing so in a way meant to intentionally dehumanize his character and provoke fear and hatred from a largely Christian audience, in part by using the trappings of the Muslim faith and of Arab culture in general ... It takes only a passing familiarity with the culture wars and identity issues of today to realize this would no longer fly—which WWE themselves realized as recently as 2005, when they faced tremendous backlash over Italian-American wrestler Marc Copani, whom they had packaged as the insidious Muhammad Hassan, a kaffiyeh-wearing Arab-American meant to be a "modern update" of the Sheik wrestling template.

It is so very important to understand that The Sheik, like so much of pro wrestling, was a product of another time. There is not a single recorded incident of public protest or controversy over his character or performances during his entire career, as the public and culture in general were simply conditioned differently. Therefore, to judge from our own present cultural ivory tower would be unwise, counterproductive, and pointless. By applying those standards, we would never have had not only The Sheik, but also the likes of the evil Nazi Fritz Von Erich (Jack Adkisson of Jewett, Texas), the devious Russian Ivan Koloff (French-Canadian Oreal Perras), Native American hero Chief Jay Strongbow (the Italian-American Joe Scarpa of Nutley, New Jersey), the childlike Polish powerhouse Mighty Igor (Hispanic-American Dick Garza), the fearsome Kamala the Ugandan Giant (Jim Harris of Senatobia, Mississippi), and many, many others. Without The Sheik, it is reasonable to imagine that Eddie Farhat might have been just a returned GI who came home to Lansing, gave pro wrestling a go for a while, and then spent the rest of his career on an auto assembly line. And thus, the history of professional wrestling, joyously subversive and rough around its edges from the start, would lose so very much of its fascinating richness and color. Better by far to celebrate The Sheik for what he brought to fans throughout his storied career in a time when such things were still possible. As Joyce herself eloquently put it in her 2007 WWE Hall of Fame acceptance speech, her husband acted as a cathartic for the fans, allowing them to work out all the frustrations of daily life, if even for just a moment, and perhaps leave the arena that night just a little bit friendlier to their fellow man, after having poured out their anger and hate into the vessel that was The Sheik.

Without question, he was ahead of his time, among those prescient few who early on recognized that whatever pseudo-sport professional wrestling may have once been, it was now first and foremost show business. While it was important to maintain the illusion for the public, he knew that it was spectacle the audiences came to see—colorful characters, wild and crazy action, over-the-top violence, and outrageous feuds. The purists like Lou Thesz and Sam Muchnick may have clutched their metaphorical pearls, but Farhat knew what put asses in seats and kept them coming back, and it wasn't scientific wrestling. When given the chance, he built his own company, Big Time Wrestling, around this philosophy, treating Midwest fans to a brand of wrestling that was uniquely their own. In a way, his brand came to be the dominant brand, as a line could very feasibly be drawn between The Sheik's approach to wrestling-as-spectacle and the WWE's reinvention of the industry as "sports entertainment." "He was probably one of the best showmen that I've ever seen in the wrestling business," remarks Jeff Walton, who saw him in action in America's very own illusion factory, Hollywood. "His legacy should never be forgotten. This was a very soft-spoken guy when he wanted to be, who was very, very intelligent about the business. He wrestled all over, and worked hard to build a phenomenal character that mesmerized so many wrestling fans. Even though in those days you wouldn't refer to wrestling as showbiz, he knew about that, and was able to put himself over everywhere he went. And that is a very hard feat. I wouldn't say he was a master wrestler or a technician of holds. He knew how to wrestle, but more than that, he knew how to draw."

Along the way, he inadvertently pioneered an entire subgenre of pro wrestling, which wound up being taken far beyond where even he would've ever imagined or preferred it would go. No one ever called The Sheik hardcore during his days in the ring, but his frequent use of copious blood, explosions of fire, constant outside-the-ring brawling, foreign objects of every stripe and size, and complete disregard for the "rule-book" in favor of wanton, unpredictable aggression, as well as the way in which he populated so much of his events with that kind of stuff up and down the card, wound up inspiring generations of performers captivated by the kind of primal reaction such antics brought out of an audience. Certainly, there had been those who had been considered violent brawlers before The Sheik, but more than anyone else, he used his mass appeal during the 1960s and '70s to sow the seeds of proto-hardcore everywhere he went. And what a crimson crop it eventually grew, leading to promotions like Memphis, FMW, CZW, and ECW, whole companies entirely dedicated to the style, in turn influencing the entire independent scene in both the US and Japan, and eventually even spilling over quite literally into the mainstream of WWE, even if the company's current fixation on an all-audiences product has resulted in a blander, safer, watering down of anything resembling the "extreme" or "hardcore." Today, to younger fans who have heard of The Sheik, this is his greatest legacy—and yet, just like the many hard rock acts who were supposedly "inspired" by Led Zeppelin and yet only ever copied the most crass, loud, and obvious trappings of that most innovative of bands, so, too, have most of those who have followed in The Sheik's footsteps favored only the blood and guts, and taken it to the tenth power, missing nearly all the other nuance of who he was and what made his act work.

And yet although he knew how to engage fans, his legacy is also a cautionary tale of how that formula can go wrong if it is never properly adapted or evolved, of how you really can have too much of a good thing, and of how rigidity and the refusal to be open to new ideas can lead to disaster. He deserves credit for making himself into one of only two major North American wrestling promoters of non-European ethnicity at a time when the industry, as nearly all fields of endeavor were, was completely dominated by white men. Yet of all the major promoters of the heyday of North American territorial wrestling, Farhat's story is one of the most unfortunate and tragic—a power broker who burned too brightly and burned out far too soon. While the territorial system was already doomed, Farhat could have continued on for years like most of his peers did, and he might have even had a decent future in the major leagues of the business during that new era like many of them did, if he hadn't been so stubborn, if he hadn't burned so many bridges, and if he hadn't allowed his personal demons to consume him. This hard fact—his fall from grace long before pro wrestling's new mainstream boom hit—is an important factor in why his name has not endured as well as those of some of his rivals.

Through the soaring highs and the crushing lows, Farhat epitomized the American dream. A first-generation citizen born to immigrant parents who traveled from a foreign land with hopes of greater opportunity for their offspring, he seized that opportunity and rode it as far as it would take him. He fought for his country just as he fought for his family, who meant more to him than anything else and, combined with his fierce ambition, gave him all the motivation he needed to excel. Like so many of his generation, he was bred with toughness and resolve, he knew the value of respect and loyalty, he loved hard yet gave his trust not easily. And like the American dream itself, his story is a complex one, as the dream would prove to be fleeting. Nothing lasts forever, but what matters is making a mark while we're here, and Ed Farhat, The Sheik, most certainly did that. In the immortal words of Theodore Roosevelt,

> The credit belongs to the man who is actually in the arena, whose face is marred by dust and sweat and blood; who strives valiantly; who errs, who comes short again and again, because there is no effort without error and short-coming; but who does actually strive to do the deeds; who knows the great enthusiasms, the great devotions; who spends himself in a worthy cause; who at the best knows in the end the triumph of high achievement, and who at the worst, if he fails, at least fails while daring greatly, so that his place shall never be with those cold and timid souls who neither know victory nor defeat.

Edward Farhat was in that arena. He sweat. He bled. And above all else, he dared greatly. In the end, that's all that matters.

THE SHEIK'S RECORD AT COBO ARENA (1962–1988)

Title changes are denoted in italics. Match times have been provided where available. Special stipulations are in parentheses where applicable.

DQ = Disqualification   DDQ = Double-disqualification
COR = Counted out of ring   DCOR = Double count out
KO = Knockout   NC = No contest

1/20/62:   Teams with Johnny Barend to defeat The Weaver Brothers
2/17/62:   Defeats Jim Hady
3/10/62:   Draw with Dick the Bruiser
5/12/62:   Loses to Lord Layton (2/3 falls)
6/23/62:   Defeats Larry Moquin
8/4/62:   Loses to Ray "Thunder" Storm
9/15/62:   Rematch with Storm (result unknown)
10/6/62:   Loses to Bruiser (DQ)
11/2/62:   Defeats Billy Red Lyons
11/24/62:   Faces Mark Lewin (result unknown)
12/8/62:   Loses to Lewin (COR)
3/2/63:   Defeats Angelo Savoldi
3/23/63:   Loses to Antonino Rocca
4/13/63:   Defeats Jim Hady
7/20/63:   Defeats Waldo Von Erich

8/10/63:	Faces Fritz Von Erich (result unknown)
2/8/64:	Defeats Lyons
2/29/64:	Loses to Layton
5/2/64:	Teams with Prof. Hiro to lose to Larry Chene and Edouard Carpentier
5/23/64:	Draw with Chene
8/8/64:	Faces Hady (result unknown)
11/27/64:	Defeats Bulldog Brower
12/13/64:	Defeats Von Erich (2/3 falls)
1/16/65:	Defeats Andy Robin
2/6/65:	*Wins US title from Johnny Valentine*
2/19/65:	Teams with Brower to lose to Brower and Bobo Brazil
3/5/65:	Defeats Mr. Kleen
3/20/65:	Defeats Sweet Daddy Siki
4/3/65:	Teams with Bruiser to lose to Valentine and Haystacks Calhoun
4/17/65:	Defeats Calhoun
5/1/65:	Defeats Art Thomas
5/15/65:	Defeats Calhoun
5/29/65:	Teams with Brower to defeat Brazil and Thomas
6/12/65:	Teams with Brower to lose to Brazil and Thomas
7/17/65:	Teams with Brower to defeat Brazil and Lewin (DQ)
7/31/65:	Draw with Brazil
8/14/65:	Loses to Brazil (DQ)
8/28/65:	Defeats Lewin (DQ)
9/11/65:	NC with Lewin
9/25/65:	Defeats Lewin (TX Death)
10/9/65:	Defeats Siki
10/30/65:	Defeats Chief Big Heart
11/13/65:	Defeats Johnny Powers
11/27/65:	Teams with Brower to defeat Brazil and Powers
12/11/65:	Teams with Brower to lose to Brazil and Powers
1/8/66:	Teams with Brower to defeat Brazil and Powers
1/22/66:	Defeats Vittorio Apollo (blood stoppage)
2/5/66:	Defeats Apollo

3/19/66: Defeats Powers

4/2/66: Teams with Killer Karl Kox to defeat Brazil and Lewin

4/16/66: Draw with Lewin

5/14/66: Loses to Cowboy Bob Ellis (DQ)

5/28/66: Defeats Lewin (TX Death)

7/9/66: Teams with Brower, NC with Lyons and Powers

7/23/66: Defeats Apollo

8/6/66: Teams with Bill Miller to lose to Brazil and Layton (DQ)

8/27/66: Teams with Miller to lose to Brazil and Layton (DQ)

9/10/66: *DDQ with Miller, US title held up*

9/24/66: *Defeats Miller to regain US title*

10/8/66: Teams with Bull Curry to defeat Lewin and Miller (DQ)

10/21/66: Teams with Bull Curry to lose to Brazil and Layton

11/5/66: Loses to Carpentier (DQ)

11/19/66: Loses to Carpentier (DQ)

12/2/66: Defeats Carpentier

12/17/66: Loses to Mighty Igor (DQ)

1/25/67: Defeats Jack Murphy

2/4/67: Draw with Igor

2/18/67: Defeats Igor

3/3/67: Teams with Kox to defeat Brazil and Igor

3/18/67: Teams with Kox to lose to Brazil and Igor

4/1/67: Draw with Brazil

4/15/67: Loses to Brazil (DQ)

5/13/67: Teams with Kox to lose to Brazil and Ernie Ladd

5/27/67: Defeats Ladd

6/10/67: Defeats Igor

7/8/67: Defeats Chief White Owl

7/22/67: Loses to Brazil (DQ)

8/5/67: *Loses US title to Brazil*

8/19/67: Defeats Layton

9/2/67: Defeats Lorenzo Parente

9/15/67: *Regains US title from Brazil in Dayton*

9/16/67: Defeats Lewin

9/30/67: Teams with Kox to lose to Brazil and Fred Curry

10/14/67:   Defeats Kox (2/3 falls)

10/28/67:   Defeats Fred Curry

11/11/67:   Defeats Fred Curry

11/26/67:   Defeats Don Leo Jonathan

12/9/67:   Loses to Brazil (DQ)

1/6/68:   Defeats Jonathan

1/20/68:   NC with Bull Curry

2/3/68:   Defeats Bull Curry

2/17/68:   Defeats Bull Curry (TX Death Cage)

3/2/68:   Defeats Bull Curry

3/23/68:   Defeats Oklahoma Kid (DQ)

4/20/68:   Defeats OK Kid

5/4/68:   Defeats Lou Klein

5/28/68:   Teams with Baron Von Raschke to lose to Lewin and OK Kid

6/7/68:   Teams with Raschke to defeat Brower and Fred Curry
            (2/3 falls, DQ)

6/22/68:   Defeats Lewin

7/27/68:   NC with Layton

8/10/68:   Defeats Layton (2/3 falls)

8/31/68:   Teams with Abdullah Farouk to lose to Layton and Brazil

9/14/68:   Loses to Brazil (DQ)

9/28/68:   Defeats Bull Curry

10/12/68:   Defeats Bull Curry (Chain)

10/26/68:   NC with Igor

11/9/68:   Defeats Igor

11/23/68:   Defeats Brower

12/7/68:   NC with Brazil

1/4/69:   Defeats Layton

1/18/69:   Defeats Jesse Ortega

2/1/69:   Defeats Ortega

2/15/69:   Defeats Carpentier

3/8/69:   Draw with Lewin

3/22/69:   Loses to Lewin (DQ)

4/5/69:   Defeats Lewin (No Time Limit/No DQ)

4/19/69:   DCOR with Rocky Johnson

5/3/69:	Defeats Johnson
5/24/69:	Defeats Dr. Jerry Graham
6/7/69:	NC with Thunderbolt Patterson
6/21/69:	Draw with Patterson
7/5/69:	Defeats Patterson (Stretcher)
7/19/69:	DDQ with Danny Hodge (NWA Jnr. Hwt.)
8/2/69:	Defeats Igor
8/16/69:	Defeats Igor
8/30/69:	Defeats Igor (Cage)
9/13/69:	Teams with Farouk to lose to Ivan Kalmikoff and Igor
10/11/69:	Defeats Billy Watson
10/25/69:	Defeats Lou Thesz
11/8/69:	Draw with Brazil
11/22/69:	Loses to Brazil (DQ)
12/6/69:	Defeats Brazil
12/27/69:	NC with Layton
1/17/70:	DCOR with Layton
1/31/70:	Defeats Layton (TX Death)
2/14/70:	DDQ with Fred Curry
2/28/70:	Defeats Fred Curry
3/21/70:	Loses to Calhoun (DQ)
4/4/70:	Defeats Calhoun (DQ)
4/18/70:	Defeats Calhoun (Cage)
5/2/70:	Defeats Calhoun (AK Death)
5/16/70:	Defeats Bull Curry (DQ)
5/30/70:	Defeats Bull Curry (Brass Knuckles)
6/13/70:	Defeats Fred Curry
7/11/70:	NC with Layton
7/25/70:	Loses to Layton (DQ)
8/22/70:	DDQ with Ladd
9/5/70:	Defeats Ladd (Igor ref)
9/19/70:	Defeats Igor
10/10/70:	Loses to Brazil (DQ)
10/24/70:	Draw with Luis Martinez (60:00)
11/7/70:	NC with Martinez (Sicilian Stretcher)

11/21/70: Defeats Martinez (Sicilian Stretcher)

12/5/70: Teams with Farouk to lose to Martinez and Layton

12/19/70: Defeats Layton

1/9/71: Loses to Tex McKenzie (DQ)

1/23/71: NC with McKenzie

2/6/71: Double KO with McKenzie

2/20/71: Defeats Martinez (Chain)

3/6/71: Defeats Fred Curry

4/3/71: Defeats McKenzie (TX Death)

4/17/71: Defeats The Stomper

5/1/71: Defeats The Stomper

5/15/71: Defeats Brazil (DQ)

5/29/71: *Loses US title to Brazil (Cage, Layton ref)*

6/12/71: Defeats Layton (Death)

7/17/71: Defeats McKenzie

9/18/71: Teams with Ladd, NC with Brazil and Fred Curry

10/2/71: Teams with Ladd to lose to Brazil and Curry (COR)

10/16/71: DDQ with Tiger Jeet Singh

10/30/71: Defeats Singh (Hindu Strap)

11/6/71: Defeats Patterson (DQ)

11/20/71: Defeats Fred Curry (DQ)

12/4/71: NC with Bull Curry

12/10/71: Defeats White Owl

12/18/71: Defeats Bull Curry (TX Death)

12/27/71: Defeats McKenzie (COR)

1/8/72: Teams with Pampero Firpo, NC with Bull Curry and McKenzie

1/22/72: Teams with Firpo, NC with Bull Curry and McKenzie

2/5/72: Teams with Firpo to lose to Bull Curry and McKenzie

2/19/72: Draw with Bruno Sammartino

2/26/72: Defeats Tony Marino

3/4/72: Draw with Martinez

3/18/72: Defeats Martinez

4/1/72: Teams with Firpo to defeat Martinez and Bull Curry (DQ)

4/8/72: Teams with Firpo to lose to Martinez and Bull Curry (Cage)

4/15/72:   Defeats The Stomper
4/22/72:   Defeats The Stomper
5/6/72:   Teams with Firpo to lose to The Stomper and Ben Justice (DQ)
5/20/72:   Defeats McKenzie (KO, Chain)
6/17/72:   Defeats Marino
7/1/72:   Draw with Jacques Rougeau
7/15/72:   Defeats Rougeau (French Death, Layton ref)
7/29/72:   DDQ with Marino
8/12/72:   NC with Marino (Italian Death)
8/19/72:   Defeats Marino
9/2/72:   Teams with Firpo to defeat Layton and Brazil (DQ)
9/16/72:   Defeats Marino
9/30/72:   Defeats Klein
10/14/72:   Teams with Firpo to defeat Brazil and Igor
11/11/72:   Defeats McKenzie
11/25/72:   Defeats McKenzie (TX Death)
12/9/72:   Defeats Dan Miller (COR)
12/23/72:   NC with Valentine
12/30/72:   *Wins US title from Brazil (Joe Louis ref)* — Pictured

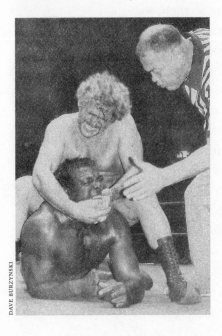

1/13/73:	*Loses US title to Brazil (Cage)*
1/27/73:	*Wins US title from Brazil (Valentine ref)*
2/10/73:	Defeats Valentine (TX Death)
2/24/73:	NC with Dory Funk Jr. (NWA World)
3/17/73:	NC with Bull Curry (Cage)
4/7/73:	NC with Bull Curry (TX Death)
4/21/73:	Defeats Bull Curry (Stretcher)
5/5/73:	Defeats Valentine (DQ)
5/19/73:	NC with Valentine
5/26/73:	Draw with Valentine
6/9/73:	Defeats Valentine (Cage)
6/23/73:	Teams with Firpo to lose to Valentine and Chief Jay Strongbow
7/7/73:	*Loses US title to Valentine*
7/21/73:	*Wins US title from Valentine*
8/18/73:	Defeats Dory Funk Jr. (DQ)
9/8/73:	Loses to Strongbow (DQ)
9/22/73:	Defeats Strongbow
10/6/73:	Defeats Strongbow
10/13/73:	Defeats Bull Curry
10/20/73:	Defeats Strongbow
11/3/73:	Defeats Bearcat Wright (DQ)
11/17/73:	Defeats Wright
12/1/73:	Defeats Brazil
12/15/73:	Teams with Firpo to lose to Igor and Valentine
12/29/73:	*DDQ with Firpo, US title held up*
1/5/74:	NC with Firpo
1/19/74:	NC with Firpo
2/2/74:	NC with Firpo
2/16/74:	*Defeats Firpo to regain US title*
3/2/74:	*Loses US title to Marino (10:15)*
3/16/74:	*Wins US title from Marino*
4/13/74:	Loses to Igor (COR)
4/27/74:	Defeats Igor (Polish Death)
5/11/74:	Teams with Killer Brooks, DDQ with Bruiser and Igor
5/25/74:	Defeats Firpo (COR)

6/15/74:	Loses to Ladd (DQ)
6/29/74:	Defeats Ladd
7/13/74:	Teams with Brooks to defeat Bruiser and Ladd
7/27/74:	Teams with Brooks to lose to Bruiser and Brazil (Cage)
9/14/74:	NC with Bruiser
9/28/74:	Defeats Bruiser (DQ)
10/5/74:	Defeats Bruiser (Cage)
10/20/74:	Teams with Justice to lose to Bruiser and Martinez
11/2/74:	Defeats Carpentier
11/30/74:	Loses to Firpo (DQ)
12/7/74:	Teams with Eddy Creatchman to defeat Bruiser and Firpo
12/21/74:	Teams with Abdullah the Butcher to lose to McKenzie and Igor
12/28/74:	Teams with Don Kent to lose to Brazil and Lewin
1/2/75:	Teams with Jacques Goulet to defeat Brazil and Thomas
1/11/75:	Defeats McKenzie
1/25/75:	*US title awarded to Brazil*
1/25/75:	Teams with Butcher to lose to Andre the Giant and McKenzie (DQ)
2/8/75:	Defeats Layton
4/19/75:	Defeats Firpo
5/3/75:	DDQ with Butcher
5/31/75:	Defeats Butcher
6/14/75:	Defeats Firpo
6/28/75:	Loses to Brazil (DQ)
7/5/75:	*Wins US title from Brazil*
7/19/75:	Loses to Hank James (COR)
8/2/75:	Teams with King Curtis to defeat Brazil and Lewin
8/16/75:	Defeats Firpo
8/30/75:	Teams with Kent to defeat Lewin and James
9/13/75:	Draw with Lewin
9/27/75:	*Loses US title to Lewin*
10/11/75:	Defeats Lewin (DQ)
10/18/75:	Defeats Firpo
10/25/75:	Defeats Lewin (US title, DQ)

11/1/75:	Defeats James
11/22/75:	Defeats Firpo (4:35)
12/6/75:	Defeats Igor
12/27/75:	Teams with Kent to lose to Lewin and Brazil (DQ)
2/14/76:	Defeats Lewin
5/1/76:	Loses to Lewin (DQ)
5/15/76:	*Wins US title from Brazil*
6/19/76:	Defeats Dominic Denucci
7/3/76:	Defeats Denucci
7/17/76:	*Loses US title to Firpo*
7/31/76:	Defeats Lewin
8/28/76:	NC with Patterson
9/4/76:	Teams with Kent to lose to Firpo and James (DQ)
9/18/76:	Defeats James
10/2/76:	Loses to James (DQ)
10/16/76:	Loses to James (Boxing Match, 5th round KO)
10/30/76:	Defeats The Spoiler (DQ)
11/6/76:	Defeats Marino
12/4/76:	Defeats James
1/8/77:	DDQ with Marino
1/22/77:	Teams with Butcher to defeat Bruiser and Marino
2/19/77:	Teams with Butcher to lose to Bruiser and Dusty Rhodes
3/19/77:	Loses to Brazil (DQ)
4/2/77:	*Wins US title from Gino Hernandez*
4/16/77:	Loses to Rhodes (DQ)
4/23/77:	Loses to Rhodes (DQ?)[1]
4/30/77:	Defeats Rhodes (DQ)
5/14/77:	Defeats James (sub for Fred Curry)
5/19/77:	Loses to Brazil (DQ)
6/11/77:	Teams with Kent to lose to Moose Cholak (Handicap)
6/25/77:	Faces Von Erich (result unknown)
7/9/77:	Loses to Terry Funk (DQ)
7/23/77:	Defeats Terry Funk
10/1/77:	Teams with Butcher to defeat Cholak and The Brute
10/15/77:	Loses to Butcher (DQ)

10/30/77:	Teams with Kent to lose to Cholak and Butcher (DQ)
11/12/77:	Defeats Butcher
11/27/77:	Defeats Crusher Verdu
12/18/77:	Defeats Peter Maivia (COR)
2/4/78:	*Loses US title to Ox Baker (Creatchman throws in towel)*
2/18/78:	Loses to Baker (DQ, US title)
3/4/78:	*Wins US title from Baker (Cage)*
3/18/78:	DCOR with Harley Race (NWA World)
4/1/78:	Loses to Mil Mascaras (DQ)
4/16/78:	Defeats Terry Funk
4/29/78:	Teams with Eric the Red to lose to Igor and Terry Funk
5/13/78:	Defeats Igor
5/27/78:	Defeats Igor (Stretcher)
6/10/78:	DCOR with Kent
6/24/78:	Teams with Brazil to defeat Kent and Nelson Royal
7/8/78:	Teams with Brazil to defeat Kent and Eric
7/22/78:	Teams with Capt. Ed George and Lewin to defeat Kent, Royal, and Stan Stasiak
8/5/78:	DDQ with Stasiak
8/19/78:	Defeats Stasiak (DQ, Andre ref)
9/24/78:	Teams with Brazil to defeat Kent and Royal
10/15/78:	Faces Stasiak (TX Death, Buddy Rogers ref, result unknown)
10/22/78:	*Wins US title from Terry Funk*
11/11/78:	Teams with Bruiser to defeat the Funks
1/1/79:	Defeats Kent (COR, Loser Leaves Town)
1/13/79:	Faces Stasiak (result unknown)
2/24/79:	Defeats Randy Savage (COR)
3/10/79:	Defeats Savage
3/31/79:	Draw with Baker (60:00)
4/14/79:	Defeats Baker
4/28/79:	Defeats Hernandez
5/19/79:	Faces Firpo and Igor (Handicap, result unknown)
6/2/79:	Defeats Igor (Chain, 44 seconds)
6/16/79:	Defeats Fred Curry (COR)
7/21/79:	Draw with Lewin

8/25/79:	Loses to Bob Backlund (COR, WWF World)
9/8/79:	Defeats Nikolai Volkoff
9/29/79:	Defeats Lewin
10/28/79:	DCOR with Backlund (WWF World)
11/11/79:	Loses to Ladd
11/24/79:	Defeats Gino Brito
1/19/80:	Teams with Butcher to defeat Strongbow and Dory Funk Jr.
2/2/80:	Teams with Butcher, DDQ with the Funks
2/15/80:	Loses to Jerry Oates (DQ)
3/1/80:	Teams with Butcher to defeat the Funks (Cage)
3/15/80:	Defeats Igor (sub for Dick Murdoch, DQ, 5:30)
3/29/80:	Defeats Igor (DQ)
4/12/80:	*Loses US title to Igor (Cage/Club)*
5/3/80:	*Wins US title from Igor (Cage)*
5/24/80:	Defeats Big Red
6/14/80:	Loses to Igor (DQ)
6/28/80:	Teams with Brooks to defeat Butcher and Ladd (DQ, Semifinals Tag Team title tournament)
6/28/80:	Teams with Brooks to lose to Giant Baba and Jumbo Tsuruta (Finals)
10/5/80:	Faces Dory Funk Jr. (Nail Board, result unknown)
10/12/80:	Defeats Bob White (sub for Brazil)
7/31/88:	Teams with Rhodes to defeat Murdoch and Kevin Sullivan (Cage, Great American Bash, 3:55)

THE SHEIK'S 127-MATCH UNDEFEATED SINGLES STREAK AT THE MAPLE LEAF GARDENS (1969–1974)

1.   2/9/69:   Bill Palmer (2:49)
2.   2/23/69:   The Mighty Igor
3.   3/16/69:   Bulldog Brower (10:30)
4.   3/30/69:   The Mighty Igor (6:26)
5.   4/13/69:   Whipper Billy Watson (DQ)
6.   5/18/69:   Whipper Billy Watson (DQ)
7.   6/1/69:   The Mighty Igor (7:34)
8.   6/29/69:   Gene Kiniski (2:39)
9.   7/13/69:   Bruno Sammartino (DQ)
10. 7/27/69:   Gene Kiniski (DQ)
11. 8/10/69:   Dominic Denucci (3:50)
12. 8/24/69:   Lou Thesz (5:04)
13. 9/7/69:   Lou Thesz (1:05)
14. 9/21/69:   Edouard Carpentier (5:36)
15. 10/5/69:   Dominic Denucci (COR, 7:32)
16. 10/19/69: Bulldog Brower (DQ, 6:52)
17. 11/2/69:   Lord Athol Layton (7:09)
18. 11/17/69: Bulldog Brower (15:33)
19. 11/30/69: Big Saka (4:48)
20. 12/14/69: Bobo Brazil
21. 12/28/69: Bobo Brazil
22. 1/18/70:   Dewey Robertson (DQ)
23. 2/8/70:   Lord Athol Layton (DDQ)

24. 2/22/70: Lord Athol Layton
25. 3/8/70: Whipper Billy Watson (COR)
26. 3/22/70: Lord Athol Layton
27. 4/5/70: "Flying" Fred Curry (COR)
28. 4/12/70: Wild Bull Curry (DQ)
29. 4/26/70: Haystacks Calhoun (DQ)
30. 5/10/70: Haystacks Calhoun
31. 5/24/70: "Flying" Fred Curry
32. 6/14/70: Lord Athol Layton (NC)
33. 6/21/70: Lord Athol Layton (COR)
34. 7/12/70: Haystacks Calhoun
35. 7/26/70: Bobo Brazil (DQ)
36. 8/16/70: Bobo Brazil (COR)
37. 8/30/70: The Mighty Igor (5:23)
38. 9/13/70: The Mighty Igor (5:12)
39. 9/20/70: "Flying" Fred Curry (DQ)
40. 10/4/70: Bobo Brazil (DQ)
41. 10/18/70: Whipper Billy Watson (DQ)
42. 11/1/70: Whipper Billy Watson (DQ)
43. 11/15/70: Whipper Billy Watson (COR)
44. 12/6/70: Lord Athol Layton
45. 12/13/70: Haystacks Calhoun
46. 12/27/70: Lord Athol Layton
47. 1/1/0/71: Tex McKenzie (DCOR)
48. 1/17/71: Tex McKenzie (TX Death)
49. 2/21/71: Tiger Jeet Singh (DQ)
50. 3/14/71: Tiger Jeet Singh (NC)
51. 3/21/71: Tiger Jeet Singh (TX Death)
52. 4/4/71: Haystacks Calhoun (Chain)
53. 4/18/71: Tex McKenzie (DQ)
54. 5/2/71: Lord Athol Layton (DDQ)
55. 5/16/71: Lord Athol Layton (Death)
56. 6/20/71: Angelo Mosca
57. 7/11/71: Masked Assassin (Stomper)
58. 7/25/71: Bobo Brazil (DQ)

59.	8/15/71:	Bobo Brazil (COR)
60.	8/29/71:	Big John Quinn (DDQ)
61.	9/5/71:	Big John Quinn (Death)
62.	9/12/71:	The Mighty Igor (DQ)
63.	9/26/71:	Tiger Jeet Singh (DCOR)
64.	10/17/71:	Tiger Jeet Singh (Indian Strap)
65.	10/31/71:	Tiger Jeet Singh (Indian Strap)
66.	11/14/71:	Luis Martinez (DQ)
67.	11/28/71:	Luis Martinez
68:	12/12/71:	Luis Martinez (Mex. Death)
69.	12/26/71:	Lord Athol Layton (DCOR)
70.	1/2/72:	Lord Athol Layton (Death)
71.	1/9/72:	Bulldog Brower
72.	2/6/72:	Carlos Rocha
73.	2/20/72:	Carlos Rocha
74.	3/5/72:	Carlos Rocha (DQ)
75.	3/19/72:	Pampero Firpo (COR)
76.	4/2/72:	Pampero Firpo (COR)
77:	4/16/72:	Carlos Rocha
78.	4/30/72:	Carlos Rocha (Port. Death)
79.	5/14/72:	Pampero Firpo (Jungle Strap)
80.	6/11/72:	Lord Athol Layton (Draw)
81.	6/25/72:	Lord Athol Layton (Death)
82.	7/9/72:	Ben Justice
83.	7/23/72:	The Beast
84.	8/13/72:	Tony Parisi (DQ)
85.	8/27/72:	The Magnificent Zulu
86.	9/10/72:	Tony Parisi (DQ)
87.	10/1/72:	The Magnificent Zulu (DQ)
88.	10/15/72:	The Magnificent Zulu
89.	10/29/72:	Sweet Daddy Siki (DQ)
90.	11/19/72:	Pampero Firpo (NC)
91.	12/3/72:	Pampero Firpo (Death)
92.	12/17/72:	Johnny Valentine (NC)
93.	12/28/72:	Tiger Jeet Singh (DDQ)

94. 1/14/73:   Tiger Jeet Singh (DCOR, 10:38)
95. 2/4/73:   Tiger Jeet Singh (7:06)
96. 2/11/73:   Tony Marino
97. 3/4/73:   Chief Jay Strongbow (NC)
98. 3/18/73:   Chief Jay Strongbow (DQ, 3:40)
99. 4/1/73:   Chief Jay Strongbow
100. 4/8/73:   Lord Athol Layton
101. 4/29/73:   Chief Jay Strongbow (20:48)
102. 5/13/73:   Bobo Brazil (Draw, 60:00)
103. 5/27/73:   Bobo Brazil (DDQ, 10:00)
104. 6/10/73:   Bobo Brazil (Death, 12:56)
105. 6/24/73:   Eric the Red (6:24)
106. 7/8/73:   Pampero Firpo (COR, 12:18)
107. 7/22/73:   Johnny Valentine (DQ, 3:18)
108. 8/12/73:   Johnny Powers (DCOR, 4:37)
109. 9/23/73:   Tony Marino (4:13)
110. 10/14/73: Johnny Powers (Death, 3:14)
111. 10/28/73: Johnny Powers (Death)
112. 11/11/73: Bearcat Wright (DQ, 2:28)
113. 11/25/73: Dominic Denucci (DCOR)
114. 12/2/73:   Dominic Denucci (Death)
115. 12/16/73: Billy Red Lyons
116. 12/30/73: Andre the Giant (DDQ, 2:58)
117. 2/10/74:   Andre the Giant (DDQ, 4:15)
118. 2/17/74:   Andre the Giant (COR)
119. 3/3/74:   Chief Jay Strongbow (DQ)
120. 3/31/74:   Chief Jay Strongbow (COR)
121. 4/7/74:   Dewey Robertson (COR)
122. 4/21/74:   Dewey Robertson
123. 5/12/74:   Edouard Carpentier (DQ)
124. 5/26/74:   Edouard Carpentier
125. 6/9/74:   Ernie Ladd (DDQ)
126. 6/23/74:   Ernie Ladd (TX Death)
127. 7/21/74:   Edouard Carpentier
     8/11/74:   *Loses to Andre the Giant (DQ)*

NOTES

CHAPTER 2

1   It's not entirely clear what the name was short for. It may have been
    Zakiya, a popular Arabic girl's name meaning "pure and innocent."
    The 1913 ship's manifest of her arrival in the US at age four lists a
    handwritten name that is not fully legible but may be "Zabnit."

2   The ship's manifest indicates that Latife was met at the port by
    "cousin" Khalil Farhat. It is unknown if this was her brother-in-law
    Assad Khalil, one of Davoud's cousins, or someone else entirely.

CHAPTER 3

1   The house, along with all the other properties on the block, would
    many years later be purchased by General Motors and razed to the
    ground to make way for new construction.

2   A matter of some conjecture: The birth certificate indicated June
    7 as the date of birth, but Eva was said to maintain that the birth
    certificate was off by two days. I choose to defer to the person who
    certainly would know better than anyone.

3   Lewie and his wife, Agnes, would later also reside in the house with
    their own children. Prior to Eva's mother's passing in February 1940,
    the house was home to eighteen people. It is not known if other
    siblings lived there with their families in later years.

4   "Nobody would say that hers has been an easy life," states an

in-depth profile in the May 10, 1953, edition of the *Lansing State Journal*, "But jolly, motherly Latifa is stronger and happier than most women of her age."

5 One particular Syrian-American Al-Ashab garden party in the summer of 1933 featured nine-year-old Edmund Farhat marveling the crowd with recitations in Arabic and English. Six years later, fourteen-year-old Edmund gave a speech in Arabic on American freedom for the opening of the Syrian-American Workmen's Association Home in Lansing—an event partly organized by his older brother Joseph.

6 As all Sheik fans know, Farhat would later bestow the ring name "Sabu" on his nephew Terry Brunk. In his 2019 autobiography, *Scars, Silence, & Superglue*, Brunk recalls that his uncle had earlier given the name to his beloved white German shepherd.

CHAPTER 4

1 Edmund was also the father of David Farhat, a prominent Michigan politician named for his grandfather.

2 Topper, Lewie, and Moses were also standout school athletes, with the first two later joining Edmund as very successful amateur softball players in their day.

3 After the war, PFC Moses Farhat was awarded the Bronze Star Medal for meritorious service in combat. He was known for his extraordinary bravery in removing the wounded from several battlefields.

4 There is reason to believe that Edward had already been trying his hand at wrestling at the local Lansing YMCA while a teen, but no records exist to corroborate this.

5 This was also the date of the execution of Benito Mussolini, former Italian dictator and one of the original pillars of the Axis powers—a major signal of the imminent end of the war.

CHAPTER 5

1 This disease was caused in many cases such as Weissmuller's by infections from bacteria that thrived on dirty ring mats and was

common among pro wrestlers in those early days. Other victims included Ed "Strangler" Lewis and "Terrible Turk" Yussif Mahmout.

2   Sandow had previously been part of the most powerful of all early wrestling syndicates, the Gold Dust Trio, along with Strangler Lewis and Joe "Toots" Mondt.

3   He would be christened "Wild Bull" Curry in later years by Houston promoter Paul Boesch.

4   Weissmuller's promotional partners Al Haft and Fred Kohler were pallbearers at his funeral.

5   With Britton as front man, Light's wrestling office also managed the booking of midget wrestling talent across North America.

6   His actual height is a matter of some debate. For example, both his close associate Dave Burzynski and daughter-in-law Kari Farhat insisted it was closer to the five-foot-eleven figure, while friend and colleague Kevin Sullivan maintained it was closer to five feet eight inches, and that Sheik was not much taller than he was.

7   Several sources, including Detroit wrestling historian Mark Bujan, have indicated as much, although it is possible this may be related to the urban legend of The Sheik being an MSU alum.

8   Klein later achieved the greatest notoriety of his pro career under the name Lou Bastien, teaming with Red Bastien as the Bastien Brothers tag team for Vincent J. McMahon's Capitol Wrestling in the early sixties.

9   Gary Cubeta's 57Talk.com. (All quotes from Eddie Jr. used in this book going forward come from that interview, unless otherwise noted.)

10 An impromptu footrace with another neighborhood youth on April 16, 1947, resulted in twenty-year-old Eddie falling flat on his face and being treated at a nearby hospital for minor bruises and lacerations. Some might call it the first time The Sheik got color.

CHAPTER 6

1   Like his future son-in-law, Fleser had also served in the war, specifically as a flight instructor for the Air Force.

2   Badui was also alleged to be the uncle of Frankie Cain ("The Great

Mephisto") and Jimmy Wehba ("Skandor Akbar"), two other "sheik" style performers Farhat would later accuse of stealing his gimmick.

3   After retiring from the ring in the 1960s, Warshawski was often used as a referee for many of Sheik's Big Time Wrestling shows at Cobo Hall and around Michigan.

4   The ubiquitous nature of the song is proven by its inclusion in the classic Jazz Age novel *The Great Gatsby* by F. Scott Fitzgerald.

5   Zieckie's husband, Solomon, had died two years prior—their teenaged son, James, was cared for by David and Latife in the big Williams Street house afterward.

CHAPTER 7

1   It is possible that this Chicago debut was the Klein match that Sheik described to Dave Burzynski as his first.

2   As relayed by Jim Lancaster to Steven Johnson and Greg Oliver in their 2007 book, *The Pro Wrestling Hall of Fame: The Heels.*

3   Joe was actually Ferdinando Carmine Muccioli (aka Joe Dorsetti, aka Fred Dorsetti), not to be confused with Gilberto Melendez, who later took on the "Gypsy Joe" moniker in the 1960s and used it till his retirement in 2011.

4   As told by Sheik to his nephew, Sabu (*Scars, Silence, & Superglue*).

5   There is some conjecture as to whether Thesz followed Sheik out into the snow. Popular legend says he did, but Thesz himself, recollecting the incident on the WrestlingClassics message board forty-five years later, didn't remember doing so: "When I didn't buckle to his antics and wanted him to wrestle, he just walked out of the ring and didn't come back. He was a great guy, but not a wrestler."

6   As testament to their revered standing in the local Syrian-American Catholic community, the celebration included a papal blessing obtained from Pope Pius XII, as well as a card of support from the Archbishop of Hauran, Syria.

CHAPTER 8

1   Often in his career, new heels would be put together with Sheik

to get the "rub" from the hated performer and cement their "evil" nature in the eyes of the fans.

2 Her name sometimes varied from place to place—she was occasionally billed as "Princess Fatima," "Princess Salome," and other variations. But Princess Salima seems to be the version most commonly used and the one she used for autographs. In her acceptance speech for The Sheik's 2007 WWE Hall of Fame induction, Joyce indicated that it was Vincent J. McMahon who first suggested she take on the princess role when her husband was brought into Capitol Wrestling.

3 McMahon had a successful track record with wrestler monikers over the years, being the man who named such stars as Blackjack Mulligan, Bruiser Brody, and even Hulk Hogan.

4 Some sources claim Light was bought out, but this seems unlikely, given that he was out of business by 1961.

5 TV tapings took place not in an arena, but in a TV studio with a small audience—an innovation credited to Barnett, which would become the standard in the industry for decades.

6 In the early sixties, Buffalo TV wrestling announcer Bill Mazer sometimes comically referred to the hold as the "Lebanese leg-up."

7 Rocca won each of these, a testament to the respect he still commanded, as he was one of the only wrestlers to consistently beat The Sheik by this point.

8 A title made popular by lifelong fan and eventual manager of The Sheik, Dave Burzynski.

9 Sonny Weaver was actually Sonny Myers, who had no qualms about working for an outlaw promotion, having successfully sued the NWA over its monopolistic practices several years earlier.

10 In his 1988 book *Drawing Heat*, Jim Freedman erroneously records the nickname as "Zip," believing it to be a reference to The Sheik's common practice of cutting himself with razor blades.

11 Sarpolis was an actual doctor, having earned his medical degree from Loyola University in 1926.

CHAPTER 9

1 Dory Funk, also on the card tag teaming with his son, had helped

get Farhat booked with Sam Muchnick, despite Muchnick's trepidations about using him.

2   As told to Steven Johnson and Greg Oliver in their 2012 book, *The Pro Wrestling Hall of Fame: Heroes and Icons*.

3   From the November 27, 1964, edition of *Body Press*, courteously provided by Detroit wrestling historian Mark Bujan. In another column penned just a few weeks prior, around the time of the sale, Doyle did an aggressive hit job on Dick the Bruiser and Wilbur Snyder, taking a parting shot at the group trying to muscle in on Detroit.

4   In addition to drawing blood from his head, Sheik was occasionally known to draw it from his arms—a practice he apparently invented and which was copied by a later heavy practitioner of the blading art, Dusty Rhodes.

5   Burzynski was first pulled into the world of wrestling as a kid through an unlikely friendship with none other than Larry Chene, who lived upstairs from Dave in the Detroit house his parents owned.

6   The present-day Sacramento Kings.

7   The title was essentially built around Valentine, Tunney bringing him in with the belt in 1962 as the first champion.

8   Strongman and fellow Lansing native Ernie Bemis, who got his wrestling name due to his resemblance to the cleaning product mascot.

9   Both letters provided by meticulous historian and NWA expert Tim Hornbaker.

10 I reached out to Bert Ruby's son Allen, now a highly successful California attorney whose clients include two-time Super Bowl champion Deion Sanders, and he declined to discuss anything having to do with The Sheik, lending credence, in my own estimation, to the notion of there having been bad blood between Farhat and his father.

11 The only place where he continued to be billed as "The Sheik of Araby."

12 This gimmick would later be infamously "borrowed" in the 1970s by Ivan Putski.

CHAPTER 10

1 Jim Freedman.

2 Terry passed away just four months after this interview was conducted, at age seventy-five.

3 The rather regal Vincent J. McMahon, who, like many, had once employed Farhat and now found himself having to share the proverbial table with him, was one of those rumored to have privately looked down their nose at him.

4 Interview conducted in November 2019, just seven months before Brooks lost his battle with cancer.

5 As told to producer, podcaster, documentarian, and wrestling historian Evan Ginzburg in 2004 for his acclaimed *Wrestling Then & Now* newsletter.

6 Coincidentally, one of the wrestlers he managed at this time was Ernie Bemis, who was using a "Mr. Kleen" gimmick.

7 Paul later reinvented himself as Chris Colt and became one of pro wrestling's most mysterious figures, exploring fetish imagery in his persona while battling drug and alcohol addiction. He vanished in the 1990s and is believed by some to have died of AIDS in a Washington halfway house, although his whereabouts were never conclusively proven.

8 The Olympic Auditorium had even been a filming location in several classic Hollywood films of the era, including *The Manchurian Candidate* and *Requiem for a Heavyweight*, both in 1962.

9 Fred Blassie had another theory about the friendship between LeBell and Sheik, which he elaborated on in his 2003 autobiography: "LeBell and The Sheik were intimate friends, and I think I know why. In addition to wrestling, The Sheik was the promoter in Detroit. That meant that he could vote for NWA president. One day, LeBell fantasized, The Sheik would help get him elected."

10 Of note to wrestling fans is that Galento holds the distinction of a second-round knockout over Fred Blassie in the future King of Men's one and only boxing effort, a June 1943 bout in Knoxville, Tennessee.

11 Items of note: their March 26 Baltimore encounter was the first steel cage match ever held in that city; for the February 24 Boston

match, Abdullah Farouk was handcuffed to Bruno's manager, Arnold Skaaland; the last meeting of the feud, on March 29, drew 15,125, setting an all-time indoor sporting event record for Boston.

12 For his part, Sammartino seems not to have been thrilled with wrestling The Sheik. In his 1990 autobiography, he wrote of the experience: "Even though he had good wrestling skills, he chose not to use them most of the time. He was an unorthodox guy who did weird things in the ring that really threw you off guard. The Sheik wasn't the type of wrestler with whom you felt you could pit your skills against and give the fans a match that could be appreciated. Instead, he would go in and out of the ring constantly. When he finally did step in to lock horns with you, just as fast he would duck out under the ropes. He made having a legitimate bout very difficult. I can honestly say I did not enjoy wrestling with The Sheik . . . because I didn't feel that I was giving the crowd the caliber of match that they had paid to see."

13 The legendary originator of this persona, El Medico (aka Medico Asesino), had met—and defeated—The Sheik in San Antonio in 1956.

14 To add insult to injury, The Sheik booked himself over Thesz yet again just a few weeks later in a thirty-five-minute match at Cobo Arena. It's almost as if Farhat were taking a victory lap or two around the ex-champion who had looked down on him all those years ago.

15 Firpo's catch-phrase "Ohhhh yeaaahhh!!" would later be adapted and coopted by another wide-eyed and wild-haired dynamo of the squared circled, Randy "Macho Man" Savage.

16 Thanks to Rogers's influence, Wrestling Show Classics was even able to get on the air in New Jersey and also in the Philadelphia area, where on October 18, 1969, they got to be the first wrestling promotion to present a show at the brand-new home of the Flyers and 76ers, the Spectrum—five years before the WWWF got there. The card was headlined by Lewin taking on Davis's "World Champion" (and best pal) Johnny Barend.

17 Now the site of an assisted living facility for seniors.

18 Father of Dwayne "The Rock" Johnson.

19 Mitchell later went on to become Jerry Valiant, joining Johnny and Jimmy in that notorious brother cooperative. After retiring, he stayed in the Detroit area to build wrestling rings, including both the main ring and the iconic motorized mini-rings used to ferry wrestlers up and down the aisle for the WWF's *WrestleMania III* in the Pontiac Silverdome.

CHAPTER II

1 Layton was unique among wrestling announcers of the time, in that he was still an active competitor as well; as a lead babyface he would often get physically involved against the heels, even while performing announcing duties.

2 Sheik superfan and future manager Dave Burzynski recalls how, at age sixteen, he was so incensed at the miscarriage of justice that he verbally called out Brazil at the next TV tapings, causing the new champion to break character and have him ejected from the crowd. (The two made up years later, after Dave joined the business himself.)

3 A son of Marion County, Indiana, Kent's decidedly non-Australian background was politely overlooked; he didn't even try to feign an Aussie accent.

4 Note the intentional spelling change, to avoid the wrath of DC Comics.

5 Sheik and Wright had wrestled several times before, including matches at Madison Square Garden and Cobo Arena, and Bearcat had even scored a rare pinfall on The Sheik in their first encounter in Montreal back in 1958, a testament to his popularity—and political deftness.

6 At the time of the match, Brazil had been temporarily divested of his United States title, which was declared vacant six days earlier after Ernie Ladd defeated him by count out in Cobo Arena. Just eight days after the LA Coliseum super-show, Brazil reclaimed the US crown by beating Ladd in a return bout.

7 This figure would be tied just one time, by a January 13, 1973, card that saw Brazil win the US title from The Sheik in a steel cage.

8   An April 17, 1965, title defense against the Masked Marvel (Joe Christie), and a February 19, 1966, defense against Bulldog Brower.

9   Finnigan's frustration over the deal may have played a part in his taking a sabbatical from Big Time Wrestling.

10 One of the label's releases was "The Ballad of Bobo Brazil," written and performed by Finnigan.

11 Dave Burzynski tells an amusing story of riding around Sheik's property with Killer Tim Brooks on mini-bikes and accidentally running them through his vegetable garden, then trying to cover it up. Just the fact that The Sheik had a vegetable garden is probably amusing enough for most.

12 Luis Martinez, another Sheik loyalist, would later switch sides as well—but be welcomed back with open arms, as always.

13 On July 26, Abdullah Farouk himself made a rare in-ring appearance alongside his protégé in Honolulu, taking on the father-son team of Bull and Fred Curry. Naturally, the weaselly manager took the fall for the team.

14 Which drew twenty-six thousand fans—a new Montreal attendance record for wrestling—to Jarry Park, home of the Montreal Expos.

15 The referee for the match was Lou Thesz, no stranger to the NWA World Heavyweight title—or to The Sheik.

16 Sheik and Morales had encountered each other several times over the years working in Hawaii, including a September 20, 1972, date they worked together, which may have planted the seeds for this brief WWWF run, including the two world title shots against the Puerto Rican champion.

17 Albano's title had its roots in reality, inspired by his role as captain of his high school football team.

18 Roth would remain with the McMahon family for the next decade, until his untimely death from a heart attack in 1983 at age fifty-seven.

19 His famous ring name was reportedly given to him by Dick the Bruiser when he first booked Andre in the WWA the year before.

20 Judging only by the participants in the match, it is possible that Farhat was being booked as a babyface on this night, which

would've been the first time since the invention of his Sheik persona.

21 Pure speculation: is it possible that the reason for the last-minute booking switch on November 29 was that The Sheik had originally been pegged to defeat Morales and be the transitional heel WWWF World Champion but backed out of the deal because he refused to be pinned by Sammartino in the middle of the ring at Madison Square Garden, and thus Stasiak was put into the role instead? It's difficult to otherwise explain why Morales would've been suddenly taken from a major arena card and sent to defend his title at a nearby high school.

CHAPTER 12

1 Prior to ever coming to Japan, Sheik had battled Baba in the LA Olympic Auditorium on September 12, 1969, in a two-out-of-three falls match for Baba's International Heavyweight title, a championship sanctioned by the National Wrestling Alliance for use in the JWA.

2 The station that helped popularize anime and sci-fi series like *Kamen Rider* and *Super Sentai* (aired in the US as *Power Rangers*).

3 Abdullah took the gold from none other than Bobo Brazil, an honor in and of itself.

4 He was also fresh off his acting turn playing Frankie the Thumper in Sylvester Stallone's wrestling picture *Paradise Alley*, the 1940s setting of which explains Terry's close-cropped hair at the time of the tournament.

5 The match would finally be aired on Japanese TV for the first time in the 1990s.

6 And there were several knockoffs floating around. Jimmy Wehba of Texas rebranded himself Skandor Akbar (Arabic for "Alexander the Great") in the mid-1960s and carried the act well into the 1980s as a manager. Iraqi wrestler Adnan Al-Kaissie, a high school buddy of Saddam Hussein, used a Native American gimmick through most of the sixties and seventies as Billy White Wolf, but by the start of the eighties was going by Sheik Adnan Al-Kaissie in the AWA. He was also notably used as a Sheik knockoff in the mid-1970s by

Antonio Inoki, who had refrained from using the real one. But of course, the most noteworthy Sheik pretender was yet to come . . .

7   Baba was by this point a three-time NWA World Champion himself, having finagled a series of very brief title reigns from the NWA committee, then headed by Jim Barnett, during tours by champions Jack Brisco and Harley Race.

8   Acclaimed AWA World Tag Team Championship duo of the 1960s.

CHAPTER 13

1   Tim Brooks told the story of getting the two together, when a nervous and shy Eddie Jr. convinced him to call Kathy and ask her out, pretending to be him. Brooks served as Eddie Jr.'s best man at the wedding, with his then-wife, Connie, serving as Kathy's matron of honor.

2   Sika is the father of Joe Anoa'i, better known as Roman Reigns, one of WWE's hottest current stars.

3   Dubois, real name Lamarche, went on to greater notoriety as Alexis Smirnoff, using a Soviet heel gimmick.

4   In one form or another, Lawler would hold the top title in Memphis a total of seventy-one times between 1973 and 1997, when the territory finally closed up for good.

5   Farhat also got his bodyguard Mike Loren booked on the Memphis card. In addition to working as a police officer, Loren wrestled regularly around the Michigan-Ontario area, for a time billed as "Porky the Pig"—no doubt a rib by his sardonic boss.

6   This was Gagne's second show at Comiskey since the AWA moved into Chicago in the mid-1960s. Still in character after the match, Sheik can be seen in locker room footage licking blood from the face of a visibly disgusted Heenan.

7   The other being a July 18, 1975, match in Vicksburg, Mississippi.

8   November 16, 1974.

9   Memphis wrestler Willie Jackson.

10 It's reasonable to assume that Einhorn may even have been working the concession stands at Comiskey for the two extravaganzas The Sheik worked for Fred Kohler in the summer of '60.

11 Dave Burzynski disputes the accuracy of Eddie Jr.'s claim, believing that The Sheik would've jumped at such a financial windfall had it been offered at that juncture.

12 Kent also took over many of the responsibilities of the retiring Lou Klein, including booking and supervising the smaller spot shows on Farhat's circuit.

13 Aka Jacques Dubois, aka Pierre Dubois, etc.

14 Title changes would sometimes be repeated for the live crowds in different towns in those days before the internet, when fans were often completely in the dark as to what had just happened in other venues on the circuit. Incidentally, this particular Sheik-Lewin match is probably the Big Time Wrestling match from over the years most commonly found on home video, YouTube, and other media sources.

15 Having been trained in shoot wrestling by consummate catch wrestler Karl Gotch, Inoki had been on a mission to demonstrate that pro wrestlers could be taken seriously as legitimate fighters, and his endeavors at this time are pointed to by many as having planted the seeds for the sport of mixed martial arts.

16 Sheik was not the only wrestler advertised in this capacity. McMahon, for example, placed his man Fred Blassie in that position as well, which was probably advantageous since Blassie was able to speak in public, as he did during a memorable *Tonight Show* appearance with Ali to help promote the fight.

17 Other highlights included Sammartino vs. Stan Hansen at Shea, NWA World Champion Terry Funk vs. Rocky Johnson in the Sam Houston Coliseum, AWA World Champion Nick Bockwinkel vs. Gagne in the International Amphitheatre, Jack Brisco vs. Dory Funk Jr. in the Omni, Gory Guerrero vs. Roddy Piper in the Olympic Auditorium, and Pat Patterson vs. Mr. Fuji in the Cow Palace.

18 Von Erich's circuit was also known as Big Time Wrestling but would eventually rebrand as World Class Championship Wrestling.

19 During his Lone Star State forays, The Sheik was not managed by Eddy Creatchman, who remained up north, but rather by Texas-based manager "Playboy" Gary Hart.

20 2017 Facebook post.

21 He'd eventually get an associate producer credit on the film as R.C. Finnigan.

22 Greenberg regrets not bringing movie cameras to the party; he did make some audio recordings, which he claims to have never played back in forty-five years.

23 Despite the abandonment of the horror film idea, some elements still survived in the script for the finished film (what there is of it), with characters heard discussing The Sheik's "Satanic" influences.

24 Greenberg recalls having to coach the nervous Andre extensively even for that one simple line, as the Frenchman had a very minimal command of the English language at the time.

25 This nevertheless didn't stop Farhat from paradoxically briefly bringing in Cannon as an on-air babyface manager for his son, proving that the wrestling business always makes the strangest bedfellows.

CHAPTER 14

1 This would place it as either the September 30, 1978, or the October 8, 1978, show, when The Sheik was in Chicago wrestling Dick the Bruiser for Verne Gagne, and Chattanooga wrestling Andre the Giant for Nick Gulas, respectively.

2 Farhat's own words as told to Jim Freedman in *Drawing Heat*: "I bought Detroit from Jim Barnett 16 years ago for $50,000 and I didn't even have to pay him any money. I could have stole it if I wanted to, but I didn't. Now you wanna know why Detroit's going down? Cause Barnett stabbed me in the back . . . I used to book my wrestlers from him. I'd pay the fee and put them on the show, and you know what happened? That'll kill your business, promising big names and the big names never show. Thank Barnett for that. I bought the territory from [him] and then he turned around and screwed the business so he could steal the business back later on."

3 The Farhats were not the only ones with marital strife, as The Sheik's in-ring archenemy but real-life best friend, Bobo Brazil, was

going through a messy divorce; in a situation that would've made any Big Time Wrestling fan's head explode, he was invited to live at the Farhat estate from late 1977 into 1978 while he battled with his wife, Kathleen, over their home and custody of their son, Randall.

4   This match marked the Cobo return of Ernie Roth, now working as the Grand Wizard, manager of Graham.

5   Greenberg recalls being disappointed when Heather was booked to wrestle Smokey, one of Dave McKigney's bears, at the December 18, 1977, Cobo show and no one from the promotion thought to alert the film crew. From then on, they made sure to be on hand whenever Heather was. As for Smokey, less than seven months later the bear was taken from McKigney's custody after escaping its cage and mauling his girlfriend to death.

6   Run by Nick Gulas's brother Gus.

7   Big Time Wrestling would return to Cincinnati just one more time, fifteen months later, with a card at the smaller Convention Center. Not even Andre the Giant and Haystacks Calhoun in a battle royal was enough to draw more than 1,650 fans.

8   Oates holds the impressive distinction of having wrestled Bruiser Brody and The Sheik in the same day, as he faced Brody that afternoon in Kansas City before traveling to Toledo for his evening match with Sheik.

9   Farhat along with Bruiser and Snyder were the only ones to choose their own counsel rather than be represented by the NWA's lawyers.

10   Also making the trip down to Puerto Rico with The Sheik and the Butcher was Don Kent, who captured the WWC Caribbean title on the same card.

11   These would be the only two times that The Sheik competed for the (W)WWF World title at his home base of Cobo Arena.

12   Rob Van Dam, a later trainee of Farhat's, remembers hearing about Eddie Jr.'s 1980 retirement from The Sheik himself: "He was trying to help book him and get him work and he said that one day Eddie just told him that's not what he wanted to do. And he was like, 'Why the fuck didn't you tell me that? You don't have to wrestle if you don't want to.'"

13　Chavo's father, Gory, like Blue Demon, had been a frequent tag team partner of the fabled Santo.

14　Another possible reason for booking Backlund in Canton was that ten days earlier, when Farhat was running Cobo, Backlund was busy at the Philadelphia Spectrum defending the title against the man who would eventually succeed him as the WWF's standard-bearer, Hulk Hogan.

15　Despite not winning the title, Backlund celebrated afterward by strapping both The Sheik's US title and the WWF World title belts around his waist, captured in an iconic photograph that made the rounds in the wrestling magazines at the time.

CHAPTER 15

1　Tunney passed away in 1983, leaving Maple Leaf Wrestling in the hands of his son Eddie and nephew Jack.

2　Occasionally, he could still use his clout to bring in some big names, as he did in March and April 1981, when he brought his one-time protégé George "The Animal" Steele, now a national headliner, to the Lincoln Park Community Center.

3　He also worked his final known match in Amarillo on April 2, 1982—against Terry Funk, fittingly enough.

4　Tales of Sheik's wild driving abound, and it was said he was well-acquainted with speed trap locations. Mickey Doyle tells a story of riding with Mike Loren and Tex McKenzie to a show in Kitchener, Ontario, with The Sheik driving sixty miles an hour through a blinding snowstorm, and McKenzie very loudly fearing for his life all the way.

5　Personal injury lawsuit filed by the Farhats on May 14.

6　Not quite old enough to have taken part in his dad's business in the way his much older brother, Eddie, had been, in the wake of Big Time Wrestling's demise, Tommy developed a passion for autobody repair, beginning what would be a successful and satisfying career.

7　Eldest child of The Sheik's brother Topper.

8　The exact timeline isn't quite clear, but it seems at some point in the 1980s, after losing their palatial mansion, the Farhats may have moved back into the home they had previously occupied on East Grand River Avenue, which they apparently had never sold. The description given in Terry's autobiography indicates that at the time he moved in with them they may have still been occupying the larger home. The obituary for Joyce's father in December 1985 lists Joyce's residence as Haslett, which might mean she and her husband were living apart at that point.

9 He probably got the bookings thanks to the Trinidad promotion's close relationship with Colon and Jovica's WWC in Puerto Rico.

10 My own personal theory which I can't prove: the name was partly inspired by Hellenic ring villain Spiros Arion, then known as "The Iron Greek."

11 This was just two months after Sawyer's "Last Battle of Atlanta" against Tommy Rich in the same building.

12 It's worth noting that McMahon had snatched The Iron Sheik from Jim Barnett, for whom he had been wrestling for about a year before coming to the WWF. Knowing that he was about to win the world title at MSG, it's possible that Barnett purposely chose to mend fences and book the true, original Sheik one night before at the Omni as an act of vindictiveness.

13 McMahon was certainly not above a little bait and switch to try and pop a new territory, such as when he acquired the services of Harley Race in 1986 and repackaged him as "King of Wrestling" partly in an attempt to move into the sacrosanct stronghold of Memphis, then still firmly held by Jerry Jarrett and Jerry "The King" Lawler. In that case, the ploy failed, as Jarrett and Lawler took legal action and won, removing Race from the card. Ironically, when Lawler himself joined the WWF ranks six years later, he was given Race's old royal entrance music for his own.

14 It's unclear whether this may have been a wrestling spot, a role as a backstage road agent, or a combination of both. McMahon was known during this period to find work for some of the older territorial headliners, either in the front office or as a means of helping draw crowds in their old stomping grounds, as he did with Mad Dog Vachon, the Briscos, The Crusher, the Funks, and others.

15 Greenberg even worked as a cameraman for director John Landis on Michael Jackson's groundbreaking *Thriller* video.

16 Home video was a natural fit for wrestling, and there were already two projects in the works at other companies: *Lords of the Ring: Superstars and Superbouts*, released in conjunction with London Publishing, publisher of *Pro Wrestling Illustrated* and other magazines; and the first volume of The Best of the WWF series, produced by Titan Sports and Coliseum Home Video. Both were released in early 1985.

17 Boone's song "Heart Punch," featured in the film, contains backward-tracked samples of actual crowd noise he recorded at Cobo Arena during his years as a fan of Big Time Wrestling.

18 Although he mentions the tour in his autobiography, and Kevin Sullivan referred to joining The Sheik there during our interview, I was not able to find any record of these matches.

19 Cannon's experience was echoed by that of other territorial promoters the WWF initially "partnered" with, such as Mike LeBell and Paul Boesch.

20 A card headlined by WWF World Champion Hulk Hogan and Ricky Steamboat against The Magnificent Muraco and Mr. Fuji. The Iron Sheik jerked the curtain that night in the opening match.

21 Shortly after her husband's death, Maivia had reportedly been assured by Vincent J. McMahon that his son's expansion plans would not extend to Hawaii. This may be another reason he waited so much longer to invade the fiftieth state.

22 Not to be confused with the Mid-South booker and father of Jake "The Snake" Roberts, of the same name.

23 A shameless knockoff of James Harris's iconic "Kamala the Ugandan Giant" gimmick.

24 During The Sheik's rampage through the frightened but sparse crowd, among those fleeing in his path can be spotted Lia Maivia herself, as well as her grandson, fourteen-year-old Dwayne Johnson.

25 In order to lay claim to the all-time indoor attendance record for sports and entertainment, the WWF inflated the number to 93,173, but this figure has long since been debunked.

26 It's been said that Gonzalez had been holding a grudge against
    Brody dating back to 1976, due to perceived liberties taken against
    him in a series of matches when they were both in the WWWF,
    Brody as a headliner and Gonzalez as enhancement talent. Due to
    the failure of the Puerto Rican justice system, Gonzalez walks free
    to this day.

27 Also in the van were popular Canadian twin brother tag team
    Victor and William Arko, aka Pat and Mike Kelly. Victor was killed
    in the crash, while William was the lone survivor. Traveling on the
    tour with his father, though thankfully not in the van at the time,
    was McKigney's eight-year-old son, Davey.

28 At one of these events, on September 25, 1987, Ronnie Garvin
    defeated Ric Flair to win the NWA World Heavyweight title,
    marking the first and only time that title had ever changed hands
    in Cobo Arena and the first world heavyweight title change of any
    kind in Detroit since Ali Baba's victory at Olympia Stadium in 1936.

29 His replacement was Larry Zbyszko, whom Crockett had recruited
    from Verne Gagne's struggling AWA ten months prior.

30 This hints at the possibility of loans having been taken out on the
    property, which would've been in the family at that point for close
    to thirty years.

CHAPTER 16

1   There is only one record of Gorgeous George and The Sheik sharing
    the same ring—a March 10, 1958, tag team bout on a Toots Mondt
    show in Charleston, West Virginia, pitting the two men, along with
    George's valet Chuck Stewart, against Chief White Eagle, Chito
    Lopez, and Billy Fox.

2   Szatkowski later learned that both Killer Kowalski and The Sheik
    had been trained by the same guy, Bert Ruby, which made his deci-
    sion that much easier.

3   The name had long obsessed Farhat—in his autobiography, Sabu
    claims that his uncle had even considered naming his second son
    Sabu before being vetoed by a horrified Joyce, who much preferred
    the name Thomas.

4   As Sheik recalled years later to Detroit-area referee and promoter Alan Haugabook.

5   The specific whereabouts of the Big Time Wrestling collection are a matter of some mystery even to this day. PM Video was sold after Ron Martinez's death in 2010, and the fate of their amassed collection is unknown. The Farhat family has also claimed to still be in possession of some master tapes, but none of the material has been made public, ostensibly due to prohibitive tape-to-digital conversion costs.

6   The Sheik and Abdullah the Butcher had their final known match against each other just six days after the TWA cage match, on September 27, 1991, at a Northeast Wrestling Federation independent card in Vermont (Sheik's only known appearance in that state). Sabu and Rob Szatkowski faced each other on the undercard.

7   In his autobiography, Sabu also recalls The Sheik joining them for bookings on the Memphis tour, but I could not find any record of his wrestling in Memphis in this period.

8   For his FMW run, Onita gave The Sheik something he had never really had before, but which had become expected in the wrestling industry by the 1990s: entrance music. His choice was the appropriately tumultuous "Night on Bald Mountain" by Russian romanticist Modest Mussorgsky.

9   The infamous taping took place before about six hundred fans and featured Sabu taking on a rookie Chris Candido with both The Sheik and ubiquitous superfan-photographer-dentist Dr. Mike Lano in his corner. The AWF folded almost immediately afterward.

10 Ironically, while The Sheik and Sabu continued to get booked in FMW in 1993, Rob Van Dam, his career beginning to take off after some TV exposure from WCW, enjoyed a run in All Japan working for Giant Baba.

11 The previous June, Sabu had also had a tryout match with WCW when the Ted Turner–owned company came through his neck of the woods with a house show in Port Huron, Michigan.

12 Taylor later achieved notoriety as Scotty 2 Hotty, one half of the tag team known as Too Cool, along with Jerry Lawler's son Brian (aka Grandmaster Sexay).

13 Farhat had good reason to trust in the power of silence, as a famous anecdote from the 1976 NWA Convention in Lake Tahoe relates: The story goes that NWA World Champion Terry Funk was making a speech about the lack of talent who knew how to cut a good promo, and how you couldn't draw money without it—at which point Farhat stood and said, "I've drawn more money than anyone in this room. And I've never cut a promo my entire career."

14 Nearly three years later, the Sultan gimmick would instead be given to already contracted WWF wrestler Solofa Fatu, who had previously worked as one half of the Headshrinkers tag team. As The Sultan, Fatu's manager would indeed be The Iron Sheik. The gimmick flopped, but he later attained WWF success as dancing sumo Rikishi. His twin sons Jimmy and Jey would go on to work for McMahon as the Usos tag team.

15 He would later shorten his name and go on to great things as Taz.

16 FMW's ability to draw for their anniversary shows was very impressive. For example, there were twenty thousand fewer fans for the largest crowd of The Sheik's North American career, his 1960 Comiskey Park match against Prince Maiava. And just one year prior to the Funk match, at the FMW fourth anniversary show, also at Kawasaki Stadium, forty-one thousand fans witnessed Sheik and Sabu taking on Dr. Hannibal and Dr. Luther.

17 The Butcher's mother was known to pass away quite often in those days.

CHAPTER 17

1 The last of these, a February 26, 1995 house show, featured Hulk Hogan's first Cobo appearance in eleven years, being only his third and final appearance there, following two 1984 defenses of the WWF World title.

2 In a 2011 article for *Jack Detroit* magazine, Jen Farhat reminisced about her grandfather with a story of teasing him at a family function when she had come home from college for a visit with some friends and he insisted on staying in character in front

of them. She also recollected on social media how he had once gifted camel pendant necklaces to all the grandkids when they were little.

3 It was at this event that WCW World Heavyweight Champion Hulk Hogan and "The Giant" Paul Wight engaged in their infamous "Monster Truck Match" on the roof of Cobo Hall right next door, culminating in The Giant ostensibly falling over the side of the building.

4 Since his last date for Jack Tunney at the Canadian National Exhibition Stadium on July 10, 1977, where he faced NWA World Champion Harley Race before a crowd of sixteen thousand.

5 This was the first time Cobo had been wired for TV since the Crockett days a decade earlier, and the closest thing to a wrestling sellout the arena had seen since the original WWF invasion in the mid-1980s.

6 Gary Cubeta's 57Talk.com.

7 In a 2010 shoot interview, he recalled specifically first hearing it when he was offered condolences by former WCW World Heavyweight Champion Bill Goldberg, also on the card that day.

CHAPTER 18

1 After his retirement in 1995, the Cauliflower Alley Club—then headed by none other than Lou Thesz—had planned to honor The Sheik at its annual banquet, but a controversy ensued when the CAC reportedly advertised The Sheik before notifying him. Feeling used, Farhat declined the offer.

2 An idea first pitched by Van Dam himself.

3 Also, a new record attendance for pro wrestling in North America at that time, ignoring the worked number for *WrestleMania III*.

4 The PWHF has since moved to Wichita Falls, Texas.

5 Tommy Dreamer and Al Snow, both close friends of his, reported that they only ever referred to him as Sabu, never by his real name, even in private conversation—echoing the practice commonly used with The Sheik himself.

6   As of this writing, the name was scheduled to change again in mid-2022 to reflect TCF's merger with Huntington Bancshares Incorporated.

APPENDIX I

1   DQ result is not one hundred percent certain. Sheik was US Champion at the time, and yet this loss did not result in Rhodes becoming champion. This leads me to surmise that the loss was via DQ.

SELECTED BIBLIOGRAPHY

Baker, David. "The Sheik (Ed Farhat) Match Results." In The Clawmaster's Archives. Sports & Wrestling. August 14, 2009. sportsandwrestling.mywowbb.com/forum2/9762.html.

Blassie, "Classy" Freddie, with Keith Elliot Greenberg. *Listen, You Pencil Neck Geeks.* New York: Simon & Schuster, 2003.

Brunk, Terry "Sabu." *The Scars that Bind: Sabu and The Sheik.* OfftheMarkShow.com, 2010.

Brunk, Terry "Sabu," with Kenny Casanova. *Sabu: Scars, Silence, & Superglue.* United States: Walking on Hot Waffles Publishers, 2019.

Burzynski, Dave. "How The Sheik Helped Heal Detroit after 1967 Riots." SlamWrestling.net, July 23, 2021.

Cubeta, Gary. 57Talk.com.

Farhat, Jen. "Life with a Madman." *Jack Detroit*, July 2011: 64–68.

Fahey, Vince. *Kayfabe Memories.* Atom Designs, 2004. kayfabememories.com.

Freedman, Jim. *Drawing Heat.* 2nd Edition. Gallatin, TN: Crowbar Press, 2010.

Hornbaker, Tim. *Capitol Revolution: The Rise of the McMahon Wrestling Empire.* Toronto: ECW Press, 2015.

———. *Legends of Pro Wrestling: 150 Years of Headlocks, Bodyslams, and Piledrivers.* 2nd Edition. New York: Sports Publishing, 2017.

————. *National Wrestling Alliance: The Untold Story of the Monopoly that Strangled Pro Wrestling.* Toronto: ECW Press, 2007.

Hornby, Fred, Scott Teal, et al. *The History of Professional Wrestling — Madison Square Garden: 1880–1999.* Hendersonville, TN: Scott Teal, 2000.

James, Mark. *Wrestling Record Book: Detroit 1964–1980.* Middletown, DE: Mark James, 2015.

Jares, Joe. *Whatever Happened to Gorgeous George?* London, England: Prentice-Hall International, 1974.

Johnson, Steven, Greg Oliver. *The Pro Wrestling Hall of Fame: Heroes and Icons.* Toronto: ECW Press, 2003.

Kreikenbohm, Philip. Cagematch: The Internet Wrestling Database. 2001, cagematch.net.

Meltzer, Dave. *Tributes II: Remembering More of the World's Greatest Professional Wrestlers.* New York: Sports Publishing, 2004.

————. *Wrestling Observer Newsletter.*

Molinaro, John F. *Top 100 Pro Wrestlers of All Time.* Toronto: Stewart House, 2002.

Nulty, Mark. WrestlingClassics.com. 1998. wrestlingclassics.com.

Oliver, Greg, and Steven Johnson. *The Pro Wrestling Hall of Fame: The Heels.* Toronto: ECW Press, 2007.

Saalbach, Axel. Wrestlingdata.com. 2001. wrestlingdata.com.

Sammartino, Bruno, with Bob Michelucci, et al. *Bruno Sammartino: An Autobiography of Wrestling's Living Legend.* Huntington, NY: Sub Entertainment, 1990.

Tanabe, Hisaharu. *Pro-Wrestling Title Histories.* Puroresu.com, 1995. wrestling-titles.com.

Wilson, Jim, and Weldon T. Johnson. *Choke Hold: Pro Wrestling's Real Mayhem Outside the Ring.* Bloomington, IN: Xlibris, 2003.

ACKNOWLEDGMENTS

T aking on a project as ambitious and unprecedented as the first biography of pro wrestling's most elusive historical figure could never have been done alone, and I am eternally grateful to so many who helped me take a project that once existed only in my wildest dreams and turn it into a reality.

First and foremost, as always, thanks must go to my family. To my endlessly supportive and reasonably patient wife, Jaimee, for allowing our lives to be taken over by all things Sheik for so long and for giving me steady and genuine feedback on my work, not as a wrestling fan, but more importantly, as a reader. To my daughter, Layla, who took time out of her nursing school studies to look over the manuscript in its early stages and provide some much-needed encouragement. To my son Jack, who helped me organize the exhaustive appendices, and probably hopes he never hears the names "Lord Athol Layton" or "Pampero Firpo" again.

To the folks at ECW Press, who were willing to get behind a book about a performer whose best days happened half a century ago, thanks for believing in this project. Above all, that means Mike Holmes, who championed *Blood and Fire* from the beginning and whose gratifying response to the finished manuscript made me realize that I just may have something special here. To Rachel Ironstone for her meticulous copy-editing work—as a former copy editor myself, I will forever be respectful of that process. And to everyone else who was so gracious in guiding me through the process and presenting my work in the best possible light, including Shannon Parr, Jessica Albert, David M. Caron, Caroline Suzuki, Michela Prefontaine, David Drummond, and Aymen Saidane.

A special thanks to Rob Van Dam, one of the coolest guys in the wrestling business, who agreed to lend his name to this project and to share his unique memories of The Sheik in a foreword that clearly came from the heart.

I knew from the beginning that this book could never be what I wanted it to be without the approval and support of the dean of Detroit wrestling, Dave Burzynski. But I never dared to hope that Dave would be as enthusiastic, helpful, and patient as he turned out be—always there to answer questions, provide valuable insight, and basically give me the rub. Not to mention providing almost half of all the pictures that appear in this book! A thousand thanks, Supermouth! Special thanks also go out to the others who provided such crucial feedback on the manuscript: my idol-turned-colleague and a man I've been proud to call a friend and peer for over twenty years, Keith Elliot Greenberg; the inimitable Jim Cornette, who put me over on his podcast and whose admiration for my work is as humbling as it gets; and The Great Brian Last, who helped me get that manuscript into the hands of Mr. Cornette, where I knew it would be most welcome.

Thanks to those whose impressive work I was able to build from, and without whose prior efforts this book would be less than what it is. To the irreplaceable Mark Bujan, keeper of the flame of Detroit wrestling fandom for so many years—I hope this book will help keep that flame burning. To Gary Cubeta for providing access to the incredible interviews he conducted years ago on 57Talk. And to one of the greatest living wrestling historians, Tim Hornbaker, who provided some fascinating historical correspondences that have been excerpted here, as well as for providing answers to some important historical questions. I hope to be half the historian he is.

Thank you to those who consented to be interviewed for this book, and whose memories and opinions on the life of such a secretive individual as The Sheik helped flesh out a story I never could've pieced together without them, including Bill Apter, John Arezzi, Mark Boone, Killer

Tim Brooks, Ernie Brown, Tom Burke, "Flying" Fred Curry, Terry Dart, Bobby Davis, Irish Mickey Doyle, Tommy Dreamer, Terry Funk, Evan Ginzburg, Bryan Greenberg, Alan Haugabook, "The Rude Boy" Rudy Hill, Jerry Jaffe (aka Dr. Jerry Graham Jr.), Dr. Mike Lano, Bernie "The Cat" Livingston, Dave Meltzer, Mark Nowotarski, James Painter (aka Big Jim Lancaster), "Leaping" Lanny Poffo, Scott Romer, Lou Sahadi, Fumi Saito, Al Snow, Kevin Sullivan, Bruce Swayze, Scott Teal, Les Thatcher, and Jeff Walton.

What would a book about The Sheik be without jaw-dropping pictures? In addition to Dave Burzynski, the all-important photography for the book came together from a number of sources. I'm grateful to Kevin McElvaney, editor-in-chief of *Pro Wrestling Illustrated*, who allowed me to abuse our friendship by nagging him endlessly for some of the beautiful shots from *PWI*'s archive, the greatest in the world. Thanks also go out to Howard Baum, Brian Bukantis, Wilson Lindsey, and John Bradford McFarlin.

And finally, thanks to the many others who came through in so many ways, whether it be answering some random questions, making important introductions, getting the word out, or just simply offering words of encouragement, including Rick Brooks, Sylvia Davis, Craig Jay Derbin, Mike Johnson, Steven Johnson, Tim Keenan, Greg Oliver, Dave Sahadi, Alissa Silver, David Torres, Scott Walton, and last but far from least, my dear departed friend Melissa Coates.